W9-CZW-514

Eighth Edition

PROBLEM SOLVING AND PROGRAMMING CONCEPTS

Maureen Sprankle
Professor Emeritus, College of the Redwoods

Jim Hubbard
HealthWare Solutions LLC

PEARSON
Prentice Hall

Upper Saddle River, New Jersey 07458

Library of Congress Cataloging-in-Publication Data

Sprankle, Maureen.
 Problem solving and programming concepts / Maureen Sprankle.—8th ed.
 p. cm.
 ISBN-13: 978-0-13-606060-4
 ISBN-10: 0-13-606060-9
 1. Computer programming. 2. Problem solving—Data processing. 1. Title.
 QA76.6.S684 2008
 006.3'33—dc22

 2008015703

> *To our spouses, Norm and Tamara*
> *and our children, Bonnie, Heidi, Tamara, John and Maliyah*
> *for their continuing support and understanding.*

Vice President and Editorial Director,
 ECS: *Marcia J. Horton*
Executive Editor: *Tracy Dunkelberger*
Assistant Editor: *ReeAnne Davies*
Editorial Assistant: *Melinda Haggerty*
Director of Team-Based Project Management:
 Vince O'Brien
Senior Managing Editor: *Scott Disanno*
Production Liaison: *Jane Bonnell*
Production Editor: *Bruce Hobart, Pine Tree*
 Composition, Inc.
Manufacturing Manager: *Alan Fischer*

Manufacturing Buyer: *Lisa McDowell*
Marketing Manager: *Erin Davis*
Marketing Assistant: *Mack Patterson*
Art Director: *Kenny Beck*
Cover Designer: *Kristine Carney*
Cover Image: *Imagezoo/Images.com*
Art Editor: *Greg Dulles*
Media Project Manager: *John M. Cassar*
Full-Service Project Management/
 Composition: *Pine Tree Composition, Inc./*
 Laserwords, Pte. Ltd.–Chennai
Printer/Binder: *Edwards Brothers*

The author and publisher of this book have used their best efforts in preparing this book. These efforts include the development, research, and testing of the theories and programs to determine their effectiveness. The author and publisher make no warranty of any kind, expressed or implied, with regard to these programs or the documentation contained in this book. The author and publisher shall not be liable in any event for incidental or consequential damages in connection with, or arising out of, the furnishing, performance, or use of these programs.

Copyright © 2009, 2006, 2003, 2001, 1998, 1995, 1992 by Pearson Education, Inc., Upper Saddle River, New Jersey 07458. All rights reserved. Printed in the United States of America. This publication is protected by Copyright and permission should be obtained from the publisher prior to any prohibited reproduction, storage in a retrieval system, or transmission in any form or by any means, electronic, mechanical, photocopying, recording, or likewise. For information regarding permission(s), write to: Rights and Permissions Department.

Pearson Education Ltd., London
Pearson Education Singapore, Pte. Ltd.
Pearson Education Canada, Inc.
Pearson Education—Japan
Pearson Education Australia PTY, Limited
Pearson Education North Asia, Ltd., Hong Kong
Pearson Educación de Mexico, S.A. de C.V.
Pearson Education Malaysia, Pte. Ltd.
Pearson Education, Upper Saddle River, New Jersey

10 9 8 7 6 5 4 3 2 1
ISBN-13: 978-0-13-606060-4
ISBN-10: 0-13-606060-9

Contents

Preface

Knowledge of problem solving and programming concepts is necessary for those who develop applications for users. Unfortunately, many students have greater difficulty with problem solving than they do with the syntax of computer languages. The art of programming is learning multiple techniques and applying those techniques to specific problems. When students learn basic programming and problem-solving techniques, they can then concentrate on the syntax when learning specific languages. These techniques may be presented in a separate class on problem solving or with a first language course that concentrates on problem solving. This approach tends to decrease students' frustration and improves their success rate.

This book is intended for a one-semester introductory course for programming majors. It can serve as a primary text or as a supplement. Although this book is written for students who have little or no computer experience, those who have studied a computer language can benefit from the generic presentation of the material.

The text provides a step-by-step progression of ideas with detailed explanation and many illustrations, from the basics of mathematical functions and operators to the design and use of techniques such as codes, arrays, pointers, other data structures, database concepts, and object-oriented programming concepts. The text uses problem-solving tools, such as problem analysis charts, interactivity charts, IPO charts, algorithms, and flowcharts, to design a solution to a problem. The appendices present additional tools, including Universal Modeling Language concepts, Nassi-Schneiderman charts, and Warnier-Orr diagrams. Putting It All Together sections illustrate a complete solution for a given problem, using the concepts previously presented. In some cases, an earlier solution is updated to incorporate more sophisticated techniques. Throughout the text, problems presented are typical of the business world and provide excellent experience for students. These problems then can be presented in a language course so that students can finish the solution on the computer.

Organization of the Text

- Unit One, *Introduction to Problem Solving and Programming*, presents basic concepts of problem solving, an introduction to how problems are solved on computers, mathematical concepts required for problem solving using a computer, and steps for analyzing a problem and designing an appropriate solution.
- Unit Two, *Logic Structures*, presents basic concepts of programming, including local and global variables, parameters, and four basic logic structures. The four basic logic structures are sequential, decision, loop, and case logic.
- Unit Three, *Data Structures*, presents the concepts of arrays, sorting techniques, stacks, queues, linked lists, and binary trees.
- Unit Four, *Database Management Systems*, presents terminology and techniques to implement an application using a database management system.
- Unit Five, *Object-Oriented Programming*, presents basic concepts in the design of a solution using object-oriented languages.
- Unit Six, *Introduction to Game Development*, presents basic concepts of game development through the use of object-oriented programming. An introduction

to assembly language is also presented because many game developers are requiring the knowledge of assembly language to make their games run faster.

- Unit Seven, *File Processing*, presents techniques of file processing. While these chapters are important to those students studying COBOL, the industry is rapidly converting to database management systems. Therefore, these chapters are not as important as they were 10 or 15 years ago.
- The appendices present the Otto the Robot problem, concepts of UML, ASCII and EBCDIC codes, blank forms, other problem-solving tools, and some common functions. Otto software is available to instructors via the Prentice Hall Instructor Resource Center. Visit www.prenhall.com for access.

New in This Edition

The eighth edition responds to suggestions from reviewers and changes in the programming industry. The following changes were made:

- New coauthor who is a software architect. This brings in perspectives from industry as well as education.
- Expanded explanation of the "Return Values" in Chapter 4.
- Rewrite of Chapter 8: Case Logic Structure to include the *Select* instruction and the use of other relational expressions.
- Update of Chapters 14 and 15 to include a more in-depth and business-oriented coverage of database management.
- A complete rewrite of Chapters 16 and 17 to include a more in-depth coverage of object-oriented programming. This is important in today's industry because most programmers develop applications using object-oriented programming techniques. Included in these chapters are VB.net examples.
- Two new chapters on game development, including object-oriented concepts and assembly language usage. Game development is a hot topic today. Students should be aware of some of the basic concepts of game development and animation.
- More problems and exercises in many chapters.
- Addition of marginal notes.
- Change of many variable names to improve readability.

Resources

Instructor Resources include lecture slides, Instructor's Manual, and Otto software. Instructor Resources are located at www.prenhall.com/sprankle. Contact your local Prentice Hall Sales Representative for access information.

Acknowledgments

We are indebted to those who reviewed the manuscript and offered suggestions and constructive comments. In particular, we thank Mardi Horton, Cerritos Community College; John Arena, Augusta Technical College (GA); Mara Casado, Manatee Community College (FL); Marty Dellinger, Catawba Valley Community College; Roy Foreman, Purdue University–Calumet; Gary Marrer, Maricopa Community College; Hazem Said, University of Cincinnati, and Melinda White, Seminole Community College. Thanks to Tracy Dunkelberger and Jane Bonnell at Prentice Hall and to Bruce Hobart at Pine Tree Composition for their support throughout the production process.

Maureen Sprankle
Jim Hubbard

UNIT ONE

INTRODUCTION TO PROBLEM SOLVING AND PROGRAMMING

Chapter 1

General Problem-Solving Concepts

Overview

Problem Solving in Everyday Life
Types of Problems
Problem Solving with Computers
Difficulties with Problem Solving

Objectives

When you have finished this chapter, you should be able to:

1. Describe the difference between heuristic and algorithmic solutions to problems.
2. List and describe the six problem-solving steps to solve a problem that has an algorithmic solution.
3. Use the six problem-solving steps to solve a problem.

Problem Solving in Everyday Life

People make decisions every day to solve problems that affect their lives. The problems may be as unimportant as what to watch on television or as important as choosing a new profession. If a bad decision is made, time and resources are wasted, so it's important that people know how to make decisions well. There are six steps to follow to ensure the best decision. These six steps in problem solving include the following:

Six Steps of Problem Solving

1. *Identify the problem.* The first step toward solving a problem is to identify the problem. In a classroom situation, most problems have been identified for you and given to you in the form of written assignments or problems out of a

3

book. However, when you are doing problem solving outside the classroom, you need to make sure you identify the problem before you start solving it. If you don't know what the problem is, you cannot solve it.

2. *Understand the problem.* You must understand what is involved in the problem before you can continue toward the solution. This includes understanding the knowledge base of the person or machine for whom you are solving the problem. If you are setting up a solution for a person, then you must know what that person knows. A different set of instructions might have to be used depending on this knowledge base. For example, you would use a more detailed set of instructions to tell someone how to find a restaurant in your city if he has a limited knowledge of the city than if he knows it well. When you are working with a computer, its knowledge base is the limited instructions the computer can understand in the particular language or application you are using to solve the problem. Knowing the knowledge base is very important since you cannot use any instructions outside this base. You also must know your own knowledge base. You cannot solve a problem if you do not know the subject. For example, to solve a problem involving calculus, you must know calculus; to solve a problem involving accounting, you must know accounting. You must be able to communicate with your client and be able to understand what is involved in solving the problem.

3. *Identify alternative ways to solve the problem.* This list should be as complete as possible. You might want to talk to other people to find other solutions than those you have identified. Alternative solutions must be acceptable ones. You could go from Denver to Los Angeles by way of New York, but this would probably not be an acceptable solution to your travel needs.

4. *Select the best way to solve the problem from the list of alternative solutions.* In this step, you need to identify and evaluate the pros and cons of each possible solution before selecting the best one. In order to do this, you need to select criteria for the evaluation. These criteria will serve as the guidelines for evaluating each solution.

5. *List instructions that enable you to solve the problem using the selected solution.* These numbered, step-by-step instructions must fall within the knowledge base set up in step 2. No instruction can be used unless the individual or the machine can understand it. This can be very limiting, especially when working with computers.

6. *Evaluate the solution.* To evaluate or test a solution means to check its result to see if it is correct, and to see if it satisfies the needs of the person(s) with the problem. (When a person needs a piece of furniture to sleep on, buying her a cot may be a *correct* solution, but it may not be very satisfactory.) If the result is either incorrect or unsatisfactory, then the problem solver must start the process again.

If any of these six steps are not completed well, the results may be less than desired.

People solve problems daily at home, or work, or wherever they go. Problems at home include such things as what to cook for dinner, which movie to see this evening, which car to buy, or how to sell the house. At work, the problems might involve dealing with fellow employees, work policies, management, or customers. The better the decisions an employee can make, the more valuable that person will be to the company. In each case, the six steps in problem solving can be followed. Most people use them without even knowing it.

Take the problem of what to do this evening.

1. Identify the problem. How do the individuals wish to spend the evening?
2. Understand the problem. With this simple problem, also, the knowledge base of the participants must be considered. The only solutions that should be selected are ones that everyone involved would know how to do. You probably would not select as a possible solution playing a game of chess if the participants did not know how to play.
3. Identify alternatives.
 a. Watch television.
 b. Invite friends over.
 c. Play video games.
 d. Go to the movies.
 e. Play miniature golf.
 f. Go to the amusement park.
 g. Go to a friend's party.
 The list is complete only when you can think of no more alternatives.
4. Select the best way to solve the problem.
 a. Weed out alternatives that are not acceptable, such as those that cost too much money or do not interest one of the individuals involved.
 b. Specify the pros and cons of each remaining alternative.
 c. Weigh the pros and cons to make the final decision. This solution will be the best alternative if all the other steps were completed well.
5. Prepare a list of steps (instructions) that will result in a fun evening.
6. Evaluate the solution. Are we having fun yet?

By going through these steps, the problem solver can be assured that he has arrived at the best possible solution and will achieve the desired results.

Types of Problems

algorithmic solution

algorithm

heuristic solution

Problems do not always have straightforward solutions. Some problems, such as balancing a checkbook or baking a cake, can be solved with a series of actions. These solutions are called **algorithmic solutions**. Once the alternatives have been eliminated, for example, and once one has chosen the best among several methods of balancing the checkbook, the solution can be reached by completing the actions in steps. These steps are called the **algorithm**. The solutions of other problems, such as how to buy the best stock or whether to expand the company, are not so straightforward. These solutions require reasoning built on knowledge and experience, and a process of trial and error. Solutions that cannot be reached through a direct set of steps are called **heuristic solutions**.

The problem solver can use the six steps for both algorithmic and heuristic solutions. However, in step 6, evaluating the solution, the correctness and appropriateness of heuristic solutions are far less certain. It's easy to tell if your completed checkbook balance is correct and satisfactory, but it's hard to tell if you have bought the best stock. With heuristic solutions, the problem solver will often need to follow the six steps more than once, carefully evaluating each possible solution before deciding which is best. Furthermore, this same solution may not be correct and satisfactory at another time, so the problem solver may have to reevaluate and resolve the same problem later. The stock that did well in January may do poorly in June.

Most problems require a combination of the two kinds of solutions.

Problem Solving with Computers

solution
results
program

In this book, the term **solution** means the instructions listed during step 5 of problem solving—the instructions that must be followed to produce the best results. **Results** means the outcome or the completed computer-assisted answer. **Program** means the set of instructions that make up the solution after they have been coded into a particular computer language.

Computers are built to deal with algorithmic solutions, which are often difficult or very time consuming for humans. People are better than computers at developing heuristic solutions. Solving a complicated calculus problem or alphabetizing 10,000 names is an easy task for the computer, but the problem of how to throw a ball or how to speak English is not. The difficulty lies in the programming. How can problems such as how to throw a ball or speak English be solved in a set of steps that the computer can understand?

The field of computers that deals with heuristic types of problems is called artificial intelligence. Artificial intelligence enables a computer to do things like build its own knowledge bank and speak in a human language. As a result, the computer's problem-solving abilities are similar to those of a human being. Artificial intelligence is an expanding computer field, especially with the increased use of Robotics.

Until computers can be built to think like humans, people will process most heuristic solutions and computers will process many algorithmic solutions. Therefore, this book will deal only with algorithmic solutions. Heuristic problem solving can help determine alternative solutions. However, for computer use, they must be transformed into an algorithmic format.

Difficulties with Problem Solving

People have many problems with problem solving. Some have not been taught how to solve problems. Others are afraid to make a decision for fear it will be the wrong one. Often, when people go through the problem-solving process, they complete one or more of the steps inadequately. They may not define the problem correctly or may not generate a sufficient list of alternatives. When choosing the best alternative, they may eliminate good alternatives or list the pros and cons too hastily. They may not use a logical sequence of steps in their solution, or they may focus on details before the framework for the solution is in place. Finally, they may incorrectly or haphazardly evaluate the solution.

The problem-solving process is not easy. It takes practice and time to perfect, but in the long run the process proves to be of great benefit.

When solving problems on the computer, one of the most difficult tasks for the problem solver is writing the instructions. Take the task of deciding which number is the largest from a group of three numbers. Almost anyone can immediately tell which is the largest, but many cannot explain the steps they followed to arrive at it. Most people will say, "I can't explain how I know, I just know it!" This explanation is not good enough for the computer. The computer is a tool that will perform only tasks that the user can explain.

The computer has a specific system of communication that programmers and users must learn. This system demands that no step in the solution to a problem be left unstated and that all steps be in the proper order. You must assume the computer knows nothing except what you tell it and think of it as an ignorant but efficient aid to problem solving.

Summary

The six steps in problem solving lead to the best possible solution to a problem. They include (1) identifying the problem, (2) understanding the problem, (3) identifying alternative solutions, (4) selecting the best solution, (5) preparing a list of instructions to solve the problem by the chosen solution, and (6) evaluating the solution. Solutions to problems are classified as algorithmic or heuristic. Algorithmic solutions are reached in a series of steps. Heuristic solutions are attained through trial and error. Algorithmic solutions are easier to define for computer use than heuristic ones.

Several things can go wrong in the problem-solving process. Sometimes the problem solver does not define the problem correctly or does not complete one or more of the steps. At other times, the list of alternatives is not sufficient or the list of instructions to the computer is incorrect. Sometimes one gets lost in details and overlooks the general framework, or does not test the solution. If the problem-solving process is incomplete, the solution will not produce the desired results.

The steps in problem solving can be applied to problems in daily life as well as to problems put on the computer. Good problem-solving techniques enable you to look at a problem logically and unemotionally, saving time and other resources.

New Terms

algorithm	heuristic solution	results
algorithmic solution	program	solution

Questions

1. What are the six steps of problem solving?
2. What is an algorithmic solution to a problem?
3. Name three current problems in your life that could be solved through an algorithmic process. Explain why each of these problems is algorithmic in nature.
4. What is a heuristic solution to a problem?
5. Name three current problems in your life that might be solved through a heuristic approach. Explain why each of these problems is heuristic in nature.
6. Name three problems that might arise at home, at school, or in a business that could be solved more efficiently with computer assistance. Do these problems require an algorithmic or heuristic solution? Why?
7. State a reason why each of the six problem-solving steps is important in developing the best solution for a problem. Give one reason for each step.

Problems

1. Complete the six problem-solving steps to solve one of the problems you listed in question 3. Follow the form outlined as follows:
 Step 1: Identify the problem.
 Step 2: Understand the problem.

a. Comments about the problem to aid in understanding it.
b. Description of the knowledge base (this list would include what you would be expected to know to follow the solution).

Step 3: Identify alternative solutions.

Solution Pros Cons

a.

b.

c.

.

.

.

Step 4: Select the best solution.

Why did you select this solution?

Step 5: List a set of numbered step-by-step instructions to attain the solution.

1.

2.

3.

.

.

.

Step 6: Test the solution.

Does this solution work?

If not, how might you change the solution so it will work?

2. For each of the following tasks, write a set of numbered, step-by-step instructions (a solution) so complete that another person could perform the task without asking questions. Define the knowledge base of this person by listing what you expect the person to know in order to follow your directions. For example, for task "a" (below), make a cup of cocoa, the knowledge base might include such things as knowledge of milk or water, a refrigerator, pan, spoon, cocoa, cup, range top or microwave, and so forth.

 a. Make a cup of cocoa.
 b. Sharpen a pencil.
 c. Walk from the classroom to the student lounge, your dorm, or the cafeteria.
 d. Start a car (include directions regarding what to do if the car doesn't start).
 e. Get a glass of water from your kitchen.
 f. Start your computer.

3. Develop the knowledge base for the following problems:
 a. Balancing your checkbook
 b. Driving a car
 c. Repairing a car
 d. Building a house
 e. Calculating the cost of using your car for a month
 f. Play a video game.

4. Write a solution to the problem of finding the largest number out of three numbers. List the specific steps that would enable another person to find the largest among three numbers presented.

5. Why do you think some of the solutions in problems 2 and 3 are harder to develop than others?

6. Appendix A contains problems dealing with Otto the Robot. Otto has a limited number of tasks that he can accomplish. Discuss the approach you would take to develop a set of instructions that will allow Otto to accomplish the problems presented in Appendix A.

7. Develop solutions for Otto's problems presented in Appendix A.

8. How does your problem solving differ between finding a solution to a problem for your own life and that of designing a solution for one of Otto's problems?

Chapter 2

Beginning Problem-Solving Concepts for the Computer

Overview

Constants and Variables
Rules for Naming and Using Variables

Data Types
Numeric Data
Character Data—Alphanumeric Data
Logical Data
Other Data Types
Rules for Data Types
Examples of Data Types

How the Computer Stores Data

Functions

Operators

Expressions and Equations
Examples

Objectives

When you have finished this chapter, you should be able to:

1. Differentiate between variables and constants.
2. Differentiate between character, numeric, and logical data types.
3. Identify operators, operands, and resultants.
4. Identify and use functions.
5. Identify and use operators according to their placement in the hierarchy chart.
6. Set up and evaluate expressions and equations using variables, constants, operators, and the hierarchy of operations.

Although problems that arise in daily life are of many types, problems that can be solved on computers generally consist of only three: (1) computational, problems involving some kind of mathematical processing; (2) logical, problems involving relational or logical processing, the kinds of processing used in decision making on the computer; and (3) repetitive, problems involving repeating a set of mathematical and/or logical instructions. This chapter explains some computer fundamentals and demonstrates ways to set up expressions and equations to solve these types of problems on the computer. Programmers, need to know these computer fundamentals (see Figure 2.1).

Two of the most fundamental concepts that you will learn in this chapter are the constant and the variable. A programmer takes the data, the unorganized facts, and the information, the organized facts, relevant to a problem and defines them as constants or variables. They are the building blocks of the equations and expressions that ultimately make up solutions to computer problems. The programmer defines each constant and variable in a problem solution as a particular data type, such as numeric or character.

Other concepts that are essential to developing computer solutions to problems are operators and functions. Operators are the many signs and symbols that show relationships between constants and variables in the expressions and equations that make up the solution. The programmer has to know all of the many operators and how to use them. The order in which operators are processed is determined by a hierarchy that programmers need to know as well.

Operators are combined with constants and variables to create expressions and equations. Expressions and equations are used in instructions that are the building blocks of the solution. Functions are sets of instructions that are so commonly used that they are built into a computer language, saving the programmer the trouble of writing them.

These are key concepts. Without an understanding of how the computer uses and defines data, without knowing what the operators are, and without knowing how to use these concepts to construct expressions and equations, a programmer cannot effectively use the computer to solve problems.

When you study this chapter, it may help to keep these pointers in mind:

- Take each topic as it is presented, and learn the concepts pertaining to it.
- Understand the examples.
- Complete the questions and problems at the end of the chapter.
- Don't skip sections.
- Don't feel that something is too hard before you make an effort to understand it.
- Take each problem one step at a time.
- Don't skip steps.
- Don't assume anything.
- Don't be afraid to read a passage over again. Once may not be enough!

Concepts to Learn

Figure 2.1 Important Concepts to Learn

Constants and Variables

constant

The computer uses constants and variables to solve problems. They are data used in processing. A **constant** is a value—that is, a specific alphabetical and/or numeric value—that never changes during the processing of all the instructions in a solution. Constants can be any type of data—numeric, alphabetical, or special symbols. (Data types are explained in more detail later.) In some programming languages and applications, constants can be named. In this case, the constant is given a location in memory and a name. During the execution of the program, this constant is given a value and then is referred to by its name. Once the constant is given a value, it cannot be changed during the execution of the program. For example, because the value of PI does not change, it would be a constant and defined within the program. This constant may be given a name, but the only way to change the value of the constant is to change the program. Any constant may be given a name. This allows an easier access to constants. Many name conventions stipulate that named constants be given names containing all capital letters in order to easily distinguish them from variables. However, this may vary between companies in which you may work.

variable
identifier

In contrast, the value of a **variable** may change during processing. In many languages variables are called **identifiers** since the name identifies what the value represents. You need to be aware of this when learning the syntax and terminology of each language. In this text the word variable will be used. A programmer must give a name to each variable value used in a solution. The programmer uses a variable name as a reference name for a specific value of the variable. In turn, the computer uses the name as a reference to help it find that value in its memory. The computer sets up a specific memory location to hold the value of each variable name found in a program. Variables can be any data type, just as constants can. For instance, consider the cost of a pair of shoes. This data item should be given a variable name because the cost of a pair of shoes may change during the processing of the program or during multiple executions of the program. The variable name should be consistent with what the value of the variable represents. In this case, the name of the variable is *ShoeCost* because it represents the cost of the pair of shoes:

ShoeCost

However, if the cost of the shoes changes during the next execution of the program, then the value of *ShoeCost* will change but the variable name will not:

ShoeCost

Notice in Table 2.1 that when the value of a constant or a variable contains alphanumeric data—that is, numbers and/or special symbols—it is surrounded by quotation marks. These marks indicate to the computer that the value is a datum, not a variable name. The computer must have some way to distinguish between the two. Also notice that the variable names stand for specific data. The variable name *Cash* has a sum of money as its value. The variable name *City* has a city name as its value. Finally, notice that there are no blank spaces between words in variable names.

Table 2.1 Constants and Variables on the Computer

Constants	Variables
Rules: Constants cannot be changed. Examples: Value `25` Value `−1.5` Value `"ARCATA"` Value `"95521"` Named Constants Rules: A constant cannot be changed after it is initially given a value. Storage location given a name. Referred to by the given name. Example: PI `3.142857`	Rules: Storage locations are given names. Values of the contents for name variable locations can be changed. Referred to by variable name in the instructions. Examples: Variable Name—*Age* Value `25` Variable Name—*Cash* Value `83.59` Variable Name—*City* Value `"Eureka"` Variable Name—*ZipCode* Value `"95501"`

Naming Conventions for Constants and Variables

Each company you work for will have naming conventions for variables and module names. The convention for naming variables may differ with companies as well as languages. It is very important to have all programmers within an environment follow the specified conventions, and it may be a requirement for employment.

There are many reasons to follow a naming convention. First, it allows several programmers to work on the same project without the problem of conflicting variable and module names. Second, it allows programs to be easily read because there is only one consistent name for a variable. It also increases the readability between applications because the form of the variable name is consistent within a company. Third, naming conventions allow the code to be easily maintained. Programmers spend most of their time on software maintenance, not development; therefore, having a convention for naming variables decreases the time and increases the reliability when updating software. In addition, most software is maintained by many different people. Naming conventions allow the software to be transferred with the least difficulty. Fourth, the software should perform more efficiently by using consistent naming of modules and variables. Fifth, there should be an increase in performance expectation. And last, naming conventions should produce a clean, well-written program.

In a solution that calculates payroll for a company, the name of the company would be a constant since it does not change. The employee name, the hours, and the rate of pay would be variables because the values of these items change for each employee. If there were no such thing as a variable, the programmer would have to write a separate set of instructions for each employee. It is far more efficient to have one rather than a thousand programs to process payroll for 1,000 employees.

The rules for naming variables differ from language to language. However, the general rule is to name the variable as near to its meaning as possible: *PayRate* for the rate of pay, *Hours* for the number of hours worked during the pay period, and the like. Some languages and applications have character-length limitations or other restrictions for names (called reserved words), so adjustments have to be made as necessary. In this book, there will be no character-length limitations for variable names.

It is important to understand the difference between the name of a variable and the value of a variable. The *name* is the label the computer uses to find the correct memory location; the *value* is the contents of the location. The computer uses the variable name to find the location; it uses the value found at the memory location to do the processing.

It is also important to be consistent in the use of variable names because the computer will go only to the location with the specified name, regardless of whether it is the one intended by the user. For example, if you use *Hours* for hours worked, then you must use *Hours* at all times in referring to hours worked, not *Hrs* or *HoursWorked*. If the computer cannot find a memory location by the specified name, it will either name a new memory location and yield an incorrect result, or it will return an error message indicating there is no location as referenced and then cease execution.

Rules for Naming Constants and Variables

Rules for Naming and Using Variables

There are a number of rules for naming and using variables, as listed below. Table 2.2 illustrates some examples of incorrect variable names.

1. Name a variable according to what it represents, that is, *Hours* for hours worked, *PayRate* for rate of pay, and so on. Create as short a name as possible but one that clearly represents the variable.
2. Do not use spaces in a variable name; for example, use *HoursWorked*.
3. Start a variable name with a letter.
4. Do not use a dash (or any other symbol that is used as a mathematical operator) in a variable name. The computer will recognize these symbols as mathematical

Table 2.2 Incorrect Variable Names

Data Item	Incorrect Variable Name	Problem	Corrected Variable Name
Hours worked	*Hours Worked*	Space between words	*HoursWorked*
Name of client	*CN*	Does not define data item	*ClientName*
Rate of pay	*Pay-Rate*	Uses a mathematical operator	*PayRate*
Quantity per customer	*Quantity/customer*	Uses a mathematical operator	*QuantityPerCustomer*
6% sales tax	*6%_sales_tax*	Starts with a number	*SixPercentSalesTax or SalesTax*
Client address	*Client_address_for_client_of_ XYZ_corporation_in_California*	Too long	*ClientAddress*
Variable name Introduced as *Hours*	*Hrs*	Inconsistent name	*Hours*
Variable name Introduced as *Hours*	*Hours_worked*	Inconsistent name	*Hours*

operators, turn your variable into two or more variables, and treat your variable as a mathematical expression.

5. After you have introduced a variable name that represents a specific data item, this exact variable name must be used in all places where the data item is used. For example, if the data item *hours worked* has the variable name of *Hours*, *Hours* must be used consistently. You may not use *Hrs* or *HoursWorked* to represent the same data item. If you do, the computer views these variables as new and different data items and will assign a new memory location to the new name.

6. Be consistent when using upper- and lower case characters. In some languages *HOURS* is a different variable name than *Hours*.

7. Use the naming convention specified by the company where you work. As stated, in this text our naming convention is upper case for the first character in each of the words in the name, with no spaces between words in the name. Named constants will be in all upper case characters. For example:

Variable Names	Constant Names
PayRate	PI
Rate	KCONSTANT
HoursWorked	MULTIPLIER
Amount	
Temperature	

Your instructor may want you to use a different naming convention. Be sure you follow the convention exactly.

Data Types

data

information

To process solutions, the computer must have data. **Data** are unorganized facts. They go into the computer as input and are processed by the program. What is returned to the user is output, or **information**. This information is printed in the form of reports. For example, when a computer calculates the balance of a checkbook, data are the checks, the deposits, and the bank charges. The information from the processing is shown on the balance sheet (see Figure 2.2).

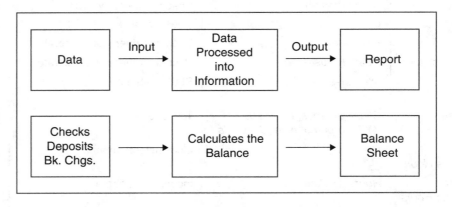

Figure 2.2 Processing Data—How a Computer Balances a Checkbook

data type

The data the computer uses are of many different types. Computers must be told the **data type** of each variable or constant. The most common data types are numeric, character, and logical. A few languages and applications also use the date as a data type. Other languages allow the programmer to define data types.

Numeric Data

numeric data

Integers
Real Number

Numeric data include all types of numbers (see Table 2.3). Numeric is the only data type that can be used in numeric calculations. The subtypes of numeric data include *integers* and *real numbers*. Integers are whole numbers, such as 5,297 or −376. They can be positive or negative. Real numbers, or floating point numbers, are whole numbers plus decimal parts. In problem solving on the computer, programmers use integers when there is no reason for using partial numbers, as when they are designing counters, expressions used for counting things, such as inventory items or people. A real number can be expressed in scientific notation, such as 2.3*E*5 or 5.4*E*–3. In scientific notation, the *E* stands for *times 10 to the power of.* Therefore, 2.3*E*5 is the same number as 2.3×10^5, or 230,000.0, and 5.4*E*–3 is the same number as 5.4×10^{-3}, or 0.0054. A number expressed in scientific notation is always considered a real data type. The computer does not use commas in a number during the processing of a calculation, only when the number is formatted as output for the user.

Numeric data are used for values, such as rate of pay, salary, angles, distance, or radius, that have calculations performed on them. Numbers such as an account number or a zip code, which would not have calculations performed on them, would not be designated by the programmer as numeric data.

Data Set

Each data type has a *data set,* the set of symbols necessary to specify a datum as a particular data type. A data set is the set of values that are allowed in a particular data type. The data set for the numeric data type includes all base 10 numbers, the plus sign (+), and the negative sign (−). The data set for the integers includes all whole numbers within the limitations of the computer or the language, and for the real numbers, all whole numbers with decimal parts within the limitations of the computer or the language, including zero as a whole number and zero as a decimal part.

Table 2.3 Data Types and Their Data Sets

Data Type	Data Set	Examples
Numeric: Integer	All whole numbers	3580 −46
Numeric: Real	All real numbers (whole + decimal)	−3792.91 4739416.0 0.00246
Character (surrounded by quotation marks)	All letters, numbers, and special symbols	"A" "a" "M" "z" "k" "1" "5" "7" "8" "0" "+" "=" "(" "%" "$"
String (surrounded by quotation marks)	Combinations of more than one character	"Arcata" "95521" "707-444-5555"
Logical	*True False*	*True False*

Character Data—Alphanumeric Data

character data

The **character data** set, sometimes called alphanumeric data set, consists of all single-digit numbers, letters, and special characters available to the computer—a, A, Z, 3, #, &, and so forth—placed within quotation marks. An upper case letter is considered a different character from a lower case letter. The ASCII (American Standard Code for Information Interchange) character set contains 256 characters. The first 128 comprise a standard set (see Appendix C for the ASCII and EBCDIC data codes), and the second 128 differ with each computer. Characters cannot be used for calculations even if they consist of only numbers. When more than one character are put together, the computer considers this item a *string*—derived from *a string of characters*. Some languages do not differentiate between characters and strings. All character data are considered string data.

String Data

Character and string data can be compared and arranged in alphabetical order in the following way. The computer gives each character a number. This numeric representation is necessary because the computer works only with numbers. The numbers are compared to see which is larger and are then arranged in ascending numeric order. Since *B* has a larger number representing it than *A, B* is placed after *A*. *C* would follow *B* by the same method, and so forth. String data can be tested in the same way to alphabetize names, cities, and the like. *Banana* is larger than *Apple* because *B* has a larger number representing it than *A*. *Joan* is larger than *James* since the letter *o* is attributed a larger number than *a*. Upper case letters have smaller numeric representations than lower case letters. It is important to bear this difference in mind when you are comparing letters to see if they are equal. Languages that differentiate between lower case and upper case are called case sensitive. When they are not case sensitive, upper- and lower case letters are treated the same. You can use functions before the comparison to ensure that data are not case sensitive by making all letters either upper- or lower case.

concatenation

Character data or string data can be joined together with the + operator in an operation called **concatenation**. When two pieces of character data are joined, the concatenation results in the second being placed at the end of the first, as in "4" + "4" = "44" (not "8"). Concatenation could be used to join a first name with a last name or to join pieces of data together to make a code for an inventory item. The concatenation operator varies with each language.

Most data in business—names, account numbers, addresses, cities, states, telephone numbers, zip codes—are string data. As a rule, items that would not have mathematical computations performed on them should be designated string data types. There is another reason for designating a zip code as string data. If you are using numeric data, there is no way to hold onto leading zeros, that is, the zeros at the front of a number, such as 00987. As a result, a zip code on the East Coast could not be entered correctly as a numeric datum. The leading zeros could be preserved only with string data.

Logical Data

logical data

Logical data consist of two values in the data set—the words *True* and *False*. (Some languages accept *yes, T,* and *Y* for *True,* and *no, F,* and *N* for *False* as part of the data set.) These are used in making yes-or-no decisions. For example, logical data type might be used to check someone's credit record; *True* would mean her credit is okay, and *False* would mean it's not okay. A home accounting system could use logical data type for check returns; *True* would mean the check has been returned, and *False* would mean it has not. There are many such uses for logical data. They are discussed further in later

chapters. Remember, the logical data set *True* and *False* are *not* string data and are considered reserved words—that is, word that cannot be used as variable names.

Other Data Types

Date Data Type

There are other data types available to most programmers, such as the date data type and user-defined data types. The date data type is a number for the date that is the number of days from a certain date in the past such as the first day of the 20th century or January 1, 1940. The use of this data type for the date allows the user to subtract one date from another date to calculate the number of days between dates. This simplifies the calculation when the dates cross over years or months. The date is printed in the date format instead of a number. The date data type is a numeric data type because you can perform mathematical calculations on any date.

User Defined Data Types

Programmers may define their own data types, such as data types that have as their data set soda pop brands, or types of cars, or computer components. The user must specify the items in the data set for each user-defined data type. If the data item is not contained within the data set, it is not part of the set. For example, if the programmer does not include *Mouse* as part of the data set for a user-defined data type of computer parts, then the computer does not recognize a *Mouse* as a computer part.

This book will use the date data type in a few places; however, user-defined data types will not be further discussed or used.

Rules for Data Types

Rules for Data Types

1. The data that define the value of a variable or a constant will most commonly be one of three data types: numeric, character (including character string), or logical.
2. The programmer designates the data type during the programming process. The computer then associates the variable name with the designated data type.
3. Data types cannot be mixed. For example, string data cannot be placed in a variable memory location that has been designated as numeric, and vice versa. When the computer expects a certain data type, the user must use that type or the computer will return an error message.
4. Each of the data types uses what is called a *data set* (see Table 2.3). The numeric data uses the set of all base 10 numbers, the plus sign ($+$), and the negative sign ($-$); the character type uses the set of all characters available to the computer; the logical data type uses the set of data consisting of the words *True* and *False*. The use of any data outside the data set results in an error.
5. Any numeric item that must be used in calculations resulting in a numeric result must be designated as numeric data type. All other numbers should be designated as character or character-string data types, even if data are all numbers, as in zip codes.

Examples of Data Types

Table 2.4 illustrates some common uses for numeric, character (including character string), and logical data types. Data are drawn from everyday life and business, and are examples of the kinds of data that are commonly used in solving various types of

Table 2.4 Examples of Data Types

Data	Data Type	Explanation
The price of an item: 7.39, 12.98	Numeric: real	The price of an item would be used in calculations. The price is money and needs decimals.
An account number: "A2453," "2987"	Character string	An account number consists of alphanumeric or simply numeric data. It is not used for calculations.
A quantity: 12389	Numeric: integer	A quantity is used for calculations. It is an integer because it normally is a whole number.
The name of a company: "Smith Corp."	Character string	A name of something is alphabetical and therefore would be character string data type.
A credit check: *True, False*	Logical	The credit check of a customer would be a choice of two answers such as *yes,* it is okay, or *no,* it is not okay. Therefore, it should be logical data.
A zip code: "95521" "76548" "00538"	Character string	A zip code would be a character string because there are no calculations to be done on a zip code, and the leading zeros need to be retained.
A date: 01/23/87 or "03/14/87"	Date or character string	If the date data type is available, then it is used; if not, then it has to be a string because it is alphanumeric.
A date: 187259	Numeric: integer	A calendar date is the number of days from a given date, such as the first day of the 20th century. It can be used for calculations.
Social Security Number "333-33-3333"	Character string	A SSN is string data because it is alphanumeric and is not used for calculations.

problems on the computer. To the right of the data examples are data types and explanations of why each type is appropriate to the data.

How the Computer Stores Data

Data Storage

The computer stores data internally in memory locations. These data are found by the variable names used by a program. Each variable name is given a memory location, and each memory location can hold one and only one value at a time. When a user enters a new value into the variable location, the previous value is destroyed. These memory locations are temporary, as the internal memory is a volatile memory. When a program completes its instructions, and/or when the computer is turned off, the values stored in the internal memory are destroyed.

Data and instructions are temporarily stored in the computer's internal memory during the processing. When data, information, or programs have to be kept for future

use, they are stored externally on an external storage medium such as a hard disk drive in storage areas called **files.** There are basically two types of files: program files and data files. Program files contain the instructions to tell the computer what to do. This book helps the programming student create programs that will be saved on the external storage device as program files. Data files contain the data required to execute the program files.

Functions

functions

Functions are small sets of instructions that perform specific tasks and return values. They are usually built into a computer language. Functions are used as parts of instructions in a solution. Because they are basic tasks that are used repeatedly in the problem-solving process, by using them a programmer or user can shorten the problem-solving time and improve the readability of the solution. Each language has a set of functions within it. This set varies with the language and the computer. Most languages allow programmers to write their own functions. Libraries of functions can be added to many languages.

The form of a function is the name of the function followed by an open parenthesis, followed by the data needed to perform the function and concluded by a closed parenthesis:

FunctionName(data)

The value of the result of the function is returned in the name of the function.

parameter

Functions use data. The data is listed as part of the function and are called **parameters.** Functions normally do not alter the parameters. Take the square root function, *Sqrt(N)*. This function will calculate the square root of *N*. *Sqrt* is the name of the function. N is the data needed to calculate the square root and, therefore, it is the parameter. Parameters are surrounded by parentheses. The maximum function, *Max(N1, N2, N3)*, will find which of three numbers is the largest. The name of the function is *Max*. The parameters, data surrounded by parentheses and needed to do the calculation, are *N1, N2,* and *N3*. Not all functions need parameters. The function *Random* generates or calculates a random number. No data are needed to do this calculation, so there are no parameters. A parameter can be a constant, a variable, or an expression. (An expression is a calculation, such as interest/100, which has not been given a permanent memory location in the computer.) The names of the functions may vary from language to language. This book will give a generic name to each function and list the parameters in parentheses.

Table 2.5 lists and defines a few of the basic functions that are found in many languages. Functions are unique to each language. As a programmer, you need to investigate the functions used in the language in which you are writing your solution. These functions have been divided into classes.

Types of Functions

1. *Mathematical functions.* Often used in science and business, mathematical functions calculate such things as square root, absolute value, or a random number. Other mathematical functions used primarily for scientific purposes have not been included in the table.
2. *String functions.* These are used to manipulate string variables. For example, they copy part of the string into another variable, find the length or the number of characters in the string, and so forth.

Table 2.5 Functions (continued on page 23)

Function*	Definition	Example	Result
Mathematical Functions			
Sqrt(N)	Returns the square root of N.	Sqrt(4)	2
Abs(N)	Returns the absolute value of N.	Abs(−3)	3
Round(N, n1)	Returns the rounded value of N to the n1 place.	Round (3.7259,2)	3.73
Integer(N)	Returns the closest whole number less than or equal to N.	Integer (5.7269)	5
Random	Returns a random number between 0 and 1, but not 1. This number is mathematically generated. To find a number N between N1 and N2, inclusive, use the following formula: $N = \text{Integer}(Random * (N2 - N1 + 1)) + N1$, where N1 is the smallest number and N2 is the largest number.	Random	0.239768
Sign(N)	Returns the sign of N: 1 when N is positive, 0 when N is zero, −1 when N is negative.	Sign(7.39)	1
String Functions			
Mid(S, n1, n2)	Returns a set of n2 characters starting at n1 in the string S.	Mid(S, 3, 2) where S = "Thomas"	"om"
Left(S, n)	Returns a set of n characters on the left side of the string S.	Left (S, 3) where S = "Thomas"	"Tho"
Right(S, n)	Returns a set of n characters on the right side of the string S.	Right (S, 3) where S = "Thomas"	"mas"
Length(S)	Returns the number of characters in the string S.	Length(S) where S = "Thomas"	6

*Definitions of symbols:
N is a numeric value—a constant, a variable, or an expression
S is a string value—a constant, a variable, or an expression
n, n1, n2 are integer values—a constant, a variable, or an expression

3. *Conversion functions.* These functions are used to convert data from one data type to another. For example, since character strings cannot be used in calculations, one of these functions would convert a string value to a numeric value.
4. *Statistical functions.* These functions are used to calculate things such as maximum values, minimum values, and so forth.
5. *Utility functions.* This class is very important in business programming because most reports require some use of utility functions. They access information outside the program and the language in the computer system. Examples of these include date and time functions.

Table 2.5 *(Continued from page 22)*

Function*	Definition	Example	Result
Conversion Functions (change data type)			
Value(S)	Changes a string value into a numeric value.	*Value*("57.39")	+57.39
String(N)	Changes a numeric value into a string value.	*String* (+57.39)	"57.39"
Statistical Functions			
Average(list)	Returns the average of a list of numbers.	*Average* (5, 3, 8, 6)	5.5
Max(list)	Returns the maximum value from a list of numbers.	*Max* (5, 3, 8, 6)	8
Min(list)	Returns the minimum value from a list of numbers.	*Min* (5, 3, 8, 6)	3
Sum(list)	Returns the sum of a list of numbers.	*Sum* (5, 3, 8, 6)	22
Utility Functions			
Date	Returns the current date from the system. The date may be in various forms: *mm/dd/yy,* day only, month only, year only, or Julian calendar.	*Date*	09/15/98
Time	Returns the current time from the system. The time may be in various forms: *hh:mm:ss,* seconds from midnight, or minutes from midnight.	*Time*	9:22:38
Error	Returns control to the program when a systems error occurs.		

Note: Other functions are listed in Appendix F.

Table 2.5 is only a partial list of functions. There are many other functions that are not listed here and may not be universal. Many languages have hundreds of functions for the programmer's use. As a programmer, you should check the function list as to the availability of the types of functions you might want to use. You also need to note that function names are not allowed to be used as variable, constant, or module names. They are considered reserved words. Using these reserved words will cause a bug in a program.

Operators

operator

The computer has to be told how to process data. This task is accomplished through the use of operators. **Operators** are the data connectors within expressions and equations. They tell the computer how to process the data. They also tell the computer what type of processing (mathematical, logical, or whatever) needs to be done. The types of operators used in calculations and problem solving include mathematical, relational, and logical operators. Without these operators very little processing can be done.

Operand
Resultant

The *operand* and the *resultant* are two concepts related to the operator. Operands are the data that the operator connects and processes. The resultant is the answer that results when the operation is completed. For example, in the expression 5 + 7, the + is the operator, 5 and 7 are the operands, and 12 is the resultant. Operands can be constants or variables. The data type of the operands and the resultant depends on the operator.

mathematical operator　　**Mathematical operators** include addition, subtraction, multiplication, division, integer division, modulo division, powers, and functions. The computer has a symbol for each of them (see Table 2.6). You are probably familiar with addition, subtraction, multiplication, division, and powers. However, you may not be familiar with integer and modulo division.

These two operations are related. In integer division, the resultant is the whole number in the quotient. In modulo division, the resultant is the whole number remainder. These two types of division are used in business to find the hours and minutes someone has worked given the total number of minutes, or the days and weeks worked given the total number of days. For example, if Jane Smith has worked 19 days during the month, then, assuming a 5-day work week, she has worked 19 \ 5 = 3 weeks and 19 MOD 5 = 4 days. Therefore, she has worked 3 weeks and 4 days. When dividing 19 by 5, the result is 3 with a remainder of 4. The 3 is the resultant of the integer division and the 4 is the resultant of the modulo division. If the dividend is less than the divisor, such as 28 MOD 379, then the resultant is always equal to the dividend, in this case 28. The resultant of 28 \ 379 is zero because the dividend is less than the divisor. When you divide 28 by 379, your resultant is zero with a remainder of 28.

Table 2.6　Operators and Their Computer Symbols

Operator	Computer Symbol	Example	
Mathematical		Operation	Resultant
Addition	+	3.0 + 5.2	8.2
Subtraction	−	7.5 − 4.0	3.5
Multiplication	*	8.0 * 5.0	40.0
Division	/	9.0/4.0	2.25
Integer division	\	9\4	2
Modulo division	MOD	9 MOD 4	1
Power	^	3 ^ 2	9
Relational			
Equal to	=	5 = 7	*False*
Less than	<	5 < 7	*True*
Greater than	>	5 > 7	*False*
Less than or equal to	<= (two key strokes)	5 <= 7	*True*
Greater than or equal to	>= (two key strokes)	5 >= 7	*False*
Not equal to	<> (two key strokes)	5 <> 7	*True*
Logical			
Not	NOT	NOT *True*	*False*
And	AND	*True* AND *True*	*True*
Or	OR	*True* OR *False*	*True*

Relational operators include the following: equal to, less than, greater than, less than or equal to, greater than or equal to, and not equal to. A programmer uses relational operators to program decisions. The operands of a relational operator can be either numberic or character (a string); however, both operands must be of the same data type. The resultant of a relational operation is logical data type *True* or *False*. The programmer designs one action or set of actions that will follow when a relational expression is *True,* and another action or set of actions that will follow when the expression is *False.* The use of relational operators is the only way for the computer to make decisions.

For example, when a credit card customer's balance is *less than $500* (*True*), then the customer can charge another purchase. When the balance is *not less than $500* (*False*), then he cannot charge another purchase. The expression would be set up as *Balance* < 500. The operands are *Balance* and 500; the operator is <; the resultant is either *True* or *False* depending on the value of the balance. The programmer would use this expression in what is called a *decision instruction.*

Relational operators are also used to control repetitive instructions called *loops.* A set of instructions to enter data for a client, which would be repeated until the data are entered for every client, is one example of a loop. When the computer processes this type of instruction, the loop repeats until the resultant changes from *True* to *False,* or vice versa. In the example, the resultant would change when the computer can find no more client data to enter.

Logical operators are the third type of operator (see Table 2.7). Logical operators are used to connect relational expressions (decision-making expressions) and to perform

Table 2.7 Definitions of the Logical Operators

NOT

A	Not A	When A Is		The Resultant Is
True	False	NOT True	Is	False
False	True	NOT False	Is	True

AND

A	B	A AND B	When A Is		When B Is		The Resultant Is
True	True	True	True	AND	True	Is	True
True	False	False	True	AND	False	Is	False
False	True	False	False	AND	True	Is	False
False	False	False	False	AND	False	Is	False

OR

A	B	A OR B	When A Is		When B Is		The Resultant Is
True	True	True	True	OR	True	Is	True
True	False	True	True	OR	False	Is	True
False	True	True	False	OR	True	Is	True
False	False	False	False	OR	False	Is	False

OR Operator

operations on logical data. For example, a store might require a driver's license or a check-cashing card on file for a customer to cash a check. When the customer has a driver's license, the check can be cashed. When she has a check-cashing card, the check can be cashed. The expression is written as *License* OR *Card. License* and *Card* are the operands. They are logical data; that is, the value of each is *True* or *False.* The operator is OR. The resultant is *True* or *False* depending on the values of the operands. When one or both of the operands is *True,* then the resultant is *True.* When both of the operands are *False,* then the resultant is *False.*

AND Operator

The OR operator is one of three logical operators. The others are AND and NOT. When the AND operator is used, the resultant is *True* only when both of the operands are *True.* When either or both of the operands are *False,* the resultant is *False.* A programmer uses AND when two requirements must be *True* in order for an action or set of actions to take place, such as when a store requires a customer to have *both* a driver's license *and* a check-cashing card to cash a check. The NOT operator is the only logical operator that requires only one operand. The resultant of the NOT operator changes in an operand from *True* to *False,* or from *False* to *True.* A programmer uses the NOT operator to change an operand to the opposite value. This operation is sometimes called *reversing* the value of the operand.

NOT **Operator**

hierarchy

These mathematical, relational, and logical operators have a **hierarchy,** or precedence, an order in which their operations take place (see Table 2.8). To reorder the normal

Hierarchy of Operations

Table 2.8 Hierarchy of Operations

Order of Operations	Operand Data Type	Resultant Data Type
() Reorders the hierarchy; all operations are completed within the parentheses using the same hierarchy.		
1. Functions		
Mathematical Operators		
2. Power	Numeric	Numeric
3. \, MOD	Numeric	Numeric
4. *, /	Numeric	Numeric
5. +, −	Numeric	Numeric
Relational Operators		
6. =, <, >, <=, >=, <>	Numeric or string or character	Logical
Logical Operators		
7. NOT	Logical	Logical
8. AND	Logical	Logical
9. OR	Logical	Logical

processing sequence, the programmer uses parentheses. The processing of the operands (as directed by the operators) always starts with the innermost parentheses and works outward, and processes from left to right. Each level of operators within a set of parentheses requires that the computer make another pass through the parentheses, until all levels have been cleared. This hierarchy is important to the programmer because the order of the operations determines the result of the expression. If the operations are not completed in the correct order, the result of the expression may be incorrect. For example, assuming a 40-hour work week and overtime pay at 1.5 times regular pay, the expression to calculate overtime pay would subtract 40 from the hours worked and multiply the result by the regular wage times 1.5. The expression would be written as

$$(Hours - 40) * Wage * 1.5$$

As you can see from the hierarchy chart, multiplication is processed before subtraction, so parentheses must be added to tell the computer to do the subtraction first, before the multiplication. If the parentheses are not added, the result will be incorrect.

In this hierarchy table the integer and modulo divisions are on a separate level from real number multiplication and division. However, many languages place these four operators on the same level. When this is true, it is important to place parentheses around the integer or modulo operations so that the integer and modulo divisions are executed before the multiplication and division. In the following example you will get two different results depending upon whether you execute the integer and modulo division on the same level or separate them with parentheses to force different levels. Look at the equation:

$$F = 6 * 2 \setminus (6 + 2)$$

If the multiplication and integer division is on the same level, the answer will be 1. When they are on different levels, where the integer division will be executed first, the answer will be 0. Remember that the execution of operators on the same level is completed from left to right. To force the integer division to be executed first, resulting in a zero resultant, the equation would have to be changed to:

$$F = 6 * (2 \setminus (6 + 2))$$

Check with the language you are working with to find out whether integer and modulo divisions are on the same or different levels. In this book we will assume they are on the different levels. However, please be aware of the difference when starting to develop equations and expressions for the language you are learning.

Each type of operator requires a certain data type for operands and determines the data type of the resultant. Mathematical operators require numeric data as the operands and have numeric resultants. When any of the relational or logical operators are used (regardless of whether they are used in conjunction with mathematical operators), the resultant is logical data. Relational operators use numeric, character, or string data types as the operands; however, the data type of the operands of an operator must be the same. The logical operators require logical data for operands.

Expressions and Equations

A knowledge of constants and variables, of the three data types, and of operators, operands, and resultants is not very valuable until you can use these concepts to create expressions and equations. The problem you are trying to solve may be calculating pay,

including tax, Social Security, and medical deductions. It may be an inventory problem with reorder quantities and cash values. It may be a problem of calculating interest or payments on a loan, or of putting a mailing list in order. These tasks all require the use of different operators and would be written as expressions and equations in order for the computer to process the data and arrive at a result. There are very few computer problems that do not use expressions and equations in their solutions.

expression

Expressions and equations make up part of the instructions in the solution to a computer problem. An **expression** processes data, the operands, through the use of operators. For example, to find the number of square feet in a room you would multiply the length of the room by the width in the expression

$$Length * Width$$

equation

An **equation** stores the resultant of an expression in a memory location in the computer through the equal ($=$) sign. The expression above would be used as part of an instruction in the equation

$$Area = Length * Width$$

The resultant of the expression *Length * Width* would then be stored in a memory location called *Area*.

As you can see in Table 2.9, expressions use no equal sign (except as a relational operator) and are used as part of an instruction, such as part of an equation. The resultant of an expression is not stored and, therefore, is unavailable for use at another time. An expression can use numeric, string, character, or logical data types.

Equations are often called *assignment statements* because the variable on the left-hand side of the equal sign is assigned the value of the expression on the right-hand side. The equal sign does not mean *equals;* instead, it means *replaced by* or *is assigned the value of.* This distinction is important because it is possible to have equations on the computer that are not allowed in a mathematics class, such as $N = N + 1$ (one is added to the old value of N to get a new value of N). This equation is the way the computer counts. There is only one variable on the left-hand side of the equal sign. On the right-hand side of the equal sign is an expression. The right-hand side is processed before the assignment is made (see Table 2.9 and the examples that follow).

For the beginning programmer, a big part of learning to solve problems on the computer is learning how to write and evaluate expressions and equations. (Recall that

Table 2.9 Expressions and Equations

Expressions	Equations
$A + B$ A and B are numeric. The resultant is numeric and is not stored.	$C = A + B$ $C, A,$ and B are numeric. The resultant is stored in C.
$A < B$ A and B are numeric, character, or string. The resultant is logical and is not stored.	$C = A < B$ A and B are numeric, character, or string. The resultant is stored in C; C is logical.
A OR B A and B are logical. The resultant is logical and is not stored.	$C = A$ OR B $C, A,$ and B are logical. The resultant is stored in C.

to *evaluate* means to test for correctness using actual data.) The following examples illustrate how to use the concepts you've learned in this chapter to write and evaluate expressions and equations.

Example 1: Setting Up a Numeric Expression

A programmer will often be given an expression to use in solving a problem. Assume the programmer has to modify the following mathematical expression for computer use:

$$X(3Y + 4) - \frac{4Y}{X + 6}$$

The appropriate computer expression would be the following:

$$X * (3 * Y + 4) - 4 * Y/(X + 6)$$

All variables, constants, and operators have to be on the same line. There must be an operator between variables and/or constants. For the computer, there are no assumed multiplication signs. Parentheses are added when the hierarchy has to be reordered or when parentheses would improve readability.

Follow these steps to complete the expression:

1. Write all parentheses, operands, and operators on a single line with the dividend first, followed by the divisor:

$$X(3Y + 4) - 4Y/X + 6$$

2. Insert all implied operators. The computer does not use any implied operators as used in mathematics. These usually include multiplication and power signs.

$$X * (3 * Y + 4) - 4 * Y/X + 6$$

3. Insert all parentheses where the hierarchy needs to be reordered. $X + 6$ needs to be calculated before completing the division, therefore parentheses need to be inserted around the $X + 6$.

$$X * (3 * Y + 4) - 4 * Y/(X + 6)$$

Example 2: Setting Up a Mathematical Equation

A mathematical equation might be given to the programmer in the following form:

$$Y + 3 = X(Z + 5)$$

The programmer has to modify the equation so that it is in the form of an assignment instruction:

$$Y = X * (Z + 5) - 3$$

Notice that there is only one variable (and no calculations) on the left side and an expression on the right side of the equal sign.

Follow these steps to complete the equation:

1. Write all parentheses, operands, and operators on a single line:

$$Y + 3 = X(Z + 5)$$

2. Use mathematical rules to complete the equation so that there is one variable on the left side of the equal sign. In this case, subtract 3 from each side:

$$Y + 3 - 3 = X(Z + 5) - 3$$
$$Y = X(Z + 5) - 3$$

3. Follow the steps in Example 1 to complete the equation.

$$Y = X * (Z + 5) - 3$$

Example 3: Setting Up a Relational Expression

A relational expression is used to make decisions. Given the expression

$$X \text{ is less than } Y + 5$$

the programmer would change its form to the following:

$$X < Y + 5$$

Because this is a relational expression, either a numeric variable, a numeric constant, or a mathematical expression is on either side of the operator. X and Y would be the same data type, in this case, a numeric data type. The resultant would be a logical data type—*True* or *False,* depending on the values of X and Y.

Example 4: Setting Up a Logical Expression

Often a computer decision is based on more than one *True* or *False* operand. For example, in order to cash a check a customer must have a driver's license *(A)* or a check-cashing card *(B)* on file at the store. As is the case with all logical expressions, this case would require a logical operator, A OR B. The operands, A and B, are logical data type; it is either *True* or *False* that the customer has a driver's license, and *True* or *False* that she has a check-cashing card. The resultant is also a logical type: The customer can cash a check (*True* or *False*).

Example 5: Evaluating a Mathematical Expression

To find out if proposed solutions are correct, it is important for the programmer to evaluate, or test, all expressions and equations. Assume the programmer has written the expression

$$5 * (X + Y) - 4 * Y/(Z + 6)$$

The programmer uses the following values to evaluate the expression:

$$X = 2 \qquad Y = 3 \qquad Z = 6$$

Notice the structure of the evaluation that follows. A dashed line leading to a circle indicates the operator. The solid lines indicate the operands. Following the illustration of the equation is a list of the operations and the resultant of each operation. The number of circles should equal the number of operators. Be sure the circles using other circles are below the circles they need to use, that is, 3 is lower than 1, 6 is lower than 3 and 5.

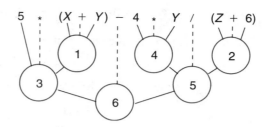

Operation	Resultant
1. $X + Y$	5
2. $Z + 6$	12
3. 5 * resultant of 1	25
4. 4 * Y	12
5. Resultant of 4 / resultant of 2	1
6. Resultant of 3 − resultant of 5	24

Illustrating the structure of the expression and listing the operations and results in this way simplifies the evaluation process for the programmer. The evaluation must be completed according to the hierarchy of operations. The operations within the parentheses would be completed first, moving from left to right—so $X + Y$ would be completed first, and $Z + 6$ second. According to the hierarchy, the programmer would then complete the multiplications and the divisions from left to right. The division would be completed after the multiplications in this expression only because it is to the right. The final operation to be completed would be the subtraction.

This evaluation shows how to test a computer expression to see if it matches an equivalent mathematical expression. It gives the programmer a correct result that can be compared to the results manually calculated by the client, or by whoever requested the computer solution to the problem, so one can be sure that the solution is correct.

Example 6: Evaluating a Relational Expression

Assume the programmer has written the expression

$$A - 2 > B$$

The programmer uses the following values to evaluate the expression:

$$A = 6 \qquad B = 8$$

The following illustration shows the structure of the evaluation:

Operation	Resultant
1. $A - 2$	4
2. Resultant of 1 > B	*False*

According to the hierarchy of operations, the mathematical operation is completed first.

Example 7: Evaluating a Logical Expression

Assume the programmer has written the expression

$$A \text{ AND } B \text{ OR } C \text{ AND } A$$

The programmer uses the following values to evaluate the expression:

$$A = \textit{True} \qquad B = \textit{False} \qquad C = \textit{True}$$

Operation	Resultant
1. A AND B	*False*
2. C AND A	*True*
3. Resultant of 1 OR resultant of 2	*True*

Example 8: Evaluating an Equation That Uses Both Relational and Logical Operators

Assume the programmer has written the following equation:

$$F = \text{NOT}(A < B) \text{ AND } (C \text{ OR } D)$$

The programmer uses the following values to evaluate the equation:

$$A = 4 \qquad B = 2 \qquad C = \textit{True} \qquad D = \textit{False}$$

The operations are completed in hierarchical order from left to right, as illustrated in the figure.

Operation	Resultant
1. $A < B$	*False*
2. C OR D	*True*
3. NOT the resultant of 1	*True*
4. Resultant of 3 AND resultant of 2	*True*
5. Store the resultant of 4 in the memory location called F.	

Example 9: Developing a Table of All Possible Resultants of a Logical Expression

It is often valuable for a programmer to figure out the resultants for all of the possible combinations of values of the variables in an expression. To create a table of all possible combinations, double the number of combinations from a table with one less unknown. For example:

- One unknown—A. Two combinations: A can be either *True* or *False*.

A
True
False

- Two unknowns—*A* and *B*. Four combinations: *B* can be either *True* or *False* for each value of *A*.

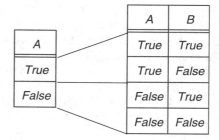

- Three unknowns—*A*, *B*, and *C*. Eight combinations.

A	B	C
True	True	True
True	True	False
True	False	True
True	False	False
False	True	True
False	True	False
False	False	True
False	False	False

A	B
True	True
True	False
False	True
False	False

Given the expression

<center>NOT A OR B</center>

the following table gives the resultants for all combinations of the values of *A* and *B*. The equation to find the number of combinations is 2^n, where *n* is the number of variables. For example, with two variables, *A* and *B*, there are four combinations; and with three variables, *A*, *B*, and *C*, there are eight combinations.

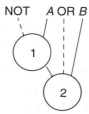

NOT *A* OR *B*

A	B	NOT *A* OR *B*
True	True	False
True	False	False
False	True	False
False	False	True

Example 10: Developing a Logical Expression from a Given Problem

Many times a programmer will be given the policies of a company and then be required to set up a logical expression from those policies. To do this, the programmer first needs to list the items on which the condition is dependent. Then the logical expression can be developed from this list.

> Problem: A large department store has its own charge card. The policy for a customer to charge an item is that the customer must have a valid charge card and either a balance of less than $500 or a charge of less than $50.

1. The first step is to list the items the charge is dependent on and their data types:
 a. the charge card (logical data type)
 b. the balance (numeric data type)
 c. the charge amount (numeric data type)
2. The second step is to write down these items as variables along with the conditions on each. Put them on one line, leaving space between, so that the logical operator can be added next. The resultant or the data type of each expression must be logical. Remember that the operators must match the data types of the operands (see Table 2.7). Do not put the logical operators in as of yet.

$$ChargeCard \quad Balance < 500 \quad Amount < 50$$

3. The third step is to put in the logical operators and parentheses:

$$ChargeCard \text{ AND } (Balance < 500 \text{ OR } Amount < 50)$$

Because the condition between the balance and the amount is one or the other, the OR operator is needed. The condition between the charge card and the other two items is both; this calls for the AND operator. Since the AND has precedence over the OR, the parentheses are added around the OR operation.
4. You have now created the logical expression. This expression can be used in various ways:
 a. In an assignment statement:

$$OkToChg = ChargeCard \text{ AND } (Balance < 500 \text{ OR } Amount < 50)$$

 b. In a decision statement (this will be explained in Chapter 6):

$$If \ ChargeCard \text{ AND } (Balance < 500 \text{ OR } Amount < 50)$$
$$Then \ Print \text{ "Okay to charge"}$$
$$Or \ Else \ Print \text{ "Not Okay to charge"}$$

Summary

This chapter explains fundamental concepts for solving problems on the computer, including constants, variables, data types, common functions, operators, expressions, and equations. It also shows the beginning programmer how to set up computer expressions and equations.

Constants are values that never change during processing, even when they are named constants; variables are values that do change. Constants and variables are assigned data

types and are used in expressions and equations. The most common data types include numeric, character, and logical.

Expressions and equations use functions to process standard tasks. Most functions are part of the computer language. Expressions and equations use operators to process the data. These operators are of three types: mathematical, relational, and logical. By using operators and the hierarchy of operations, a programmer can design calculations and decisions, which are the key to solving problems on the computer.

New Terms

character data	file	mathematical operator
concatenation	function	numeric data
constant	hierarchy	operator
data	identifier	parameter
data type	information	relational operator
equation	logical data	variable
expression	logical operator	

Questions

1. Name the reasons it is important to maintain a naming convention in a company.
2. Name the rules for naming constants and variables.
3. What is a constant? What is a variable?
4. Fill in the following table with the variable name and data type needed to solve an inventory problem for White Auto Supplies.

Data Item	Variable Name	Data Type
a. Name of vendor company		
b. Inventory item name		
c. Inventory number		
d. Quantity		
e. Price		
f. Address of company		
g. Date last ordered		
h. Reorder quantity		
i. Obsolete item (yes/no)		

5. Name the data type for each of the following constants. Explain your answer.
 a. 5.38
 b. "87654"

 c. *True*
 d. "A"
 e. "707-434-5555"
 f. "New York"
 g. −389
 h. 2.45E6
 i. 48976.0
 j. *False*

6. What is a function?

7. Why are functions used?

8. What is the difference between the operators /, \, and MOD? Give an example of each.

9. Find the result of the following operations:
 a. 5 + 4
 b. 10/2
 c. *True* OR *False*
 d. 20 MOD 3
 e. 5 < 8
 f. 25 MOD 70
 g. "A" > "H"
 h. NOT *True*
 i. 25\70
 j. *False* AND *True*
 k. 20 * 0.5
 l. 35 <= 35
 m. 35/7
 n. *False* OR *False*
 o. *True* AND *True*
 p. 50 MOD 5
 q. −35 < 67
 r. $4.0 ^ 3$
 s. 60\9
 t. 35 < 35
 u. *True* AND *False*

10. Using the hierarchy chart (Table 2.8), list the order in which the following operations would be processed. (Remember: Operations are processed left to right within a level in the hierarchy table.)
 a. +, −, *
 b. /, \, =
 c. OR, *, <
 d. NOT, AND, *
 e. NOT, >, +
 f. AND, OR, NOT
 g. <, AND, >, +
 h. *, ^, +
 i. NOT, +, \
 j. MOD, \, <

11. Name the data type of the operands and the resultant of each of the following expressions or equations.

	Data Types of Operands	Data Types of Resultant
a. $A * B$		
b. $D > R$		
c. NOT C		
d. B AND F		
e. $G = B$		

12. What is the difference between an expression and an equation?

13. What does the equal sign mean in an equation? Is the meaning of the equal sign as a relational operator different from that in an assignment statement? If so, in what way?

Problems

1. Evaluate the following equations, given the values $A = 12, B = 3, C = 6, D = 2$:
 a. $F = A + B/C - D^\wedge 2$
 b. $F = (A + B)/C - D^\wedge 2$
 c. $F = A + B/(C - D^\wedge 2)$
 d. $F = (A + B)$ MOD C
 e. $F = (A + B)\backslash D^\wedge 2$

2. Write the following equations in computer form:
 a. $X = Y + 3Z - \dfrac{Z + Y}{Z - 3}$

 b. $X = 5Y + \dfrac{3Z - 1}{4(3Z + 1) - Y}$

 $X = (X - Y)^2$

 c. $X = (X - Y)^2$

3. Is the $=$ sign an assignment instruction or a relational operator in the following equations? Justify your answer.
 a. $A = B + 2 + C$
 b. $A - B = 2 + C$

4. Set up an equation to calculate the following (create your own variable names):
 a. The area of a room.
 b. The wall area of a room including windows and doors.
 c. The wall area of a room not including two windows and a door.
 d. The number of miles given a number of feet. (Use 5,280 feet per mile.)
 e. The percent increase (or decrease) of a value given the beginning number and the ending number. How would the result differ between increase and decrease?
 f. The average of five numbers.
 g. The sale price of an item given an original price and a percentage discount.

5. Evaluate the following equations given $A = 5, B = 4, C = 3, D = 12$:
 a. $E = A * B + D/C$
 b. $E = D$ MOD $A * B$

 c. $E = 5 * A \backslash D * (B + 1)$
 d. $E = D/B * ((A + 4) \backslash (C + 1))$

6. An employee came in to work and clocked in at *MorningIn,* clocked out at *NoonOut* for lunch, clocked back in at *NoonIn,* and clocked out to go home at *NightOut* (all in minutes since midnight). Set up equations to calculate the number of hours and the number of minutes the employee worked for the day. (You will develop two equations.)

7. Steve Thompson bought and charged an electric saw on *Date1* and made the first payment on *Date2*. Write an equation to calculate how many days (*Days*) elapsed between the two dates.

$$Days =$$

8. Eureka Lumber Company gives a 2% discount if the remaining balance is paid within 10 days of purchase. Write a logical expression to verify whether a customer qualifies for this discount. Use the following variable names:

 BuyingDate: date the customer purchased the merchandise

 PaidDate: date the customer made the final payment

9. A part-time employee worked 20 hours in the first week and 15 hours in the second week of a two-week pay period. He is paid a weekly salary based on a 40-hour week. What is his full-time equivalent for the two weeks based on a 40-hour week (i.e., what percentage of full time did he work)? Write a general equation that could be used to express and store the full-time equivalent of any hours worked per week.

$$FullTime =$$

10. Roger would like to know the average of his test scores. Write an equation that would calculate the average given five test scores. Write the equation with and without using a function.

11. Sharon is traveling from city A to city B. The distance between the two cities is a variable because she would like to use the equation to use for other cities. She knows that 50% of the time she will be traveling 30 miles an hour and the remaining 50% she will be traveling 65 miles per hour. Write an equation that will calculate the time it will take to travel from one city to the next.

12. Evaluate the following equations, given $A = $ *False*, $B = $ *True*, $C = $ *False*, $D = $ *True*. (Include the structure of the order of processing—see page 32 for example.)
 a. $R = A$ AND B OR C AND D
 b. $R = $ NOT $(A$ AND $B)$ OR NOT $(D$ AND $C)$
 c. $R = (A$ OR $B)$ AND $(D$ OR $C)$
 d. $R = $ NOT $(A$ AND B OR $C)$ AND $(A$ OR B AND $D)$
 e. $R = C$ OR NOT $(A$ AND $D)$ AND $(A$ OR $B)$ OR NOT $(A$ OR $C)$

13. Create a table that gives all possible answers for the following logical equations. (Include the structure of the order of processing—see page 33 for example.) Make clear how you set up the table.
 a. $R = A$ OR B
 b. $R = $ NOT A OR B
 c. $R = A$ AND B AND $(B$ OR $C)$
 d. $R = $ NOT $(A$ OR $B)$ AND NOT $(B$ OR $C)$
 e. $R = B$ AND NOT $(A$ OR $C)$ OR NOT $(B$ AND $C)$

14. Evaluate the following for the values $A = 5, B = 2, C = True, D = False$. (Include the structure of the order of processing.)
 a. $R = A + 3 > B - 1$ AND C OR D
 b. $R =$ NOT C OR D OR $A - 3 <= B$

15. Set up a logical expression for the following conditions. A company gives a bonus at the end of each fiscal year. For an employee to get a bonus, the following must be true:
 a. The employee has been working at the company for more than six months with no negative reports.
 b. The employee has earned more than $5,000 during the fiscal year.

16. Set up a logical expression for the following conditions. A retail store has this check-cashing policy:
 a. The customer must have a driver's license.
 b. When the check is for more than $50, the customer must have a check-cashing card on file.

WHAT'S WRONG WITH THIS?

1. What is wrong with these variable names? Can you correct them?
 a. *City Name* referencing the name of a city.
 b. *Client-name* referencing a client name.
 c. *City/State* referencing a city and state.
 d. *LN* referencing a last name.
 e. *Street address*
 f. *Q* for a quantity of books
 g. *Street_Address_for_Joe's_Hardware_Supply_Incorporated_Client*

2. The answers given are wrong. What is the correct answer and why are the answers wrong?

 The answer to: is:
 a. 5 MOD 255 0
 b. 250\100 2.5

3. What is wrong with the following expressions? Can you correct them?
 a. "L" < 5
 b. "D" * "5"
 c. *True* < "F"
 d. *False* >= 5

Chapter 3

Planning Your Solution

Overview

Communicating with the Computer

Organizing the Solution
 Analyzing the Problem
 Developing the Interactivity Chart
 Developing the IPO Chart
 Writing the Algorithms
 Drawing the Flowcharts
 Internal and External Documentation

Using the Tools

Testing the Solution

Coding the Solution

Objectives

When you have finished this chapter, you should be able to:

1. List and describe the six basic tools used in this book to aid in the development of a solution to a problem.
2. Use a problem analysis chart to consolidate data for a problem.
3. Use an interactivity chart to designate the modules to be used in the solution of a problem.
4. Use an IPO chart to designate the input, processing, module number, and output for a solution of a problem.
5. Use algorithms and flowcharts to develop the instructions for each module in the solution of a problem.
6. Describe the importance of internal and external documentation.

Computers are only as good as their hardware, their software, and the people using them. Assuming the hardware has been engineered to accomplish a given job, the efficiency of the computer relies on the effectiveness of the programmer.

The computer must be told what to do. It needs a set of instructions, the solution, in order to process data in the correct sequence and reach the desired results. For greatest efficiency, the programmer or the user has to be able to easily read and interpret the solution. The solution will be most effective if the programmer follows certain steps and rules that have been developed over the years. The solution becomes a program when it is coded into a computer language during the final stages of programming.

Programmers have three resources that they need to optimize for cost effectiveness: computer memory, computer time, and programmer time. Early computers were much less useful and efficient than they are today. Programmers worked alone, and only when they left a company did their programs go to others. Since computers were slow and had small memories, conservation of computer time and memory was of utmost importance. For these reasons and the fact that the profession was new, programs were often hard to read and maintain. Over the years, both computers and programming methods have changed. Because programs are larger and more complex, and need to be completed in less time than ever before, today many programmers work together on the same program. As a result, readability is now what's most important. Because computers are much faster with much more memory, programmers may sacrifice these resources somewhat in favor of improved readability. Cost effectiveness, decrease in programmer frustration, and increase in programmer satisfaction are the rewards.

The type of problem the computer can solve best is one that can be solved algorithmically—that is, the problem can be solved with a single sequence of instructions. These instructions must be written in a way the computer can understand, and the computer executes them in the order presented in the program. If the instructions are written according to the appropriate rules and they correctly follow the syntax of the computer language, then the computer will complete the task. Although this scrupulous adherence to the instructions is usually what the programmer wants, it is also, believe it or not, the most frustrating thing about the computer. If the instructions make sense to the computer, it will complete them. If the programmer has made an error in the instructions, the results are not likely to be what was intended. The computer does not reason, nor does it read minds; it only follows instructions.

Communicating with the Computer

Since the computer does not speak English as you do, you have to learn its system of communication or language. For the computer to "understand" a message, its system of communication requires instructions governed by specific rules. If the instructions you write are incorrect, the computer will give an error message, the wrong answer, or no answer at all. If the instructions are not properly sequenced, the computer will, nevertheless, execute them in the order given, and the result will be wrong.

syntax
bug
debugging

The meaning of an instruction is essentially the same in any computer language or application. The differences between instructions from one language and another are in how they are set up. **Syntax** refers to the rules governing the computer operating system, the language, and the application. An error is called a **bug.** A bug must be found and corrected, a process called **debugging.** Many bugs are a result of syntax errors, but some are logic errors. You can find and correct most logic errors during the problem-solving process. You will find and correct syntax errors when you enter your

program into the computer. All syntax errors must be corrected before you execute and test your program.

Although a set of instructions must be in a correct order to lead to the correct result, there may be several "correct" orders, just as there are several routes leading from New York to San Francisco. Whether the routes are equally efficient doesn't affect the result. When efficiency is important, then and only then should each route be examined and kept or discarded. People employ different logic and different ways of thinking. Two programmers may develop equally good solutions to a problem, but the solutions may look entirely different. There is nothing wrong with this. Computers are exact machines, but the people working with them are not.

Organizing the Solution

problem analysis chart
structure chart
interactivity chart
IPO chart
algorithms
flowchart

Certain organizational tools will help you learn to solve problems on the computer. The tools used in this book and illustrated in this chapter include the **problem analysis chart,** which shows a beginning analysis of the problem; the **structure chart** or **interactivity chart,** which shows the overall layout or structure of the solution; the **IPO chart,** which shows the input, the processing, and the output; the **algorithms,** which show the sequence of instructions comprising the solution; and the **flowcharts,** which are graphic representations of the algorithms. To analyze a problem and set up the most efficient solution, a programmer organizes the solution by using all or some of these tools. When the programmer does not use these tools during the problem-solving process, the solution takes longer to program, and the final program is less efficient, lacks readability, and increases programmer frustration.

Analyzing the Problem

To organize a solution, the programmer first has to understand and analyze the requirements of the problem. A good way to analyze a problem is to separate it into four parts, shown in the problem analysis chart (PAC) in Figure 3.1:

1. The given data
2. The required results
3. The processing that is required in the problem
4. A list of solution alternatives

Given Data	Required Results
Section 1: Data given in the problem or provided by the user. These can be known values or general names for data, such as price, quantity, and so forth.	Section 2: Requirements for the output reports. This includes the information needed and the format required.
Processing Required	Solution Alternatives
Section 3: List of processing required. This includes equations or other types of processing, such as sorting, searching, and so forth.	Section 4: List of ideas for the solution of the problem.

Figure 3.1 Problem Analysis Chart

(A blank problem analysis chart for student use appears in Appendix D, Figure D.1). As a problem unfolds (in a textbook or in the real world), the programmer can use this form to sort it out. The PAC allows the problem solver to eliminate the words and glean only the facts from the problem. Data, constants and variables, would be entered in the Given Data section. Variable data are the input values. Requirements for the output reports would be entered under Required Results. Any equations or other processing requirements would be listed in the Processing Required section. Finally, the programmer would write any other ideas that spring to mind concerning the solution in the Solution Alternatives section.

The following problem illustrates the use of the problem-solving tools: Calculate the gross pay of an employee given the hours worked and the rate of pay. The gross pay is calculated by multiplying the hours worked by the rate of pay.

Figure 3.2 shows how the problem solver would fill in the PAC for this problem. The hours worked and the pay rate are the data given and are put into the Given Data box. The gross pay is what needs to be calculated and given to the user; therefore it is put into the Required Results box. The formula used is

$$GrossPay = Hours * PayRate$$

It is put into the Processing Required box. The Solution Alternatives are as follows:

1. Define the hours worked and the pay rate as constants.
2. Define the hours worked and the pay rate as input values.

The second alternative will be used, as signified by the asterisk in the figure, since the program will not need to be changed in order to calculate the gross pay for another employee.

The problem analysis chart is an aid to clear thinking because it helps the problem solver to identify the essential data and information in a problem and to disregard the nonessentials. Most problems programmers work with are word problems. This is true whether they are working in a classroom situation or out on the job. The PAC helps to pare down the words.

Developing the Interactivity Chart

module

The next step in organizing your solution is to divide the processing into subtasks called **modules** and then to connect these modules together to show the interaction of processing between the modules. Each module should contain the tasks to accomplish one

Given Data	Required Results
Hours Pay Rate	Gross Pay
Processing Required	Solution Alternatives
*GrossPay = Hours * PayRate*	1. Define the hours worked and pay rate as constants. *2. Define the hours worked and pay rate as input values.

Figure 3.2 Problem Analysis Chart for the Payroll Problem

function, such as entering data, printing results, or calculating results. There will be one module that controls the flow to most of the other modules. This will be called the *Control* or *Main* module. Each module should contain no more than 20 instructions. This breakdown enables you to view a complex problem in simpler parts and to program smaller, simpler parts of a program rather than one large, complex program. This chart is called the interactivity chart or structure chart. In the rest of the text, we will refer to this chart as the interactivity chart since it really shows how the modules interact with each other.

Today's programmer will use two different ways of looking at a solution to a problem. Before the advent of the graphic user interface, all solutions were procedural in nature. Solutions were developed using a top-down method to develop a procedural program that was executed from the first lines of code to the end. The user had very little to do with the order of execution of the modules. The program was in complete control. However, with the advent of the graphic user interface, which allows the user to choose what to do next, programming changed from procedural to object-oriented programming. In object-oriented programming, execution is completed through an interactivity between the computer and the user. The user is in control, not the program. Modules are still used, and are basically the same. Within each module the execution is procedural. The difference lies in when each module will be executed. In procedural programming, there is a direct order of processing. In object-oriented programming, there is no preconceived order. The user directs the order of execution of the modules. Object-oriented programming is discussed in Chapters 16 and 17. The Object Oriented Activity Chart will be discussed in these chapters.

In developing the procedural interactivity chart, use the top-down method. The top-down method simply means that as you divide the problem into subtasks, you illustrate them in the order in which they will be processed from the top to the bottom of the chart. When using the top-down method, the module that encompasses the complete solution becomes what is called the *Control* module because it controls the processing of all the data. The subtasks of this module are then located below it in the structure chart. The interactivity chart shows what will happen, not how it will happen.

As you can see in Figure 3.3, the interactivity chart shows the relationships of the parts of a problem to each other and to the whole. The programmer indicates duplicate modules by darkening the upper left-hand corner of each module and writing the name of the module

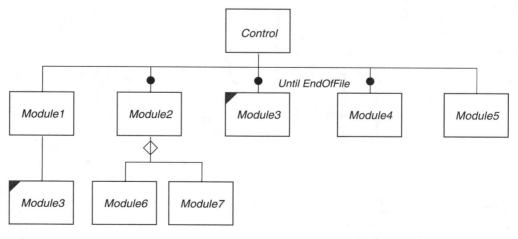

Figure 3.3 The Interactivity Chart

inside the rectangle, giving the same name to identical tasks. Notice in Figure 3.3 that *Module3* is found in two places, indicating that it is processed at two different points in the solution. Since it is the same module in both places, it carries the same name.

A module processes only those tasks connected to it by a network of horizontal and vertical lines. In Figure 3.3, the *Control* module processes *Module1, Module2, Module3, Module4,* and *Module5.* The darkened circles indicate that the module is part of a set of modules that are processed many times—those in a loop. At the level below the *Control* module, *Module1* processes *Module3,* and *Module2* processes *Module6* and *Module7.* However, only one of these modules will be processed since they are part of a decision. That is, the instructions in *Module2* and the appropriate data would lead the computer to choose one of the two modules. The diamond on the vertical line above the box indicates which modules are involved in a decision. Annotation may be placed beside the circle or diamond to indicate the condition. (Appendix D, Figure D.2 is an interactivity chart for student use.)

Dividing a solution into modules is not an easy job. When you approach a solution to a problem, you need to think about the basic things you want to accomplish, during the processing, in general terms. Some of these might be input of data, initialization of data, types of processing such as calculations or putting data in order, and completing the solution. In most solutions you will have a control module that controls the processing of the solution. In Figure 3.4, the modules include:

1. The control module (Control) to control the processing of the solution.
2. An initialize module (Initialize) to process data that needs to be accomplished only once in the solution and at the beginning.
3. A read module (Read) to enter data needed in the solution.
4. Two modules (Salaried and Hourly) to enter data needed for two different types of employees.
5. A calculation module (Calculate) to process the data for each employee.
6. A print module (Print) to print the processed information.
7. A wrap-up module (WrapUp) to process any data that should be done only once in the solution and at the end of the solution.

These are some of the standard modules. In the next several chapters you might start with four modules. The control module, the read module, the calculation module, and the print module are basic to most programs. From there, add other modules as needed

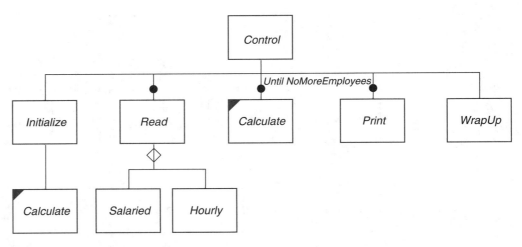

Figure 3.4 The Completed Interactivity Chart

along with the addition of processing symbols showing which modules are duplicates, which are part of a decision, and which are repeated in a loop. In Figure 3.4, the Calculate module is duplicated in two places as indicated by the shaded in corner; the Salaried and Hourly modules are part of a decision as indicated by the diamond; and the Read module, the Calculate module, and the Print module are repeated until the NoMoreEmpolyees (when there are no more employees to process) as indicated by the filled-in circle. These concepts will be discussed further in Chapter 4.

Figure 3.5 shows the interactivity chart for the payroll problem. The top rectangle is the *Control* module, which processes the *Read,* the *Calc,* and the *Print* modules.

Developing the IPO Chart

The IPO (input-processing-output) chart extends and organizes the information in the problem analysis chart. It shows in more detail what data items are input, what processing takes place on that data, and what information will be the end result, the output (see Figure 3.6). The IPO chart also shows where in the solution the processing takes place. The output is the first to be completed in an IPO chart. The next is the input, and the last is the processing. This may sound backwards, but it is really very logical. An analogy to completing an IPO chart would be planning a trip. The first thing you need to know is the destination—San Francisco, Paris, New York. This information is the output. Then you can plan what to pack, your means of transportation, and all the other essentials for starting out—the input. Finally, you plan the route—the processing. How can you know what to pack or what route to follow if you don't know where you're going?

The IPO chart has four sections: the Input, the Processing, the Module Reference, and the Output. The Input section contains all input data from the problem analysis chart. The input includes all given data from Section 1 on the problem analysis chart. The

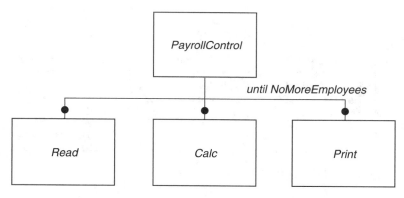

Figure 3.5 The Interactivity Chart for the Payroll Problem

Input	Processing	Module Reference	Output
All input data (from Section 1 of the problem analysis chart)	All processing in steps (from Sections 3 and 4 of the problem analysis chart)	Module reference from the interactivity chart	All output requirements (from Sections 1 and 2 of the problem analysis chart)

Figure 3.6 The IPO Chart

Processing section contains all processing, evident and implied, from Sections 3 and 4 of the problem analysis chart. The Module Reference section contains the number from the interactivity chart of the module in which each step in the processing is to be completed. The Output section includes all required output as designated by the problem and/or the user; it comes from Section 2, along with the needed input items from Section 1, of the problem analysis chart. (An IPO chart for student use appears in Appendix D, Figure D.3.)

To illustrate how to use an IPO chart, Figure 3.7 shows one for the payroll problem. The input, the processing, and the output are taken from Figure 3.2, the problem analysis chart for the payroll problem. The module references are taken from Figure 3.5, the interactivity chart for this problem. They show which module will perform each step in the processing. Notice also that these steps are numbered in the order to be processed.

Writing the Algorithms

After using the structure chart and the IPO chart, the next step in organizing a solution is for the programmer to develop sets of instructions for the computer, called *algorithms* (see Figure 3.8). **Pseudocode** is very similar to algorithms, and many times the words are used interchangeably. Pseudocode usually includes some syntax of the language. Since this book is generic in nature, we will use the word *algorithm* to indicate the set of instructions needed to solve the problem.

To complete all of the algorithms needed to solve a problem, the programmer writes a separate set of instructions for each module in the structure chart. To be understood by the computer, the instructions have to be written according to certain rules that will be explained in future chapters throughout this book. Setting up the algorithms is probably the hardest part of problem solving on the computer. *The instructions cannot assume anything, cannot skip steps, must be executable one step at a time, and must be complete.* The modules are taken from the interactivity chart, and the processing is taken

Input	Processing	Module Reference	Output
Hours Worked Pay Rate	1. Enter Hours Worked 2. Enter Pay Rate 3. Calculate Pay 4. Print Pay 5. End	*Read* *Read* *Calc* *Print* *PayRollControl*	Gross pay

Figure 3.7 The IPO Chart for the Payroll Problem

```
Control Module              Name of Module (list of parameters)

1. Instruction              1. Instruction

2. Instruction              2. Instruction

3. ..                       3. ..

4. ..                       4. ..

  ..                          ..

—. end                      —, exit
```

Figure 3.8 The Form of an Algorithm

from the IPO chart. The number of instructions in an algorithm is determined by the way the programmer chooses to solve the problem. The algorithms pull the interactivity chart and the IPO chart together to give a logical step-by-step solution. Note in Figure 3.8, the *Control* module uses an *End* since this is the end of the processing. The other modules use *Exit* because the processing continues.

There are four algorithms and flowcharts for the payroll problem because there are four different modules in the structure chart. Figure 3.10 shows how the flowcharts and algorithms correspond for the payroll problem. Figure 3.11 shows the order of processing from module to module.

Flowchart Symbol	Explanation
Flowlines	Flowlines are indicated by straight lines with optional arrows to show the direction of data flow. The arrowhead is necessary when the flow direction might be in doubt. Flowlines are used to connect blocks by exiting from one and entering another.
Start End/Stop/Exit	Flattened ellipses indicate the start and the end of a module. An ellipse uses the name of the module at the start. The end is indicated by the word *end* or *stop* for the top or *Control* module and the word *exit* for all other modules. A start has no flowlines entering it and only one exiting it; an end or exit has one flowline entering it but none exiting it.
Processing	The rectangle indicates a processing block, for such things as calculations, opening and closing files, and so forth. A processing block has one entrance and one exit.
I/O	The parallelogram indicates input to and output from the computer memory. An input/output (I/O) block has one entrance and only one exit.
Decision	The diamond indicates a decision. It has one entrance and two and only two exits from the block. One exit is the action when the resultant is *True* and the other exit is the action when the resultant is *False*.

Figure 3.9 Flowchart Symbols (*continued on page 50*)

Drawing the Flowcharts

Flowchart

From the algorithms the programmer develops the flowcharts, graphic representations of the algorithms. The algorithms and the flowcharts are the final steps in organizing a solution. Using them, the programmer can test the solution for bugs and go on to code the problem into a computer language for entry into the computer. A flowchart will show errors in logic not readily visible in the other charts. Also, a set of data can be tested easily using a flowchart.

There are flowchart symbols for use with various types of processing. Figure 3.9 shows and explains some general flowchart symbols. There are many specific symbols, such as printer output, monitor output, and so forth, that are used in systems flowcharts.

A flowchart shows the flow of the processing from the beginning to the end of a solution. Each block in a flowchart represents one instruction from an algorithm. *Flowlines* indicate the direction of the data flow. Most blocks have one or more *entrances*, flowlines directing the flow of the data into the block. Most blocks have only one *exit*, flowlines directing the data out of the block, since, in most cases, data can flow

Flowchart Symbol	Explanation
Process Module	Rectangles with lines down each side indicate the process of modules. They have one entrance and only one exit.
Counter A B S — Automatic-Counter Loop	The polygon indicates a loop with a counter. The counter starts with *A* (the beginning value) and is incremented by *S* (the incrementor value) until the counter is greater than *B* (the ending value). *Counter* is a variable. *A*, *B*, and *S* may be constants, variables, or expressions.
On-Page Connectors* / Off-Page Connectors*	Flowchart sections can be connected with two different symbols. The circle connects sections on the same page, and the home base plate connects flowcharts from page to page. Inside these two symbols the programmer writes letters or numbers. The on-page connector uses letters inside the circle to indicate where the adjoining connector is located. An *A* connects to an *A*, a *B* to a *B*, etc. The off-page connectors use the page number where the next part or the previous part of the flowchart is located. This allows the reader to easily follow the flowchart. On- and off-page connectors will have either an entrance or an exit.

* These connectors should be used as little as possible. They should be used to enhance readability. Overuse decreases readability and produces a cluttered effect.

Figure 3.9 Flowchart Symbols (*continued from page 49*)

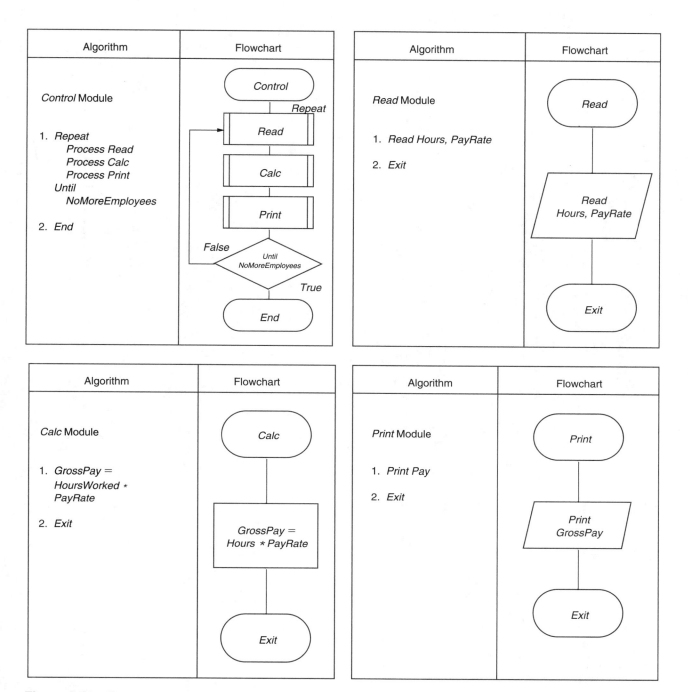

Figure 3.10 The Algorithms and Flowcharts for the Payroll Problem

to only one other block. The exception to this rule is a block representing a *decision instruction,* an instruction that enables the computer to make one of two choices. A decision block has two exits, one for each choice.

Besides the decision instructions, Figure 3.9 refers to another type of instruction that you will learn to use later, but it does deserve a brief explanation here. A *loop* enables the computer to perform a task repeatedly during the processing of a solution. An *automatic-counter loop* is a type of loop that enables the computer to count in increments of a given value; the increment can be 1, 2, 5, or whatever. That given value is the *incrementor* referred to in Figure 3.9.

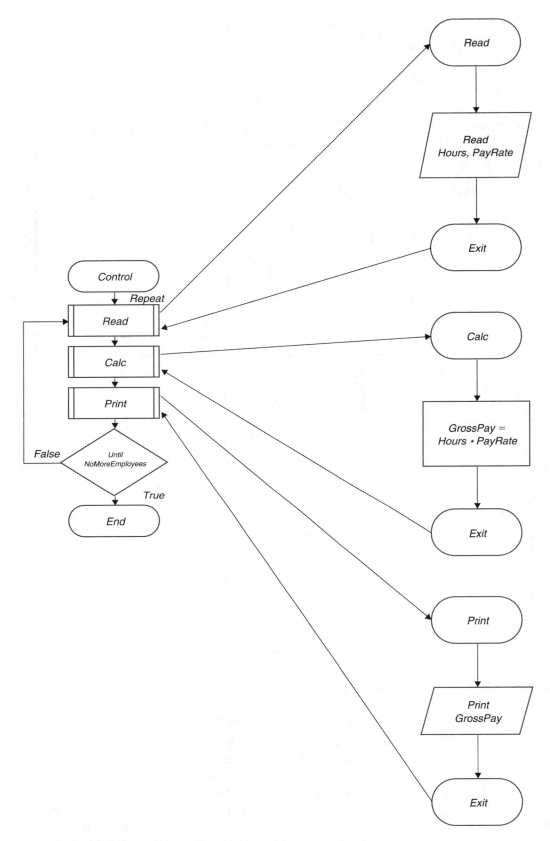

Figure 3.11 Order of Execution of Instructions

The following are some of the rules for drawing flowcharts:

1. You should write the instructions inside the blocks.
2. If there is something you need to remember, you can write a note beside a block. Test values of variables also can be placed beside flowchart blocks. This makes the flowchart an **annotated flowchart.**
3. A flowchart always starts at the top of the page and flows to the bottom. If you need more than one page for a flowchart, start another column on the same page or go on to another page. On- and off-page connectors are used to connect parts of the flowchart. A flowchart should not flow up, or sideways, or all over the page.
4. Use a computer program, or a template and a straightedge, to draw the flowchart. When you use a computer program or a template, the symbols are the same size and your flowchart will be neater and easier to read.
5. Make the blocks big enough to write instructions so they can be easily read.
6. Put the module number and name from the interactivity chart in the upper right-hand corner of the page for quick reference to the correct module.
7. Have plenty of paper on hand since the final copy of the flowchart normally will not be the first draft.
8. Use a pencil with a large eraser.

It is helpful to keep the algorithm and the flowchart of a module on the same page. Figure 3.12 shows a form (also in Appendix D, Figure D.4) you can use to develop your algorithms and flowcharts. Notice the last four sections of the form. The first is the Annotation section. Here you put notes about the algorithms and the flowcharts including test data, information about variables, things to remember, and so forth. The Test section is used to test the solution with sample data. The other two sections, Internal Documentation and External Documentation, are for notes to refer to later when you are completing the internal and external documentation. The last four sections of Figure 3.12 are optional but helpful in many cases.

Internal and External Documentation

Internal documentation consists of remarks written with the instructions to explain what is being done in the program. **External documentation** is made up of the manuals or help menus written about the solution. Documentation of your program is very important.

Good programming techniques require a program to be easily read by another programmer. The majority of the time, a program is passed from one programmer to another programmer. Proper internal documentation ensures that the new programmer will be able to learn about the program in the least amount of time. Internal documentation should include such things as people who have worked on the program, an abstract of the program, variable usage, notes about the development of the program, and anything else that will enable the new programmer to understand this program in the least amount of time. Internal documentation is written as the program is coded. Be careful not to overdo the internal documentation. Write enough information to help readability, but not so much that the instructions are lost in the remarks.

External documentation is for the user of the program. The end user will use the program to help solve problems. Proper external documentation ensures that the end user will have good instructions in order to learn to use this program in the least amount

Algorithm	Flowchart	Annotation	Test	Internal Documentation	External Documentation

Figure 3.12 Algorithm and Flowchart Form

of time. External documentation should also allow the end user to find answers to questions arising while using the program. Good external documentation increases productivity for the end user. External documentation should include such things as tutorials, input definitions, usage instructions, installation instructions, command explanations, and anything else that will allow the end user to learn to use this program in the least amount of time. External documentation may be printed or electronic, such as help menus.

Using the Tools

The problem-solving tools used in this book are the problem analysis chart, the structure chart or interactivity chart, the IPO chart, the algorithm, and the flowchart. There is much duplication in these tools. Because of this duplication, you will find that after the first few weeks you will drop the use of some of these tools. However, for the first few problems, you should use all of the tools. In this way you will know which ones help you the most. You should end up using at least four of the six tools:

1. The PAC or the IPO chart
2. The structure chart or interactivity chart
3. The coupling diagram (presented in Chapter 4)
4. The algorithm or the flowchart

Other tools are presented in Appendix E.

Testing the Solution

Testing a Solution

When a solution is complete, it is important to test it to make sure it meets the requirements of the user, and to check for errors in logic or in the setup of the expressions and equations. To test a solution, the programmer selects test data, a set of values for the input data, and works them through every step in the solution. It is important to select test data carefully, so the correctness of the results can be checked with as much accuracy as possible. The values of the input data should be capable of checking logic and calculations thoroughly. For example, to test the expression X/Y, the test data should be numbers other than 1. Since 1/1 is 1, and 1 * 1 is also 1, this set of data would not accurately test the expression.

A solution should never be assumed correct. If a bug is detected, the solution has to be modified to correct it, and then the testing process is started again at the beginning. Logic errors, such as incorrect loop conditions or wrong conditions in a decision statement, are the hardest to find and correct. It takes only a few logic errors to produce a program that is unreadable and a programmer who is frustrated. It is far easier to correct the solution in the problem-solving stages of program development than after the program is put into the computer.

Coding the Solution

Coding the Solution

Once you have completed the steps described so far, you have finished analyzing the problem and organizing the solution. This book stops with testing the solution. The next step is writing the solution of the problem into a computer language—that is, *coding* the solution. You will learn to code solutions when you take language courses.

If the programmer follows the proper steps in developing the solution, there should be few logic errors in the program, and the testing and coding should go quickly. Most bugs will be syntax errors or will stem from a misunderstanding of the original problem. Often the process will appear shorter and easier if you skip these problem-solving steps and code directly into the computer. The experienced programmer knows the fallacy of this shortsighted reasoning; this approach is almost always more time consuming, and the resulting program is less readable and less efficient.

Summary

The efficiency of the computer relies on the effectiveness of the programmer or the user. The programmer must write solutions that are clear, organized, and correct. A solution is a sequence of instructions for solving a problem. A program is a solution after it has been coded into a computer language. Data are stored internally in memory locations according to variable names and externally on a magnetic disk. External data are stored in sections called files, which are divided into records, which are further divided into fields. The file must be opened before accessing the data and closed when the user has finished with it.

The steps in organizing the solution to a problem start with problem analysis, a process whereby you separate a problem into four parts, including given data, required results, processing needs of the problem, and solution alternatives. The problem analysis chart is an aid to completing this first step. Second, the interactivity chart is developed showing the breakdown of the whole problem into subtasks called modules. The IPO chart is the third step; it shows the input, the processing, and the output. The algorithms are developed fourth, showing in detail the sequence of instructions in the solution. Finally, from the algorithms the programmer draws the flowcharts, showing graphic representations of the algorithms. After completing these steps, the programmer can test, code, and implement the solution.

New Terms

algorithm	flowchart	problem analysis chart
annotated flowchart	interactivity chart	pseudocode
bug	internal documentation	structure chart
debugging	IPO chart	syntax
external documentation	module	

Questions

1. What is a program?
2. Why is problem analysis important?
3. What are the tools of problem solving described in this chapter?
4. What are the relationships of the problem-solving tools to each other?
5. How would each of the flowchart symbols be used? Include an example in your explanation.

6. What type of flowchart symbols would you use for Otto's instructions? (See Appendix A.)

7. How do the problem-solving tools help in leading to a solution?

8. What is the difference between internal documentation and external documentation?

9. Why is it important to test a solution before coding the solution?

Problems

1. Develop a PAC for a solution to balance your checkbook. Include in the PAC various solutions for solving this problem.

2. List the various modules that you might include in the solution in problem 1. Put these modules together in an interactivity chart. Why did you choose these modules?

3. Draw the flowchart for your solution to problem 5, Appendix A.

4. Draw the flowchart for your solution to problem 6, Appendix A.

5. After completing problem 3 or 4, list three advantages to using an algorithm and three advantages to using a flowchart. Justify your answer. You may want to discuss the answer to this problem with other classmates.

6. Draw an algorithm and a flowchart for a solution to find the smallest of two numbers.

7. List the modules you might use to solve the following problems:
 a. Putting a list of names in alphabetical order.
 b. Calculating the average of a series of numbers.
 c. Calculating the total mileage given the distance between cities.

Unit One

Supplementary Exercises

1. Write a set of numbered step-by-step instructions to plan a trip to San Francisco. Be sure to take into account the knowledge base of those who are going.

2. Write a set of numbered step-by-step instructions to plan a summer vacation to a place of your choice.

3. Write a set of instructions for Otto to walk in a square figure 8.

4. Define the data types of the following data items. Justify your answers.
 a. Sum of money
 b. Telephone number
 c. Zip code
 d. Quantity of shoes
 e. Check okay on a client
 f. Account number

5. Define a variable name for each of the items in exercise 4.

6. Evaluate for $A = 6$, $B = 4$, and $C = 2$.
 a. $F = A \wedge 2/3 * B$
 b. $F = 3 * B/A \wedge 2$
 c. $F = A * C \backslash (A + C)$
 d. $F = (A + 7 - C) \text{ MOD } B$
 e. $F = (C * (B + 3 * A) + 5 * A)/C$

7. a. Joe Brown's Shoe Store expects to increase its sales by 5% during the next year. Write an equation to calculate the projected sales at the end of the year.

 Hint: The standard expression to increase a number by a percentage is

 $$Number * (1 + Percentage)$$

 b. However, inflation will decrease his profit increase. Expected inflation is $4\frac{1}{2}\%$, and 50% of Joe's expenses are directly affected by inflation. Joe's expenses are equal to 80% of his sales. Modify the equation in exercise 7a to calculate the projected profit, taking into consideration inflation.

8. Evaluate for $A = True$, $B = True$, $C = False$, $D = False$.
 a. $R = (A \text{ OR } B) \text{ AND } C$
 b. $R = A \text{ AND } B \text{ OR } C$
 c. $R = B \text{ AND } C \text{ OR } A$
 d. $R = \text{NOT } C \text{ AND NOT } D \text{ OR } A$
 e. $R = \text{NOT } C \text{ OR NOT } D \text{ AND } A$

9. Set up a logical expression for the following policy on using a company credit card. The card may be used if the
 a. Balance plus sales amount is less than the maximum allowable amount.
 b. Last payment was less than 45 days ago.
 c. Credit card has not expired.

10. Set up a logical expression to check data using the following criteria. The data are assumed correct when
 a. Number is <1000.
 b. Number is positive.
 c. Number is divisible by 2.

11. Develop a flowchart for the instructions to balance your checkbook. Be sure to include all steps, such as repeating the addition of each check.

12. Select one of the problem-solving tools and answer the following questions:
 a. How does this tool help in the solution of a problem?
 b. Why would you use this tool?

13. Which tool do you think will be hardest for you to learn to use? Why?

14. What type of information do you think should go into external documentation?

15. What type of information do you think should go into internal documentation?

WHAT'S WRONG WITH THIS?

The following problems have errors in them. Find the error, explain what is wrong, and correct the error.

1. Set up the following equations for the computer:

Mathematical Equation	Computer Equation
a. $A + B = 5D$	a. $D = A + B/5$
b. $\dfrac{X + Y}{4} = Z$	b. $(X + Y)/4 = Z$
c. $5X - 3Y = Z$	c. $Z = 5X - 3Y$

WHAT'S WRONG WITH THIS (*continued*)

2. What is the order of processing of the following equations:

Computer Equation	Order of Processing
a. $D = A + B/5$	**a.** $D = A + B/5$
b. $S = 5/D + 6 * (C + B)/E$	**b.** $S = 5/D + 6* (C + B)/E$
c. $R = A < B \text{ AND } C * F > G + 3$	**c.** $R = A < B \text{ AND } C * F > G + 3$

3. Write a truth table for the following equation:
$R = A \text{ AND } B \text{ OR NOT } C$

$R = A \text{ AND } B \text{ OR NOT } C$

A	B	C	R
False	False	False	False
True	True	True	True
False	False	True	False
True	False	True	True
True	False	False	False
False	True	True	False

UNIT TWO

LOGIC STRUCTURES

Chapter 4

An Introduction
to Programming Structure

Overview

Pointers for Structuring a Solution

The Modules and Their Functions

Cohesion and Coupling

Local and Global Variables

Parameters

Return Values

Variable Names and the Data Dictionary

The Four Logic Structures

Objectives

When you have finished this chapter, you should be able to:

1. Explain the need for structured programming.
2. Explain how to design modules and functions in terms of cohesion and coupling.
3. Explain the difference between local and global variables.
4. Explain the use of parameters.
5. List and describe the four logic structures: sequential, decision, loops, and case.

The tools described in Chapter 3 help programmers organize programs as they arise in the business world or in a textbook. The techniques explained in Chapters 4 through 8 of Unit Two provide ways to structure solutions so the computer can efficiently read and process the finished programs. That is, the techniques explained in these chapters help you write the several types of instructions that make up algorithms

Pointers for Structuring a Solution

The computer should be a tool to help people find solutions to their problems and to increase their productivity. The solutions must be developed according to methods that accomplish these goals. You can develop efficient computer solutions to problems if you heed the following pointers:

1. Use modules—break the whole into parts, with each part having a particular function.
2. Use the four logic structures to ensure that the solution flows smoothly from one instruction to the next, rather than jumping from one point in the solution to another.

 sequential logic structure

 a. The **sequential structure** executes instructions one after another in a sequence. See Figure 4.1.

 decision logic structure

 b. The **decision structure** branches to execute one of two possible sets of instructions. See Figure 4.2.

 loop logic structure

 c. The **loop structure** executes a set of instructions many times. See Figure 4.3.

 case logic structure

 d. The **case structure** executes one set of instructions out of several sets. (This is a special case of the decision structure. Many textbooks include the case structure with the decision structure; however, because of the unique uses of the case structure, it has been placed in a separate chapter in this text.) See Figure 4.4.
3. Eliminate the rewriting of identical processes by using modules.
4. Use techniques to improve readability, including the four logic structures, proper naming of variables, internal documentation, and proper indentation.

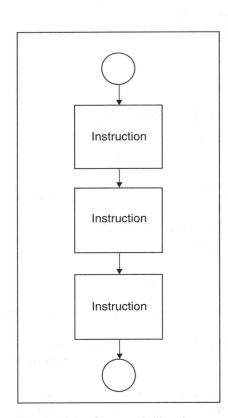

Figure 4.1 Sequential Logic Structure

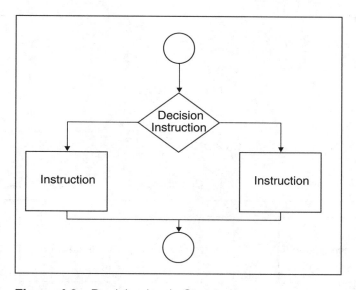

Figure 4.2 Decision Logic Structure

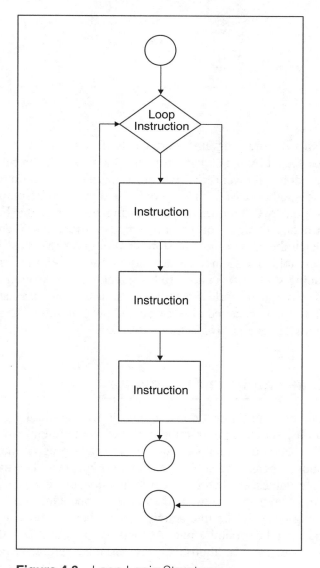

Figure 4.3 Loop Logic Structure

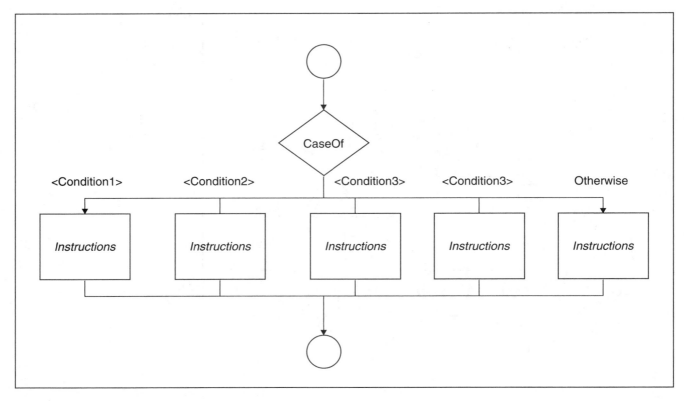

Figure 4.4 Case Logic Structure

You can structure programs more easily if you build a library of techniques that have been perfected by the experts over the years. One of the rules for programming a computer is don't reinvent the wheel. Experienced programmers are productive because, among other reasons, they have learned good programming techniques.

In addition to techniques for structuring programs, the beginning programmer needs to learn the techniques of working with data structures. Techniques used with data structures teach the student how to store data in order to access and process it as efficiently as possible. These include techniques for processing arrays, linked lists, and trees. Beginning students also need to learn techniques for programming in a graphical user interface computer world where instructions are not necessarily executed in a procedural manner. This is called object-oriented programming. These techniques are discussed in Units Three and Five in this textbook.

The Modules and Their Functions

Just as an author would not sit down and write without thinking about the structure of the book, neither should a programmer write without thinking about the structure of the program. First, an author thinks about the subject. A programmer studies the problem. Next, the author breaks the subject matter into chapters. The programmer breaks the problem into modules, each with a specific function. Once the chapters are in the correct order, then the author starts to write them, one by one. Once the modules are in the correct processing order in the interactivity chart, then the programmer writes the algorithm for each module, one by one. A good programmer tests the algorithm for each module for correctness, as thoroughly as possible, before writing the next one. It is

much easier to write and test many small modules than a single large one. Not only that, but when the program needs to be modified, it is much easier to test and change small modules.

Rules for Designing Modules

Follow these rules for designing modules when you design your own solutions:

1. Each module is an entity in itself. There is one entrance and one exit. That is, the processing starts at the top and ends at the bottom of the module. Processing does not jump out of the middle of a module to another module, nor does it jump into the middle of a module. The only way to go from one module to another module is through the exit instruction or through the use of the *Process* module instruction.
2. Each module has a single function, such as printing, calculating, or entering data.
3. Each module is short enough to be easily read and modified.
4. The length of a module is governed by its function and the number of instructions to be executed to perform that function.
5. A module is developed to control the order of processing. This may be where the interface of an object-oriented program is introduced or where the instructions to the computer are given as to the order of processing of the modules in a procedural-oriented program.

The types of modules needed for the solutions to most problems in this unit are the following:

control module

1. The ***Control*** module shows the overall flow of the data through the program. All other modules are subordinate to it.

initialization module

2. The ***Initialization*** module processes instructions that are executed only once during the program, and only at the beginning. These instructions include opening files and setting the beginning values of variables used in processing.

process module

3. The ***Process*** modules may be processed only once, or they may be part of a loop, which is processed more than once during the solution. There are several kinds of *Process* modules:

calculation module

 a. ***Calculation*** modules do arithmetic calculations, accumulating (summing to calculate totals), counting, or manipulating numerical data in some other way, such as putting numbers in numerical order. Sometimes *Calculation* modules manipulate string data to perform tasks such as putting a list of values in alphabetical order.

print module

 b. ***Print*** modules print output lines (the results of the processing, line by line), including headings and summaries.

read module
data validation module

 c. ***Read*** and ***Data Validation*** modules read or input the data into the internal memory of the computer, validate data (check the accuracy of the data), enter data from the keyboard, and so forth. *Validation* modules are usually separate from *Read* modules.

wrapup module

4. ***Wrapup*** modules process all instructions that are executed only once during the program and only at the end. These instructions include closing files and printing totals, among others.
5. Modules in an object-oriented program may include event modules such as mouse down, mouse up, key entry, and so on.

Different types of modules are often combined in one solution. A module can be broken into several smaller modules to make the parts of a program more manageable. One module performing a specific function can be used by one or more other modules

in which that same function is needed. Other types of modules are introduced in later chapters. The types on the previous page are the most frequently used.

Cohesion and Coupling

One of the most difficult tasks in the development of a solution to a problem is to divide the solution into modules. The question arises as to what should be included in each module. Modules should be functionally independent and perform a single task. However, modules will need to be connected, primarily through the data needed to complete the specified task within the modules. These opposing concepts are called *cohesion* and *coupling*. These concepts describe conflicting principles that lead to program design compromise.

cohesion **Cohesion** is the ability for a module to work independently from all other modules. Each module should have a function such as data entry, printing information, specific calculations, and so forth. To work independently, each module should have a single entry and single exit (see Figure 4.5). As nice as this is, it is not realistic. Modules

Figure 4.5 Cohesion and Coupling

need to share data from other modules in order to complete the modular tasks. This sharing of data is called coupling. **Coupling** is accomplished by some type of interface between modules that enables data to be passed from one module to another with the minimum interruption of the modular independence. Coupling allows for the communication between modules.

Cohesion and coupling are important concepts to the modern programmer, who in all probability will be working with many other programmers on the same problem. Cohesion allows a programmer to write a module of a larger program and test it independently. This module can then become a "black box" in a large program. Coupling allows all programmers to use necessary variables without losing the cohesion of the module. For example, if *Module1* performs task 1 successfully, it may be required to provide data to *Module2*. Cohesion results from having separate modules; coupling results when data are passed from *Module1* to *Module2*. Another example of cohesion and coupling would be the use of the square root function. A function is another name for a module. The square root function is a set of instructions to calculate the value of the square root of a number. The independence of these instructions is *cohesion*. The function is basically a black box. The programmer really doesn't worry about what the instructions are as long as a correct value is returned. However, in order to calculate the square root, the function needs a value to calculate the square root, and a value to return to the programmer. These data links, the number and the square root of the number, are what connects or *couples* the function to the rest of the program. This is *coupling*. There are three ways to couple modules: global variables, parameters, and return values. These are presented in the next sections. The preferred methods of coupling modules are parameters and return values.

Local and Global Variables

The concept of local and global variables is important in many languages. Programmers use the concept of local and global variables to allow cohesion and coupling to occur. Global variables are defined outside of the individual modules. Local variables are defined within a module. The major difference between the two is in the *scope* of the variables. The scope of the variables designates where the value of the variable can be used.

Local variables may be used only by the module itself. Other modules have no knowledge of these variables. This allows cohesion to take place. Through the use of local variables the programmer does not have to worry about variable name duplication in modules created by other programmers. If other modules need to use the value of a variable, the modules must be coupled through the use of parameters or return values.

All modules have knowledge of **global variables.** They are global to the program because they can be seen by all modules. The use of global variables defeats one of the purposes of cohesion, that is to allow for the duplication of variable names in different modules. Although global variables allow data coupling through the entire program, they should be used with caution. Only those variables that will be used in all modules should be designated as global variables. The programmer must be careful not to use the same variable name for a local variable and a global variable, since the hierarchy of use is to search the local variable list first, the parameter list second, and the global variable list last. The use of parameters and return values is not necessary since global variables couple the data from module to module.

Figure 4.6 shows a typical small interactivity chart. Figure 4.7 shows the scope of the variables found in this program. The variables *A, B,* and *C* are global. All modules

Figure 4.6 Interactivity Chart

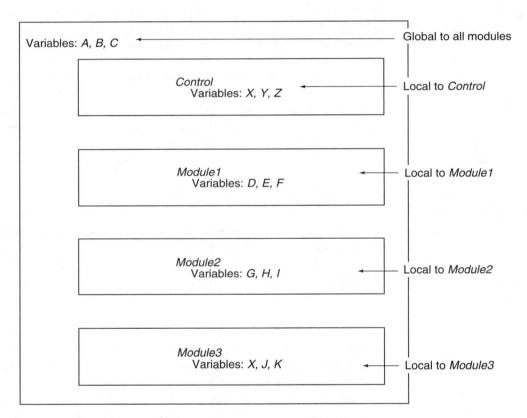

Figure 4.7 Scope of Local and Global Variables

can use and change the values of these variables. All other variables are local. Only the *Control* module can see the values of *X*, *Y*, and *Z*. The values of *D*, *E*, and *F* can be seen only by *Module1*. *Module2* can see *G*, *H*, and *I*. *Module3* can see only *X*, *J*, and *K*. Notice the duplication of the variable name *X*. In this case, there are two memory locations named *X*, one that can be used by the *Control* module and the other that can be used by *Module3*. The computer will not get confused by this duplicity, since each *X* is linked to its own module.

Parameters

Parameters are one of the hardest and most important concepts to understand and to use in programming. Through the use of parameters, programmers may work independently in groups, each developing a section of a very large program without the worry of duplicating variable names. In this way, a program can be developed in a relatively short amount of time. Each section is developed as a cohesive module, coupled together mainly through the use of parameters. In learning about parameters, new terminology will be introduced and discussed: the formal versus actual parameter listings, the calling module versus the called module, and call-by-value versus call-by-reference parameters. Refer to Figure 4.8 as you are reading the information about these terms.

parameters

Parameters are local variables that are passed or sent from one module to another. Parameters are another way of facilitating coupling that allows the communication of data between modules. They are placed after the module name and within parentheses, for example: *Read(A, B, C)*. The *calling module* is the module that processes another module. The *called module* is the module being processed. In Figure 4.8, the calling module is the *ControlPay* module since it processes the *Read* module, the *Calc* module, and the *Print* module. The *Read* module, the *Calc* module, and the *Print* module are the called modules since they are the ones being processed by the *Control* module. The

Actual Parameter
Listing
Formal Parameter
Listing

actual parameter listing is the list of parameters that follows the module name being processed in the calling module. The *formal parameter listing* is the list of parameters that follow the module name at the beginning of the module. Notice that the variable names in the actual parameter listings may or may not be the same as those in the formal parameter listings. The values are sent and received according to the position in the listings; the first variable in the actual listing corresponds to the first variable in the formal listing, the second to the second, and so forth. In Figure 4.8, *Hours* in the *ControlPay* module corresponds to *Hrs* in the *Read* and *Calc* modules. Likewise, *Pay Rate* in the *ControlPay* module corresponds to *Rate* in the *Read* and *Calc* modules, and *Pay* in the *Control* module corresponds to *Pay* in the *Calc* and *Print* modules.

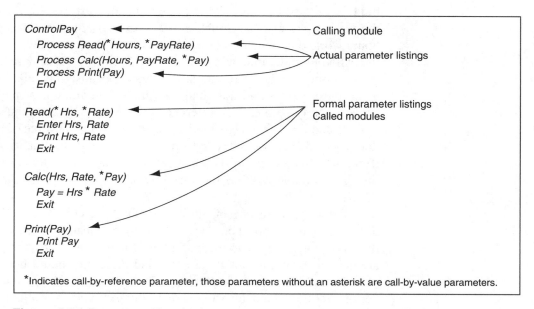

Figure 4.8 Parameter Terminology

There are two ways to send data from one module to another through the use of parameters. The first is to send the *value* of the variable, a *call-by-value parameter*. The second is to send the *address* of the variable, a *call-by-reference parameter* that is specified by the use of an asterisk (*) in front of the variable name in both the actual and the formal parameter listings. A variable name that has no asterisk in front of the name is assumed to be a call-by-value parameter. When a call-by-value parameter is used, the value of the variable is sent to the called module by the calling module. The called module will then make a new memory location (or address—a memory location is an address) for this variable since it has no knowledge of where the variable is stored by the calling module. Therefore, when the called module makes a change in the variable, the change will not be made in the calling module because the parameter has a different memory location in the called module than it does in the calling module (see Figure 4.9). The call-by-value parameters (referenced by circled 2s) have a memory location number in both modules. When a call-by-reference parameter (referenced by circled 1s in Figure 4.9) is used, the memory location is sent, not the value. The called module refers to the memory location to find the value. When the called module changes the value of the parameter, the calling module will see the change because they are using the same memory location—the one designated by the calling module. The call-by-reference parameters share the same memory location. When using parameters, variables might have the same location but two or more names referenced from different modules, or two memory locations may have the same name used in two different modules. Figure 4.10 shows another example of parameters.

Figure 4.11 shows the coupling diagram for Figure 4.9. A *coupling diagram* indicates how data couples modules together. A coupling diagram has a rectangle for each module and a line connecting the modules for each datum sent from one module to another. In this case, there is a rectangle for *Module1* and another for *Module2*. Notice the connecting lines. Two double-headed arrows are drawn from the *ControlPay* module to the *Read* module, one for the hours worked and the other for the rate of pay. The double-headed arrows indicate that these parameters are call-by-reference parameters and changes can be seen by both modules. In Figure 4.11, two single-headed arrows and one double-headed arrow are drawn from the *ControlPay* module to the *Calc* module; the single-headed arrows are for the hours worked and the rate of pay and the double-headed arrow is for the amount of pay. In this case, hours worked and the rate of pay have single-headed arrows with the arrowheads into the called module, indicating that these are call-by-value parameters and changes can be seen only by the called module. This is because the called module, *Calc,* will be using these values and not changing them. The amount of pay has a double-headed arrow, specifying a call-by-reference parameter. This is because *Pay* will be changed in *Calc* and the *ControlPay* module needs to know the value of the change in *Pay.* One double-headed arrow is drawn from the *ControlPay* module to the *Print* module, specifying that the amount of pay is a call-by-value parameter for this module since only the *Print* module will use the variable. See Figure 4.12 for the coupling diagram for Figure 4.10.

Parameters are one of the best methods of coupling modules. The programmer does not have to worry about variable name duplication in modules that other programmers are developing. Parameters in the formal parameter listing (in the called module) are neither local nor global variables and therefore should not be declared as local or global variables. In the event of variable name duplication, the local variable has precedence over the parameter variable, and the parameter variable has precedence over the global variable. When the program is looking for the variable name, it first looks at the

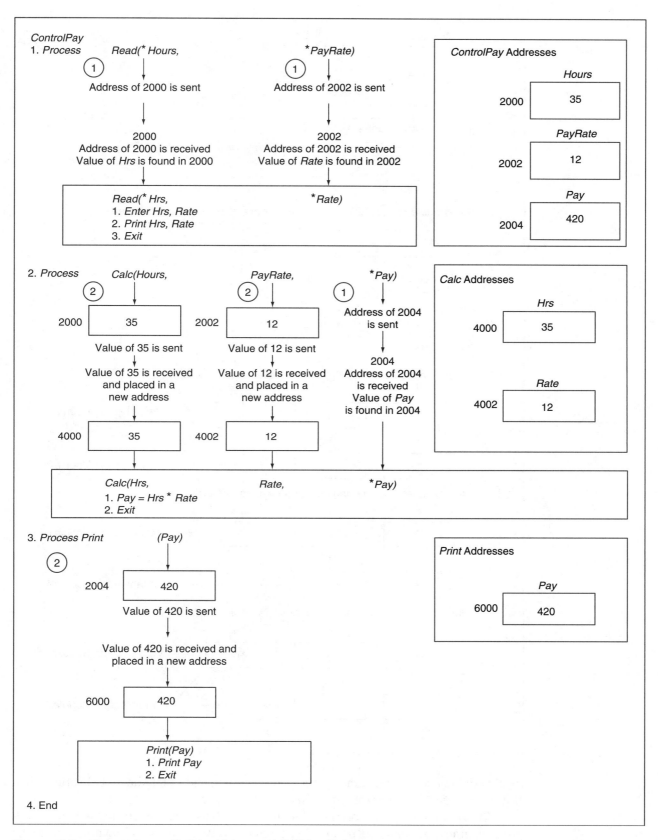

Figure 4.9 Parameters—Call-by-Value and Call-by-Reference

Figure 4.10 Parameter Example

local variable list, second at the formal parameter list, and last at the global variable list. If it is not found at any of the three lists, an error occurs.

Many of the programs presented in this text will use parameters and will have coupling diagrams presented as part of the solution. Likewise, many of the problems at the end of the chapters will require the use of parameters. As a programmer it is very important that you learn how to use parameters.

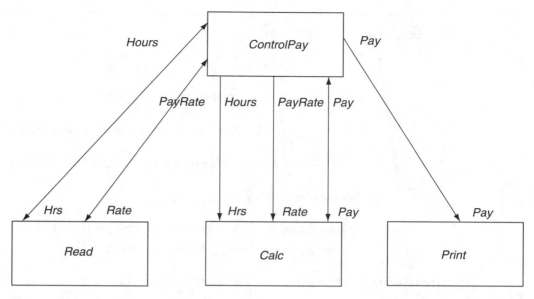

Figure 4.11 Coupling Diagram for Figures 4.8 and 4.9

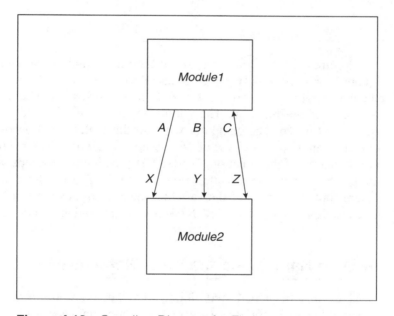

Figure 4.12 Coupling Diagram for Figure 4.10

Return Values

Return Values

The three ways to couple modules are through the use of global variables, parameters, and return values. As we learned in Chapter 2, when functions are used within another instruction, they have a return value. The return value is the result of the function. This is accomplished through the name of the function. At the conclusion of the execution of the function, the result is placed temporarily in the name. The function must be used as part of another instruction. The value of the name of the function is no longer available once the instruction has been executed. In the case of the return value, the value is only sent out of the called module into the calling module. In a coupling diagram the arrow-head would be a single-headed arrow, but pointing to the calling module.

SquareRoot = 5 + SQRT(16)

9

SQRT(X)

X takes on the value of 16

The function will calculate the square root of 16.

The resultant will be placed in SQRT, thus SQRT will equal 4

The value of SQRT is now 4.

The processing is then transferred back to the calling module where it continues with the addition of 5 to 4, giving a resultant of 9.

The resultant, 9, is then assigned to the variable SquareRoot.

Figure 4.13 Return Value

Figure 4.13 illustrates the use of the return value in an equation. In the equation SquareRoot = SQRT(16) + 5. SquareRoot is the variable in which the result of the calculation will be placed in memory to be saved for later use in the solution. SQRT is the name of the function. The parameter, which is the data needed to calculate the square root, is 16. The computer will call the SQRT function first. Next, the function will calculate the square root of 16, giving a result of 4. The resultant, 4, is then placed into the name of the function, SQRT. The processing proceeds with the equation. The number 5 is then added to the value of SQRT. The resultant value is then placed in SquareRoot. The value of the variable SquareRoot is stored in memory. After the 5 is added to SQRT, the value of SQRT is no longer available to be used.

Variable Names and the Data Dictionary

Data Dictionary

Variables must be named according to what they represent. If they represent *hours*, then the variable name should be *Hours*. When the variables are all local or used as parameters, variable names must be unique to the module in which they are defined. If variables are global, they must be unique to the total program. When you name a variable, that name must be used whenever you are referring to that item. You cannot use *Hours* in one place and *Hrs* in another place in one module, or again, if the variable is global, throughout the whole program. The computer references values by their names. Therefore, if you change the name, the computer assumes the new name represents a new item. A data dictionary is a great help to keep track of the variable usage in your program. It contains a list of all items, their variable names, their data types, the module in which they are found, pseudonyms and the module in which each pseudonym is found, and any error check that needs to be made on the variable. Figure D.5 in Appendix D is a form to use for your data dictionary. Figure 4.14 shows an example of a data dictionary. If you are using different names in different modules, you must also show the coupling diagram.

Data Dictionary

Item	Variable Name	Data Type	Module	Scope	Pseudonym/Module	Error Check
Hours worked	*Hours*	Numeric—real	*ControlPay*	Local	*Hrs*	None
Hours worked	*Hrs*	Numeric—real	*Read/ Calc*	Parameter	*Hours*	Hours $<$ 0
Pay rate	*PayRate*	Numeric—real	*ControlPay*	Local	*Rate*	None
Pay rate	*Rate*	Numeric—real	*Read/ Calc*	Parameter	*PayRate*	Pay rate $<$ 4.00
Net pay	*Pay*	Numeric—real	*ControlPay*	Local	None	None
Net pay	*Pay*	Numeric—real	*Calc/ Print*	Parameter	None	None

Figure 4.14 Example of a Data Dictionary

The Four Logic Structures

logic structures

Four Logic Structures

Up to now, this book has discussed the structure of the *problem*—that is, how to break a problem into parts, or modules, and arrange them so the data flow in a solution is logical. There are other types of structures used to design the modules themselves. These structures are called **logic structures,** and they control the logic of the data flow though the module. The instructions that make up the algorithms and the flowcharts are combinations of the four logic structures.

Chapters 5, 6, 7, and 8 in this unit are devoted to the four basic logic structures:

1. The sequential logic structure
2. The decision logic structure
3. The loop logic structure
4. The case logic structure

A brief explanation of each of these logic structures follows.

The sequential logic structure processes data one instruction after another. This logic structure is the most widely used, and it is normally used in conjunction with others. The programmer uses the decision logic structure to program the computer to make choices. The programmer uses calculations that use relational or logical operators to design these choices. The third logic structure is the loop, which enables the computer to repeat tasks. The last logic structure, the case logic structure, enables the programmer to request that the computer pick one of a set of tasks through a code or through an option using a number, a letter, or a string. When a problem is broken down in modules, the appropriate logic structures can be applied to each module. Effective use of the four logic structures results in efficient and readable solutions.

Summary

Unit Two consists of several chapters on how to structure solutions for particular computer languages and applications. You will learn four logic structures for designing programs for problem solving, plus additional techniques for record processing. These techniques are extremely important because they can greatly increase productivity. They help you effectively organize the instructions in each of the algorithms that make up your solution. As a result, the computer can read the solution easily and process your program efficiently.

Cohesion is designing a module to be as independent of the rest of the modules as possible. Coupling refers to how data connects the modules. The three ways to couple modules are through the use of global variables, parameters, and return values. Global variables are those variables known to other modules. Local variables are those variables known to only one module. The computer searches for variables first in the local variable list, then the parameter list, and finally the global list.

Parameters are local variables that are shared with other modules. Call-by-reference parameters pass the address or location of the variable to the other module. Call-by-value parameters pass the actual value of the variable to the other module. The calling module can recognize a change made by the called module when using a call-by-reference parameter. The calling module, when using a call-by-value parameter, does not recognize a change made by the called module. It is very important for a programmer to learn how to effectively use parameters.

To make a computer problem manageable, break your solution into modules. For Unit Two, the types of modules you will need include *Control, Initialization, Process,* and *Wrapup.* There are several kinds of *Process* modules, including *Calculation* modules, various *Print* modules, *Read* modules, and *Data Validation* modules.

New Terms

cohesion	loop structure	*Process*
coupling	case structure	*Calculation*
global variables	parameters	*Print*
local variables	types of modules:	*Read*
logic structures:	*Control*	*Data Validation*
sequential structure	*Initialization*	*Wrapup*
decision structure		

Questions

1. Name the four logic structures.
2. What is a module? How is it used?
3. Name the major types of modules and explain their functions.
4. List the kinds of *Process* modules.
5. What is meant by the cohesion of a module?
6. What is meant by coupling modules?
7. Why are cohesion and coupling important to programmers?

8. How are modules coupled?

9. What does a coupling diagram show?

10. Define the two types of parameters. How do they differ? Under what circumstances would you use each type?

11. How can you use a return value later in your solution?

12. What is the difference between using a return value and a call-by-reference parameter?

Problems

1. Create a calling module name and parameters for the following. (Remember that the asterisk before the parameter name indicates a call-by-reference parameter.)
 a. *Process Print(Average, Count)*
 b. *Process Calc(AgeSum, Count, *Average)*
 c. *Process Calc(Length, Width, Height, *Volume)*
 d. Process Init(*Number)
 e. Maximum = Max(Test1, Test2, Test3, Test4)
 f. Process Calc(Sqrt(A), C, *D)

2. Using the modules in problem 1, answer the following questions:
 a. Which of the parameters are call-by-value parameters?
 b. Which of the parameters are call-by-reference parameters?
 c. Are there any parameters that cannot be changed by the called module? If so, which ones? Justify your answer.
 d. Which parameters, if changed by the called module, will the calling module recognize as changed values?
 e. Which parameters have more than one location in the computer; one associated with the calling module and the other associated with the called module?
 f. Which parameters have one location in the computer, that of the calling module?
 g. Where is the return value placed?
 h. In problem 1f., what are the two modules? Which is called first?

3. Create a data dictionary for the parameters in problem 1.

Chapter 5

Problem Solving with the Sequential Logic Structure

Overview

Algorithm Instructions and Flowchart Symbols

The Sequential Logic Structure

Solution Development
 Problem Analysis
 The Interactivity Chart
 The IPO Chart
 Coupling Diagram and Data Dictionary
 Internal and External Documentation
 The Algorithms and Flowcharts

Objectives

When you have finished this chapter, you should be able to:

1. Use the sequential logic structure to develop a solution to a problem.
2. Use the proper form for instructions in an algorithm and a flowchart.
3. Use the seven problem-solving tools to develop a solution to a problem.

Algorithm Instructions and Flowchart Symbols

The computer's system of communication dictates how the programmer designs algorithms and flowcharts. Recall that an algorithm is a set of instructions telling the computer how to process a module in a solution. You will write an algorithm for each module in a program. A flowchart is a visual illustration of an algorithm. You will draw a flowchart to accompany each algorithm. This chapter begins with only a few of the specific algorithm instructions and flowchart symbols you will use as a trained

programmer, those required to solve problems using the sequential structure. They are found in Table 5.1 and include the instructions to start and stop each module, to enter data, to output data, to process modules, and to perform calculations.

You write an instruction in two parts: a general instruction followed by specifications regarding what is to be processed. In Table 5.1 the general instruction is the first word in the Algorithm Instruction column, that is, *Start, Enter, Variable =,* and so forth. The specifications—a specific module name, a list of variable names, a specific

Table 5.1 Algorithm Instructions and Flowchart Symbols

Algorithm Instruction	Flowchart Symbol	Definition (What the instruction tells the computer)
Start module name list of parameters (module number)		Start processing a module. The word *Start* is optional and is not used in this text.
Enter list of variable names		Enter data from a data block or from the keyboard into the following variable memory locations.
Variable = expression		Assign the value of the following expression to a variable location. This is called an *assignment instruction*. A module may be processed as part of an expression, if there is a return value.
Write list of variable names		Write to the printer the values represented by the following variable names.
Print list of variable names		Print on the screen the values represented by the following variable names.
Process module names (list of parameters)		Execute the instructions in the named module, and then return to execute the next instruction.
End/Exit		Stop the processing of the module. Processing ceases with the *End*; with the *Exit*, processing continues with the next instruction after the *Process*.
Return (variable)		Stop the processing of the module, place the value of the variable in the module name, and continue with the instruction containing the module call.

expression, and so forth—follow the instruction. They are data and ways of processing drawn from the problem and collected for the problem and information from the structure chart and the other charts you completed prior to the algorithms.

The *Start* instruction is always understood, if not stated, at the beginning of an algorithm and flowchart and indicates where the module begins. The oval is the flowchart symbol for the *Start* instruction. The instruction includes the name of the module and all parameters. For example

Init (Hours, PayRate)

or

Print (Hours, Pay)

The name of the module also may be written at the beginning of the algorithm, which is the case throughout this text.

The *Enter* instruction enables the user to enter data into memory locations with variable names. The list of variable names follows the *Enter* instruction. For example,

Enter Name, Age

Data are entered from the keyboard as specified in the program.

Variable = (commonly called the *assignment instruction*) enables a user to instruct the computer to store a constant, a variable, or an expression in a named variable memory location. The order of the instruction is the variable name followed by the equal sign followed by a constant, a variable name, or an expression, as in

*Pay = Hours * Wage*

A module, called a function, may be processed in an expression if and only if the module or function has a return value. For example, the square root function is used in an assignment statement as follows:

$$A = Sqrt(X) + 7$$

If we were to look at the instructions for the square root function, we would see that the result of the square root of *X* would be returned in the name of the function, in this case *Sqrt*. This value is added to 7 and then stored in *A*.

The *Write* instruction outputs values to the printer. The list of information to be printed follows the *Write,* as in

Write Name, Age

The *Print* instruction is similar to the *Write* instruction except that the output is directed to the screen rather than the printer.

The *Process* instruction tells the computer to process the instructions of a named module before continuing. The name of the module to be processed follows the *Process* instruction. The list of parameters, enclosed in parentheses, follows the module name. For example

Process Init (Hours, PayRate)

or

Process Calc (Hours, PayRate)

If there are no parameters, the parentheses are not included.

The *End, Exit,* or *Return* instruction specifies the completion of a module. *End* is used to end the *Control* module and indicates that the processing of the solution is complete. *Exit* is used to end a subordinate module if there is no return value, and indicates that the processing will continue in another module, the module where the *Process* instruction originated.

The *Return* (variable) is used to place a value in the name of the module. The *Return* is used when the module is to be processed within an expression. The only way to preserve the value of the function name is either to use it in an expression or to place the value in a variable through the use of the assignment statement. The processing continues in the calling module, the module in which the instruction that contained the expression originated. The programmer writes each instruction in its entirety within the appropriate flowchart symbol. The list of instructions in Table 5.1 will be expanded in future chapters.

The Sequential Logic Structure

Sequential Logic Structure

The most commonly used and the simplest logic structure is the sequential structure. All problems use the sequential structure, and most problems use it in conjunction with one or more of the other logic structures. To illustrate how to use this structure, this chapter develops a sample problem solution demonstrating each of the computer problem-solving steps explained in Chapter 3.

A programmer who uses the sequential logic structure is asking the computer to process a set of instructions in sequence from the top to the bottom of an algorithm. In general, the form of the algorithm looks like this:

> *ModuleName* (list of parameters)
> 1. *Instruction*
> 2. *Instruction*
> 3. . . .
> . . .
> XX.*End, Exit,* or *Return* (variable)

The algorithm begins with the *Start* instruction represented by the name, the list of parameters, and number of the module. The numbered instructions following the *Start* might be any of the instructions other than *Start* and *End/Exit/Return* depending on the problem. The form of the flowchart corresponds to the form of the algorithm (see Figure 5.1). The first block is the *Start* block. Other instruction blocks follow. These blocks can be of any type other than the flattened ellipse, which indicates *Start* or *End/Exit/Return.* The final block is the *End, Exit,* or *Return* block. See Figure 5.2 for an example of the algorithm and the flowchart for a solution that enters a name and an age into the computer and prints them to the screen.

The name of the module is *NameAge.* There are no parameters. The flowchart uses the flattened ellipse to indicate that this is the start of this module. The first instruction to be executed is the *Enter* instruction. The instruction is in the form of the word *Enter* followed by the list of data items whose values will be entered from the keyboard, a data block. The flowchart uses a parallelogram to designate that this is an input instruction. The second instruction to be executed is the *Print* instruction. This instruction is in the form of the word *Print* followed by the list of data items whose values will be printed to

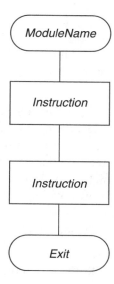

Figure 5.1 Flowchart Diagram for the Sequential Structure

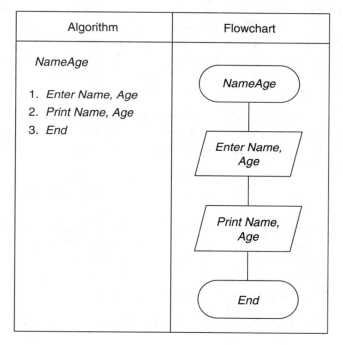

Figure 5.2 Algorithm and Flowchart to Enter and Print Two Variables

the screen. The flowchart uses the parallelogram to indicate that this is an output instruction. The input and output instructions both use the parallelogram in the flowchart. The last instruction is the *End* instruction. This signals the end of the list of instructions and to stop the execution of the program. The end is placed in a flattened ellipse in the flowchart. All of the start and ending instructions use the flattened ellipse in the flowchart. Notice that the algorithm instructions are numbered starting with the first instruction after the name of the module.

Solution Development

Solution Development

In Chapter 3, the tools for organizing problems were introduced. Now you will use them to solve problems from the business world. These organizing tools are used in the first six steps of developing a solution.

1. The problem analysis chart—helps you define and understand the problem, develop ideas for the solution, and select the best solution.
2. The interactivity chart—breaks the solution to the problem into parts.
3. The IPO chart—helps define the input, the output, and the processing steps.
4. The coupling diagram and the data dictionary designate the data flow between modules. The data dictionary records information on the items.
5. The algorithms define the steps of the solution.
6. The flowcharts are a graphic form of the algorithms.

The seventh step in solving the problem is to test the solution to catch any errors in logic or calculation. Remember, the charts are aids to the efficient development of a well-written program. They will not be perfect the first time around and will often need several revisions.

As you follow the solution to the sample sequential structure problem that follows, take the time to think through each step. Photocopy the forms in Appendix D to complete the seven steps. The solution to the following problem will be developed. This may seem like a lot of work for this simple of a problem; however, it is easier to learn on a simple short problem than on a long difficult one. If you can understand this problem and the use of the tools involved in the solution of this problem, you will be able to solve more difficult problems as they come up.

The Problem

Problem: Mary Smith is looking for the bank that will give the most return on her money over the next five years. She has $2,000 to put into a savings account. The standard equation to calculate principal plus interest at the end of a period of time is

$$Amount = P * (1 + I/M)^{\wedge}(N * M)$$

where P = *Principal* (amount of money to invest, in this case $2,000)
 I = *Interest* (percentage rate the bank pays to the investor)
 N = *Number of Years* (time for which the principal is invested)
 M = *Compound Interval* (the number of times per year the interest is calculated and added to the principal)

(Refer to Table 2.5 to review the meanings of the operators used here.)

Problem Analysis

Problem Analysis

The first step in analyzing the problem is to understand what is needed and what is given and to separate them from all of the nonessential information in the problem. Write down the input in the Given Data section and the output in the Required Results section. Record the processing that the problem demands in the section of the problem analysis chart headed Required Processing. Finally, write possible solutions for the problem and any ideas related to the solution in the Solution Alternatives section. Generate solution ideas through brainstorming and creative thinking. When you are first learning problem-solving skills, brainstorming is best accomplished in groups of two to three people. The more ideas, the easier it is to develop a good solution.

Given Data	Required Results
Principal—$2,000 Interest Number of Years—5 Compound Interval (#/year)	Principal plus Interest at the end of the time period

Required Processing
$Amount = P * (1 + I / M)\char`^(N * M)$

Solution Alternatives
*1. Enter all data as variables. 2. Enter principal and interest as constants and the other data as variables. *3. Process one bank in one run. 4. Process all banks in one run. *Processes selected for the best solution.

Figure 5.3 Problem Analysis Chart—Interest Problem

In Figure 5.3, the problem analysis chart has been filled in for the interest problem given in the previous section. The given data are the *Principal* ($2,000), the *Interest* (variable), the *Number of Years* the *Principal* is to be invested (5), and the *Compound Interval* (variable). The required result is the *Amount* of *Principal* plus *Interest* at the end of the time period. The required processing is the equation for the *Amount.* Solution ideas include the following:

1. Enter all input data as variables.
2. Enter the principal and interest as constants and the other values as variables.
3. Enter the data for one bank per run.
4. Enter the data for all banks per run.

Figuring out the best solution involves weighing the ideas and alternatives in the Solution Alternatives section of the problem analysis chart. Since a solution should be as flexible as possible, it would be better to enter all the data as variables. Variables provide flexibility because their values can be changed, whereas the values of constants cannot. It is best to use variables wherever there is a possibility that the data might change, and constants only if it is known that the data won't change. Furthermore, since the user probably will not have all data from all banks at once, entering one bank per run would be best for this solution.

The Interactivity Chart

Interactivity Chart

At this point, you can develop the interactivity chart. To complete the interactivity chart you have to answer the question: How can I divide this problem into smaller, more manageable parts? In Figure 5.4, the interest problem is broken into four modules:

1. The *InterestControl* module, which controls the solution
2. The *Read* module, which enters the data
3. The *Calc* module, which calculates the amount
4. The *Print* module, which prints the result

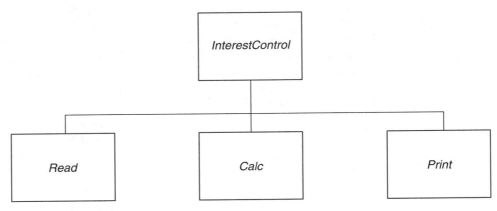

Figure 5.4 The Interactivity Chart—Interest Problem

The interactivity chart shows that the *InterestControl* module processes the other three modules in the following order—the *Read, Calc,* and *Print* modules, respectively. These four modules are the only ones in this solution. There is no *Init* module since there is nothing to be initialized (no files to open, no headings to print, or the like), nor is there a *Wrapup* module since there is nothing to be done at the conclusion of the processing (no files to close, no totals to print, or the like). The solution requires only that data be entered, that a calculation be performed, and that the results be printed. Each box represents a module. Each module has a function and represents two or more instructions. The modules are numbered according to their level.

The IPO Chart

IPO Chart

Now the IPO chart can be developed from the problem analysis chart and the interactivity chart. To complete the IPO chart you have to answer the question: How can the input be processed to achieve the required output? You will provide general instructions for the solution on the IPO chart. You will not write the specific instructions to the computer until you complete the algorithms and the flowcharts.

Remember to start with the output, next specify the input, and then develop the processing method required to calculate the output from the input. In Figure 5.5, the output is the amount of the *Principal* plus *Interest* after five years. The input required to

Input	Processing	Module Reference	Output
1. Beginning Principal	1. Enter data (Change interest rate to hundredths)	*Read*	1. Ending Principal plus Interest
2. Interest Rate			
3. Number of Years	2. Calculate ending Principal and Interest	*Calc*	2. All input data
4. Number of Times Interest is Compounded Yearly	AMOUNT = PRINCIPAL * (1 + INTEREST / TIME)^(YEARS * TIME)		
	3. Print required results	*Print*	

Figure 5.5 The IPO Chart—Interest Problem

produce this result includes the beginning *Principal,* the *Interest Rate* (changed to hundredths after it is input), the *Number of Years Invested,* and the *Compounded Time Interval.* The processing includes entering the data (found in the *Read* module), calculating the amount (found in the *Calc* module), and printing the amount (found in the *Print* module).

Coupling Diagram and Data Dictionary

Figure 5.6, the coupling diagram, and Figure 5.7, the data dictionary, are interrelated. The coupling diagram shows which variables are passed from one module to another.

The data dictionary shows which modules use each variable and the scope of each variable (whether the variable is local or global.) In this problem, all variables are local, therefore, all coupling will be done through parameters. The variables that couple the *InterestControl* module and the *Read* module are the *Principal,* the *Interest,* the *NumberOfYears,* and the *CompoundingTime.* These are all call-by-reference parameters since the variables sent to the *Read* module must have values assigned to them. Because the memory locations of *Principal, Interest, Years,* and *Time* were sent to the *Read* module, both modules are using the same memory locations. Therefore, when the *Read* module enters values into *Principal, Interest, Years,* and *Time,* the *InterestControl* module will be able to see the new values. The same four are call-by-value parameters when coupling the *InterestControl* module to the *Calc* module. In this case the values of *Principal, Interest, Years,* and *Time* are sent to the *Calc* module. The *Calc* module then assigns new memory locations for these variables. Since the *InterestControl* module and the *Calc* module have different memory locations for these variables, the *InterestControl* module will not be able to see any changed values and will retain the original values even if the *Calc* module were to change them. This is because they will not be changed, only used, in the *Calc* module. The amount, however, needs to be a call-by-reference parameter since the value of the *Amount* will be calculated in the *Calc* module and the *InterestControl* module needs the new value. All five variables couple the *InterestControl* module to the *Print* module. They are call-by-value parameters since the *Print* module

Figure 5.6 Coupling Diagram

Data Dictionary

Item	Variable Name	Data Type	Module(s)	Scope	Pseudonym/ Module	Error Check
Principal	*Principal*	Numeric—real	*InterestControl/ Read/Calc/Print*	Local Parameter	None	None
Interest	*Interest*	Numeric—real	*InterestControl/ Read/Calc/Print*	Local Parameter	None	None
Number of years	*Years*	Numeric—real	*InterestControl/ Read/Calc/Print*	Local Parameter	None	None
Compounding time	*Time*	Numeric—real	*InterestControl//Read/ Calc/Print*	Local Parameter	None	None
Amount	*Amount*	Numeric—real	*InterestControl/ Calc/Print*	Local Parameter	None	None

Figure 5.7 Data Dictionary

only needs to use them. The five variables will not be changed in the *Print* module. Usually, to determine which variables are call-by-reference parameters and which are call-by-value parameters, the programmer needs to see which variables will be changed in the called module. If the variable is changed, then it needs to be a call-by-reference parameter. If the called module is going to use only the value of the variable, then it needs to be a call-by-value parameter.

Internal and External Documentation

Documentation

Documentation is useful to everyone involved with the program, so it is important that the programmer or the user of the application package write down important details about the program. The programmer's colleagues need to know what was done, how it was done, and where, in order to finish and maintain the program. The user needs to know what has been done and how, in order to use the program or application effectively, and, further, to make sure the processing is correct. Internal documentation involves noting within the instruction set what the instructions do. This is accomplished through the use of remark or comment statements. These statements appear only in the listing of the statements and nowhere else. They are for the use of the programmer only. The end user never sees them. External documentation involves writing manuals (either printed or electronic) with detailed explanations of the program and how to use it.

You take notes for internal and external documentation during problem solving because it is easy to forget the details that you need later when you are writing the documentation. There is an Annotation section for these notes on page 465 of Figure D.4—Algorithm and Flowchart, Appendix D. You write the notes for the documentation as you develop the algorithms and the flowcharts, including any important information that is not already part of the algorithms and flowcharts. In the *InterestControl* module in Figures 5.8a–d, the exact task of each of the Process modules (the *Read,* the *Calc,* and the *Print* modules) is not specified. The remarks in the Annotation section specify those tasks. For example, the *Read* module enters all data from the keyboard. The Annotation

section is the only place you can explain such things in any depth. Only after the module has been developed completely can you tell all that belongs in the documentation, so it is best not to finish the notes on each module until then. The Annotation and Documentation sections of the Algorithm and Flowchart form are optional, but are often useful later.

The Algorithms and Flowcharts

Once the structure chart and the IPO chart are completed, you can proceed with the algorithms and the flowcharts. To complete an algorithm, you have to answer the question: How can this module complete its function? To draw the flowchart, you answer the question: How does the algorithm look graphically? By using the completed algorithms and the flowcharts, you can find and correct logic errors.

Figures 5.8a–d show the four algorithms, one for each module in the structure chart, and their corresponding flowcharts. The *InterestControl* module uses a sequential structure to execute the instructions, as do each of the other modules. Notice how the instructions simply flow in order from the top to the bottom of each algorithm. Remember, you

Algorithm	Flowchart	Annotation	Test
InterestControl 1. *Process Read* *(*Principal, *Interest* **Years, *Time)* 2. *Process Calc* *(Principal, Interest,* *Years, Time, *Amount)* 3. *Process Print* *(Principal, Interest,* *Years, Time, Amount)* 4. *End* * Specifies call-by-reference parameters.	(InterestControl) [Read] [Calc] [Print] (End)	 Enters all data from keyboard Calculates amount Prints data and amount	1. Start 2. Transfer to *Read* 3. Transfer to *Calc* 4. Transfer to *Print*

Internal Documentation		External Documentation	
1. Remark at top: Calculates principal and interest given, beginning principal, interest rate, number of years, and compounded time interval. 2. Include annotations		1. Same as 1 in Internal Documentation	

Figure 5.8a Algorithm and Flowchart for *InterestControl* Module

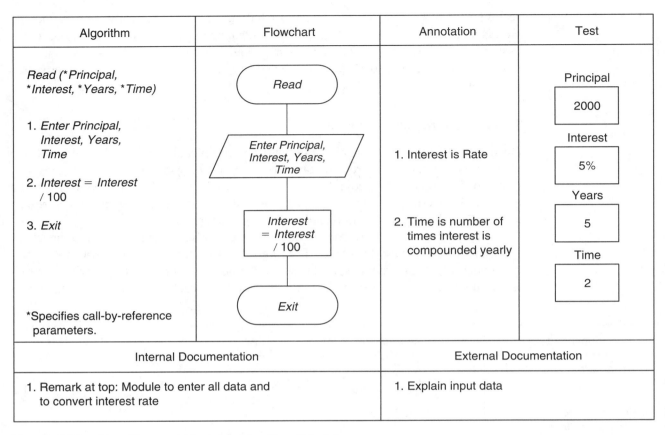

Algorithm	Flowchart	Annotation	Test
*Read (*Principal, *Interest, *Years, *Time)* 1. *Enter Principal, Interest, Years, Time* 2. *Interest = Interest / 100* 3. *Exit* *Specifies call-by-reference parameters.	Read → Enter Principal, Interest, Years, Time → Interest = Interest / 100 → Exit	1. Interest is Rate 2. Time is number of times interest is compounded yearly	Principal 2000 Interest 5% Years 5 Time 2

Internal Documentation	External Documentation
1. Remark at top: Module to enter all data and to convert interest rate	1. Explain input data

Figure 5.8b Algorithm and Flowchart for *Read* Module

Algorithm	Flowchart	Annotation	Test
*Calc (Principal, Interest, Time, *Amount)* 1. *Amount = Principal * (1 + Interest/Time) ^ (Years * Time)* 2. *Exit* *Specifies call-by-reference parameters.	Calc → Amount = Principal * (1 + Interest/Time) ^ (Years * Time) → Exit	None	Amount = 2000 * (1 + .05 / 2) ^ (5 * 2) Amount = 2000 * (1 + .025) ^ 10 Amount = 2560

Internal Documentation	External Documentation
1. Remark at top: Module to enter all data and interest	1. Specify equation

Figure 5.8c Algorithm and Flowchart for *Calc* Module

Algorithm	Flowchart	Annotation	Test
Print (Principal, Interest, Years, Time, Amount) 1. *Print Amount, Principal, Interest, Years, Time* 2. *Exit*	Print * Print Amount, Principal, Interest, Years, Time Exit	1. Print each variable on a separate line with a label.	Prints what is required

Internal Documentation		External Documentation	
1. Remark at top: Module to print required output		1. Specify output	

*Specify only what and when the information is printed, not how it is printed.

Figure 5.8d Algorithm and Flowchart for *Print* Module

must only use the algorithm instructions in Table 5.1, and each instruction must be in the form presented. The same is true for the flowcharts. The Annotation and Documentation sections of this figure have been completed to show how to use these sections in the Algorithm and Flowchart form.

The next step in developing the solution is to take a set of test data and work it through the algorithm instructions on a piece of paper or in the section provided on the Algorithm and Flowchart form. Do not skip any steps. It is important to process the data as you have instructed the computer to do it, starting at the beginning of the *InterestControl* module and working a set of data through the instructions in the algorithms for each module, one by one. As you process each module, write down the results. The solution is correct if the output matches the desired results. In this problem, the output should match the hand-calculated value of the amount. If the correct output is produced, then the analysis is complete. If not, you need to make corrections in the algorithm until you reach the correct output. At that point the analysis will be complete and coding into a language or application can begin. Coding is done in a language or applications course.

Summary

The instructions in every algorithm must use particular logic structures in order to increase readability for the programmer or user. The first logic structure is the sequential structure, in which the processing flows from one instruction to the next from start to end. The particular instructions used with the sequential structure include *Start, Enter* data, *Print* and *Write* data, assign a value to a variable (variable =), *Process* another module, and *End/Exit/Return*.

A solution to a problem is developed in seven steps:

1. Analyze the problem.
2. Develop the structure chart.
3. Develop the IPO chart.
4. Develop the coupling diagram and the data dictionary.
5. Develop the algorithms.
6. Develop the flowcharts.
7. Test the solution.

These steps will help you develop a solution that is efficient and easy to understand, code, and maintain.

After preparing the structure chart and the IPO chart, and while developing the algorithms and flowcharts, the programmer takes notes for the internal and external documentation that will be completed later. The internal documentation will be written within the program. The external documentation will be written in the form of manuals explaining the program.

Questions

1. What is the sequential logic structure?
2. Which flowchart symbols are used for the sequential logic structure?
3. Why is documentation important?
4. What is meant by solution development? Why is it important?

Problems

Complete the seven steps of solution development for the following problems:

1. A painter wants to know the amount of paint needed to paint only the walls and the interior side of the door in a room. The chosen paint covers 100 square feet per gallon. There are two windows. Test the problem with the following data:

 The room is 12 feet long, 10 feet wide, and 8 feet tall.

 The two windows are 5 by 3 feet, and 6 by 2 feet, respectively.

2. One of the jobs that Joe Roberts has been given at work is to order special paper for a report for a board meeting. The paper comes in reams of 500 sheets. He always makes five more copies than the number of people that will be there. Joe wants to know how many reams of paper he needs for a meeting. He can order only whole, not partial, reams. Assume the required number of pages will not equal an exact number of reams. Test your solution with the following data:

 The report is 140 pages long.

 There will be 25 people at the meeting.

3. An instructor calculates grades by dropping the lowest homework score and the lowest test score and adding the remaining scores together. He then calculates the final points as a percentage of the total points possible. The instructor needs to know the final points for a given student.

(*Hint:* Use the minimum function, that is, the function that returns the minimum value in a list of values.) Test your solution with the following data:

Total points possible—500 points

Tom Johnson

Homework scores—45, 46, 41, 31, 44

Test scores—95, 84, 75, 98

4. **a.** Develop a solution that would return the fewest coins in change from a purchase of under one dollar. (Include pennies, nickels, dimes, quarters, and half dollars.)

Example:	purchase	63¢
	change	37¢
	coins	1 quarter
		1 dime
		2 pennies

 b. Develop a solution that would return the fewest bills and coins for a purchase under $50.

5. Mary Williams needs to change a Fahrenheit temperature to Celsius. Use the Fahrenheit temperature of 80 degrees to test your solution.

(*Hint:* $C = 5/9(F - 32)$)

6. Write a solution to print the number of months (use 30 days to a month) and remaining days given the number of days between two dates.

7. A sweater is on sale for 25% off the original price. The original price is $50. Write a solution to calculate and print the sale price.

8. Bob would like to know what percentage of his income his rent is. Write a solution that would calculate and print this percentage.

(*Hint:* Percentage = Number/Total * 100)

9. An instructor calculates the grade percentage based on the highest score on a test. Given the highest score and one student's score, write a solution to calculate and print that student's test percentage.

(*Hint:* Percentage = Score/Highest Score * 100)

10. Joe would like to build several bookcases that are different heights and widths. All will be 12 inches in depth. The bookcases will have three shelves, in addition to the bottom and the top. Write a solution to print the number of feet of 12-inch-wide boards that will Joe need to complete a bookcase, given the height and width.

11. Given three numbers, print the maximum value.

(*Hint:* Use the Maximum function.)

12. Given three numbers, print their sum and their product.

13. Have the computer "throw" a pair of dice and print out the resulting numbers.

(*Hint:* Use the random number generator twice, once for each die. There are six different numbers on a die.)

14. Sharon would like to know how much gas will cost for her to take a trip to her vacation home 180 miles away. She knows the average price of gas and the average miles per gallon for her car. Write a solution to calculate the cost of the gas for her trip. (Remember she has to travel back.)

15. Michael has designated 5% of his paychecks for the year for presents (birthday, Mother's Day, etc.). Write a solution to calculate the amount of money he can spend given the amount of money he earns.

16. Jim is going to replant his lawn. He would like to know how much the sod will cost, given cost of the sod and the length and width of two different lawn areas. Write a solution to calculate this cost.

WHAT'S WRONG WITH THIS?

Correct the following algorithm instructions:

1. $A + B = C$
2. Output A, B, C
3. Input A, B, C
4. Enter $a, b,$ and c
5. Stop
6. *Goto Calc*
7. $A = 5 B \times C$

Chapter 6

Problem Solving
with Decisions

Overview

The Decision Logic Structure
Multiple *If/Then/Else* Instructions
Using Straight-Through Logic
Using Positive Logic
Using Negative Logic
Logic Conversion
Which Decision Logic?
Decision Tables
Putting It All Together

Objectives

When you have finished this chapter, you should be able to:

1. Develop problems using the decision logic structure in conjunction with the sequential logic structure.
2. Use the seven problem-solving tools when developing a solution using the decision logic structure.
3. Use nested decision instructions to develop a problem solution.
4. Distinguish the different uses of straight-through, positive, and negative nested decision logic structures.
5. Convert a positive decision logic structure to a negative decision logic structure.
6. Develop decision tables given a set of policies.
7. Develop a decision logic structure from a decision table.

The logic structures will almost always be used in some combination with each other in a program. In this chapter you will learn how to use a second logic structure, the decision structure, as a way to design instructions. The decision structure is one of the most powerful because it is the only way that the computer can choose between two or more sets of actions. Without decisions, the computer would be nothing more than a fast calculator.

The decision logic structure is relatively easy to understand since it works much like the way humans think. Because of the complexity of some of the decisions a programmer has to design, however, it is often one of the most difficult structures to implement. The difficulty goes back to the fact that people make decisions without understanding the reasoning involved. Also, a decision can be written in many different ways, which can add to the confusion.

The Decision Logic Structure

If/Then/Else instruction The decision logic structure uses the ***If/Then/Else*** **instruction.** It tells the computer that *If* a condition is true, *Then* execute a set of instructions, or *Else* execute another set of instructions. The *Else* part is optional, as there is not always a set of instructions if the conditions are false. When there are no instructions for true, a *Continue* statement must be used. The following algorithm instruction for the decision structure (the decision instruction) should be added to the list in Table 5.1. Notice the brackets and the indentation in the illustration of the algorithm of the decision instruction. Programmers use these features when they are writing instructions in the decision structure because they improve readability.

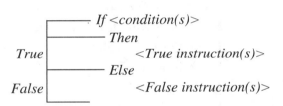

The *True* instructions are processed when the resultant of the condition is *True,* and the *False* instructions are processed when the resultant of the condition is *False.* A condition can be one of four things: a logical expression, that is, an expression that uses logical operators (AND, OR, and NOT); an expression using relational operators (greater than, less than, greater than or equal to, less than or equal to, equal to, and not equal to); a variable of the logical data type (*True* or *False*); or a combination of logical, relational, and mathematical operators.

Some examples of conditional expressions are as follows:

1. $A < B$ (A and B are the same data type—either numeric, character, or string)
2. $X + 5 > = Z$ (X and Z are numeric data)
3. $E < 5$ or $F > 10$ (E and F are numeric data)
4. *DataOk* (*DataOk* is a logical datum)

Logical operators are used to link more than one condition together. For example, consider a store policy requiring that to cash a check, a customer must have a driver's license, AND the check must be under $50. Two conditions are linked by the

logical operator AND. (See Tables 2.6, 2.7 and 2.8 for the definitions and the hierarchy of all the operators.)

The programmer can set up the conditions for a decision through the use of operands and various operators. These conditions can be used alone or linked with other conditions for use in the instruction. The programmer derives the information needed to set up the condition(s) for a decision from the problem itself during problem analysis.

Figure 6.1 shows a simple flowchart illustrating the decision structure. In the figure, the resultant of the condition(s) can be *True* or *False* depending on the data. From the decision block (the diamond), there will be a flowline, a branch for each set of instructions: one branch for the instructions to be executed if the resultant is *True,* and another branch for the instructions to be executed if the resultant is *False.* There can never be more than two flowlines coming from a decision block since there are only two possibilities for the resultant of the condition(s). The *True* branch and the *False* branch can come from any of the lower three points of the diamond. It is best to be as consistent as possible in choosing the points of the diamond on which these branches are placed. The convention is to draw the *True* branch on the right and the *False* branch on the left or bottom, although it depends on the decisions to be made. This book follows that convention whenever possible. The processing flow from both the *True* branch and the *False* branch must connect to the rest of the processing somewhere before exiting the module. There can be no dangling flowchart blocks—blocks with no flowlines leading to another block. The processing must flow somewhere. Each module can have only one entrance and one exit. The only way to get to another module is through a *Process* instruction, that is, by telling the computer to process the instructions in another module and then return to continue processing in the current module.

Single Condition

A simple decision with only one condition and one action or set of actions (one instruction or set of instructions) for *True* and another for *False* is relatively simple. For example, assume you are calculating pay at an hourly rate and overtime pay (over 40 hours) at 1.5 times the hourly rate. The decision to calculate pay would be stated in the following way: *If* the hours are greater than 40, *Then* the pay is calculated for overtime, or *Else* the pay is calculated in the usual way (see Figure 6.2).

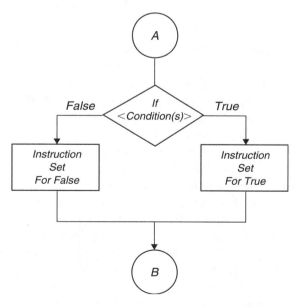

Figure 6.1 Flowchart Diagram of the Decision Structure

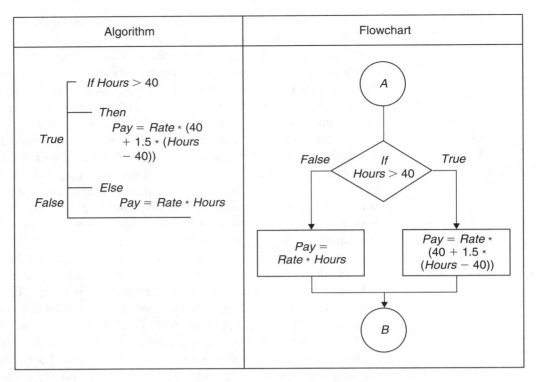

Figure 6.2 Single Condition—Two Possible Actions or Sets of Actions

Multiple Condition

Decisions in which you have *multiple* conditions that lead to one action or set of actions for *True* and another action or set of actions for *False* are slightly more complicated than those with single conditions. In these decisions you will use logical operators to connect the conditions. As with decisions based on a single condition, the resultant will determine whether the *True* or the *False* actions are taken.

The decision structure becomes more complicated as the number of conditions and/or the number of actions for a *True* or *False* resultant increases.

Multiple *If/Then/Else* Instructions

Multiple *If/Then/Else* Instructions

There are three types of decision logic you will use to write algorithms for solutions consisting of more than one decision. These types of decision logic include straight-through logic, positive logic, and negative logic.

straight-through logic

Straight-through logic means that all of the decisions are processed sequentially, one after the other. There is no *Else* part of the instructions; the *False* branch always goes to the next decision, and the *True* branch goes to the next decision after the instructions for the *True* branch have been processed.

On the other hand, with positive logic not all of the instructions are processed.

positive logic

Positive logic allows the flow of the processing to continue through the module instead of processing succeeding decisions, once the resultant of a decision is *True*. Whenever the resultant is *False* (the *Else* part of the decision), another decision in the sequence is processed until the resultant is *True,* or there are no more decisions to process. At that time, the *False* branch processes the remaining instructions.

negative logic

Negative logic is similar to positive logic except that the flow of the processing continues through the module when the resultant of a decision is *False*. Whenever the

resultant is *True,* another decision is processed until the resultant is *False,* or there are no more decisions to process. At that time, the *True* branch processes the remaining instructions. Negative logic is the hardest to use and understand.

Some series of decisions will require a combination of two or more of these logic types. The use of each decision logic type will be further explained and illustrated later in this chapter.

nested If/Then/Else instructions

In algorithms containing multiple decisions, you may have to write **nested If/Then/Else instructions.** Decisions using positive and negative logic use nested *If/Then/Else* instructions. Decisions using straight-through logic do not. Nested *If/Then/Else* instructions are sets of instructions in which each level of a decision is embedded in a level before it; like nesting baskets, one goes inside the next. You use the nested *If/Then/Else* structure only when one of several possible actions or sets of actions are to be processed (see Figure 6.3). In composing an *If/Then/Else* instruction, draw a large bracket around each *If/Then/Else* in the algorithm to ensure that each instruction is in the proper place. The top part of the bracket indicates the condition. The middle section of the bracket indicates the *True* branch, or the *Then* part of the decision. The bottom part of the bracket indicates the *False* branch, or the *Else* part of the decision.

In Figure 6.3, the decision is *If PayType* = "Hourly" and says, Is the value of the variable *PayType* equal to the string constant "Hourly"? If the two are equal, then the resultant is *True* and the instruction set for the *True* is processed. If the resultant is *False,* the instruction set for the *False* branch is processed. The *True* branch uses a nested *If/Then/Else* instruction; the decision is embedded in the *True* branch of the first decision. This decision says, Are the hours worked greater than 40? If the answer is "yes," the resultant is *True,* and the pay is processed at the overtime rate. When the resultant is

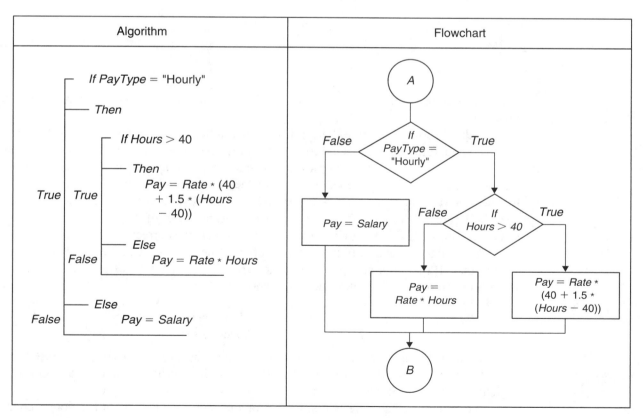

Figure 6.3 Nested *If/Then/Else* Instructions

False, that is, when the hours are not greater than 40, the pay is processed at the normal rate. When the resultant of the first decision is *False,* that is, when the *PayType* is not equal to "Hourly," then the pay is processed at the salary rate. (Notice that when the *PayType* is not equal to "Hourly," the embedded decision on the *True* branch cannot be processed—an example of negative logic.) A good programmer thoroughly tests algorithms that use decision logic with many sets of test data. Every path in every algorithm is checked, and a separate set of data is used for each path. It is important to test each path so errors will be eliminated.

Using Straight-Through Logic

Straight-Through Logic

With decisions following straight-through logic, all conditions are tested. To test a condition means to process a condition to get a *True* or *False* resultant. Straight-through logic is the least efficient of all types of decision logic because all the decisions must be processed. However, you must use it to solve certain problems—those that require two or more unrelated decisions and those in which all decisions must be processed. It is often used in conjunction with the other two logic types and in data validation (checking data to make sure it is correct). It is also used with languages that have limited features in their decision instruction.

The problem illustrated in Figure 6.4 is to find the amount to charge people of varying ages for a concert ticket. When the person is under 16, the charge is $7; when the person is 65 or over, the charge is $5; all others are charged $10. The conditions are the following:

Age	Charge
$Age < 16$	7
$Age >= 16$ and $Age < 65$	10
$Age >= 65$	5

Notice in Figure 6.4 that even when the age is less than 16, the other decisions must be processed.

In the algorithm and flowchart in Figure 6.4, notice that there is no *Else* in straight-through logic. If the resultant of the condition is *False,* then the processing flow drops to the next instruction. There is no need for the *Else* since there are no instructions for the *False* branch. If the resultant of the condition is *True,* then the set of instructions for the *True* part is processed, and the processing flow then drops to the next instruction. The set of conditions in Figure 6.4 is more efficiently executed by using either of the other types of logic since only one condition has to be met in order to execute the correct set of instructions.

The problem found in Figure 6.5 is to change the value of *X* to 0 when *X* becomes greater than 100, and to change the value of *Y* to 0 when *Y* becomes greater than 250. Each decision is independent of the other. The conditions are

$$X > 100 \qquad X \text{ becomes } 0$$
$$Y < 250 \qquad Y \text{ becomes } 0$$

Straight-through logic is required when all the decisions have to be processed, and when they are independent of each other. Based on these criteria, the only appropriate logic type for the decision in Figure 6.5 would be straight-through logic.

The following example is a similar problem, but with two sets of actions rather than one. When the age of a person is greater than 18, the person can vote; when the age

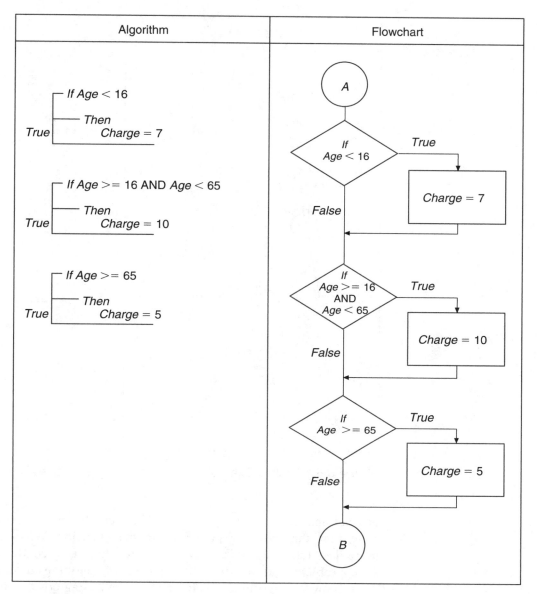

Algorithm	Flowchart

Figure 6.4 Straight-Through Logic—Example 1

is greater than 21, the person can have alcoholic beverages. Both decisions are contingent on the age of the person; however, the two actions take place at different ages. At the age of 20, a person can vote, but cannot be served alcoholic beverages. In this case, straight-through logic is required because all the decisions have to be processed and because they are independent of each other.

Using Positive Logic

Positive Logic

Positive logic is the easiest type for most people to use and understand because it is the way we think. Positive logic always uses nested *If/Then/Else* instructions. In general, when you use positive logic, you are telling the computer to follow a set of

Algorithm	Flowchart

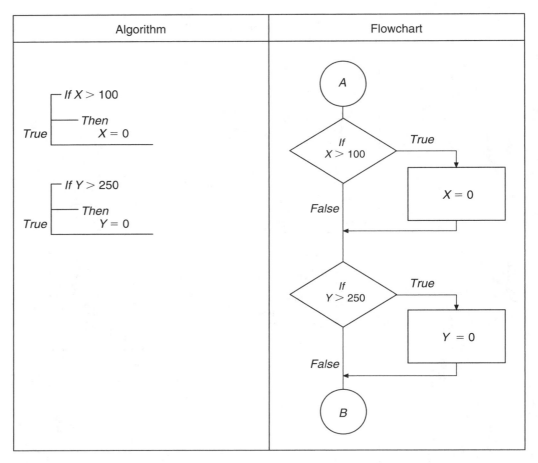

Figure 6.5 Another Example of Straight-Through Logic—Example 2

instructions and continue processing if the condition is *True;* if the condition is not *True,* then the computer processes another decision. When you use this logic, no more decisions are processed once the resultant of a condition is *True.* Taking the same problem, and therefore, the same set of conditions as in Figure 6.4, Figure 6.6 shows how the algorithm would be structured using positive logic. Notice that there are fewer decisions processed than in Figure 6.4—two compared to three—even if all the decisions are processed. There is no need to process the third decision because the resultant of the third condition statement has to be *True* once you have processed the second statement and found it *False.* That is, when the age is NOT less than 16, it has to be greater than or equal to 16. Therefore, this test can be eliminated if nested *If/Then/Else* instructions are used. Likewise, if the age is NOT less than 65, it must be greater than or equal to 65. Therefore, the third decision in the set of conditions is not necessary.

Figure 6.7 illustrates another set of conditions using positive logic and a nested *If/Then/Else* structure. The problem illustrated in this figure is to calculate the commission rate for a salesperson, given the amount of sales. When the salesperson has sold less than or equal to $2,000 worth of goods, the commission is 2%. When the sales total is more than $2,000 and less than or equal to $4,000, the commission is 4%. When the sales total is more than $4,000 and less than or equal to $6,000, the commission is 7%.

Algorithm	Flowchart

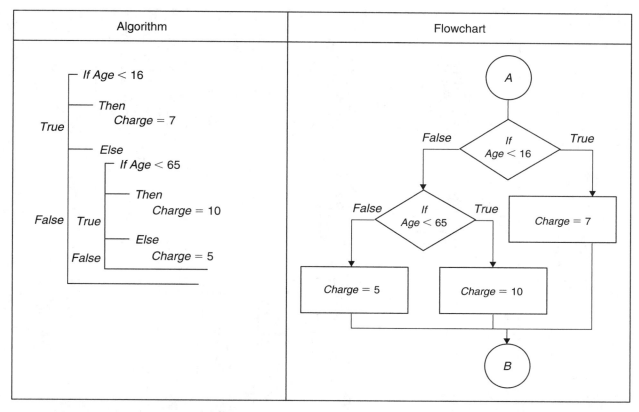

Figure 6.6 Positive Logic—Example 1

When the person has sold more than $6,000, the commission is 10%. The conditions are the following:

Sales	Commission
$< = 2000$.02
2001–4000	.04
4001–6000	.07
> 6000	.10

Notice that in Figure 6.7 there are only three decisions. The fourth decision is not necessary; when the sales are NOT $< = 6000$ they have to be > 6000. Remember, when setting up an expression, you must have an operand on each side of the operator. *Sales* = 2001–4000 does not mean this is true for any sales amount between 2001 and 4000. The computer will subtract 4000 from 2001 first, then it will compare *Sales* to the resultant, –1999. The proper expression for this condition is *Sales* > 2000 and *Sales* $< = 4000$. Also, remember that if this is the second decision in a nested decision and the first decision is *Sales* $< = 2000$, the expression in the second decision will be *Sales* $< = 4000$ since *Sales* > 2000 will always be true. Any *Sales* $> = 2000$ will have dropped out of the nested *Ifs* during the first decision.

Figure 6.7 is easy to read and understand because of the structure of the algorithm: Brackets and indentation are used with positive logic to show the nested levels of the decision structure. These features are important to readability.

Figure 6.7 Positive Logic—Example 2

To test positive logic for correctness, choose data to test every path. In the Test section of the algorithm and flowchart in Figure 6.7, there are four separate sets of data tested, one for each commission. You should arrive at the correct commission (hand calculated) by working each piece of test data through the flowchart. Notice that when *Sales* = 1500, there is only one decision to be processed; the resultant is *True,* the *Commission* is replaced by .02, and the processing continues at on-page connector B. When the *Sales* is equal to 3500, two decisions are processed before the resultant of one of them is found to be *True.*

There are times when it is more efficient to start an algorithm with one condition rather than another. The general rule is that the condition that will have a resultant of *True* most of the time should be the first. This way you will have to process the fewest decisions. See Figure 6.8 for another way to set up a solution for the conditions found in the sales commission problem illustrated in Figure 6.7. Notice the changes in the operators and in the order of the decisions. If you are unable to judge the condition that is most likely to be *True,* then it really does not matter how the logic starts.

Using Negative Logic

Negative Logic

Negative logic is the hardest for most people to comprehend because they do not think in negative terms. In general, when you use negative logic you are telling the computer to process another decision when the resultant of the condition is *True;* if the resultant is *False,* then the computer processes a consequent set of instructions and continues processing the module. It is often advantageous to use negative logic to decrease the number of tests or to improve the readability of a program.

In Figure 6.9, negative logic is used with the same set of conditions as in Figure 6.4. Notice that the actions take place on the *False* part of the instruction unless there are no more tests. Again, the algorithm uses brackets and indentation for readability. With the indentations the algorithm makes a sideways V. If a nested *If/Then/Else* instruction using negative logic does not form a sideways V, then either the indentation is wrong, or some of the instructions for each *True* or *False* are set up incorrectly. The top section of each bracket indicates a condition or conditions. The middle section indicates the instructions processed when the resultant of the condition(s) is *True.* This section is much larger when a decision uses negative logic than when the decision uses positive logic. The bottom section indicates the instructions to process when the resultant of the condition(s) is *False.* This section is much smaller when a decision uses negative logic than when the decision uses positive logic. The brackets make the nested *If/Then/Else* instruction easier to read by partitioning the conditions, the *True* section, and the *False* section.

For example, in the algorithm and the flowchart in Figure 6.9, when the resultant of the first condition (*Age* < 16) is *True,* another decision is processed (Age > = 65). When the resultant of the first condition is *False,* the charge of the ticket is $7; after this decision the processing continues through the rest of the module. When the resultant of the second condition is *True* the charge is $5; when *False,* the charge is $10.

Figure 6.10 shows the solution from the positive logic illustration in Figure 6.7 if we were to use negative logic. The conditions are the following:

Sales	Commission
< = 2000	.02
2001–4000	.04
4001–6000	.07
> 6000	.10

Figure 6.8 The Conditions in Figure 6.7 Set Up in a Different Way

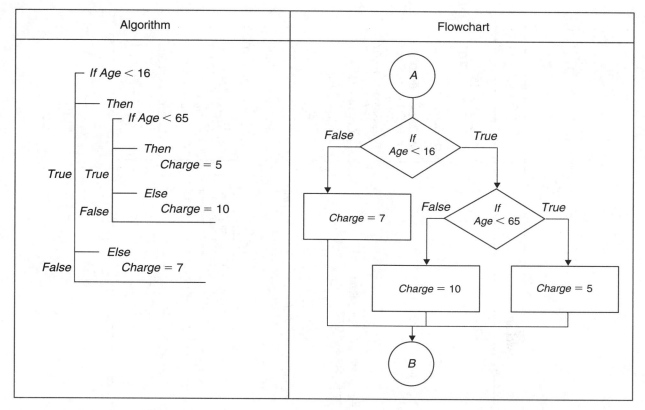

Algorithm	Flowchart

Algorithm:

If Age < 16
　Then
　　If Age < 65
　　　Then
　　　　Charge = 5
　　　Else
　　　　Charge = 10
　Else
　　Charge = 7

True / True / False / False / False labels as shown in figure

Figure 6.9　Negative Logic—Example 1

Notice how the testing takes place. Without proper testing, the problem-solving process is useless. Testing the algorithm or the flowchart reveals errors in logic, so corrections can be made before proceeding. It is far easier to make corrections during problem solving than after the coding has been done.

Figure 6.11 shows another way to organize the set of conditions in Figure 6.10 using negative logic. Here again, the rule is to have the computer make as few tests as possible.

Logic Conversion

Logic Conversion

There are times when it is necessary to change the logic from positive to negative or vice versa in order to improve the efficiency or readability of a solution. Sometimes the structure of a solution simply does not lend itself to the logic type that you've used, either because of the number and nature of the instructions to be processed, or because there are no instructions to be processed. In a decision, there must always be instructions for a *True* section, but not always for a *False* section. If there are no instructions for the *True* section of a decision instruction, then it is better to convert the logic type.

To convert from positive logic to negative logic or vice versa, do the following:

1. Change all $<$ to $>$ =.
2. Change all $<$ to $>$.
3. Change all $>$ to $<$ =.

Algorithm	Flowchart	Test

Figure 6.10 Negative Logic—Example 2

Figure 6.11 The Conditions in Figure 6.10 Set Up in a Different Way

The image contains three columns:

Algorithm

```
If Sales < = 6000
        Then
True            If Sales < = 4000
                        Then
          True                  If Sales < = 2000
                                        Then
                          True                  Commission = .02
                                        Else
                          False                 Commission = .04
                        Else
          False                 Commission = .07
        Else
False           Commission = .1
```

Flowchart

(A) → If Sales < = 6000 — True → If Sales < = 4000 — True → If Sales < = 2000 — True → Commission = .02
 — False → Commission = .1 — False → Commission = .07 — False → Commission = .04
→ (B)

Test

1. Sales = 1500
 Is Sales < = 6000?
 True
 Is Sales < = 4000?
 True
 Is Sales < = 2000?
 True
 Commission = .02

2. Sales = 3500
 Is Sales < = 6000?
 True
 Is Sales < = 4000?
 True
 Is Sales < = 2000?
 False
 Commission = .04

3. Sales = 5500
 Is Sales < = 6000?
 True
 Is Sales < = 4000?
 False
 Commission = .07

4. Sales = 7500
 Is Sales < = 6000?
 False
 Commission = .1

4. Change all $>$ $=$ to $<$.
5. Change all $=$ to $<>$.
6. Change all $<>$ to $=$.
7. Interchange all of the *Then* set of instructions with the corresponding *Else* set of instructions.

If you are using the convention to keep all *Trues* to the right and all *Falses* to the left in the flowchart, then reverse flowchart sections (see Figure 6.12). Figure 6.12 revisits the problem regarding the charge for a concert ticket based on age, illustrated in Figure 6.6. Notice that first, the relational operators are changed in the conditions. Second, the *True* sections of the algorithms and flowcharts are exchanged with the *False* sections.

Which Decision Logic?

How do you decide which type of decision logic to use? The general rule is to evaluate all three types for each solution and choose the one that is most readable, requires the fewest tests, and is easiest to maintain. It is easy to fall into the trap of always using the same logic type. It is also easy to fall into the habit of accepting and using a set of conditions exactly as the customer has given them. Such habits are not the most efficient ways of solving problems.

Figure 6.13 contains flowcharts showing four ways to set up the same conditions. The problem is to calculate a pay bonus given the set of conditions in the figure. From the data given, which logic type is the most efficient? Since the first and second solutions (the examples of positive logic) are easy to read, and the second solution requires the fewest tests, the second solution would be the best.

To analyze which type of decision logic would be most efficient for a particular solution, answer the following questions:

1. Which type would make the solution most readable?
2. Which type would make the solution the easiest to maintain or change?
3. Which would require the fewest tests when you don't know anything about the data?
4. Which would require the fewest tests when you're given some data?

If you find at the end of the analysis that more than one of the logic types could be equally effective, then simply choose one.

Decision Tables

Decision Tables

You may have a problem with multiple conditions and multiple consequent actions. In such a case discovering all of the actions that correspond to particular conditions—and discovering which combination of conditions, if any, leads to meaningful actions—can be complicated. A good way to simplify this process is to draw a decision table. You would draw a decision table during problem analysis. It is an excellent tool to use as a communication vehicle with a customer or with the person for whom you are solving the problem. You can also use it to test the algorithm and the flowchart.

decision table

A **decision table** consists of four parts:

1. The conditions
2. The actions

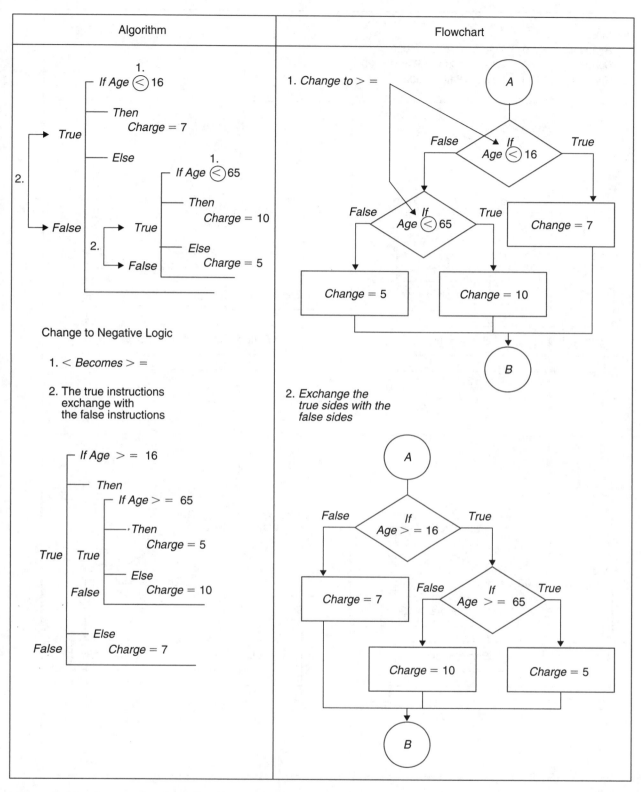

Figure 6.12 Conversion from Positive Logic to Negative Logic

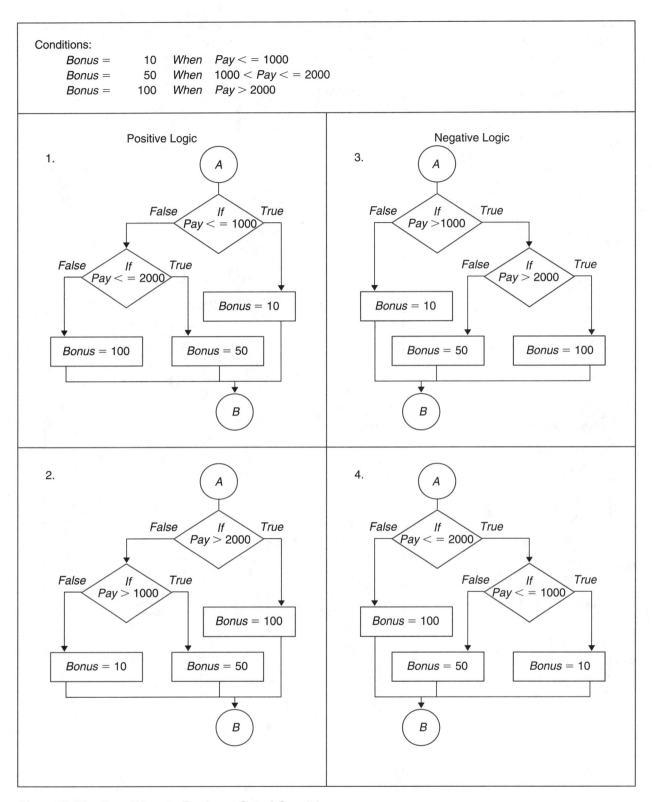

Figure 6.13 Four Ways to Design a Set of Conditions

3. The combinations of *True* and *False* for the conditions

4. The action to be taken or the consequences for each combination of conditions

Draw a decision table in the form of a rectangle divided into the four major sections. Each section is divided into smaller sections, as needed, according to the number of possible combinations of *True* and *False* (see Table 6.1). The total number of possible combinations of *True* and *False* for the conditions is two to the power of the number of conditions. That is, if there are two conditions, then there are $2 \wedge 2$, or 4 possible combinations of *True* and *False*. If there are three conditions, then there are $2 \wedge 3$, or 8 possible combinations. If there are four conditions then there are $2 \wedge 4$, or 16 possible combinations.

A flowchart must then be developed from the decision table. Figure 6.14 shows the flowchart development from the decision table in Table 6.1. The first step in the development of the flowchart is to draw in all decisions. Figure 6.14a shows the starting flowchart. Notice that the first decision is the first condition. The second decision is the second condition and is repeated on the true side and the false side of the first decision. The third decision is the third condition. This decision is repeated four times, once for each true and false for the second decision. This will allow all combinations of true and false values. Step two is to look at both sides of each decision, starting with decision one. Figure 6.14b shows the comparison of sides. If both sides are the same the decision is not needed. Notice that the true side of decision one is exactly the same as the false side. Therefore, this decision is not needed. The decision and the false side can be eliminated. The true side and the false side of the second decision are different and therefore, they need to stay. The same is true for the third decision. Figure 6.14c shows the final algorithm and flowchart. The four steps to develop a flowchart from the decision table are the following:

1. Draw all decisions in flowchart form.

2. Compare the true and false sides of each decision, starting with the first one.

3. Eliminate any decisions that have the same instructions on both the true and false sides, keeping the true consequence or action.

4. Redraw the flowchart.

The decision table is a graphical way of stating a policy for a company, such as a policy for cashing a check or for giving a bonus. Only the manager of the company can instruct the programmer regarding the company policy, so the programmer must work with the manager to complete the decision table. The manager tells the programmer the conditions and the actions, or consequences, of the decisions. The only

Table 6.1 Decision Table Format

List of Conditions									
Condition1	True	True	True	True	False	False	False	False	
Condition2	True	True	False	False	True	True	False	False	
Condition3	True	False	True	False	True	False	True	False	

List of Actions									
Action1		X				X			
Action2	X			X	X			X	
Action3			X				X		

All Possible Combinations of *True & False*

Consequences

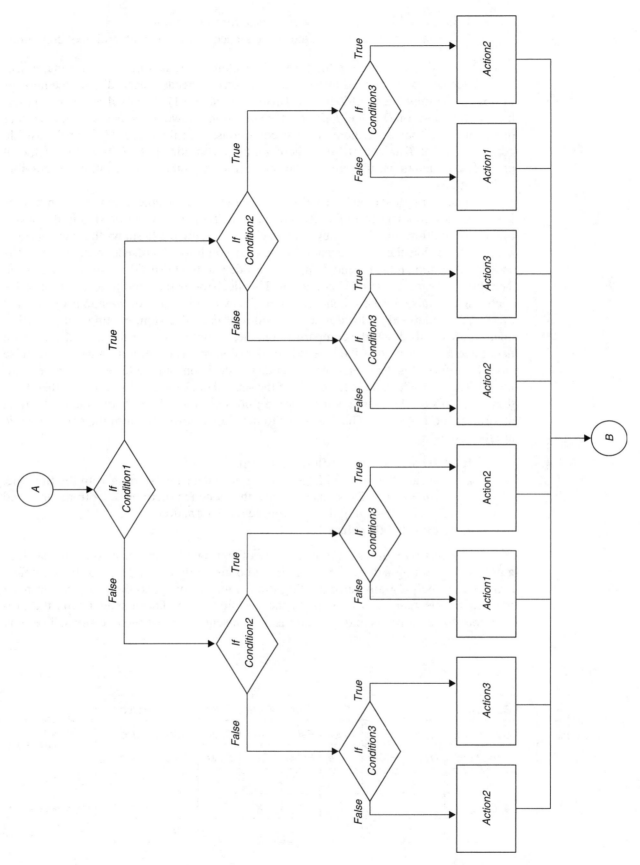

Figure 6.14a Starting Flowchart from Table 6.1

Figure 6.14b Elimination of Conditions

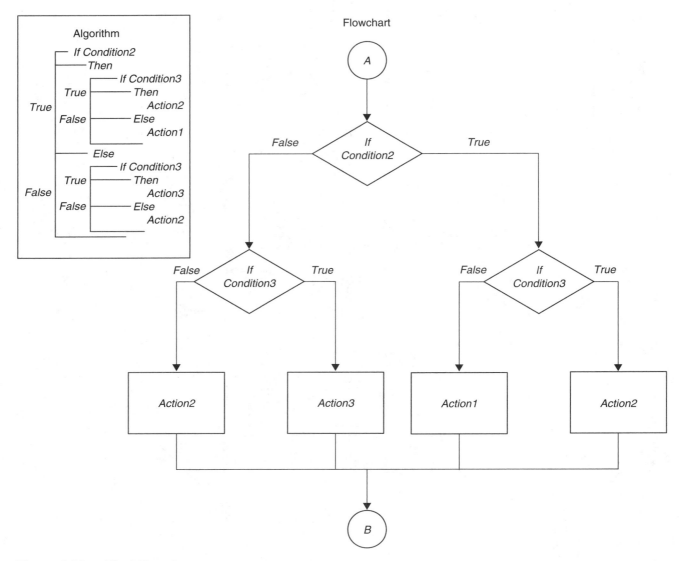

Figure 6.14c Final Flowchart

part the programmer fills in is the upper right-hand section showing the possible combinations of *True* and *False*. It is important for the programmer to work with the customer to make sure all combinations have the correct set of actions. From the decision table, the programmer proceeds to write the algorithm and the flowchart to solve the problem. The major difficulty in designing the algorithm is to make decision structure as efficient as possible by weeding out all unnecessary tests and putting the conditions in the best possible order. It often takes several experiments to come up with the best structure.

Table 6.2 shows a decision table for a store policy for charging a purchase. There are three conditions:

1. The purchase is less than $100.
2. The last payment to the account was made in the last 30 days.
3. The balance of the account is less than $1,000.

Table 6.2 Decision Table

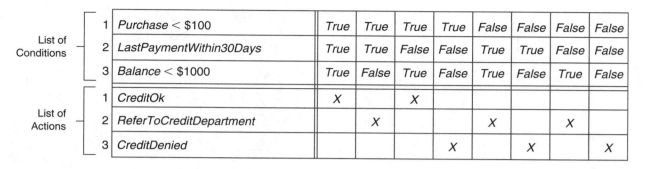

	List of Conditions								
1	Purchase < $100	True	True	True	True	False	False	False	False
2	LastPaymentWithin30Days	True	True	False	False	True	True	False	False
3	Balance < $1000	True	False	True	False	True	False	True	False

	List of Actions								
1	CreditOk	X		X					
2	ReferToCreditDepartment		X			X		X	
3	CreditDenied				X		X		X

Each of these three conditions could be *True* or *False* depending on the customer. The following actions could be taken:

1. Credit is okay, and the customer can charge the item.
2. Refer the customer to the credit department.
3. Credit is denied and the customer cannot charge the item.

These conditions and actions are supplied by the manager of the credit department. The manager also states when each of the actions will take place. The policy illustrated in Table 6.2 specifies that a customer can charge an item when all three conditions are *True,* or when the first and third conditions are *True* and the second one is *False.* The customer is referred to the credit department in the following cases: when conditions 1 and 2 are *True* and 3 is *False;* when 2 and 3 are *True* and 1 is *False;* and when 1 and 2 are *False* and 3 is *True.* Credit is denied in these cases: when conditions 2 and 3 are *False* and 1 is *True;* when 1 and 3 are *False* and 2 is *True;* and when all three are *False.*

Figure 6.15 shows the development of the flowchart from Table 6.2. Figure 6.15a shows the complete flowchart with all decisions. The condition *Purchase* < $100 is the first decision. *LastPaymentWithin30Days* is the second condition and is repeated twice, once each for the true and false in the first decision. The third decision is *Balance* < $1000. This decision is repeated four times, once for each true and false in decision two. This will give the actions for all combinations of true and false. Figure 6.15b shows the decisions that have the same true and false actions. Notice that the second decision on the false side of the first decision has identical actions on the true side and the false side. This indicates that this decision is not necessary and can be eliminated. After all, if the same action takes place whether the decision is true or false, the decision is not needed. Figure 6.15c shows the redrawn flowchart and the associated algorithm.

Putting It All Together

Example

The Putting It All Together (PIAT) sections in this book are designed to show students how to pull together and use the concepts from a previous section or sections. The following PIAT demonstrates how to use the six steps of problem solving on the computer to develop a solution that uses the sequential and the decision logic structures. The problem is as follows:

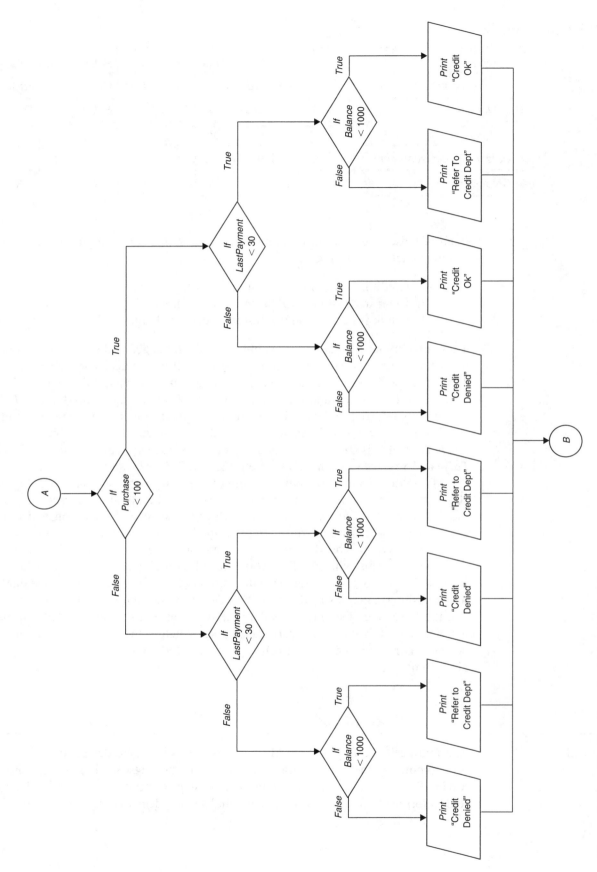

Figure 6.15a Starting Flowchart from Table 6.2

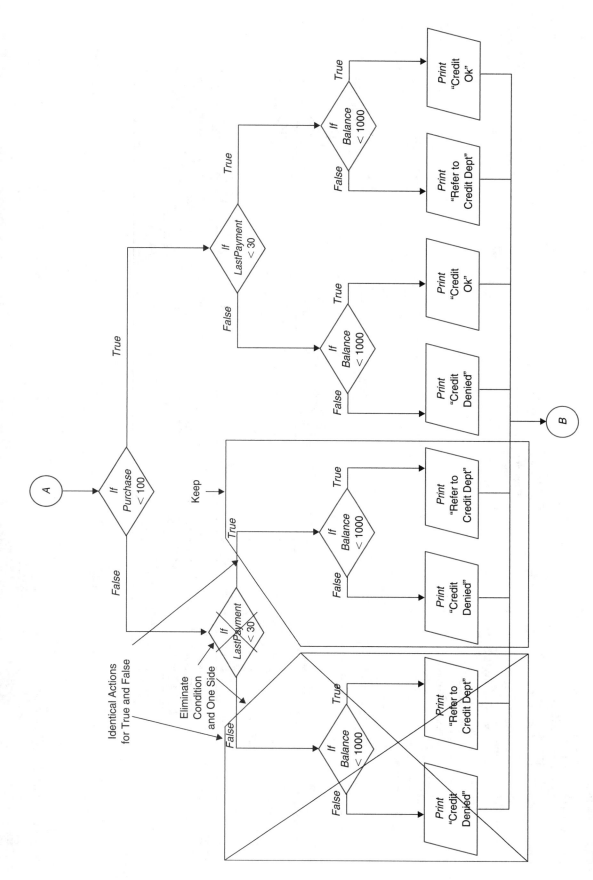

Figure 6.15b Elimination of Conditions

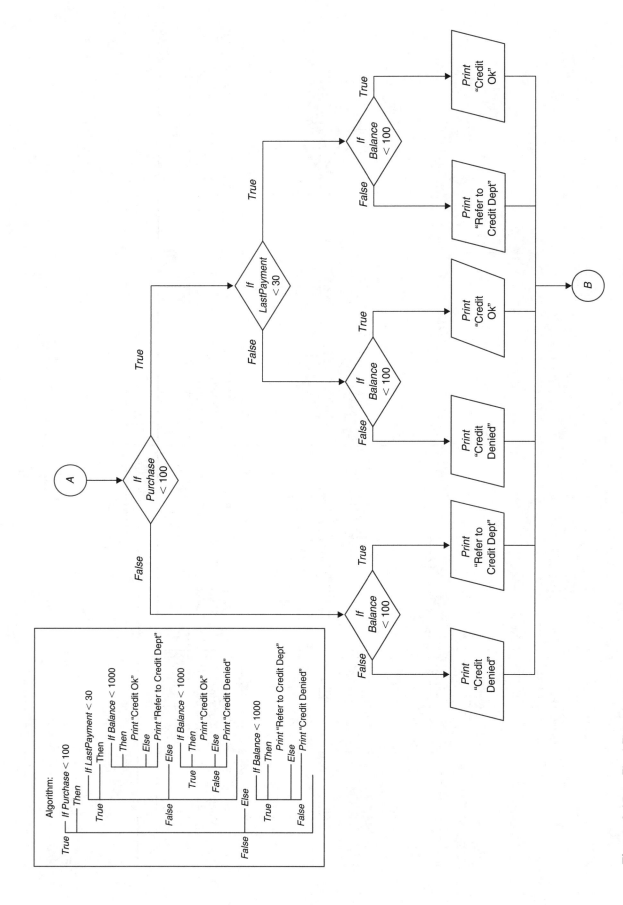

Figure 6.15c Final Flowchart

The Fantastic Floral Company sells to wholesale and retail buyers. The wholesale buyer needs a resale number in order to buy at no tax and to receive discounts. The retail buyer pays 6% tax. These are the discounts to the wholesale buyer:

Amount < $100	Discount = 2%
Amount > = $100 AND < $500	Discount = 5%
Amount > = $500	Discount = 10%

Given an amount of purchase, how much will the customer owe the company? (See Figure 6.16a–h.)

Given Data	Required Results
Wholesale buyers: • Must have resale number. • Amount of purchase discount < 100 2% > = 100 AND < 500 5% > = 500 10% Retail buyers: • No discount Amount of purchase (AP) 6% Tax	Amount owed
Processing Required	**Solution Alternatives**
Retail = 1.06 * AP Wholesale = (1 − D) * AP	*• Use positive logic for discount • Use negative logic for discount • Use straight-through logic for discount *This solution was chosen because it results in the fewest number of tests and it is easily read.

Figure 6.16a Fantastic Floral Company—Problem Analysis Chart

Figure 6.16b Fantastic Floral Company—Structure Chart

Input	Processing	Module Reference	Output
1. Amount of purchase 2. Resale number (If 0 then a retail customer)	1. Enter input data 2. Calculate discount 3. Calculate amount owed 4. Print output information	*Read* *Calc* *Calc* *Print*	1. Amount of purchase 2. Resale # 3. Amount owed

Figure 6.16c Fantastic Floral Company—IPO Chart

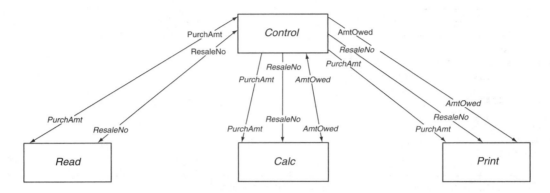

Item	Variable Name	Data Type	Module	Scope	Pseudonym	Error Cks.
Purchase Amount	*PurchAmt*	Numeric	All	Local	None	None
Resale Number	*ResaleNo*	Numeric	All	Local	None	None
Amount Owed	*AmtOwed*	Numeric	*Control, Calc, Print*	Local	None	None

Figure 6.16d Coupling Diagram and Data Dictionary

Algorithm	Flowchart	Annotation	Test
Control 1. *Process Read (*PurchAmt, *ResaleNo)* 2. *Process Calc* 3. *Process Print* 4. *End* *Specifies call-by-reference parameters.*	Control → Read → Calc → Print → End	Enters data Calculates amount owed Prints output	*GoToRead* Module *GoToCalc* Module *GoToPrint* Module *Stop*

Internal Documentation	External Documentation
1. Title: calculates amount owed given amount of sale and resale #	1. Same as internal documentation 2. Explain problem

Figure 6.16e The Algorithms and Flowcharts—*Control* Module

Algorithm	Flowchart	Annotation	Test
*Read (*PurchAmt, *ResaleNo)* 1. *Enter PurchAmt* 2. *Enter ResaleNo* 3. *Exit* *Specifies call-by-reference parameters.*	Read → Enter PurchAmt → Enter ResaleNo → Exit	PurchAmt = amount of purchase ResaleNo = resale number (0 means retail purchase)	*PurchAmt* 300 *ResaleNo* 27505 *Return*

Internal Documentation	External Documentation
1. Title: Enters data from keyboard 2. See annotations	1. Same as internal documentation

Figure 6.16f The Algorithms and Flowcharts—*Read* Module

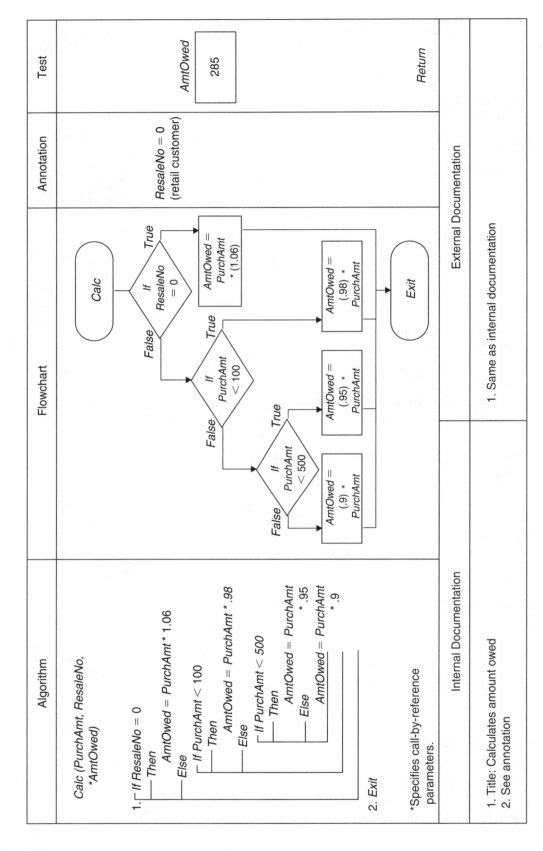

Figure 6.16g The Algorithms and Flowcharts—*Calc* Module

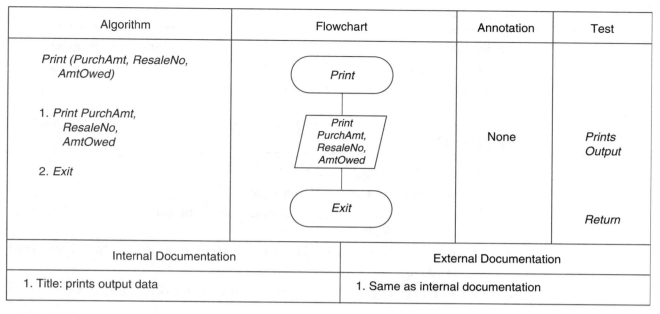

Algorithm	Flowchart	Annotation	Test
Print (PurchAmt, ResaleNo, AmtOwed) 1. *Print PurchAmt, ResaleNo, AmtOwed* 2. *Exit*	*Print* *Print PurchAmt, ResaleNo, AmtOwed* *Exit*	None	*Prints Output* *Return*

Internal Documentation	External Documentation
1. Title: prints output data	1. Same as internal documentation

Figure 6.16h The Algorithms and Flowcharts—*Print* Module

Summary

The decision logic structure is the second basic logic structure used to design algorithms, the first being the sequential logic structure. You now know the following types of instructions for communicating with the computer:

- *Start*
- *Stop*
- *Print*
- assignment
- *If/Then/Else*
- *Process* module
- *End/Exit*
- *Return*
- *Continue*

The instruction added in this chapter was *If/Then/Else,* the decision instruction. This instruction is powerful because it enables the computer to make decisions. It is an instruction that is easy to understand but more difficult to put to work.

There are three decision logic types: straight-through, positive, and negative logic. The programmer evaluates the conditions that arise in the problem to decide which logic type to use.

When you are using the decision structure, a decision table is a tool to help you develop the best set of decision instructions. You can use it to find the consequences following from every condition in a decision, so you can design the most efficient algorithms to solve the problem.

New Terms

decision table

If/Then/Else instruction

negative logic

nested *If/Then/Else* instruction

positive logic

straight-through logic

Questions

1. What is the decision logic structure?
2. What are the three types of decision logic?
3. Without specific data, outline an algorithm and a flowchart for each of the three types of decision logic.
4. What factors should determine which decision logic type to use for a specific problem?
5. How do you use a decision table?
6. When should you use single decision logic over nested decision logic?

Problems

1. Set up four different algorithms and flowcharts for calculating a student's letter grade given the following (do not use straight-through logic):

$$90-100 = A$$
$$80-89 = B$$
$$70-79 = C$$
$$60-69 = D$$
$$\text{below } 60 = F$$

2. Which of the four solutions from problem 1 would be the best? Justify your answer.
3. Using first positive and then negative logic, write the algorithms and draw the flowcharts for the following set of conditions:

$$R = 50 \text{ for } S <= 1000$$
$$R = 100 \text{ for } S = 1001-4000$$
$$R = 250 \text{ for } S = 4001-8000$$
$$R = 75 \text{ for } S > 8000$$

4. Change the positive logic algorithm and flowchart from problem 3 to reflect the following:

$$R = 100 \text{ for } S = 1000-4000$$
$$R = 250 \text{ for } S = 4001-8000$$
$$\text{otherwise } R = 75$$

5. a. Write the *Calculation* module to choose the largest number from a set of three numbers *A*, *B*, and *C*. Write the algorithm and draw the flowchart. Do not use the maximum function.

 b. Modify the logic in the calculation module to print *A*, *B*, and *C* in the correct order.

6. Complete the seven problem-solving steps to calculate the water bill given the cubic feet of water used for Eureka Water Company, which charges the homeowner one of the following:
 a. A flat rate of $15.00 for usage up to and including 1000 cubic feet.
 b. $0.0175 per cubic foot for usage over 1000 cubic feet and up to and including 2000 cubic feet.
 c. $0.02 per cubic foot for usage over 2000 cubic feet and up to and including 3000 cubic feet.
 d. A flat rate of $70.00 for usage over 3000 cubic feet.

 Test your flowchart with actual data.

7. A company that issues check-cashing cards uses an algorithm to create card numbers. The algorithm adds the digits of a four-digit number, and then adds a fifth digit of 0 or 1 to make the sum of the digits even. The last digit in the number is called the *check digit.* Complete the seven problem-solving steps to develop a solution that accepts a four-digit number into one variable, adds the check digit, and prints the original number and the new number. Test your flowchart with the following data: Original number = 4737 (47371) and 4631 (46310).

 Hint: You may use any or all of these functions and the principle of concatenation of strings.

 Integer(X)—Integer function

 String(X)—Numeric to string

 Value(A)—String to numeric

 Note: The *Integer(X)* gives the whole number value of the real number X. When X is 546.43, the *Integer(X)* is 546; when X is 23.899 the *Integer(X)* is 23. The *String(X)* and *Value(A)* are conversion functions. The resultant of the function *String(X)* is the string value of the numeric X. The resultant of *Value(A)* is the numeric value of the string A. Concatenation is the combining of strings by placing the first string in front of the second one. For example, the resultant of "4" + "5" would be "45."

8. Create a decision table, flowchart, and algorithm for problem 8 in Chapter 2.

9. An admission charge for The Little Rep Theater varies according to the age of the person. Develop a solution to print the ticket charge given the age of the person. The charges are as follows:
 a. Over 55: $10.00
 b. 21–54: $15.00
 c. 13–20: $10.00
 d. 3–12: $5.00
 e. Under 3: Free

10. A customer needs a specific amount of paper. The charges on the paper are $0.10 for single sheets, $0.055 for amounts in multiples of 100 sheets, $0.04 in multiples of 500 sheets, and $0.03 in multiples of 1000 sheets. Develop a solution to calculate the type and number of package(s) for the least amount of money the customer should buy, given the minimum amount of sheets the customer needs. For example, if the customer needs 380 sheets, the amount she would pay when buying in multiples of 100 would be $22.00. However, if the customer bought 500 sheets, the cost would be $20.00. It would be cost effective for the customer to buy a package of 500 sheets.

11. A hotel has a pricing policy as follows:
 a. 2 people: $85
 b. 3 people: $90
 c. 4 people: $95
 d. Additional people: $6 per person

 If the customer is staying on company business, there is a 20% discount. If the customer is over 60 years of age, there is a 15% discount. A customer does not receive both discounts. Given the above data, print the cost of the room.

12. A manufacturer would like to have a device for a car that will turn on a light when the temperature is between 34 and 40 degrees Fahrenheit (F) and sound a warning signal when the outside temperature is 34 degrees F or below. The light and the sound are never going simultaneously. Write a solution to this problem.

 (*Hint:* Use the enter statement to input the present outside temperature. Print out what should happen, instead of actually turning on the light and the signal.)

13. Joan is planning her vacation. She is considering two different destinations. She would like to go to the one that will be less expensive for the total trip including gas, hotel room for six nights, and meals for seven days. Write a solution to tell her which of the destinations would be the less expensive.

14. Monica needs to buy a present for her best friend. She can buy it online or she can travel 30 miles to buy at the store. She is not sure which would be less expensive considering shipping and handling costs to buy online and gas costs to travel to the store. The cost is the same in both places. Write a solution to tell Monica which would be the best way to buy the present.

WHAT'S WRONG WITH THIS?

1. a. Is the following nested *If/Then/Else* statement valid? Why or why not?

 $$If \ X < Y$$
 $$Then$$
 $$If \ Y < Z$$
 $$Then$$
 $$X = X + 1$$
 $$Else$$
 $$Y = Y + 1$$

 b. Which *If* does the *Else* go with? Explain your answer.
 c. How would you change the statement to clarify the statement?
 (*Hint:* Use a *Continue* statement.)
 d. Discuss your answer with your classmates and your instructor.

2. Correct the following algorithmic instructions:
 a. *If A* < *B* + *C Then*
 Else
 A = 5
 b. *If Len*(*S*) < "5" *Then*
 Print S
 c. *If Width* = *Length Then*
 Print "Object Is a Square."
 Otherwise
 Print "Object Is Not a Square."

Chapter 7

Problem Solving with Loops

Overview

The Loop Logic Structure
Incrementing
Accumulating
While/WhileEnd
Putting It All Together
Repeat/Until
Putting It All Together
Automatic-Counter Loop
Putting It All Together
Nested Loops
Indicators
Algorithm Instructions and Flowchart Symbols
Recursion

Objectives

When you have finished this chapter, you should be able to:

1. Develop problems using the loop logic structure in conjunction with the decision and sequential logic structures.
2. Use the seven problem-solving tools when developing a solution using the loop logic structure.
3. Use counters and accumulators in a problem solution.

4. Use nested loop instructions to develop a problem solution.
5. Distinguish the different uses of three types of loop logic structures.
6. Use recursion in a simple problem.

The Loop Logic Structure

loop logic structure

A third logic structure for designing decisions is the loop structure. The loop logic structure is the repeating structure. Most problems in business involve doing the same task over and over for different sets of data, so this structure is extremely important. Through the loop structure, a program can process many payroll records or inventory items, or put a mailing list in alphabetical or zip code order. This structure is harder to understand than the decision structure, but easier to use. The main difficulty in using it as part of a solution is identifying what instructions should be repeated. Besides being used to repeat instructions in a solution, the loop structure is also used to return the processing to an earlier point in the solution. When it is used in this way, it is a replacement for the *GoTo* statement. (The *GoTo* is an instruction that tells the computer to transfer to another instruction in the solution instead of processing the next instruction in sequence.) Replacing the *GoTo* statement in this way increases the readability of the program.

There are three types of loop structures, and each of them can be written in another way as a set of instructions using the *If/Then/Else* structure and the *GoTo* instruction. However, the *If/Then/Else* is a decision logic structure and generally should not be used to facilitate a loop. The loop structure is easier to read and to maintain than the *If/Then/Else* and *GoTo* combination. Since you already understand the decision logic structure, the decision equivalence to each loop structure will be illustrated to aid your understanding of loops.

The first type of loop structure is the *While/WhileEnd* loop, which repeats instructions while a condition is *True* and stops repeating when a condition arises that is not *True*. The second type is the *Repeat/Until* loop, which repeats instructions while a condition is *False* or until a condition is *True*. The third is the automatic-counter loop in which a variable is set equal to a given number and increases in equal given increments until it is greater than an ending number. Each of the three loop structures has a specific use according to the language and/or the problem.

The algorithm and the flowchart differ with each type of loop structure. It is extremely important to indent the instructions in algorithms using the loop structure—as it is with the decision structure—to improve readability. Also, nested loops are common, and in these solutions indentation with bracketing allows you to easily identify each loop.

Several standard types of tasks are accomplished through the use of the loop structure. Two of these are counting (also called incrementing and decrementing) and accumulating (also called calculating a sum or a total). In both tasks a number is added or subtracted from a variable and the result is stored back into the same variable. The basic difference between counting and accumulating is in the value that is added or subtracted. When counting, the value is a constant; when accumulating, the value is a variable. In each case the resultant variable is assigned the value of zero before starting the loop. This is called *initializing* the variable.

An updated table of the Algorithm instructions and Flowchart symbols is found in Table 7.1 on pages 149–150. These have either been introduced in the previous chapters or will be introduced in this chapter. Please use this table as a reference to the instructions you will be using in this chapter.

Incrementing

incrementing

The task of **incrementing,** or counting, as we said, is done by adding a constant, such as 1 or 2, to the value of a variable. To write the instruction to increment a variable, you use an assignment statement. For example,

$$Counter = Counter + 1 \text{ or } C = C + 1$$

when counting by ones. An assignment statement allows the variable on the left side of the equal sign to be assigned the value of, or to be replaced by, the resultant of the expression on the right side of the equal sign. The counter or incrementor instruction is a special version of the assignment instruction. This instruction enables the programmer to count the number of items, people, temperatures, and so on, as part of the solution to a problem.

Notice the structure of the assignment instruction for incrementing. The same variable name is on both sides of the equal sign; the amount the variable is to be incremented follows the plus sign. This instruction takes the value of the counter, adds one to it, and then replaces the old value of the counter with the new. The increment can be one, two, or any other constant, including negative numbers if you want to decrement rather than increment. In this example *Counter* or *C* must be initialized to zero before starting the loop.

Accumulating

accumulating

Another task that a program must often perform is **accumulating,** or summing, a group of numbers. The process of accumulating is similar to incrementing, except a variable instead of a constant is added to another variable, which holds the value of the sum or total. The instruction for accumulating is the following:

$$Sum = Sum + Variable \text{ or } S = S + V$$

For example, the instruction to find total sales would be

$$TotalSales = TotalSales + Sales$$

Like the instruction to increment, the instruction to accumulate is a special version of the assignment instruction. As in incrementing, the same variable name appears on both sides of the equal sign (*TotalSales*) but in accumulating, a variable rather than a constant is on the right-hand side of the plus sign (*Sales* in this case). In other words, with an accumulator you are adding a variable (the item you are accumulating) to the value of another variable, which holds the sum or total. In these examples *Sum* and *TotalSales* must be initialized to zero before starting the loop.

Products

Calculating the product of a series of numbers is similar to finding the sum of a series of numbers with two exceptions. First, the plus sign is replaced by the multiplication sign (*). Second, the product variable must be initialized to 1 instead of 0. For example

$$Product = 1$$
$$Product = Product * Number$$

Finding the product of a series of numbers is used very little. However, it will be used in the discussion on recursion at the end of this chapter.

While/WhileEnd

while/whileend

The first of the three types of loop structures is the ***While/WhileEnd*** structure. This type of loop tells the computer that while the condition is *True,* repeat all instructions between the *While* and the *WhileEnd.* The form of the algorithm is the following:

When you design *While/WhileEnd* loops, use brackets and indentation to improve the readability of the algorithms. In the illustration, notice how the bracket connects the beginning (*While*) and the end (*WhileEnd*) of the loop, and how the instructions are indented within the brackets to make the algorithm easily readable. The general form of the *While/WhileEnd* flowchart is shown in Figure 7.1.

The symbol used for the *While* part of the instruction is the diamond, the symbol for a decision. Since this flowchart shows only part of an algorithm, on-page connectors are used. The completed algorithm would have one part that would connect to *A* and another part that would connect to *B*.

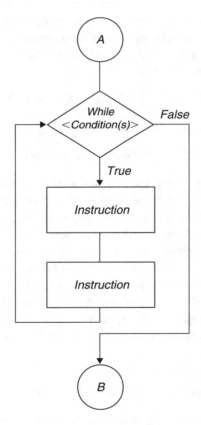

Figure 7.1 Flowchart Diagram of *While/WhileEnd*

At the beginning of the *While/WhileEnd* loop, the program processes the condition in order to decide whether to execute the loop instructions, as illustrated in the diamond at the top of the flowchart. When the resultant of the condition is *False* at the start, the instructions within the loop will not be executed. When the resultant of the condition is *True,* the complete set of instructions will be executed, and then the computer will go back to the beginning of the loop and process the condition again. The loop will repeat until the resultant of the condition is *False,* at which time the processing will continue with the instruction following the *WhileEnd.*

Figure 7.2 shows the decision-structure equivalent to the *While/WhileEnd* loop structure. Notice that the decision structure requires a separate *GoTo* instruction to return to the top of the loop. Also notice that when the condition is *False,* the line of execution transfers to the instruction after the loop instructions.

Use the *While/WhileEnd* structure when you do not know the number of times the instructions will be repeated, or if there are cases when the instructions in the loop should not be processed. In those cases, the resultant of the condition is *False* at the start of the loop, so the loop is not processed. Examples of such cases are when you are entering information on clients and you don't know the number of clients; when you are finding

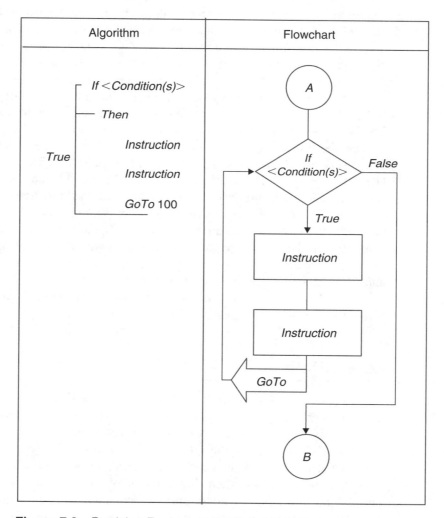

Figure 7.2 Decision Equivalent to *While/WhileEnd*

the total amount of sales for the day and you don't know the number of sales; or when you are calculating test averages for each student in a class. In the case of calculating test averages, the loop instructions should not be executed for students who for some reason have no test grades. To calculate the average you would accumulate and count the test scores and then divide the total score by the number of tests. Since the number of grades would be zero for the student who didn't take any tests, the computer would try to divide by zero, and an error would result. The *While/WhileEnd* loop would enable the processing to pass over the student and go on to the next student.

Putting It All Together

Example

Problem: Create the algorithm and the flowchart to find the average age of all the students in a class.

Figure 7.3 demonstrates the use of a *While/WhileEnd* structure to calculate the average age of a group of people. The first instruction initializes the value of the *Sum* (the total of all ages) to zero. The second instruction initializes the value of the counter variable to zero. Next the first age is entered. An age must be entered before the loop so that the condition has data to use to get a resultant. This is called a ***primer Read*** because it gives the *While/WhileEnd* loop a valid value for the variable *Age* in order for the conditions to be true the first time through the loop. If there is no primer *Read,* the value of *Age* is unknown. The next read is at the end of the loop for two reasons. First, the first value of *Age* must be included in the calculations. Second, the test for the trip value (the value of age that makes the condition false and signals the end of the list of students) must be just before the condition, so the trip value will not be calculated as part of the average age. The *While* begins the loop and processes the condition *Age* < > 0. When the resultant is *True,* the instructions in the loop are processed; when the resultant is *False,* the processing continues with the calculation of the average. The first loop instruction accumulates the ages by adding each age to the total, followed by an instruction that counts the people by adding one to the counter variable. The final instruction in the loop enters the next age. The processing then returns to process another condition. The last age should be zero. This zero is called a *trip value,* or a *flag.* It allows the value of *Age* to control when to stop the looping process and continue with the rest of the solution. When the looping process stops, the processing continues at the calculation of the average age, and finally, the printing of the average age.

The data for this problem can be entered from the keyboard; the user enters a 0 when there are no more ages to enter.

primer read

Repeat/Until

repeat/until

The second type of loop structure is the ***Repeat/Until*** structure. This type of loop tells the computer to repeat the set of instructions between the *Repeat* and the *Until,* until a condition is *True.* There are two major differences between this instruction and the *While/WhileEnd.* First, in the *While/WhileEnd* loop, the program continues to loop as long as the resultant of the condition is *True;* in the *Repeat/Until* loop, the program stops the loop process when the resultant of the condition is *True.* Second, in the *While/WhileEnd* loop, the condition is processed at the beginning; in the *Repeat/Until* loop, the condition is processed at the end. When the condition is processed at the end,

Algorithm	Flowchart

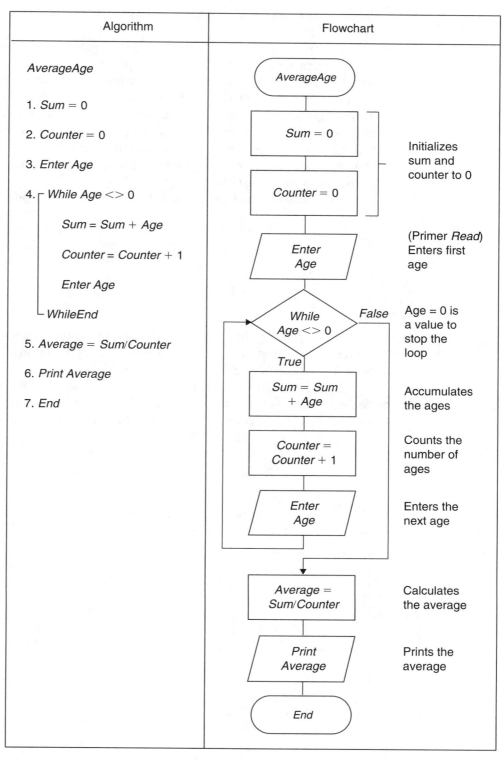

AverageAge

1. *Sum* = 0

2. *Counter* = 0

3. *Enter Age*

4. ┌ *While Age* <> 0

 Sum = *Sum* + *Age*

 Counter = *Counter* + 1

 Enter Age

 └ *WhileEnd*

5. *Average* = *Sum/Counter*

6. *Print Average*

7. *End*

Flowchart (right column):

AverageAge

Sum = 0 — Initializes sum and counter to 0

Counter = 0

Enter Age — (Primer *Read*) Enters first age

While Age <> 0 — False — Age = 0 is a value to stop the loop

True

Sum = Sum + Age — Accumulates the ages

Counter = Counter + 1 — Counts the number of ages

Enter Age — Enters the next age

Average = Sum/Counter — Calculates the average

Print Average — Prints the average

End

Figure 7.3 Average Age of a Class—*While/WhileEnd*

the instructions in the loop are processed entirely at least once, regardless of whether it is necessary.

It is important that you be able to distinguish between the loop structures so you can use them appropriately. Both the setup and the uses for the two loop structures are different. When you are using the *While/WhileEnd,* you must initialize the data so that the resultant of the condition is *True* the first time through the loop. Otherwise, the loop instructions will never be processed. With the *Repeat/Until,* you can set the operands of the conditions anywhere within the loop since the condition is processed at the end. If there is any reason that the loop instructions should not be processed the first time, then the *While/While-End* must be used because the *Repeat/Until* always processes the instructions at least once.

The format of the *Repeat/Until* algorithm is the following:

$$
\begin{array}{l}
\textit{Repeat} \\
\quad \textit{Instruction} \\
\quad \textit{Instruction} \\
\quad . \\
\quad . \\
\textit{Until<Condition(s)>}
\end{array}
$$

Here again, use brackets and indentation to improve readability. Figure 7.4 shows the form of the flowchart. When you are designing a *Repeat/Until* flowchart, write the word *Repeat* above the first instruction of the loop.

Figure 7.5 shows the equivalent decision structure. Unlike the *While/WhileEnd* decision equivalent, in which the processing of the condition is always at the beginning of the instructions to be repeated, with the *Repeat/Until* decision equivalence, the processing of

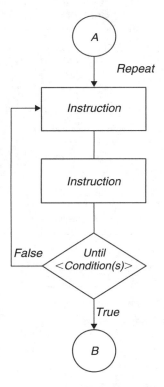

Figure 7.4 Flowchart Diagram of *Repeat/Until*

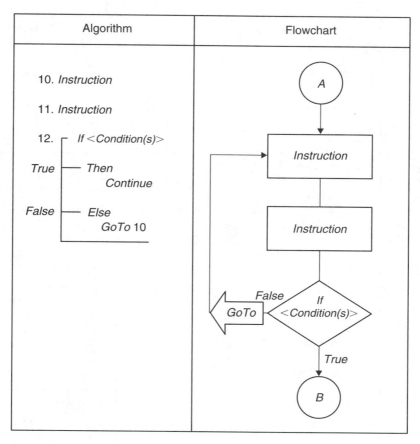

Algorithm	Flowchart

10. *Instruction*

11. *Instruction*

12. *If <Condition(s)>*

True *Then*
 Continue

False *Else*
 GoTo 10

Figure 7.5 Decision Equivalent to *Repeat/Until*

the condition always takes place at the end of the instructions to be repeated. Also notice that there is no evidence of a loop until the condition is reached. The loop structure provides a solution that is easier to read and understand.

 Use the *Repeat/Until* structure when you do not know the number of times the instructions will be executed, when you know they will be executed at least once, or when you do not know the condition for repeating until after the instructions in the loop are processed. Usually, the problem will dictate which loop to use.

Putting It All Together

Using the *Repeat/Until* loop structure, this section illustrates the same problem as in the Putting It All Together section for the *While/WhileEnd* loop.

Example

 Figure 7.6 demonstrates the use of the *Repeat/Until* structure to calculate the average age of a group of people. The first instruction initializes the value of the *Sum* (the total of all ages) to zero. The second instruction initializes the value of the counter variable to zero. Next the first age is entered. An age must be entered so that there is a value for *Age* to use in the calculations the first time through. The data must be entered just before processing the condition, or the trip values will be used in the last calculations in the solution. This is the primer *Read*. However, unlike the *While/WhileEnd* loop structure, when a zero is entered at this place in the processing, the instructions within the loop will be executed at least once, depending on what is entered at the second *Enter*

Algorithm	Flowchart

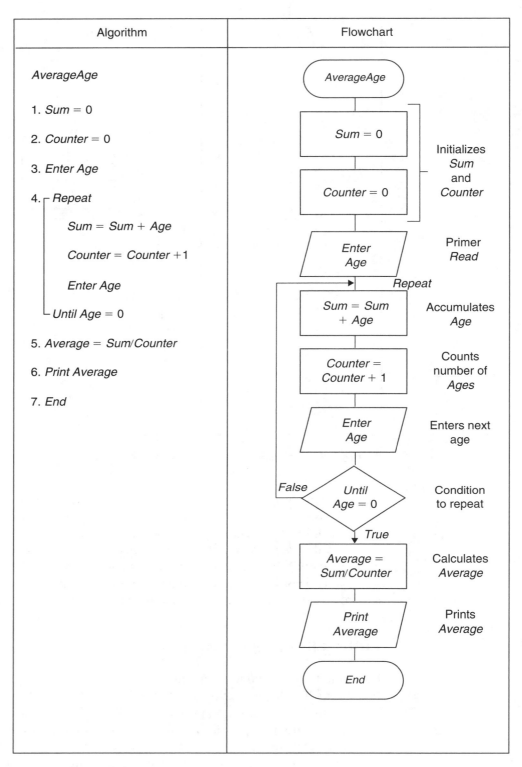

AverageAge

1. *Sum* = 0

2. *Counter* = 0

3. *Enter Age*

4. ┌ *Repeat*

 Sum = *Sum* + *Age*

 Counter = *Counter* +1

 Enter Age

 └ *Until Age* = 0

5. *Average* = *Sum/Counter*

6. *Print Average*

7. *End*

Figure 7.6 Average Age of a Class—*Repeat/Until*

instruction. For this reason, the *While/WhileEnd* loop structure is often the preferred choice. The *Repeat* begins the loop. The first instruction in the loop accumulates the ages by adding each age to the total, followed by an instruction that counts the people by adding 1 to the counter variable. The last instruction in the loop enters the next age. The next instruction is the loop-end instruction. This instruction processes the condition *Age* = 0. When the resultant is *False* the instructions in the loop are processed; when the resultant is *True* the processing continues with the calculation of the average. The last age is a zero, the trip value or dummy value. It allows the value of *Age* to control when to stop the loop process and continue with the rest of the solution. When the looping process stops, the processing continues at the calculation of the average age, and finally, the printing of the average age.

The programmer or the language dictates which loop structure to use. Sometimes the *While/WhileEnd* and the *Repeat/Until* could be used with equal efficiency. The choice is then a matter of the programmer's preference.

Automatic-Counter Loop

automatic-counter loop

The third type of loop structure is the **automatic-counter loop.** This type of loop increments or decrements a variable each time the loop is repeated. To design an automatic-counter loop, the programmer uses a variable as a counter that starts counting at a specified number and increments the variable each time the loop is processed. The amount to be incremented is specified by the instruction. The set of instructions within the loop repeats until the counter is greater than an ending number. The beginning value, the ending value, and the increment value may be constants, variables, or expressions (calculations). They should not be changed during the processing of the instructions in the loop. They may be changed after the loop is completed. The test for whether to process the loop instructions in an automatic-counter loop will be found at the beginning or at the end of the loop depending on the language or the version of the language.

The form of the algorithm for the automatic-counter loop is the following:

> ┌─ *Loop: Counter = Begin To End Step StepValue*
> │ *Instruction*
> │ *Instruction*
> │ .
> │ .
> │ .
> └─ *Loop-End: Counter*

Here again, a bracket connects the beginning (*Loop*) and the end (*Loop-End*) of the algorithm, and the instructions are indented to improve readability, just as in the other loop structures.

The flowchart in Figure 7.7 shows the automatic-counter loop structure. *Counter* is the variable used for the counter, *Begin* is the beginning value, *End* is the ending value, and *StepValue* is the value by which the counter is to be incremented. To decrement, *StepValue* needs to be a negative number and *Begin* must be greater than *End*.

Figure 7.8 shows the decision equivalents to the automatic-counter loop structure. There are two solutions illustrated since there are two places the decision can be processed: at the beginning of the loop or at the end of the loop. Which decision equivalent

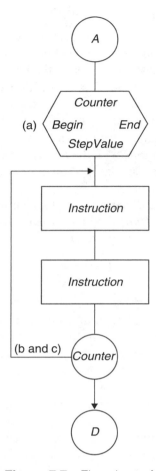

Figure 7.7 Flowchart of Automatic-Counter Loop

would be used depends on the language or the version of the language. You will not find both versions in the same language or language version.

Figure 7.9 shows the equivalent algorithms and flowcharts of the *While/WhileEnd* and *Repeat/Until* loops for the automatic-counter loop. Note that both these loops require a counter instruction (*Counter = Counter + StepValue*) and initialization of the counter (*Counter = Begin*). The decision for both loops involves the use of the ending value (*While Counter <= End and Until Counter > End*). The automatic-counter loop takes care of these instructions automatically. The *While/WhileEnd* loop executes the test at the beginning of the loop, and the *Repeat/Until* executes it at the end. When *Begin* is greater than *End* at the beginning of the loop, the *While/WhileEnd* will not execute any internal instructions, whereas the *Repeat/Until* will execute the instructions once. When you know the starting and ending values of the counter and you need a counter to run through a group of instructions multiple times, the use of the automatic-counter loop is preferred.

There are rules that the computer follows when processing the automatic-counter loop. The rules are simple, and it is important that the user understands and follows them when testing a solution.

When incrementing the counter, remember the following rules:

1. When the computer executes the *Loop* instruction, it sets the counter equal to the beginning number (see a, a_1, and a_2 in Figures 7.7 and 7.8).

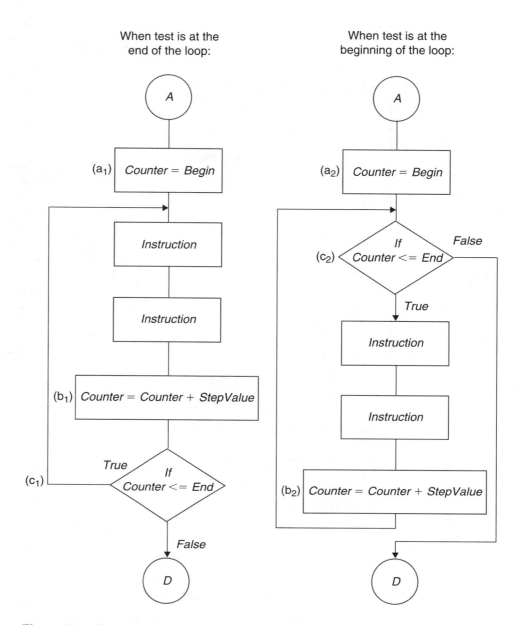

Figure 7.8 Decision Equivalents to Automatic-Counter Loop

2. When the computer executes the *Loop-End,* it increments the counter. Since the counter is usually incremented before the condition is processed, this book assumes the incrementing of the counter at *Loop-End* (see b, b_1, and b_2 in Figures 7.7 and 7.8).

3. When the counter is less than or equal to the ending number, the processing continues at the instruction that follows the *Loop* instruction. When the counter is greater than the ending number, the processing continues at the instruction that follows the *Loop-End* instruction (see c, c_1, and c_2 in Figures 7.7 and 7.8).

There are two differences in these rules when decrementing the counter. First, the counter is decremented instead of incremented at the end of the loop. Second, when the counter is greater than or equal to the ending value, the loop continues, instead of when

Algorithm	Flowchart
10. *Counter = Begin* 11. *While Counter <= End* *Instruction* *Instruction* *Counter = Counter + StepValue* *WhileEnd* 12	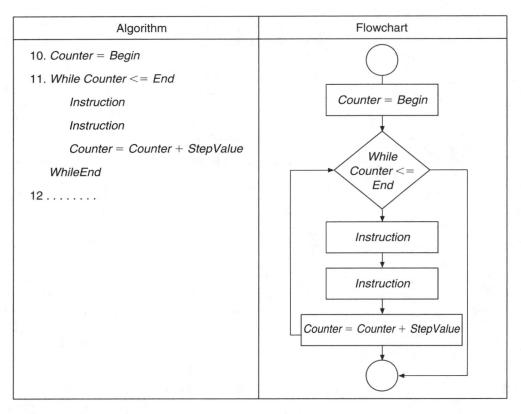

Figure 7.9a *While/WhileEnd* Loop Equivalent of the Automatic-Counter Loop

Algorithm	Flowchart
10. *Counter = Begin* 11. *Repeat* *Instruction* *Instruction* *Counter = Counter + StepValue* *Until counter + End* 12	

Figure 7.9b *Repeat/Until* Loop Equivalent of the Automatic-Counter Loop

it is less than or equal to the ending value when incrementing. It is important to understand these rules in order to use this structure correctly.

Use the automatic-counter loop structure when you know from the start the number of times the loop will be executed—for example, when you know the exact number of people in the group for the average-age problem. Do not use a decision to exit from this loop. A decision cannot be used to exit a loop since to do so would require a *GoTo* instruction. *GoTo* instructions tend to decrease readability, so they are used as little as possible in structured programming. If a decision instruction is necessary, then consider using one of the other types of loop structures for your solution. Counter loops are overused because they are easy to code. A good programmer is careful not to fall into this trap. It is important to choose the best loop structure for the problem.

Putting It All Together

Example

This section illustrates the same problem, using the automatic-counter structure that the previous two Putting It All Together sections did, using the other two types of loop instructions. The solution calculates the average age of a group of people. The programmer would use the automatic-counter loop structure for this solution only if the number of students in the class—in this case, 12—is known.

In the automatic-counter loop in Figure 7.10, as in the other two loop structures, the first two instructions initialize the variables *Sum* and *Counter.* The next instruction begins the loop. The *A* is the counter variable. The counter begins at 1 and is incremented by 1 until the counter is greater than 12, so the loop will be repeated 12 times. Notice that there is no increment value. When the increment value is left out, the computer assumes the value to be 1. When the counter increases to a value greater than 12, the average age is calculated and printed. Also notice the absence of the primer *Read.* The primer *Read* is not necessary because there is no trip value needed since the number of students is known. Whenever the number of items to be counted is known, the automatic-counter loop is preferred. If that number is not known, then one of the other loop structures is preferred.

Nested Loops

Nested Loops

Loops can be nested like decisions can. Each loop must be nested inside the loop just outside it. The general rules regarding loops, such as where the condition is processed and how indentation and brackets are used, hold true for nested loops as well as single loops. The inner loops do not have to be the same types of loop structures as the outer loops; that is, a *While/WhileEnd* may be nested inside a *Repeat/Until* loop, or vice versa.

Examples of nested loops are found in Figure 7.11. Notice that the nested loop in each flowchart results in the same output. The output for all four nested loops is the following:

OuterLoop	InnerLoop
(outer loop counter)	*(inner loop counter)*
1	1
1	2
1	3
2	1
2	2
2	3

Algorithm	Flowchart

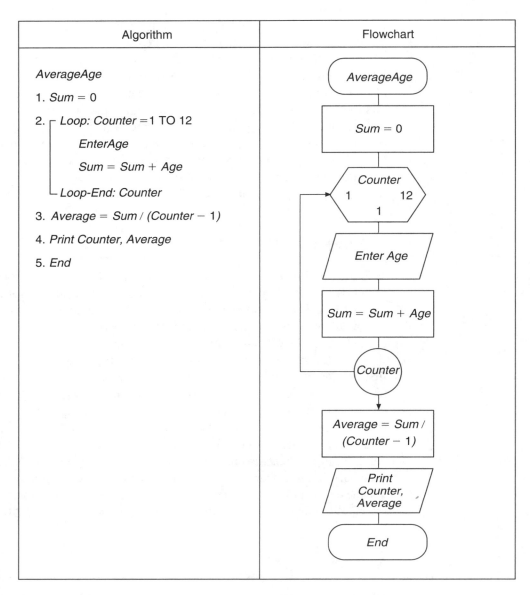

AverageAge

1. *Sum* = 0

2. ⌐ *Loop: Counter* =1 TO 12

 EnterAge

 Sum = Sum + Age

 └ *Loop-End: Counter*

3. *Average = Sum / (Counter − 1)*

4. *Print Counter, Average*

5. *End*

Figure 7.10 Example of an Algorithm and Flowchart for a Problem Using an Automatic-Counter Loop

In the first flowchart in Figure 7.11, the nested loops are both *While/WhileEnd* structures. The inner loop will be processed as long as the value of InnerLoop is less than 3. The inner loop increments InnerLoop and, later, prints the values of OuterLoop and InnerLoop. During the processing of the inner loop, the value of OuterLoop does not change. When InnerLoop becomes equal to 3, the inner loop has completed the processing, and the processing continues with the outer loop. The OuterLoop increments OuterLoop, sets InnerLoop equal to 0, and then processes the InnerLoop. When OuterLoop becomes equal to 2, processing continues at *B*. This whole process is essentially what happens in the other three examples of nested loops. The outer loop increments OuterLoop, sets InnerLoop equal to 0 or 1, and processes the inner InnerLoop loop. The InnerLoop increments InnerLoop and prints the values of OuterLoop and InnerLoop.

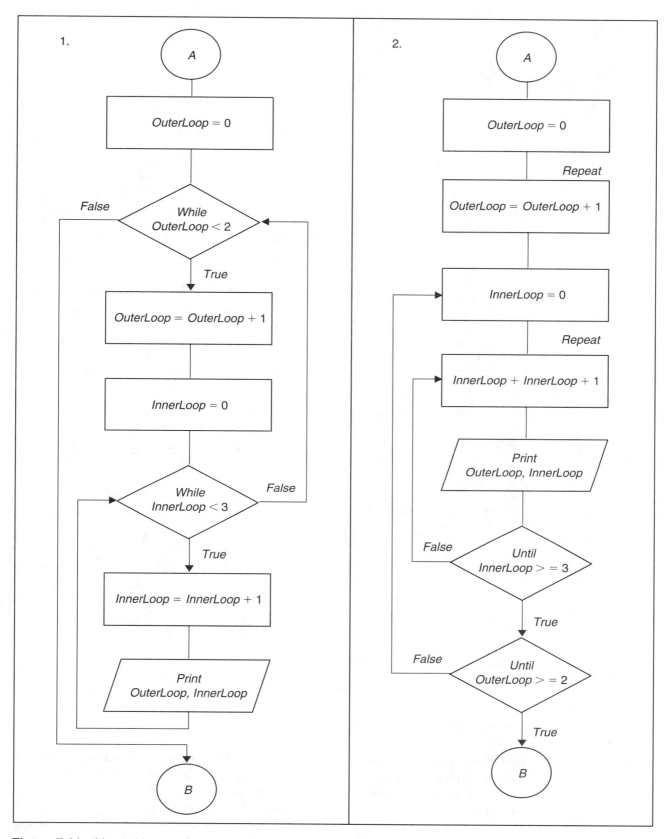

Figure 7.11 Nested Loops *(continued on page 148)*

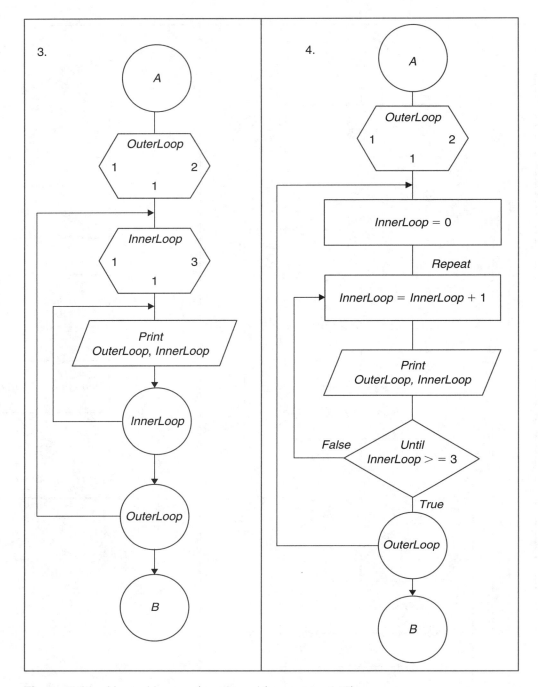

Figure 7.11 Nested Loops *(continued from page 147)*

Indicators

indicators

Indicators are logical variables that a programmer sets within a program to change the processing path or to control when the processing of a loop should end. They are sometimes called *flags, switches,* or *trip values.* The user has no knowledge of these indicators during processing. These indicators are used to detect changes in the output line, in the processing of data, and so forth. An error indicator designates that an error has occurred in the input or the output. An end-of-data indicator designates that there are no more data to be entered.

The main thing to remember about indicators is that they are set internally to change the processing. An indicator was used in the average-age problem in Figures 7.3 and 7.6 (the zero value of *Age*) to stop the looping when there were no more ages to be entered. An indicator can be a variable of logical data type or a value that the variable can never equal. For example, an indicator for *Age* might be 0 or 500 or −300. An indicator for an error could be a variable with the value *True* when an error has occurred, and *False* when there have been no errors.

Algorithm Instructions and Flowchart Symbols

Table 7.1 is an update of the Algorithm Instructions and Flowchart Symbols table, last seen in Chapter 5. The new instructions and logic structure instructions are found in Chapters 4 and 5.

- Decision Logic Structure *If/Then/Else*
- Instructions:
 Incrementing *Counter = Counter + 1*
 Accumulating *Sum = Sum + Variable*
 Product Product *= Product * Number*
- Loop Logic Structures *While/WhileEnd*
 Repeat/Until
 Loop: Counter = Begin To End
 Step S
 Loop-End: Counter

Table 7.1 Algorithm Instructions and Flowchart Symbols *(continued on page 150)*

Algorithm Instruction	Flowchart Symbol	Definition (What the instruction tells the computer)
Start module name (module number)		Start processing a module.
Enter list of variable names		Enter data from a data block or from the keyboard into the following variable memory locations.
Variable = expression		Assign the value of the following expression to a variable location. This is called an *assignment instruction*. A module may be processed as part of an expression, if there is a return value.
Write list of variable names		Write to the printer the values represented by the following variable names.
Print list of variable names		Print on the screen the values represented by the following variable names.
Process module name (list of parameters)		Execute the instructions in the named module, and then return to execute the next instruction.

Table 7.1 Algorithm Instructions and Flowchart Symbols *(continued from page 149)*

Algorithm Instruction	Flowchart Symbol	Definition (What the instruction tells the computer)
End/Exit		Stop the processing of the module. Processing ceases with the *End;* with the *Exit*, processing continues with the next instruction after the *Process*.
Return (variable)		Stop the processing of the module, place the value of the variable in the module name, and continuing with the instruction continuing the module call.
If/Then/Else		When the condition is *True,* use one set of instructions; when the condition is *False,* use another set of instructions.
Continue	or no box	A placeholder. Does *no* processing and continues to next instruction.
Counter = Counter + 1 (*C = C + 1*)		Increments the counter *C*.
Sum = Sum + Variable (*S = S + V*)		Accumulates the values of the variable *V*.
*Product = Product * Number*		Finds the product of a group of numbers.
While/WhileEnd		Repeat a set of instructions as long as a condition is *True*.
Repeat/Until		Repeat a set of instructions as long as a condition is *False*.
Loop: Counter = Begin To End Step Step Value *Loop-End: Counter*	C A B S	Repeat a set of instructions using a counter *C* that starts at *A(Begin)* and increments by *S(Step)* and *C* is greater than *B(End)*.

Recursion

recursion

Another type of loop structure is **recursion.** Recursion occurs when a module or a function calls itself. The condition that ends the loop must be within the module. Recursive procedures can be replaced by conventional loop structures; however, recursive procedures are usually faster. Figure 7.12 is an example of a recursive function that calculates a factorial number such as 5! (5! = 5 * 4 * 3 * 2 * 1). Notice that *Factorial(N)* continues to call itself until $N = 1$. There must be a way to stop the recursion. See Figure 7.13 for the execution of this problem where $N = 4$.

Recursion is difficult to use in a solution; however, it is needed more and more in today's programming. A recursive technique is used, for example, in finding the power of a number, sorting large amounts of data, and selecting the correct form from many report forms. The main problem in using a recursive technique is to figure out what goes before the calling of the function (or module) or after. The previous problem did not have anything happening after the *If/Then/Else* instruction. However, this is not true in most cases. Figure 7.14 shows the instructions for printing out the following using a recursive technique.

```
*
**
***
***
**
*
```

The first four lines are printed before the *If/Then/Else* instruction, and the last four are printed afterwards. The middle line is printed in the *Else* section of the *If/Then/Else* instruction. Because there are no values to be returned, the procedure will take place in a *Process Module* instruction. See Figures 7.14 and 7.15 for the algorithm, flowchart, and execution of this problem.

Summary

The third basic logic structure is the loop logic structure. By using this structure a programmer can design solutions that repeat processes.

There are three common tasks associated with the loop logic structure. The first is counting, or incrementing, to determine a total number of items. The second is summing, or accumulating, to find totals. The third is processing arrays, which are presented in Chapter 9.

The loop logic structure includes three types of loops. The *While/WhileEnd* loop repeats a set of instructions as long as the resultant of a condition is *True*. The condition is processed before the first instruction of the loop. The second type of loop structure is the *Repeat/Until* loop. This loop repeats the instructions until a condition is *True*. The condition in this case is processed after the last instruction in the loop. The third loop structure is the automatic-counter loop. In this case the instructions are repeated a given number of times, directed by a loop counter, which starts at a beginning number and is increased by a given increment until the counter is greater than an ending number. The condition can be processed at the beginning or the end of an automatic-counter loop

Algorithm	Flowchart

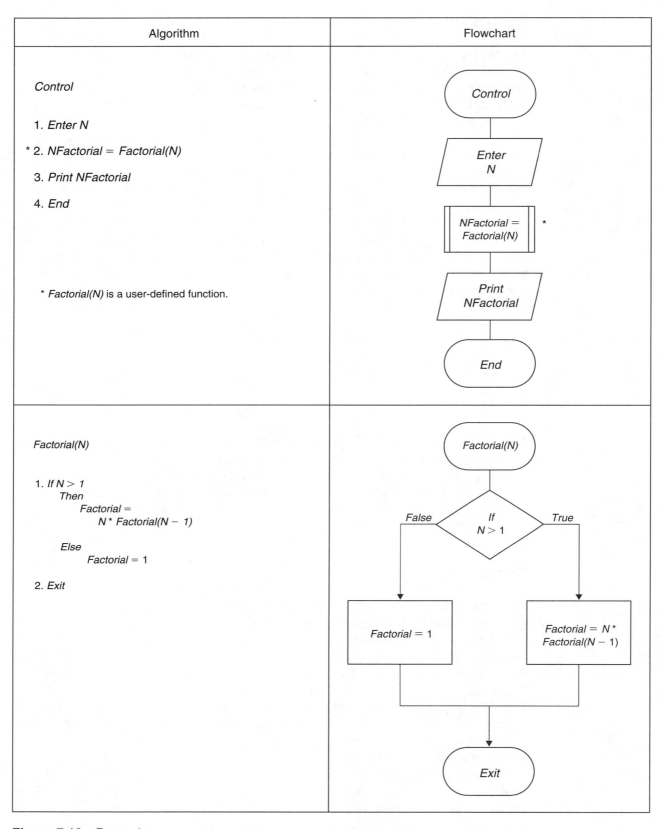

Control

1. *Enter N*

* 2. *NFactorial = Factorial(N)*

3. *Print NFactorial*

4. *End*

* *Factorial(N)* is a user-defined function.

Factorial(N)

1. *If N > 1*
 Then
 Factorial =
 *N * Factorial(N − 1)*

 Else
 Factorial = 1

2. *Exit*

Figure 7.12 Recursion

This figure shows how recursion works during execution. $N = 4$ in this processing and therefore variables will be replaced by the actual numbers.

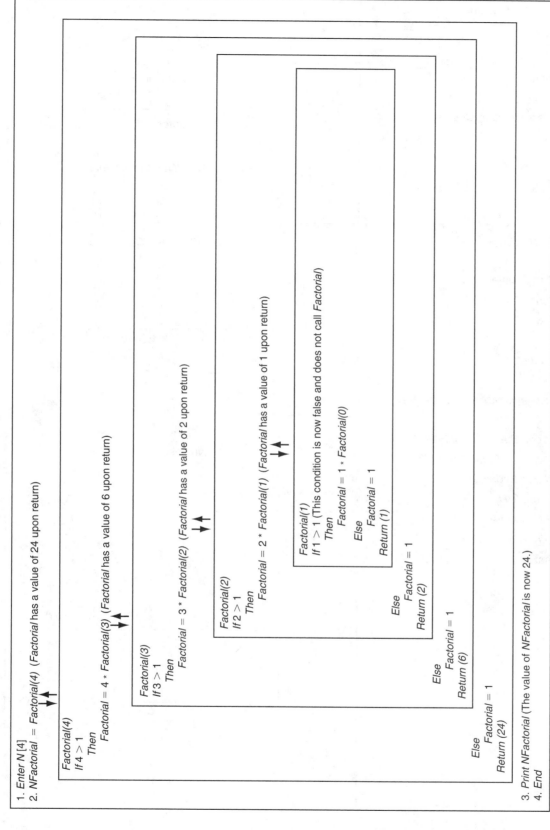

1. Enter N [4]
2. NFactorial = Factorial(4) (Factorial has a value of 24 upon return)

Factorial(4)
If 4 > 1
 Then
 Factorial = 4 * Factorial(3) (Factorial has a value of 6 upon return)

 Factorial(3)
 If 3 > 1
 Then
 Factorial = 3 * Factorial(2) (Factorial has a value of 2 upon return)

 Factorial(2)
 If 2 > 1
 Then
 Factorial = 2 * Factorial(1) (Factorial has a value of 1 upon return)

 Factorial((1)
 If 1 > 1 (This condition is now false and does not call Factorial)
 Then
 Factorial = 1 * Factorial(0)
 Else
 Factorial = 1
 Return (1)

 Else
 Factorial = 1
 Return (2)

 Else
 Factorial = 1
 Return (6)

 Else
 Factorial = 1
 Return (24)

3. Print NFactorial (The value of NFactorial is now 24.)
4. End

Figure 7.13 Execution of a Recursion Problem

Algorithm	Flowchart
Control *1. Enter Number* *2. Counter = 1* *3. Process Stars(Number, Counter)* *4. End*	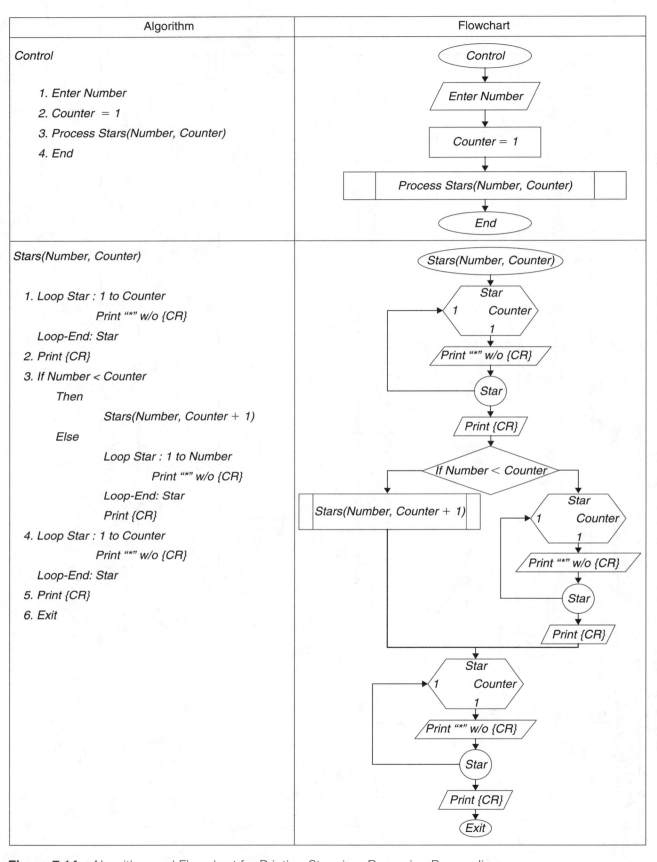
Stars(Number, Counter) *1. Loop Star : 1 to Counter* *Print "*" w/o {CR}* *Loop-End: Star* *2. Print {CR}* *3. If Number < Counter* *Then* *Stars(Number, Counter + 1)* *Else* *Loop Star : 1 to Number* *Print "*" w/o {CR}* *Loop-End: Star* *Print {CR}* *4. Loop Star : 1 to Counter* *Print "*" w/o {CR}* *Loop-End: Star* *5. Print {CR}* *6. Exit*	

Figure 7.14 Algorithm and Flowchart for Printing Stars in a Recursion Proceeding

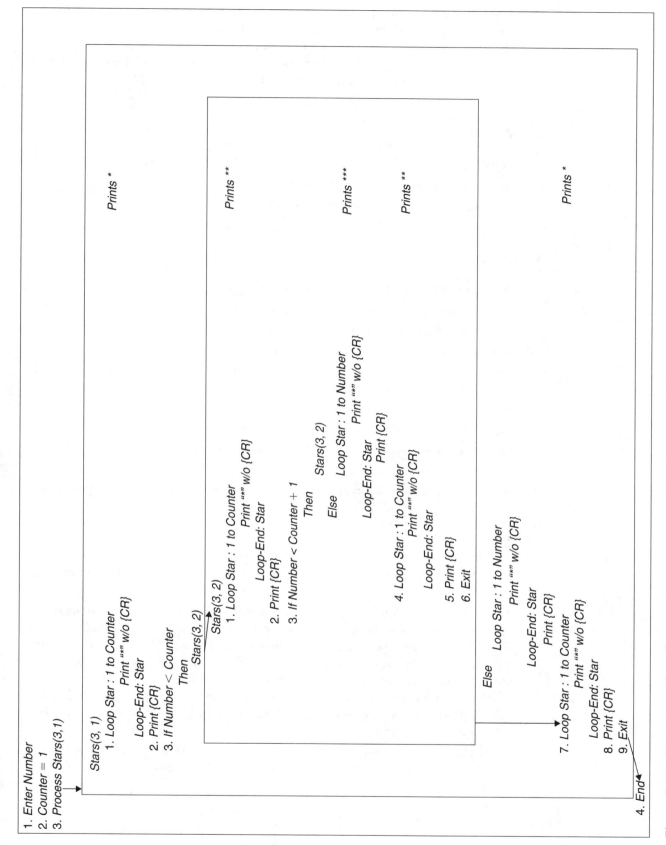

Figure 7.15 Execution of Star Recursive Procedure

depending on the language. For a programmer, the type of loop to use is determined by the problem and the language or application.

Indicators are used with loop structures to change the course of processing and to control the ending of a loop. Indicators are written in the instructions within the solution and normally are not entered externally by the user.

New Terms

accumulating	indicators	*Repeat/Until*
automatic-counter loop	primer *Read*	*While/WhileEnd*
incrementing	recursion	

Questions

1. Write the instruction to increment a variable by 1.
2. Write the instruction to accumulate a variable *A*.
3. Name the three types of loop structures.
4. State the major differences in the three types of loop structures.
5. Write the equation to find the product of a group of numbers entered into the variable *A* each time through a loop.
6. Why would you use a *While/WhileEnd* over the other two?
7. Why would you use a *Repeat/Until* over the other two?
8. Why would you use an automatic-counter loop over the other two?
9. Explain a recursive procedure.
10. What do you have to do to stop the continued recalling of a recursive procedure?

Problems

Complete the seven steps of solution development and a data dictionary for the following problems:

1. The Last Stop Boutique is having a five-day sale. Each day, starting on Monday, the price will drop 10% of the previous day's price. For example, if the original price of a product is $20.00, the sale price on Monday would be $18.00 (10% less than the original price). On Tuesday the sale price would be $16.20 (10% less than Monday). On Wednesday the sale price would be $14.58; on Thursday the sale price would be $13.12; and on Friday the sale price would be $11.81. Develop a solution that will calculate the price of an item for each of the five days, given the original price. Test the solution for an item costing $10.00.

2. Make changes in the solution to problem 1 to *set* the price at wholesale when the sale price drops below the wholesale price. Test the solution with the following prices:

Retail Prices:	$20.00, $25.00
Wholesale Prices:	$10.00, $20.00

3. Develop a solution that will calculate the average temperature, given a set of temperatures. The number of temperatures may differ from time to time. (Use a trip value to stop the processing of the loop.) Test the solution with the following 10 temperatures:

78°	90°
85°	80°
87°	83°
75°	90°
86°	70°

4. Mr. Brown has given a test to his class. He would like to have the average score for the class as well as the highest and lowest scores. Develop a solution to calculate and print out these values. (Use a trip value to stop the processing of the loop.)

5. Mary Smith, a student, has borrowed $3,000 to help pay her college expenses. After setting up a budget, $85 was the maximum monthly payment she could afford to make on the loan. Develop a solution to calculate and print the interest, the principal, and the balance on the loan per month. Other information she would like to know is the number of years and months it will take to pay the loan back and the total interest she will pay during that period. The interest rate is 1% per month on the unpaid balance. Keep in mind these formulas:

$$\text{interest normal} = \text{balance} * \text{interest rate}$$
$$\text{payment} = \text{balance} - \text{interest}$$
$$\text{new balance} = \text{balance} - \text{payment}$$

6. Develop a solution to flip a coin a given amount of times and then print the number of heads and the number of tails. The equation to toss the coin is

$$Coin = Integer(Random * 2) + 1$$

(See page 22 for explanation of this formula.) When $Coin = 1$ the toss is heads, and when $Coin = 2$ the toss is tails. $Random$ returns a number between 0 and 1, including 0 but not 1. Therefore, when $Random$ is less than 0.5, $Coin$ will equal 1: and when $Random$ is greater than or equal to 0.5 and less than 1, $Coin$ will equal 2.

7. Develop a solution to calculate a student's grade average for one semester. The letter grades should be entered and the grade average printed out. An A is equivalent to 4 grade points, a B is 3 grade points; a C is 2 grade points, a D is 1 grade point, and an F is zero grade points.

8. Write a solution to tell the user whether a number is a palindrome. (A palindrome is a number that is the same written both forward and backward, such as 81318.)

9. Write a solution to tell the user whether a string is a palindrome. (A palindrome string is a list of characters that spell the same word(s) forward or backward, such as *wow* or *radar.*)

10. Write a solution to tell the user whether a number is a prime number.

 (*Hint:* A prime number can be divided only by one and itself. There are no other factors.)

11. Write a solution to print out all of the factors of a number. Specify to the user whether the number is a prime number, that is, if the only factors are one and itself.

12. Using the recursion technique, develop a solution to calculate the power of a number, given the number and the exponent.

13. Write a solution to find the average miles per gallon on a car after six fillups at a gas station. Additional data kept included the number of gallons of gas at each fillup, the starting odometer reading, and the odometer reading at each fillup.

14. In problem 13, which loop did you use? Justify why you used that particular loop and not one of the other two. Did you need all of the data that was collected? Why or why not?

15. Mr. Jones, a history instructor, would like to know the percentage increase in the population of the United States per decade given the first decade and the last decade. Other given data include the population at the beginning of each decade.

 (*Hint:* Percentage = (present decade population − previous decade population)/ *present population* * 100.)

16. In problem 15, which loop did you use? Justify why you used that particular loop and not one of the other two. Did you need all of the data that was collected? Why or why not?

17. Jerry would like to know the balance in his checkbook given the beginning balance, the deposits, the check amounts, and the bank fees. Write a solution to print out the ending balance.

18. Modify your solution in problem 17 to print out the deposits, the check amounts, and the bank fees.

19. Using a recursive technique, print out the numbers starting with an input value of *Start* and ending value of *End*, then going backward to the starting number.

WHAT'S WRONG WITH THIS?

1. Correct the following set of instructions:

 Counter = 1
 While Counter < 5
 Enter Score
 Total = Total + Score
 Counter = Counter + 1

 WhileEnd

2. Correct the following set of instructions:

 Counter = 1
 Repeat
 Enter Score
 Total = Total + Score
 Counter = Counter + 1
 Until X < 5

WHAT'S WRONG WITH THIS?

3. Correct the following set of instructions:

> *Sum* = 0.0
> *Loop: Counter* = 10 TO 100 *Step* 15
> *Sum* = *Counter*
> *Loop-End: Counter*
> *Print* "Sum of the Numbers =", *Sum*
> *End*

Chapter 8

Problem Solving with the Case Logic Structure

Overview

The Case Logic Structure
Codes
Putting It All Together
Another Putting It All Together

Objectives

When you have finished this chapter, you should be able to:

1. Develop problems using the case logic structure in conjunction with the loop, decision, and sequential logic structure.
2. Use the seven problem-solving tools when developing a solution using the case logic structure.

Sometimes a solution to a problem requires the computer to select one action from a set of actions. This kind of solution can be designed through the decision logic structure, but the case logic structure is more efficient for this purpose. The case logic structure is a special variation of the decision structure, although it is different enough to present here separately. This structure is used in many business-related problems, such as those dealing with types of accounts in a bank, types of insurance available to an employee, or the selection of a bonus.

161

The Case Logic Structure

The case logic structure is made up of several sets of instructions, usually only one of which will be selected by a condition and then executed by the computer. Through the use of the case logic structure, a programmer can enable a user to enter the value of a variable from the keyboard, from a file, or use a calculated value to select one of several options in a list. Then the instruction following the *EndOfCase* instruction is executed. (The *EndOfCase* instruction is the last instruction in the case logic structure.) The case logic structure does not enable the program to loop back to select another option. If the solution requires looping back, then the programmer has to use the loop logic structure. The form of the case logic structure is the following:

> *CaseOf*
> > <Condition1>
> > > actions for <Condition1>
> >
> > <Condition2>
> > > actions for <Condition2>
> >
> > <Condition3>
> > > actions for <Condition3>
> >
> > .
> > .
> >
> > *Otherwise:*
> > > actions when all other conditions are *False*
>
> *EndOfCase*

Notice how the indentation improves the readability of the algorithm.

When the case logic structure is processed, the first condition is evaluated. If it is *True* then the actions for the first condition are executed. For most languages, the processing then continues after the *EndOfCase*. If the first condition is *False,* then the processing continues with the second condition. If this is *True*, then the actions for the second condition are processed. If *False*, the processing continues on with the next condition until no more conditions are available. When all conditions are *False*, then the actions for *Otherwise* are processed before dropping out of the *CaseOf* instruction. The *EndOfCase* signals the end of the *CaseOf* instruction. This would be equivalent to nested *If/Then/Else* instructions. However, a few languages allow more than one set of actions to take place. Therefore, when a condition is *True*, the actions for that condition are processed and then the next condition is evaluated. This would be equivalent to straight-through logic of *If/Then/Else* instructions. You will need to check your language manual to determine the type of case logic structure you will be using. Figures 8.1 and 8.2 shows the flowchart diagram for the CaseOf instruction. Figures 8.3 and 8.4 demonstrate the *If/The/Else* equivalencies of this instruction.

Examples of the use of this instruction include the determination of a bonus, a medical insurance deduction, a vendor, a paycheck, or income tax deduction. The number of possible options or sets of instructions in the case logic structure is limited only by the language in use. When using the *CaseOf* instruction, the conditions may be in any order, with the *Otherwise* always last. However, the best order is to place them is the order of most used. This will speed up your program by limiting the number of instructions.

There are some pitfalls when using the *CaseOf* instruction. You need to make sure that the order that you place the conditions will allow the correct condition to occur. For example, if you have one set of actions for Salary < 1000 and another set of instructions for Salary < 500, the condition Salary < 500 needs to be first or it

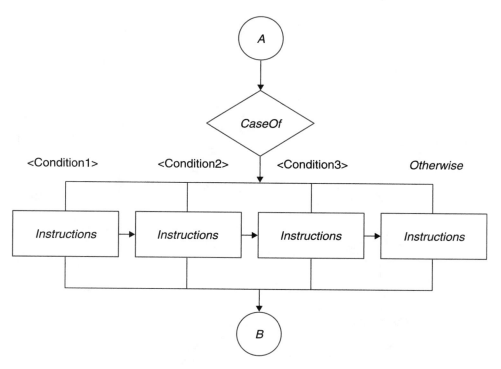

Figure 8.1 Flowchart Diagram for the Case Logic Structure

will never execute a salary of 450 because 450 is also less than 1000. If you are using a *CaseOf* instruction that allows you to test all conditions, then you want to make sure you drop out of the instruction by putting a *GoTo* instruction at the end of each set of actions. There are times that you want to have more than one condition's actions take place. In this case, do not use the *GoTo* or *Continue* instruction and make sure you do not change the variables in the conditions during the execution of a set of actions.

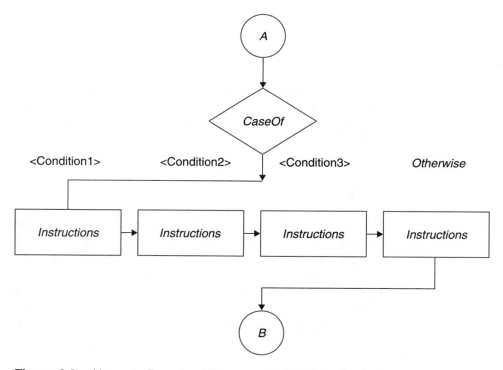

Figure 8.2 Alternate Flowchart Diagram for the Case Logic Structure

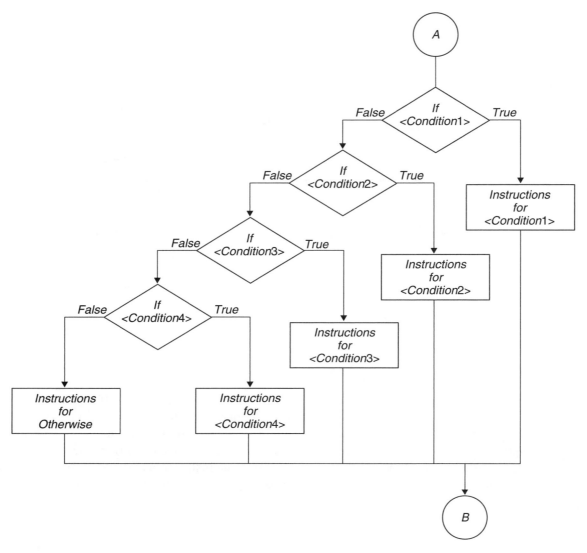

Figure 8.3 Nested Decision-Structure Equivalent to the Case Logic Structure

There are other instruction names and relational operators that you may encounter. Instead of *CaseOf*, you may find *Select* or *Choose*. Other operators may include *Inbetween* or *InSet*. There are many varieties of this instruction. Check your language to find what is available for you to use.

Codes

codes

Codes are characters, character strings, numbers, or some combination of these types of data that a programmer uses to name the options, the constants, in a case structure. They are abbreviations for each of the options. They direct the processing path just as indicators do by specifying the choice that the user prefers—and, therefore, that the computer will make, such as a particular employee medical plan out of many plans: *B* for Best Medical Insurance Company, *D* for Direct Medical Insurance Company, and the like.

The major differences between indicators and codes are the following:

1. Codes are data to be entered by the user. Indicators are internal signals to change the processing path.

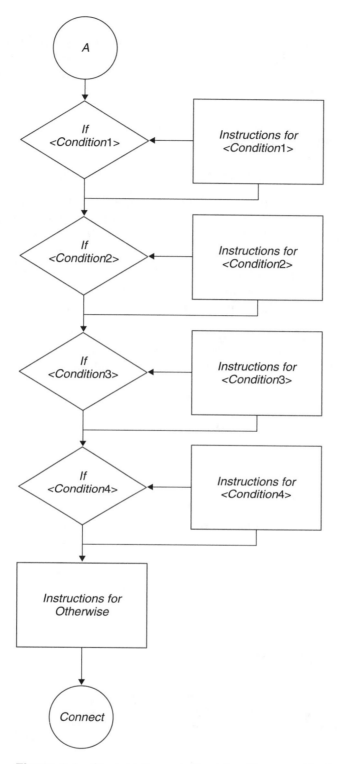

Figure 8.4 Straight-through Decision Structure Equivalent to the Case Logic Structure

2. A code can have a value of many different types. The value of an indicator can be logical data, *True* or *False,* or it can have an implausible value for the variable it represents in the solution.

A code is used to indicate choices such as the type of insurance an employee is buying, the gender of an individual, or the vendor in an inventory problem. When using codes, the *Otherwise* option indicates an error. Without the use of codes, solutions requiring a choice from among several options would be longer, harder to read, and more difficult to maintain.

Putting It All Together

This PIAT illustrates the use of codes in a solution using the case logic structure.

> Problem: A company has four different medical plans. The programmer has given each plan a code corresponding to the beginning initial of the company: Plan 1 = *F*, Plan 2 = *B*, Plan 3 = *K*, Plan 4 = *E*.

> The company pays for all of Plan 1. The individual has to pay for part of the others. The payroll deduction for Plan 2 = 4.65, for Plan 3 = 7.85, and for Plan 4 = 5.50. Any other codes are considered in error. Write the algorithm and draw the flowchart for a module to determine the payroll deduction.

Figure 8.5 shows the module to calculate the insurance deduction. The variable name for the medical plan code is *MedCode*. *MedCode* can have only the value of *F*, *B*, *K*, or *E*. Any other value is unacceptable, and therefore an error. When *MedCode*

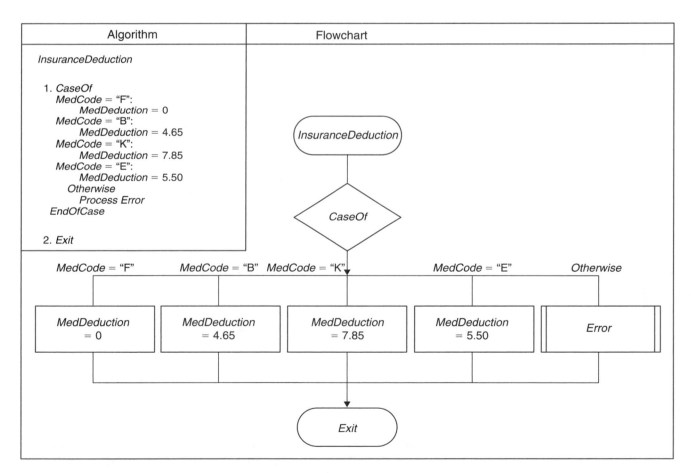

Figure 8.5 Using Codes—Medical Insurance Problem—*InsuranceDeduction* Module

has the value of *F*, then *MedDeduction*, the medical deduction, is 0; when it has the value of *B*, *MedDeduction* is 4.65; when it has the value of *K*, *MedDeduction* is 7.85; when it has the value of *E*, *MedDeduction* is 5.50. If *MedCode* has any other value, then an error module is processed. An error module is simply the module that prints out an error message.

Another Putting It All Together

This PIAT illustrates the use of a pay-type code to calculate an employee's pay. The codes are as follows:

H =	Hourly	pay =	rate * hours
P =	Piece work	pay =	rate * number of pieces
C =	Commission	pay =	commission * sales
S =	Salary	pay =	salary

The module to calculate an employee's pay is illustrated in Figure 8.6. Notice that there is an instruction box for each pay type that explains how to calculate each employee's pay. The *Otherwise* instruction processes an error module to catch any keyboard entry errors. If there is an error, the processing returns to an instruction that reenters the employee's data.

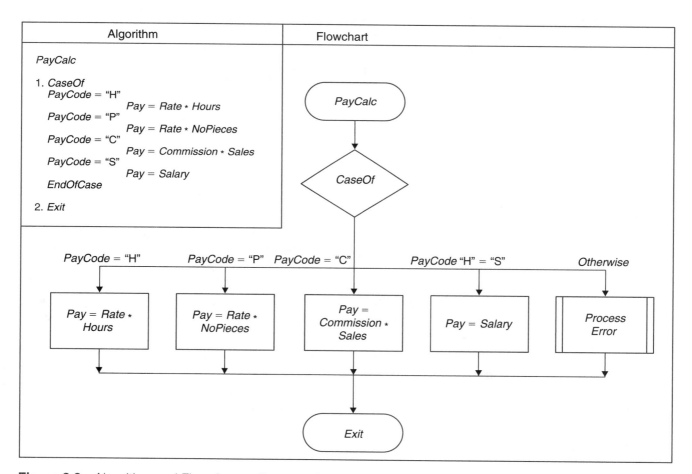

Figure 8.6 Algorithm and Flowchart to Illustrate *Pay* Module

Summary

The case logic structure is the fourth basic logic structure. It enables the computer to select one set of actions from many by selecting an integer or a character from a list of coded choices designed by a programmer. Codes are one of the tools of the case logic structure. The case structure replaces a multiple nested *If/Then/Else* instruction that uses positive logic and the relative operator *equals*. By using the case structure rather than the nested *If/Then/Else* alternative, a programmer can improve the readability and reduce the complexity of the program.

New Terms

codes

Questions

1. Why would the case logic structure be used instead of the decision structure?
2. What are the differences between an indicator and a code?
3. For what type of problems would you use the case logic structure?
4. For which of the following would you use the case logic structure? State why or why not.
 a. The cost of a car given 10 models.
 b. The cost of a car given 7 ranges of the cost of cars.
 c. Population of a state given 50 states.
 d. Average temperature of a given month.
 e. Months having a given average temperature.
 f. Bonus given commission.
 g. Temperature zone given a city's average temperature.
 h. Cost of books for a semester.

Problems

1. Develop the other modules to complete the pay-type problem in the second PIAT. Allow the user to enter as many employees as needed. Develop a trip value to end the execution of the program. Remember that when an error occurs in the pay code, the execution for that employee is ignored and the employee's information must be reentered. The information to enter includes the employee's name, social security number, pay-type code, and pay information (commission, hours, or number of pieces—do these have to be three entries?).
2. Modify problem 1 so that only the pay-type code is reentered when an error in the code is entered.
3. Develop the algorithm and flowchart for a module that calculates the retirement deduction rate according to the following codes:

$$R = 10\%$$
$$P = 8\%$$
$$G = 5\%$$

4. Develop a solution to change Roman numerals into their decimal equivalents. Consider all possibilities of Roman numerals—no letters, only one letter, two letters, and so forth. Assume that the Roman numerals are in correct order. One Roman numeral character is entered at a time. The Roman numeral is entered from left to right. Roman numeral equivalents are as follows:

$$I = 1$$
$$V = 5$$
$$X = 10$$
$$L = 50$$
$$C = 100$$
$$D = 500$$
$$M = 1000$$

Examples of input numbers are IV, XIX, MMCDXL, and CCLV.

5. A student wants to know his grade point average for the semester. The grades are given in letter grades with numeric equivalents. Develop a solution to calculate a grade point average given the letter grades. (Remember, the grade point average is figured per unit of credit, not per course.) An $A = 4.0$, $B = 3.0$, $C = 2.0$, $D = 1.0$, $F = 0.0$. Test the solution with the following data:

History	B	3 units
Economics	A	3 units
PE	A	1 unit
Chemistry	C	4 units
Art	B	3 units

(*Hint:* Use a trip value to stop the processing of the loop and a case structure to find the grade points.)

6. A bank has five different types of savings accounts. The interest rates on these accounts change often. The bank manager would like to have the computer print out information about the account type of her choice. Develop a solution to solve the manager's problems.

7. Mr. Johnson would like to know how many As, Bs, Cs, Ds, and Fs his students received on a test. He has 200 students who took the test. He would like to enter the student number and the number grade for the test for each student. Develop the solution to print out each student's student number, number grade, letter grade, and the total number of As, Bs, Cs, Ds, and Fs. His grading scale is as follows: 90–100 is an A, 78–89 is a B, 65–77 is a C, 50–64 is a D, and below 50 is an F.

8. How would you modify problem 7 to process any number of students?

9. John Smith is a new car salesperson. He would like to have the computer calculate the total cost of a car given the following:

initial price of the car

0 to 10 accessories (the computer would select the price according to the accessory)

sales tax

10. Rewrite problem 1 in Chapter 6 using the *CaseOf* instruction.

11. Rewrite problem 6 in Chapter 6 using the *CaseOf* instruction.

12. Rewrite problem 9 in Chapter 6 using the *CaseOf* instruction.

WHAT'S WRONG WITH THIS?

Correct the following sets of algorithm segments:

1. *Enter L*

 CaseOf

 $L < 10$:

 Process M5

 $L < 5$:

 Process M10

 Otherwise

 Process MOtherwise

 EndOfCase

2. *Enter V*

 CaseOf

 = Car1

 Process MCar1

 = Car2

 Process MCar2

 = Car3

 Process MCar3

 EndOfCase

Unit Two

Supplementary Exercises

Develop a complete solution and a data dictionary for the following problems:

1. Draw a solid diamond on the screen using a single character. The size of the diamond should be entered from the keyboard:

 Example: *Size* = 5, *Character* = "*"

   ```
         *
        ***
       *****
        ***
         *
   ```

2. Draw the same diamond except make it hollow:

 Example: *Size* = 5, *Character* = "*"

   ```
         *
        * *
       *   *
        * *
         *
   ```

3. Modify problem 4 in Chapter 5 so that the program stops when the remaining change becomes zero.

4. Reverse the digits of a number such that 1234 becomes 4321.

5. Calculate the ending balance of your checking account, given the beginning balance, the checks written, the deposits made, and the bank charges.

6. Create your own dice game. Print directions and rules. Have the user play against the computer.

7. Print all prime factors of a number entered from the keyboard.

8. Print out four cards dealt randomly from a 52-card deck. Differentiate between hearts, spades, clubs, and diamonds.

9. Calculate the average rainfall over a two-week period.

10. The counselor of a camp would like to know the average age of those attending a camp, and who the oldest and the youngest are. The number of people attending a camp can vary from 50 to 100.

11. Flowchart your solutions to the problems presented in Appendix A: Otto the Robot. Are there any changes in your solutions that you might want to make? Explain what changes you would make and why.

12. Using a recursive technique, write a solution to exercise 1.

13. Using a recursive technique, write a solution to exercise 2.

UNIT THREE

DATA STRUCTURES

Chapter 9

Processing Arrays

Overview

Objectives

When you have finished this chapter, you should be able to:

1. Develop problem solutions for the computer using one-dimensional and two-dimensional arrays.
2. Develop problem solutions requiring table look-ups, sequential and binary searches, frequency distributions, and cross-tabulations.

Arrays

Data are stored in the computer in a logical way in order to find values as quickly as possible. The way data are stored is called the structure of the data, hence the term *data structures*. The only data structure you have used so far in this text is the single variable. Using this data structure, a single value is stored in a single named location. This is the simplest of all data structures. Another type of data structure is the array.

It is often advantageous for a user to store several values for the same variable in the internal memory of the computer because it decreases processing time. This multiple storage means there has to be more than one memory location in the computer for each variable name. When more than one memory location is designated for a single variable, it is called an **array.** Sometimes these variables are called *subscripted variables.* This term comes from mathematics, where subscripts are used to designate multiple values. Arrays are also called *tables,* a term from business, where data are often put into tables. For the purposes of this book, *array* will be used because it is universal and is becoming the most common term. The other two terms may be used in other sources.

arrays
Subscripted Variables
Tables

Arrays are used in the problem-solving process. A programmer who has many values of data of the same kind—many ages, temperatures, names, or the like—can store them in the computer in the form of an array, which makes them easier to read and use. The programmer can also use the values in one array to point to values in another array. This is the way the computer tallies the number of times a value appears in an array. Without arrays this task would be very difficult.

A programmer uses arrays when more than one value of a variable is used in the solution—for example, when calculating the percentage of each store's sales out of the total company's sales or when calculating each student's test grade based on the highest and lowest scores. The store sales or the student grade would be the variable with more than one value—a value for each store or for each student. If the user does not need to use the data more than once in the solution, then there is no need for the programmer to use arrays. Their overuse is a common mistake for beginning programmers.

Dimensioning
the Variable

The programmer tells the computer how many memory locations to save for an array through a special instruction or within the definitions of the data types. In many languages this is called *dimensioning the variable.* The number of memory locations to be saved is equal to or greater than the number of locations used in the solution. If it is less than the number of locations used, an error will result. For problem-solving purposes, this number is part of the annotation of the flowchart.

static arrays

Most languages use **static arrays.** This means that once the computer is told how many locations to save, that number cannot be changed unless the instruction is changed. In most languages, the number in the instruction is a constant. However, some languages allow the number to be a named constant, which is set once, and only once, during the execution of the solution. In this case, the number of memory locations saved

for an array can change from execution to execution, but it cannot change during an execution. This type of array is still considered static.

dynamic arrays

Some languages allow **dynamic arrays.** When using dynamic arrays, the programmer designates the number of array locations as a variable, which can be expanded or contracted during the execution of the solution. Dynamic arrays are more flexible and use less memory space than static arrays, but are usually more time consuming during processing.

If the number of the designated memory locations is a constant, then the programmer has to know how big the array will be, at its largest, while writing the solution. When that number is a variable but cannot be changed during execution, then the size of the array is part of the input data. This kind of static array allows more flexibility in the solution and in the use of memory than the static array in which the number of memory locations is a constant. The most flexible arrays are dynamic. The solution itself determines the size of a dynamic array, and thus, the programmer does not have to predict the size of the array.

Element

Each array memory location is called an *element* and is given a number or numbers corresponding to the position of the location in the array. This number is a reference number relative to the location of the first value of the array. The name of the element has two parts. The first part is the variable name; the second part is the reference number, also called the *index number,* an *element number* or subscript in parentheses.

base-zero system

base-one system

Because computers are zero-based, for counting purposes, many programming languages are also zero-based. This means that the first array element is numbered *zero,* and not *one;* it is a **base-zero system.** In this way, the computer adds the element number to the memory location number of the beginning box to locate the needed value. If the language uses the **base-one system,** then to identify a specific data memory location, add the element number minus one to the beginning number (see Figure 9.1). Base

Base 0 A			Base 1 A		
A(0)	0		A(1)	1	
A(1)	1		A(2)	2	
A(2)	2		A(3)	3	
A(3)	3		A(4)	4	
A(4)	4		A(5)	5	
A(5)	5		A(6)	6	
A(6)	6		A(7)	7	
A(7)	7		A(8)	8	
.	
A(N)	N		A(N)	N	

Figure 9.1 Base-Zero Versus Base-One Arrays

one is easier for the programmer to understand because the first element is the first box, the second element is the second box, and so on. When using zero-based arrays, the zero element is the first box, the first element is the second box, and so on. Often programmers will avoid zero elements in an array because they make it more difficult to keep track of element numbers. In this chapter, base one will be assumed.

You do not have to use an array in any special order. The data used as the actual values of the elements must have the same data type as you have identified for the variable name of the array. By using the assignment instruction, you can assign the value of a constant, a variable, or an expression to an element.

One-Dimensional Arrays

one-dimensional array

The simplest array structure is the **one-dimensional array.** This array consists of one column of memory locations. In Figure 9.2, there is a one-dimensional array named *Age*. In mathematics, the reference name for each of the equation elements would be age_1, age_2, age_3, and so forth. Array elements are given similar reference names. Since the computer has trouble with subscripts (because it is hard to roll the screen up a little to print subscripts), the reference names are written as *Age*(1), *Age*(2), *Age*(3), and so forth. The number in the parentheses is a reference number only and can be a constant, a variable, or an expression. *Age*(5) would be the fifth element of the *Age* array. In most languages the reference numbers must be of the integer data type, although a few computer languages allow any data type for the index or reference value. Since this practice is not common, and since the use of each of the data types is very similar to the use of integers as element numbers, this book will use only integers for the index.

	Array *Age*	Variable Reference Name	
1	32	*Age*(1)	The number in the parentheses refers to the box number in the array, the element number.
2	54	*Age*(2)	
3	25	*Age*(3)	
4	36	*Age*(4)	
5	45	*Age*(5)	
6	20	*Age*(6)	
7	28	*Age*(7)	
8	50	*Age*(8)	
9	42	*Age*(9)	

Figure 9.2 One-Dimensional Array

parallel arrays

Parallel arrays are two or more arrays in which values in the same elements relate to each other. For example, in Figure 9.3 there are three arrays. The first array contains area numbers, the second array contains temperatures for day 1, and the third, temperatures for day 2. The data in the first elements in the second and third arrays pertain to the area in the first array; the data in the second elements in the second and third arrays pertain to the area in the second element of the first array, and so forth. They are called parallel arrays because the same element number in all arrays has data pertaining to the same subject.

Entering Data

Entering Data

When you enter data into an array, or *load an array,* you use a loop. If you know the number of elements, then use the automatic-counter loop. If you do not know the number of elements, then use an indicator code with the *Repeat/Until* or the *While/WhileEnd* loop. Use a counter to keep track of how many elements are entered into the array.

Figure 9.4 shows the loop process for entering the data into an array. In Figure 9.4a, the number of elements in the array is known to be the value of *NElements*. The counter *Element* of the loop allows the computer to increase the element number by 1 each time a piece of data is entered into a memory location. The computer can find a particular memory location for an element in the array by first finding the set of locations for the array *Array,* and then using the reference number, which has the value of *Element*. Figure 9.4b shows the use of the *Repeat/Until* loop structure. Here, the elements are counted to find the total number of elements *(NElements)* in the array. The number *NElements* is then used for the number of elements through the rest of the solution. Figure 9.4c shows the use of the *While/WhileEnd* loop structure. Here again, the elements are counted to find the total number of elements. Notice that in the *Repeat/Until* and the *While/WhileEnd* loops, the indicator element number (indicating the end of the array) is not included in the total number of elements since it is not needed. The number of elements is known and, therefore, the indicator is not needed to signal the end of the array.

AreaNo			Day1			Day2	
1	5		1	82		1	80
2	9		2	75		2	72
3	15		3	80		3	82
4	35		4	90		4	87
5	50		5	95		5	92
6	73		6	78		6	80
7	88		7	85		7	83

Figure 9.3 Parallel Arrays

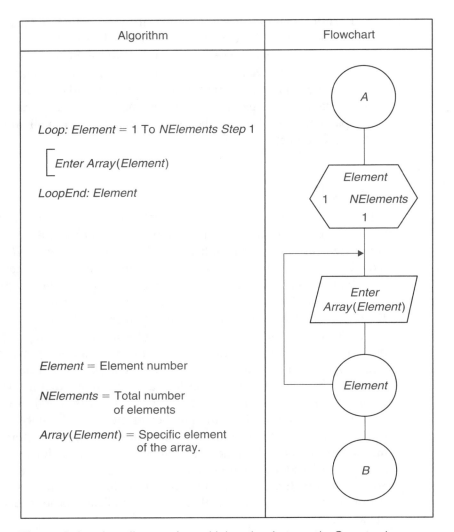

Algorithm	Flowchart
Loop: Element = 1 To *NElements Step* 1 ⎡ *Enter Array*(*Element*) *LoopEnd: Element* *Element* = Element number *NElements* = Total number of elements *Array*(*Element*) = Specific element of the array.	

Figure 9.4a Loading an Array Using the Automatic-Counter Loop

Printing

Printing

After the array is loaded, it can be used in other calculations or printed. You write the algorithm to print an array by using the automatic-counter loop since the number of elements in the array is now known (see Figure 9.5). The array will be printed one element at a time down the page. To print the array across the page, you must use the *Write* or *Print* instruction without a carriage return. With parallel arrays, the corresponding elements will be printed in columns on the same line. The headings to the columns have to be printed before the processing starts into the automatic-counter loop.

Accumulating the Elements

Accumulating
Elements in an Array

Often you need the sum of the elements in an array. Use the accumulation instruction to total the sum (see Figure 9.6). Initially, set the variable containing the value of the sum to zero. The accumulation instruction (*Sum* = *Sum* + *Array*(*Element*)) tells the computer to add the value of the element *Array(Element)* to the old value of the sum *(Sum)*

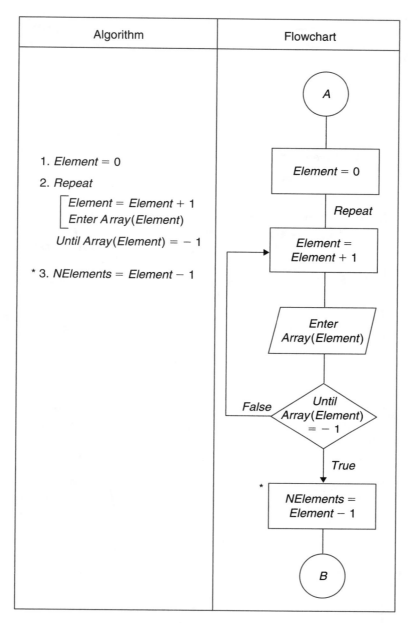

Algorithm	Flowchart
1. *Element* = 0 2. *Repeat* ⎡ *Element* = *Element* + 1 ⎣ *Enter Array(Element)* *Until Array(Element)* = − 1 * 3. *NElements* = *Element* − 1	

A

Element = 0

Repeat

Element = Element + 1

Enter Array(Element)

False ← *Until Array(Element) = − 1*

True

* *NElements = Element − 1*

B

* The number of elements in the array should
not include the trip value of −1.

Figure 9.4b Loading an Array Using the *Repeat/Until* Loop

and to store the result in the sum memory location *(Sum)*. The value of the element number *Element* changes as the loop counter progresses from one element to the other during summing.

Observe the testing of the flowchart in Figure 9.6 through the use of the various variable memory locations. The first time the loop is processed, the value of *Element* is 1, and the value of *Array(Element),* or *Array*(1), is 2. This value is added to the previous value of the *Sum,* which is zero since the value of *Sum* is zero at the start. The resultant is 2, which is placed into the *Sum* memory location. The second time the

Algorithm	Flowchart
1. *Element* = 1 2. *Enter Array(Element)* 3. *While Array(Element)* <> −1 ⎡ *Element = Element + 1* ⎣ ENTER *Array(Element)* *WhileEnd* * 4. *NElements = Element − 1*	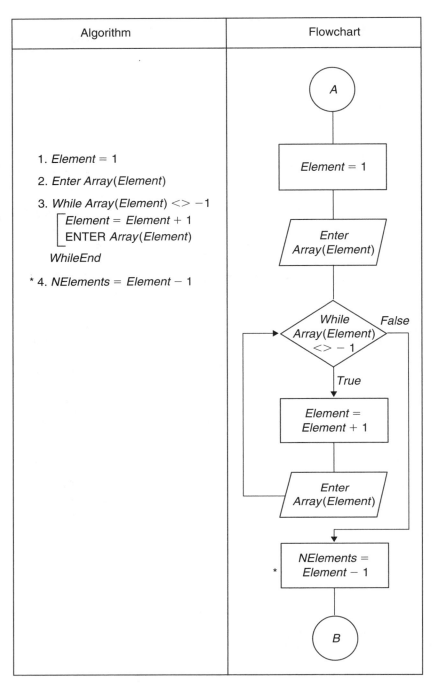

* The number of elements in the array should
not include the trip value of −1.

Figure 9.4c Loading an Array Using the *While/WhileEnd* Loop

loop is processed, *Element* is incremented to 2 and the value of *Array(Element),* or *Array(2)*, is 4. This value is added to the previous value of *Sum,* which is 2, and placed into the *Sum* memory location. *Sum* now has the value of 6. The third time the loop is processed, *Element* is incremented to 3, and *Array(Element),* which has the value of 6, is added to *Sum* and placed into the *Sum* memory location. The value of *Sum* is now 12.

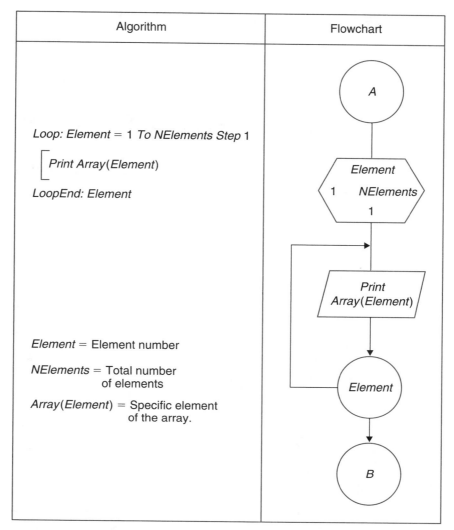

Algorithm	Flowchart
Loop: Element = 1 To NElements Step 1 *Print Array(Element)* *LoopEnd: Element* *Element* = Element number *NElements* = Total number of elements *Array(Element)* = Specific element of the array.	

Figure 9.5 Printing a One-Dimensional Array

This sequence is repeated each time the loop is processed until the value of *Element* has increased to a number greater than the value of *NElements*. The final value of *Sum* is 42.

Putting It All Together

Example

This PIAT illustrates how to enter, use, and print one-dimensional arrays.

Problem: The president of the Too Little Variety Stores would like to know each store's percentage of the total sales of the corporation. There are 15 stores altogether.

Figure 9.7 shows the complete solution to this problem. Diagrams d–g show the algorithms and flowcharts for each module. The *Control* module processes each of the modules, *Init, Read, Calc,* and *Print.* The *Sum* is set equal to zero in the *Init* module. The *Read* module enters the values of the sales per store into the *Sales* array. The value of *R* becomes the store number. In the *Calc* module, the sum of the sales for all 15 stores is calculated through the use of a loop and the accumulation instruction. The next loop

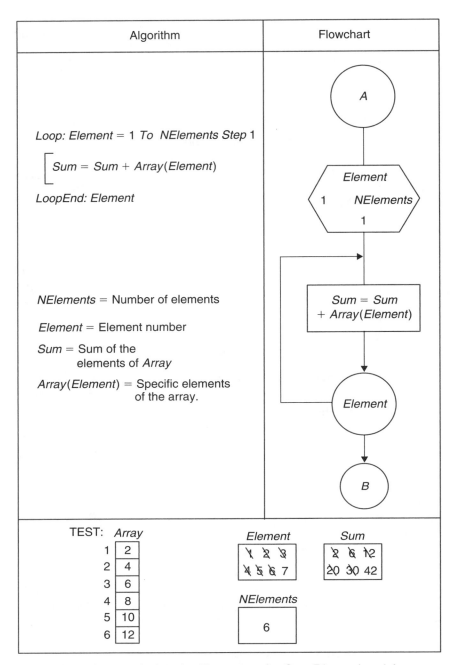

Algorithm	Flowchart
Loop: Element = 1 To NElements Step 1 \quad Sum = Sum + Array(Element) \quad LoopEnd: Element $\quad\quad\quad$ NElements = Number of elements \quad Element = Element number \quad Sum = Sum of the $\quad\quad$ elements of Array \quad Array(Element) = Specific elements $\quad\quad\quad\quad$ of the array.	

Figure 9.6 Accumulating the Elements of a One-Dimensional Array

Given Data	Required Results
1. 15 stores 2. Sales per store	Percent of total sales per store
Processing Required	Solution Alternatives
Percent (store) = sales (store)/total sales	Must use arrays

Figure 9.7a Problem Analysis Chart

Interactivity (Structure) Chart

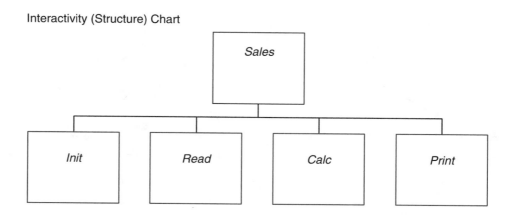

IPO Chart

Input	Processing	Module Reference	Output
1. Sales per store	1. Enter data 2. Set sum to 0 3. Accumulate sales 4. Calculate percent 5. Print output	*Read* *Init* *Calc* *Calc* *Print*	For each store: 1. Store number 2. Sales 3. % of total sales

Figure 9.7b Interactivity Chart and IPO Chart

calculates the value of the percentage for each store and places that value in the *Percent* array. The *Sales* array and the *Percent* array are parallel arrays since each element corresponds to the same store. The values of the store number, the *Sales,* and the *Percent* are printed, element by element, in the *Print* module.

Two-Dimensional Arrays

two-dimensional array

A **two-dimensional array** is a block of memory locations associated with a single memory variable name and designated by row and column numbers. Each element number is written as *Array* (Row #, Column #). The row number is always first and the column number second. As in one-dimensional arrays, the row and column numbers can be constants, variables, or expressions, and they are of the integer data type. Whatever processing takes place, the row and column numbers always remain in the same positions in the parentheses. As with one-dimensional arrays, you can change the values in a two-dimensional array by using the assignment instruction.

Two-dimensional arrays are used for tables of values. They can replace parallel arrays if the data are of the same data type in all of the arrays. In Figure 9.8, the two-dimensional array *Array* is shown. This figure shows the general form of a two-dimensional array, and of reference names (including the variable name and the row and column numbers), for each location. For example, *Array*(3,2) is found at the intersection of row 3 and column 2.

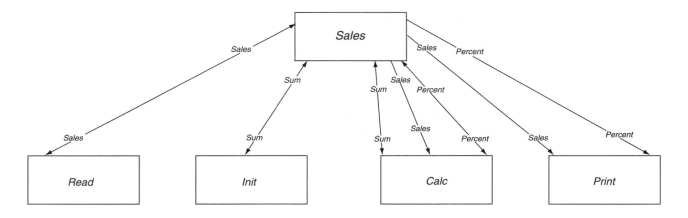

Figure 9.7c Coupling Diagram and Data Dictionary

Item	Variable Name	Data Type	Module	Scope	Pseudonyms	Error Cks.
Sum of Sales	*Sum*	Numeric	*Control, Init, Calc*	Local	None	None
Sales Array	*Sales*	Numeric	All	Local	None	None
Sales Percentage	*Percent*	Numeric	*Control, Calc, Print*	Local	None	None
Element No.	*Element*	Numeric	*Read, Calc, Print*	Local	None	None

Entering Data

Entering Data

You load a two-dimensional array with nested loops (see Figure 9.9). The data are normally loaded row by row. When you load the data row by row, the outer loop represents the row, and the inner loop represents the column. This order of the loops allows the row number to remain constant while the column number varies. In Figure 9.9, compare the data block to the array block. In the flowchart, notice that the first four numbers in the data block are read into the first row of the array, the second four into the second row, and the last four into the third row. The array is now loaded with the numbers 1 to 12.)

Printing

Printing

After the array is loaded, it can be used in calculations, or it can be printed. As in loading, use nested loops to print a two-dimensional array. Normally, the array is printed row by row. For example, in Figure 9.10 the outer loop (*Row* loop) is the row loop and the inner loop (*Column* loop) is the column loop. Notice that the flowchart is designed so that the element is printed without a carriage return. The carriage return is executed after a row is printed, that is, after the end of the column loop. Place the *Cursor Return*

Algorithm	Flowchart	Testing

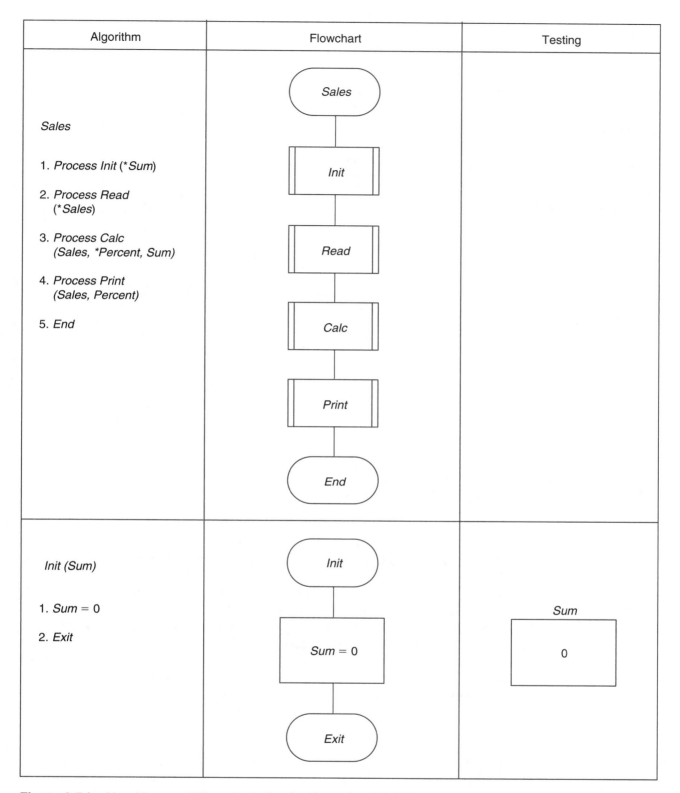

Sales

1. *Process Init (*Sum)*

2. *Process Read (*Sales)*

3. *Process Calc (Sales, *Percent, Sum)*

4. *Process Print (Sales, Percent)*

5. *End*

Init (Sum)

1. *Sum = 0*

2. *Exit*

Figure 9.7d Algorithms and Flowcharts for the *Control* and *Init* Modules

Algorithm	Flowchart	Testing

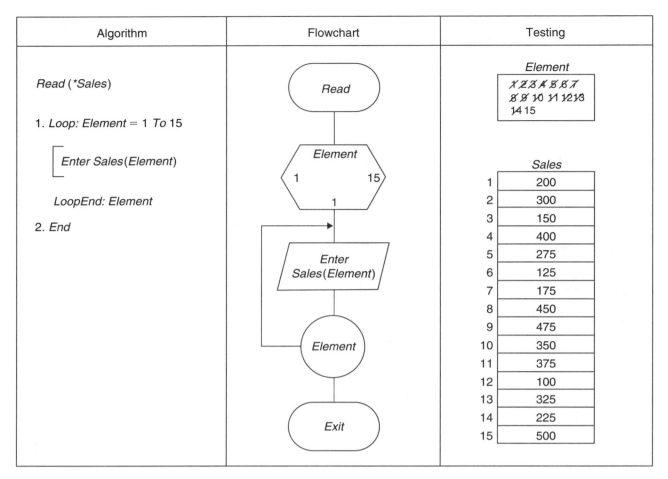

Figure 9.7e Algorithm and Flowchart for the *Read* Module

instruction between the two *LoopEnd* instructions. The column headings are printed before either loop is executed. Each row heading is printed between the two beginning loop instructions.

Follow the execution of the loop in Figure 9.10 to see how the array is printed. Notice that the column headings are printed first. Then the row loop (*Row* loop) prints row 1 and continues to print through row *NRows*, the total number of rows. Within each row, the row heading must be printed first. Then, through the use of the *Column* loop, each element of the row, designated by the column number (*Column*), is printed without a cursor or carriage return. Once the elements of the row are printed, the cursor or carriage has to be returned before the next row can be printed.

Accumulating the Rows and Columns

Accumulating

In many solutions you need a total of rows, columns, and the grand total of all elements in a two-dimensional array, and as in the one-dimensional array, you use the assignment statement to do so. In the solution, you can use a row following the last row of the array for the sums of the columns, and a column to the right of the last column for the sums of

Algorithm	Flowchart	Testing

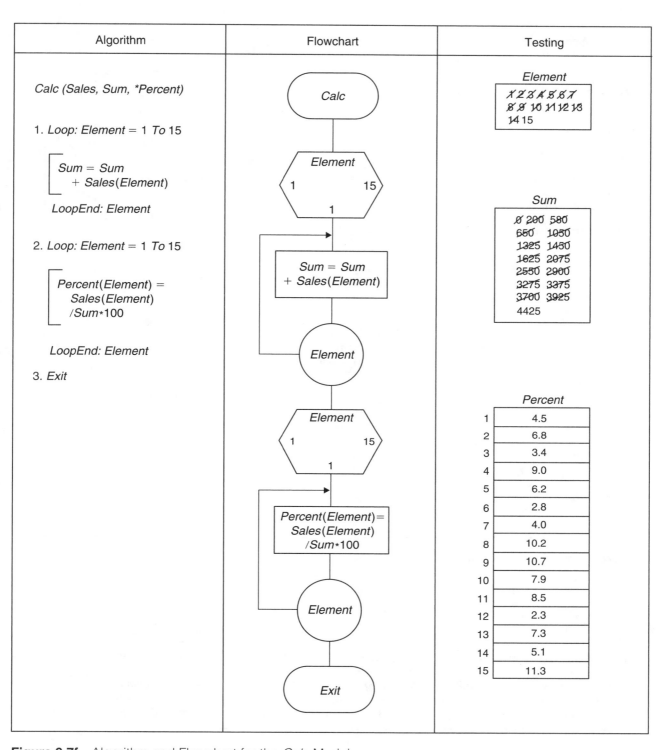

Figure 9.7f Algorithm and Flowchart for the *Calc* Module

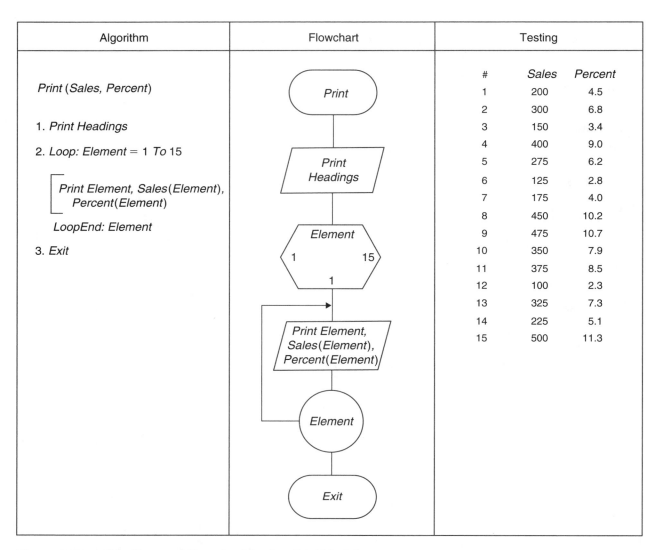

Algorithm	Flowchart	Testing
Print (Sales, Percent) 1. Print Headings 2. Loop: Element = 1 To 15 Print Element, Sales(Element), Percent(Element) LoopEnd: Element 3. Exit	Print → Print Headings → Element (1 ... 15) → Print Element, Sales(Element), Percent(Element) → Element → Exit	# Sales Percent 1 200 4.5 2 300 6.8 3 150 3.4 4 400 9.0 5 275 6.2 6 125 2.8 7 175 4.0 8 450 10.2 9 475 10.7 10 350 7.9 11 375 8.5 12 100 2.3 13 325 7.3 14 225 5.1 15 500 11.3

Figure 9.7g Algorithm and Flowchart for the *Print* Module

A

Row \\ Column →	1	2	3	4	. . .	C
1	Array(1,1)	Array(1,2)	Array(1,3)	Array(1,4)	. . .	Array(1,Column)
2	Array(2,1)	Array(2,2)	Array(2,3)	Array(2,4)	. . .	Array(2,Column)
3	Array(3,1)	Array(3,2)	Array(3,3)	Array(3,4)	. . .	Array(3,Column)
.
R	Array(Row,1)	Array(Row,2)	Array(Row,3)	Array(Row,4)	. . .	Array(Row,Column)

Figure 9.8 General Form of a Two-Dimensional Array

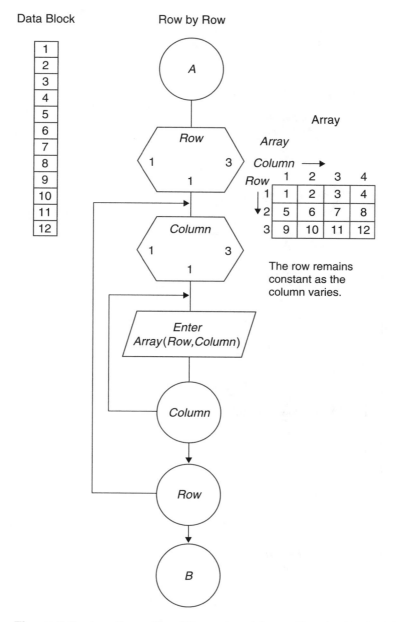

Figure 9.9 Loading a Two-Dimensional Array, Row by Row and Column by Column

the rows (see Figure 9.11). For the grand total, use the intersection of the last row and the last column. This placement of row, column, and grand totals facilitates printing them in the printout of the array.

In the array in Figure 9.11, the fourth row is used for the sum of each column, and the fifth column is used for the sum of each row. The element in the lower right-hand corner—*Array*(4,5)—holds the grand total. In the solution, the sum of both the rows and columns can be done in the same nested loop. It does not make any difference if the sum of a single row is completed before the start of the sum of the next row, or if the sums of all rows are done at the same time, column by column. Notice in Figure 9.11 that the final sum is the same if you accumulate a whole row at one time or all of the rows at the same time. Either way, the sum of the first row is 10, the sum of the second row is 26, and the sum of the third row is 42. The same is true of the columns.

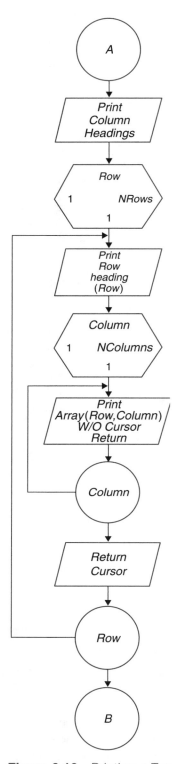

Figure 9.10 Printing a Two-Dimensional Array

In Figure 9.12, the algorithm and the flowchart are shown for summing the rows and columns of the array in Figure 9.11. Notice the differences between the assignment instructions for summing the rows, the columns, and the grand total. The only difference is in the reference numbers of the array elements containing the sums. The

Array

Column →

	1	2	3	4	5
Row 1	1	2	3	4	~~4~~ ~~8~~ ~~6~~ 10
2	5	6	7	8	~~5~~ ~~11~~ ~~18~~ 26
3	9	10	11	12	~~9~~ ~~19~~ ~~30~~ 42
4	~~1~~ ~~6~~ 15	~~2~~ ~~8~~ 18	~~3~~ ~~10~~ 21	~~4~~ ~~12~~ 24	~~10~~ ~~36~~ 78

- Column 5 holds the sum of each of the rows.
- Row 4 holds the sum of each of the columns.
- *Array*(4,5) holds the grand total.

Figure 9.11 Accumulating a Two-Dimensional Array

grand total is the sum of the last column since the sum of the rows is complete at the end of the inner loop.

In the instruction to sum the rows in Figure 9.12, the element numbers are represented by the variable *Row* for the row number, and the expression *NColumns* + 1 for the column number containing the sum of the rows. In the instruction to sum the columns, the element numbers are represented by the expression *NRows* + 1 for the row containing the sum of the columns, and the variable *Column* for the column number. The element numbers of the box containing the grand total, at the intersection of the sums of the rows and the columns, are *NRows* + 1 and *NColumns* + 1. When the rows are summed in the outer loop, they are summed one row at a time; the columns are summed when all the rows have been processed. The summation of the grand total is placed between the two *LoopEnds* because it is the summation of the sums of the rows. The elements to be accumulated for the grand total are the row sums in *Array*(*Row*, *NColumns* + 1).

Putting It All Together

Example

This PIAT illustrates how to enter, use, and print a two-dimensional array.

Problem: The president of the Too Little Variety Stores has collected sales data on the 15 stores in the corporation for seven days. He would like to know the total sales for each store for the week, the total sales for the company for each of the seven days, and the total sales for the company for the week (see Figure 9.13).

In this problem the data can be stored in a two-dimensional sales array; the sum of the store sales per week can be stored in a one-dimensional array; the sum of the store sales per day can be stored in another one-dimensional array; and the grand total for the week can be stored in a single variable. An alternative way to store the data would be to place the totals in an additional row and column in the two-dimensional sales array. The latter would be the better alternative since there is only one array to keep track of and to print. This makes the processing easier and more readable.

The problem is divided into five modules: the *Control, Init, Read, Calc,* and *Print* modules. The *Control* module uses the sequential logic structure to process the modules.

Algorithm	Flowchart

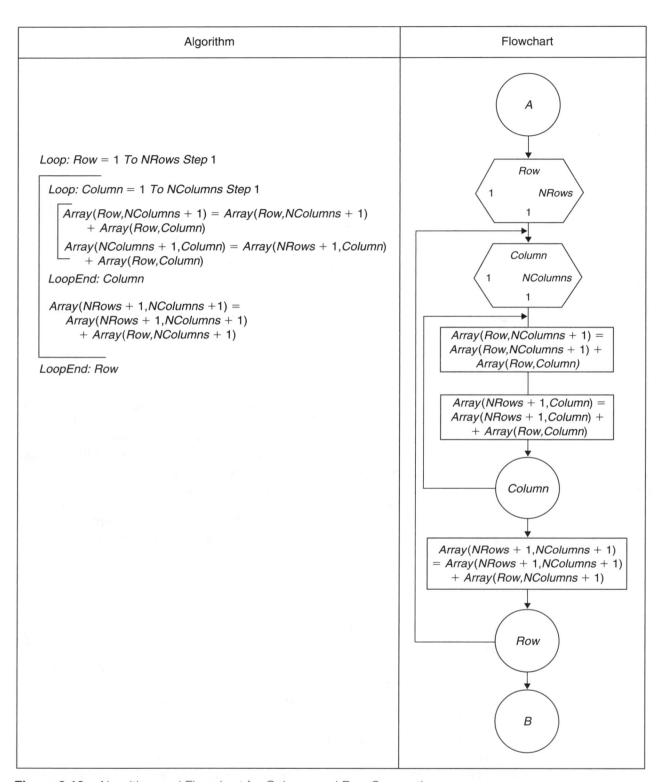

Loop: *Row* = 1 *To NRows Step* 1

 Loop: *Column* = 1 *To NColumns Step* 1

 Array(Row,NColumns + 1) = Array(Row,NColumns + 1)
 + Array(Row,Column)

 Array(NColumns + 1,Column) = Array(NRows + 1,Column)
 + Array(Row,Column)

 LoopEnd: Column

 Array(NRows + 1,NColumns +1) =
 Array(NRows + 1,NColumns + 1)
 + Array(Row,NColumns + 1)

LoopEnd: Row

Figure 9.12 Algorithm and Flowchart for Column and Row Summation

Given Data	Required Results
1. 15 stores 2. Sales for all stores for seven days	1. Total sales for each store for the week 2. Total sales for the company for each day 3. Total sales for the company for the week
Processing Required	**Solution Alternatives**
1. Summing store sales 2. Summing day's sales 3. Summing all sales	1. Use two-dimensional array for data, one-dimensional array for store totals and day's totals, and a single variable for grand total 2. Use a two-dimensional array to store all values

Figure 9.13a Problem Analysis Chart for Array Problem

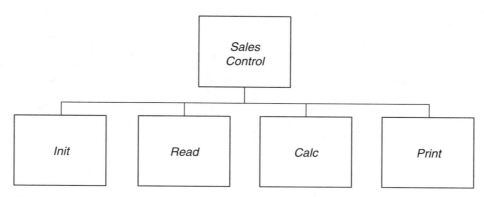

Figure 9.13b Interactivity Chart

Input	Processing	Module Reference	Output
1. Sales/day/store 2. 15 stores	1. Enter data 2. Set array = 0 3. Calculate totals 4. Print output	*Read* *Init* *Calc* *Print*	1. Total sales for each store for the week 2. Total sales for each day for company 3. Total sales for week for company

Figure 9.13c IPO Chart for Array Problem

The *Init* module sets the elements of the array to zero. The *Read* module enters the sales data into the *Sales* array, row by row. The *Calc* module sums the rows to give the totals for each store, the columns to give the totals for each day, and the grand total for the total sales for the company for the week. The *Print* module prints the *Sales* array including the totals.

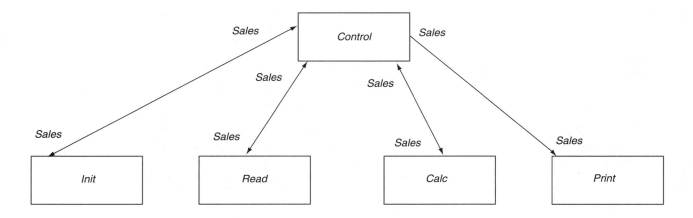

Item	Variable Name	Data Type	Module	Scope	Pseudonyms	Error Cks.
Sales Array	*Sales*	Numeric	All	Local	None	None
Row No.	*Row*	Numeric	*Read, Calc, Print*	Local	None	None
Column No.	*Column*	Numeric	*Read, Calc, Print*	Local	None	None

Figure 9.13d Coupling Diagram and Data Dictionary

Algorithm	Flowchart
Control	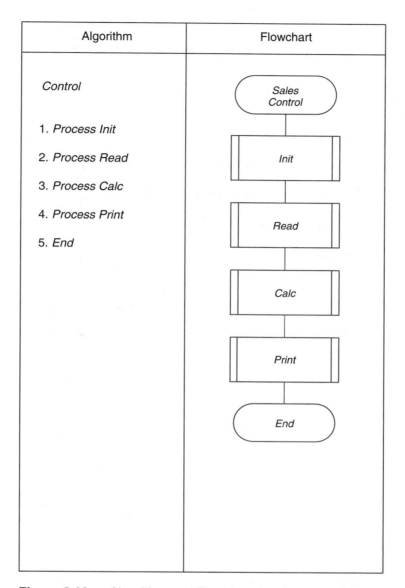
1. *Process Init*	
2. *Process Read*	
3. *Process Calc*	
4. *Process Print*	
5. *End*	

Figure 9.13e Algorithm and Flowchart for *Control* Module

Algorithm	Flowchart
Init 1. Loop: *Row* = 1 *To* 16 *Loop: Column* = 1 *To* 8 *Sales(Row,Column)* = 0 *LoopEnd: Column* *LoopEnd: Row* 2. *Exit*	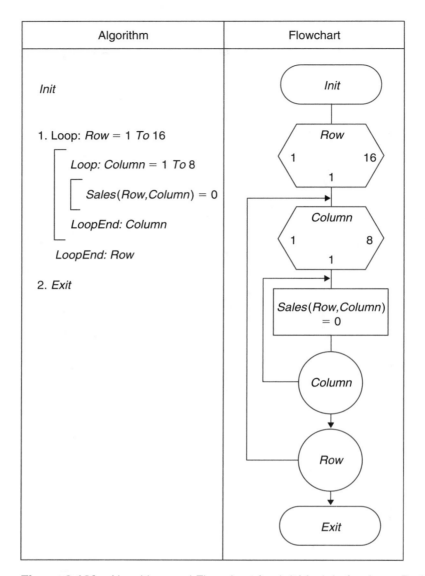

Figure 9.13f Algorithm and Flowchart for *Init* Module for Array Problem

Algorithm	Flowchart
Read 1. *Loop: Row* = 1 *To* 15 *Loop: Column* = 1 *To* 7 *Enter Sales(Row,Column)* *LoopEnd: Column* *LoopEnd: Row* 2. *Exit*	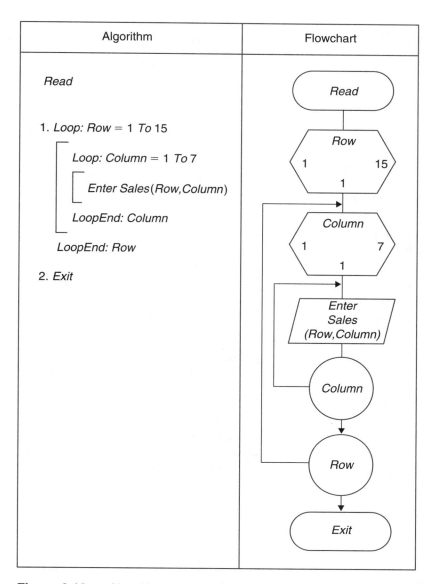

Figure 9.13g Algorithm and Flowchart for *Read* Module for Array Problem

Algorithm	Flowchart	Annotation

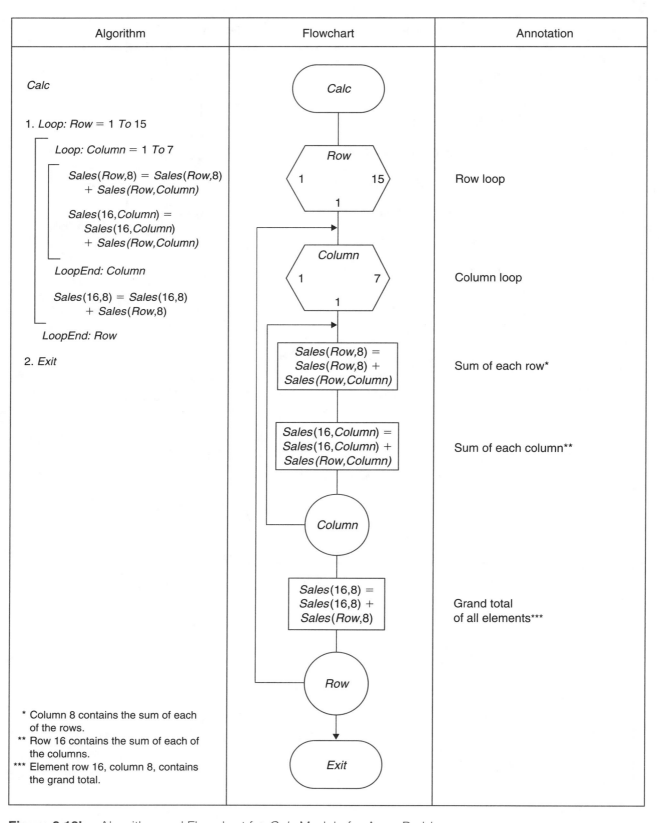

Calc

1. *Loop: Row* = 1 *To* 15

 Loop: Column = 1 *To* 7

 Sales(*Row*,8) = *Sales*(*Row*,8)
 + *Sales*(*Row*,*Column*)

 Sales(16,*Column*) =
 Sales(16,*Column*)
 + *Sales*(*Row*,*Column*)

 LoopEnd: Column

 Sales(16,8) = *Sales*(16,8)
 + *Sales*(*Row*,8)

 LoopEnd: Row

2. *Exit*

* Column 8 contains the sum of each
 of the rows.
** Row 16 contains the sum of each of
 the columns.
*** Element row 16, column 8, contains
 the grand total.

Figure 9.13h Algorithm and Flowchart for *Calc* Module for Array Problem

Algorithm	Flowchart

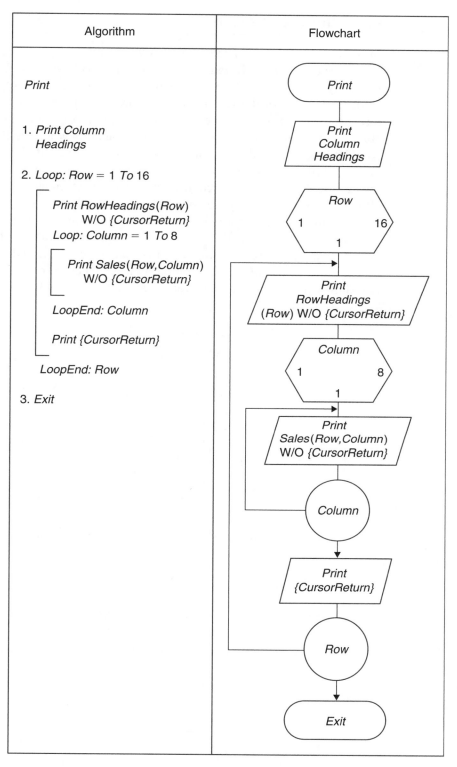

Print

1. *Print Column Headings*

2. *Loop: Row = 1 To 16*

 Print RowHeadings(Row)
 W/O {CursorReturn}
 Loop: Column = 1 To 8

 Print Sales(Row,Column)
 W/O {CursorReturn}

 LoopEnd: Column

 Print {CursorReturn}

 LoopEnd: Row

3. *Exit*

Figure 9.13i Algorithm and Flowchart for *Print* Module for Array Problem

Multidimensional Arrays

multidimensional arrays

In some cases there is a need for arrays with a third or even a fourth dimension. These arrays are called **multidimensional arrays.** You will use these multidimensional arrays relatively infrequently. They can facilitate an understanding of the data, improve the readability of algorithms, and facilitate processing since the data can be processed through the use of three or more nested loops. For example, with input data on temperatures referenced by day, city, county, and state, *day* would be the first dimension, *city* would be the second dimension, *county* would be the third dimension, and *state* would be the fourth dimension of the array. In any case, any temperature could be found as long as the day, the city, the county, and the state are known. A multidimensional array allows the programmer to use one array for all the data.

Figure 9.14 shows a block of memory locations and their reference names for a three-dimensional array. The recommended variable names for the indexes of a three-dimensional array are *Row* for row, *Column* for column, and *Depth* for depth. For a fourth dimension, *Volume* for volume is used. These arrays are processed much like two-dimensional arrays, and, therefore, are not discussed further.

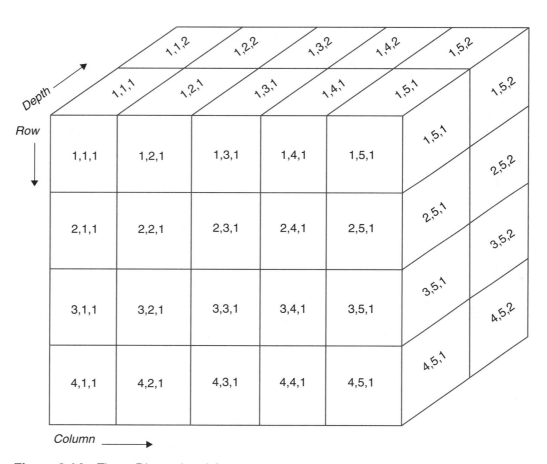

Figure 9.14 Three-Dimensional Array

Table Look-Up Technique

Table Look-up

A common application for arrays is using a value to look up another value in a table. A one-dimensional array would be used if the element number can be utilized as the given value (see Figure 9.15). A two-dimensional array with two columns would be used if the element number cannot be utilized. In this case the first column would contain the values to compare with the given value, and the second column would contain the values to be located. Figure 9.15 illustrates a one-dimensional array and the algorithm and flowchart for a table look-up problem. In this problem we need to find the number of days in a month given the month number. In this case we can utilize the element number as the month number. For example, given month number 3, the number of days in the month would be 31.

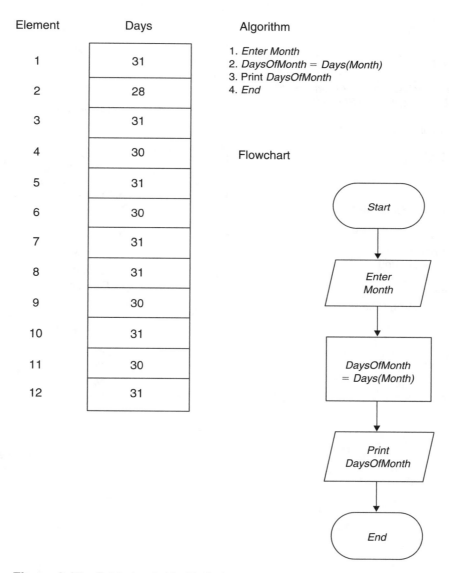

Figure 9.15 Table Look-Up Technique

Sequential Search

sequential search

There are instances when you do not know the element number, but you do know the value of the element. In this case a search must be made on the array to find the correct element. The easiest way to search an array is called a **sequential search.** Figure 9.16 shows the algorithm and the flowchart of a sequential search. The methodology is simple. Given the search value of the element you want to find, element number one is tested to see if it matches the search variable. If it does, the flow of the program drops out of the loop with the desired element number. If it doesn't match, the element number is incremented and loops back to test again.

Algorithm	Flowchart

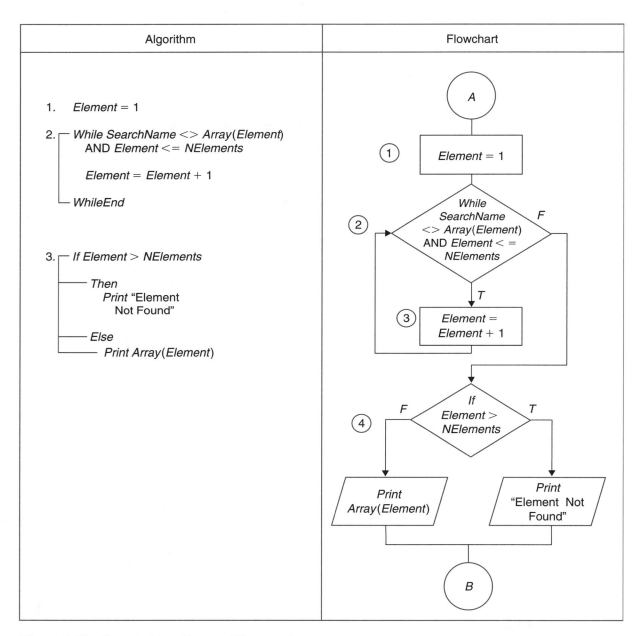

Figure 9.16 Search Algorithm and Flowchart

Notes on Figure 9.16

The numbers of the notes correspond to the circled numbers in Figure 9.16.

1. The element number is set to 1.
2. A loop is set up to test the search value against the value of the present element of the array. This test also includes a test to make sure the element number is less than or equal to the number of elements in the array. If the element number is greater than the number of elements, then the value was not found.
3. The element number is incremented.
4. A test is made on the element number. If the element number is greater than the number of elements in the array, an error message is printed; if not, the value of the element is printed.

Binary Search

binary search

A faster method of finding the desired element of an array is the **binary search.** Figure 9.17a shows the algorithm and flowchart of the binary search. The binary search technique involves comparing the mid-element of all or part of the array. If it compares, the flow of the program drops out of the loop with the desired element number. If it does not compare, the program checks to see if the value is lower or higher than the middle value. The boundaries are then reset to select a new section of the array in which the search value should be found. The midpoint of this new section is then checked. The program continues to divide the remaining elements by half until the desired element is found. At that time the program drops out of the loop with the element number of the desired element. Even with 1,000 elements, this method will take less than 10 comparisons. Figure 9.17b shows an example of a binary search using the algorithm and flowchart in Figure 9.17a.

Notes on Figure 9.17a

The numbers of the notes correspond to the circled numbers in Figure 9.17a.

1. The lower boundary is set at 1 (lowest element number).
2. The upper boundary is set at the maximum number of elements in the array.
3. The flag is set at zero. This flag is set at 1 when the element is found and 2 when the element could not be found. The flag is zero until one of the two preceding conditions is met.
4. The loop is started and will continue as long as *Flag* = 0.
5. The mid-element number is calculated. This always rounds down because the *Int* function is used.
6. This is the test to see if the mid-element is equal to the value of the desired element. If it is, *Flag* is set equal to 1, and the flow goes back to the *While* statement. The condition at the *While* statement is now false so the flow drops out of the loop. If the mid-element is not equal to the desired value, then the flow of the program will need to loop again to test another element against the search value.
7. The next test is made so the upper or lower boundaries can be reset. This will designate the new section of the array. This is accomplished by testing the value of the element against the search value. If the search value is greater

Algorithm	Flowchart

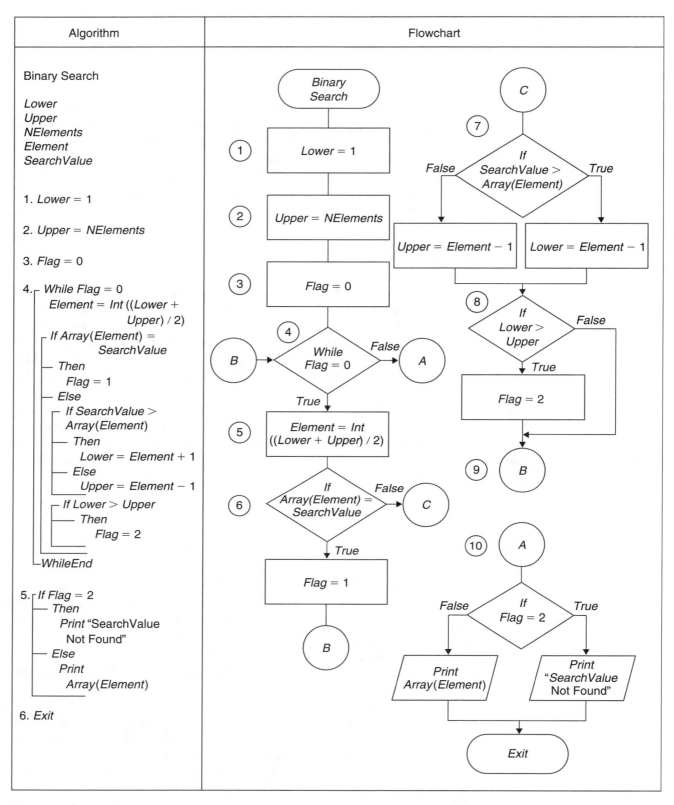

Binary Search

Lower
Upper
NElements
Element
SearchValue

1. *Lower* = 1

2. *Upper* = *NElements*

3. *Flag* = 0

4. While *Flag* = 0
 Element = *Int* ((*Lower* + *Upper*) / 2)
 If *Array*(*Element*) = *SearchValue*
 Then
 Flag = 1
 Else
 If *SearchValue* > *Array*(*Element*)
 Then
 Lower = *Element* + 1
 Else
 Upper = *Element* − 1
 If *Lower* > *Upper*
 Then
 Flag = 2
 WhileEnd

5. If *Flag* = 2
 Then
 Print "*SearchValue* Not Found"
 Else
 Print *Array*(*Element*)

6. *Exit*

Figure 9.17a The Binary Search

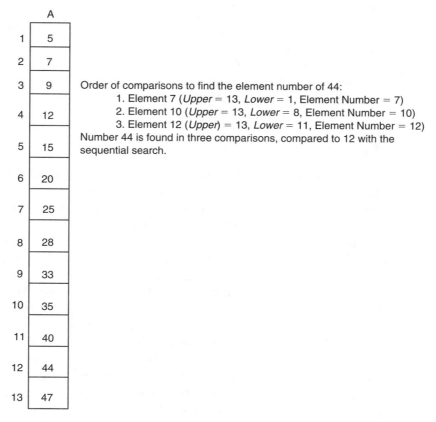

A

1	5
2	7
3	9
4	12
5	15
6	20
7	25
8	28
9	33
10	35
11	40
12	44
13	47

Order of comparisons to find the element number of 44:
1. Element 7 (*Upper* = 13, *Lower* = 1, Element Number = 7)
2. Element 10 (*Upper* = 13, *Lower* = 8, Element Number = 10)
3. Element 12 (*Upper*) = 13, *Lower* = 11, Element Number = 12)

Number 44 is found in three comparisons, compared to 12 with the sequential search.

Figure 9.17b Example of a Binary Search

than the value of the mid-element number, then the lower boundary is set to one more than the midpoint. This means that the desired element is in the upper half of this section. If not, the upper boundary is set to one less than the midpoint. This means the desired element is in the lower half of the section.

8. This test is to make sure there are still elements in the section to be tested. If the lower boundary is less than the upper boundary, the flag is set to 2, indicating that the element could not be found.

9. The flow then returns to the *While* statement and continues or drops out of the loop according to the value of *Flag*.

10. After the flow of the program drops out of the loop, the flag is checked. When the *Flag* is 1, the element (or elements if using parallel arrays or multidimensional arrays) information is printed. If *Flag* is equal to 2, an error message is printed.

The Pointer Technique

pointer technique

Another way to use arrays is to specify the value of an element in one array as the element number in another array. This use of array is called the **pointer technique** because the value of the element in the first array points to the element in the second. The pointer technique is used in frequency distributions. A *frequency distribution* is a tally of one type of value in an array, such as how many students in a school are in each class or how many of a company's customers live in each zip code area. The result of a

frequency distribution is a one-dimensional array that contains the tally for the value of each element number. The pointer technique is also used for calculating statistics from a questionnaire by cross-tabulating items, such as how many students are in each major and each class. The result of this cross-tabulation is a two-dimensional array containing the tally for the combination of the majors and the classes; the majors would be the rows and the classes would be the columns.

Frequency Distribution

Frequency
Distribution

In the development of the solution for a frequency distribution, the arrays must be defined. First, you define the array from which the frequency distribution is to be calculated. This array contains data that are coded using the numbers from 1 to the number of different values in the array. For example, when doing a frequency distribution on grades in a class, the grades must be coded numerically, such as, $1 = A, 2 = B, 3 = C, 4 = D, 5 = F$. Or if the frequency distribution deals with the number of first-, second-, third-, and fourth-year students, including graduate students in a college, each class would be given a number from 1 to 5. The number of values of the code then becomes the number of elements in the frequency distribution array.

Figure 9.18 illustrates the solution to the following problem: Using a grading scale of 1 to 10, design a solution to find the number of students out of a class of 30 who received each grade (1 through 10) on a test. The *Grade* array contains 30 elements, one element for each student, which have the values of 1, 2, 3, 4, 5, 6, 7, 8, 9, or 10, depending on the student's grade. The *F* (frequency distribution) array contains 10 elements, one for each different grade: The first element contains the number of students who received a 1, the second element contains the number of students who received a 2, the third element contains the number of students who received a 3, and so forth (see Figure 9.18d).

Figures 9.18a–c demonstrate the use of pointers for a frequency distribution. Notice in the *Calc* module that the value of the *Grade* array element is the element number of the frequency distribution array. The *Grade* array element value points to the location of the element in the frequency distribution array that needs to be incremented, an example of the pointer technique. Follow the notes for Figures 9.18a–c for an explanation of each major step in the solution to the frequency distribution problem. Figure 9.18d shows an example of data and outcomes of this problem.

Notes for Figures 9.18a–c

The following notes explain the flowcharts for a frequency distribution. The numbers of the notes correspond to the circled numbers in Figures 9.18a–c.

1. The *Init* module initializes the variables to zero.
2. The *Read* module enters the data.
3. The *Calc* module calculates the frequency distribution.
4. The *Print* module prints the frequency distribution.
5. The frequency distribution array *(Frequency)* is 10 elements long since there are 10 grades. Each element in this array is set to zero because each element is a counter.
6. There are 30 elements in the *Grade* array since there are 30 students. This loop enters the grades into the *Grade* array. There is one element per student.

7. In this loop the ending number is the number of students, since that will determine the frequency distribution.

8. Through the pointer technique, the value of the *StudentGrades(Student)* points to the element number of the frequency distribution array to indicate which element will be incremented. The *Grade* variable is the pointer variable. It has the same value as the grade of student number *Student*.

9. The *Grade* element of the frequency array is incremented. At the conclusion of the loop, the frequency array will contain the values of the number of students receiving each of the 10 grades.

10. This loop executes 10 times since there are 10 elements in the frequency array.

11. This loop prints the number of the element *(Student)*, which is equal to the grade and the value of the *Student* element of the frequency array *(Frequency)*, which is the number of students receiving the grade *(Student)*.

Figure 9.18a Algorithm and Flowchart of *Control* Module for a Frequency Distribution

Algorithm	Flowchart
Init 1. *Loop: Student* = 1 *To* 10 *Frequency*(*Student*) = 0 *LoopEnd: Student* 2. *Exit* *Read* 1. *Loop: Student* = 1 *To* 30 *Enter StudentGrades* (*Student*) *LoopEnd: Student* 2. *Exit*	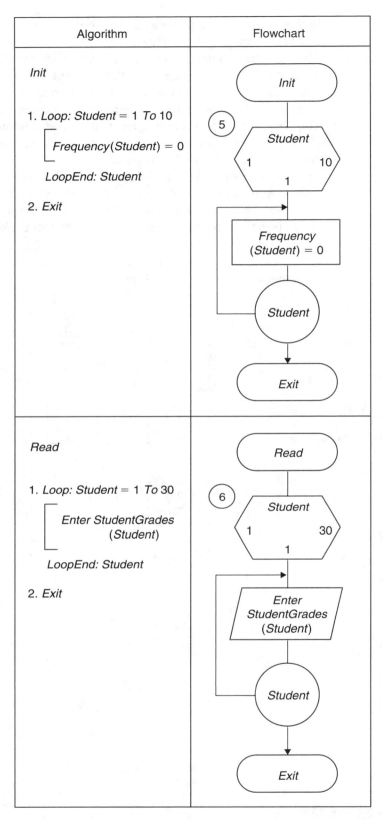

Figure 9.18b Algorithms and Flowcharts of *Init* and *Read* Modules for a Frequency Distribution

Algorithm	Flowchart
Calc 1. *Loop: Student* = 1 *To* 30 *Grade* = *StudentGrades* *(Student)* *Frequency(Grade)* = *Frequency(Grade)* + 1 *LoopEnd: Student* 2. *Exit*	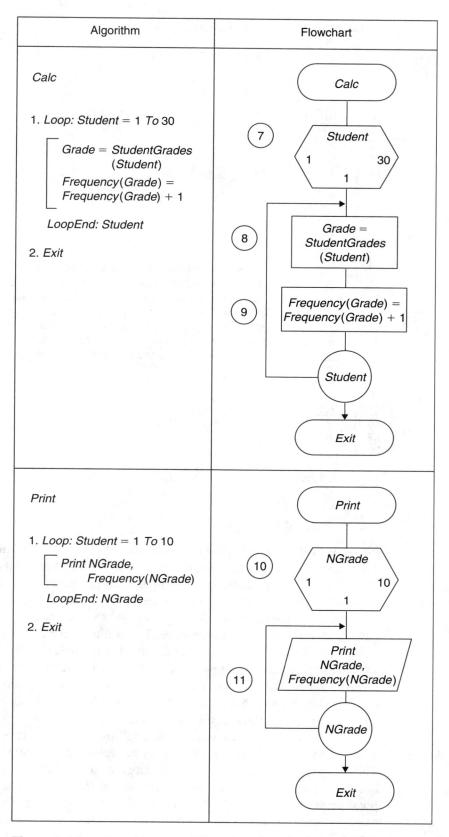
Print 1. *Loop: Student* = 1 *To* 10 *Print NGrade,* *Frequency(NGrade)* *LoopEnd: NGrade* 2. *Exit*	

Figure 9.18c Algorithms and Flowcharts of *Calc* and *Print* Modules for a Frequency Distribution

StudentGrades

1	10
2	8
3	5
4	10
5	9
6	10
7	6
8	1
9	3
10	8
11	7
12	7
13	10
14	9
15	8
16	9
17	9
18	6
19	7
20	4
21	3
22	2
23	7
24	6
25	8
26	9
27	10
28	9
29	8
30	10

Frequency

1	1
2	1
3	2
4	1
5	1
6	3
7	4
8	5
9	6
10	6

The *element* number of the frequency distribution array is the number of points correct and the *value* of the element is the number of students that received that grade. Therefore, the frequency distribution array *Frequency* shows that there is 1 student who received 1 point, 1 who received 2 points, 2 who received 3 points, 1 who received 4 points, 1 who received 5 points, 3 who received 6 points, 4 who received 7 points, 5 who received 8 points, 6 who received 9 points and 6 who received 10 points.

Figure 9.18d Example of a Frequency Distribution

Cross-Tabulation

Cross-Tabulation

Figure 9.19 demonstrates the use of pointers for a cross-tabulation. Notice that in this case, one value points to the row and another value points to the column in the cross-tabulation array. The data for cross-tabulation problems come from questionnaires. A cross-tabulation shows the number of people who gave the same responses to two questions from the questionnaire. A frequency distribution shows the number of people who gave the same answer to one question. For example, in a frequency distribution, a set of test scores would be separated into the number of students who received each grade. In a cross-tabulation, a set of test scores could be separated into the number of females that received each test grade and the number of males that received each test grade, or the number in each class that received each test grade. A cross-tabulation allows the user to have more detail in the analysis of the data.

Figure 9.19 shows the algorithms and flowcharts for a cross-tabulation for the following problem: A questionnaire has been sent out by a company that conducts polls. The company needs a program to calculate the cross-tabulation for any two items on the questionnaire. The questionnaire has five items. Items 1 and 2 are *age* and *education* (5 possible answers). Items 3 through 5 are *yes* or *no* questions. There were 150 questionnaires returned. The following would be a sample output given option 1 = gender and option 2 = question 1.

Algorithm	Flowchart

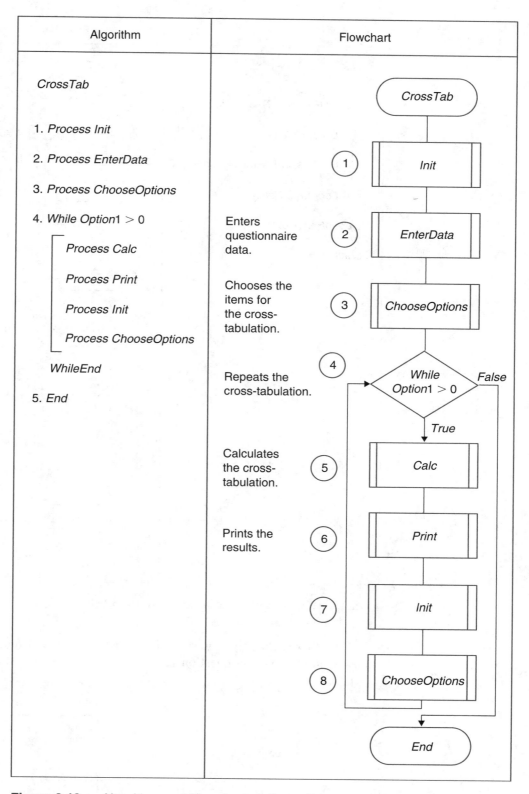

Algorithm

CrossTab

1. *Process Init*

2. *Process EnterData*

3. *Process ChooseOptions*

4. *While Option1 > 0*

 Process Calc

 Process Print

 Process Init

 Process ChooseOptions

 WhileEnd

5. *End*

Flowchart

CrossTab

1. Init

2. EnterData — Enters questionnaire data.

3. ChooseOptions — Chooses the items for the cross-tabulation.

4. While Option1 > 0 — Repeats the cross-tabulation. False / True

5. Calc — Calculates the cross-tabulation.

6. Print — Prints the results.

7. Init

8. ChooseOptions

End

Figure 9.19a Algorithm and Flowchart of *Control* Module for Cross-Tabulation Solution

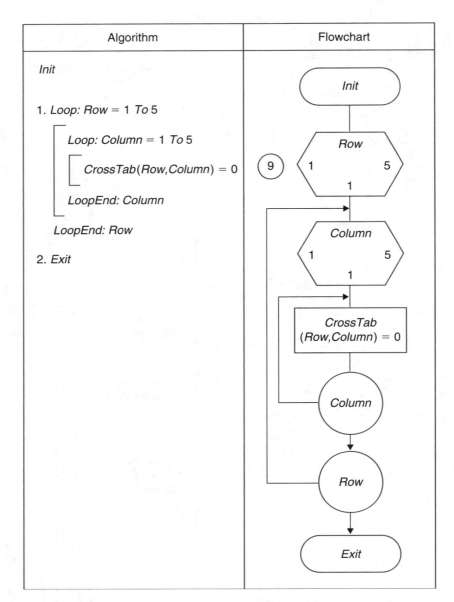

Figure 9.19b Algorithm and Flowchart of *Init* Module for Cross-Tabulation Solution

The *CrossTab* array represents the output where row 1 represents females; row 2, males; column 1, yes for question 1; and column 2, no for question 1.

CrossTab	1 Yes	2 No
1 Females	32	25
2 Males	51	42

Algorithm	Flowchart

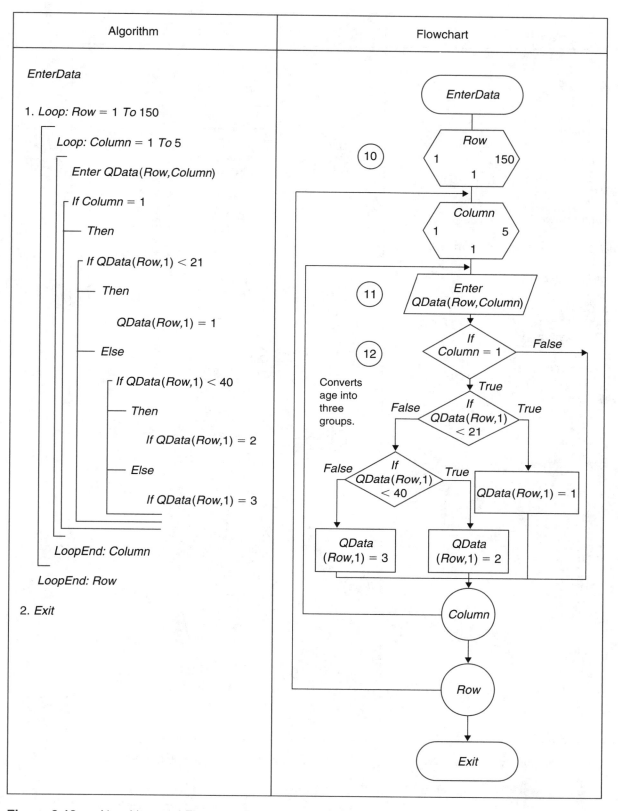

EnterData

1. *Loop: Row* = 1 *To* 150

 Loop: Column = 1 *To* 5

 Enter QData(Row,Column)

 If Column = 1

 — *Then*

 *If QData(Row,*1) < 21

 — *Then*

 *QData(Row,*1) = 1

 — *Else*

 *If QData(Row,*1) < 40

 — *Then*

 *If QData(Row,*1) = 2

 — *Else*

 *If QData(Row,*1) = 3

 LoopEnd: Column

 LoopEnd: Row

2. *Exit*

Figure 9.19c Algorithm and Flowchart of *Enter* Module for Cross-Tabulation Solution

Algorithm	Flowchart

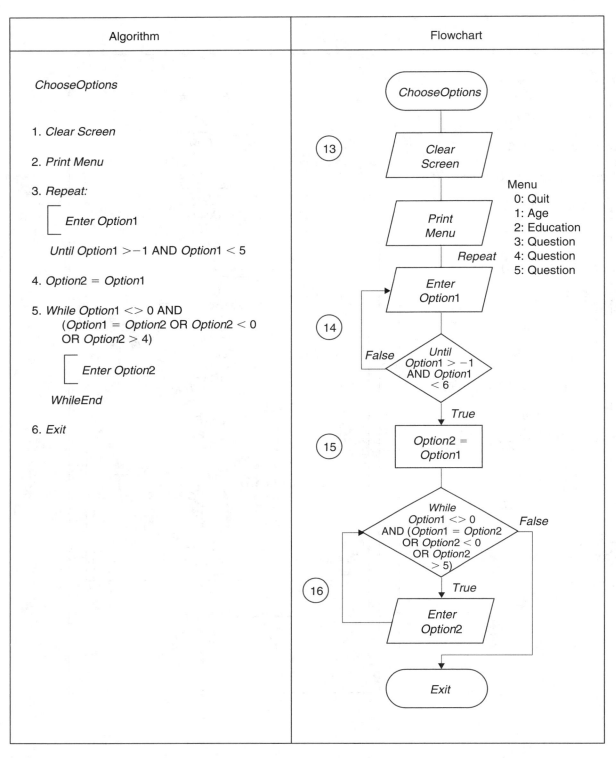

Figure 9.19d Algorithm and Flowchart of *ChooseOptions* Module for Cross-Tabulation Solution

Algorithm	Flowchart

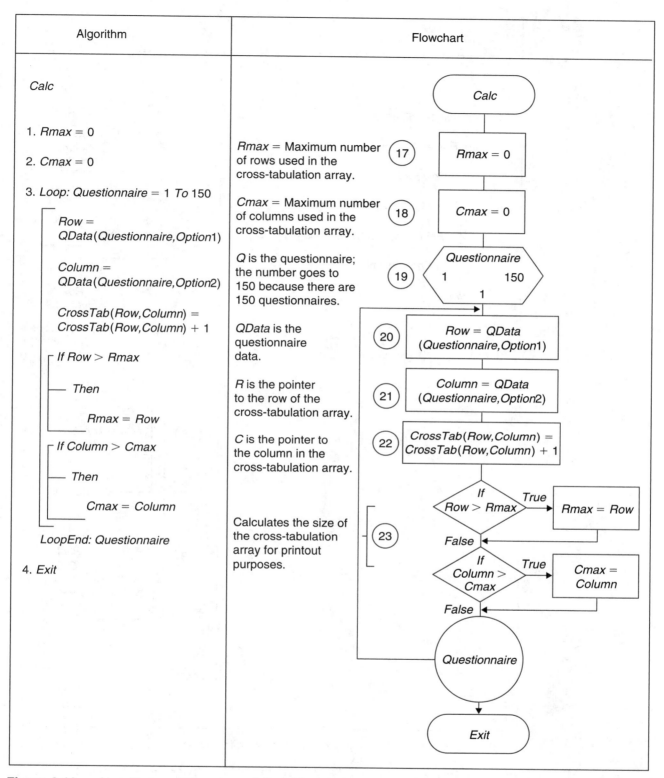

Calc

1. *Rmax* = 0

2. *Cmax* = 0

3. *Loop: Questionnaire* = 1 *To* 150

 Row =
 QData(Questionnaire,Option1)

 Column =
 QData(Questionnaire,Option2)

 CrossTab(Row,Column) =
 CrossTab(Row,Column) + 1

 If Row > *Rmax*

 Then

 Rmax = *Row*

 If Column > *Cmax*

 Then

 Cmax = *Column*

 LoopEnd: Questionnaire

4. *Exit*

Flowchart annotations:

Rmax = Maximum number of rows used in the cross-tabulation array. ⑰

Cmax = Maximum number of columns used in the cross-tabulation array. ⑱

Q is the questionnaire; the number goes to 150 because there are 150 questionnaires. ⑲

QData is the questionnaire data.

R is the pointer to the row of the cross-tabulation array.

C is the pointer to the column in the cross-tabulation array.

Calculates the size of the cross-tabulation array for printout purposes. ㉓

Figure 9.19e Algorithm and Flowchart of *Calc* Module for Cross-Tabulation Solution

Algorithm	Flowchart

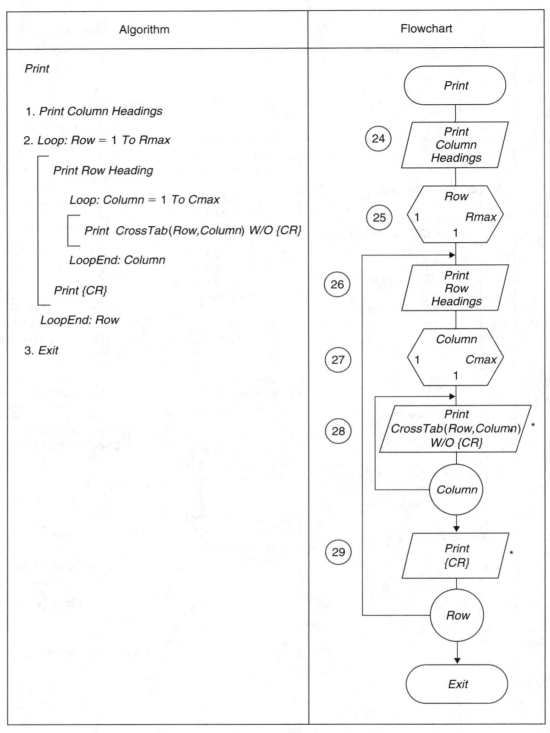

Print

1. *Print Column Headings*

2. *Loop: Row = 1 To Rmax*

 Print Row Heading

 Loop: Column = 1 To Cmax

 Print CrossTab(Row,Column) W/O {CR}

 LoopEnd: Column

 Print {CR}

 LoopEnd: Row

3. *Exit*

* *{CR}* = Cursor return for monitor or carriage return for printer.

Figure 9.19f Algorithm and Flowchart of *Print* Module for Cross-Tabulation Solution

The values of the four elements add up to the total number of questionnaires. The *CrossTab* array shows that 32 females answered yes to question 1, 25 females answered no, 51 males answered yes, and 42 males answered no.

Notes on Figure 9.19

The following notes explain the flowcharts in Figure 9.19. The numbers of the notes correspond to the circled numbers in Figures 9.19a–f.

1. The *Init* module initializes the variables.
2. The *EnterData* module enters the questionnaire data.
3. The *ChooseOptions* module chooses the two items for the cross-tabulation.
4. This loop repeats the cross-tabulation until no more cross-tabulations are desired by the user.
5. The *Calc* module calculates the cross-tabulation.
6. The *Print* module prints the results of the cross-tabulation.
7. The *Init* module, processed at this point, reinitializes the variables for another cross-tabulation on the same data.
8. This *ChooseOptions* module chooses the two items for the next cross-tabulation.
9. This nested automatic-counter loop sets the elements of the cross-tabulation array to zero.
10. These loops are set so that the rows *(Row)* are the questionnaires (1 to 150) and the columns *(Column)* are the items (1 to 5).
11. This instruction enters the questionnaire data, one element at a time.
12. This decision instruction checks to see if the column number is 1; if it is, then the instruction changes the ages to age groups: 1 = under 21, 2 = between 21 and 40, 3 = over 40.
13. These instructions clear the screen and print the menu of the questionnaire items.
14. This loop enters the first item number *(Option1)* for the cross-tabulation option. It repeats until the number entered is within the limits of the options of the menu (0 to 5).
15. This instruction initializes *Option2* to prepare for the next loop.
16. This loop enters the second item number *(Option2)* and repeats until the answer is within the limitations of the number of items (1 to 5) and is not equal to *Option1*.
17. *Rmax* is the maximum number of rows used in the cross-tabulation. It is set to zero since the maximum number of rows has to be greater than zero.
18. *Cmax* is the maximum number of columns used in the cross-tabulation. It is set to zero since the maximum number of columns has to be greater than zero.
19. This loop is set up for the number of questionnaires (150).
20. *Row* is the pointer to the row of the cross-tabulation array. The value comes from the value in the *Option1* column for that questionnaire. *Option1* is the first item number entered by the user.
21. *Column* is the pointer to the column of the cross-tabulation array. The value comes from the value in the *Option2* column for that questionnaire. *Option2* is the second item number entered by the user.
22. This instruction increments the element in the cross-tabulation array specified by the pointers *Row* and *Column*.

23. These decisions calculate the maximum row number and the maximum column number for printing.
24. This instruction prints column headings.
25. This loop specifies the number of rows to print, determined by *RMax*.
26. This instruction prints the row heading each time through the loop.
27. This loop specifies the number of columns to print, determined by *CMax*.
28. This instruction prints an element without a carriage return, as specified by *Row* and *Column*.
29. This instruction returns the carriage after a row is printed.

Putting It All Together

Example

This PIAT illustrates the use of arrays in the solution to a cross-tabulation problem.

Problem: A company has data on the number of days each employee was absent during the previous year. The data also include gender (1 = female, 2 = *male*), pay type (1 = salary, 2 = hourly wage, 3 = commission), education (1 = no diploma or degree, 2 = high school diploma, 3 = *associate degree,* 4 = *bachelor's degree,* 5 = graduate degree), and age group (1 = below 30, 2 = 30–50, 3 = over 50). The personnel manager would like a cross-tabulation on these data giving the average number of days absent. The company has 55 employees (see Figure 9.20).

In this example output, the *CrossTab* array represents the average absences, where row 1 represents salary pay type; row 2, hourly pay type; row 3, commission pay type; column 1, females; and column 2, males.

CrossTab	1 Females	2 Males
1 Salary pay type	2.4	5.6
2 Hourly pay type	5.2	4.8
3 Commission pay type	6.1	5.3

The *CrossTab* array shows that the average number of absences for females having salary pay type is 2.4; males had 5.6. Females having hourly pay types had an average number of absences of 5.2; males had 4.8. Females who were under commission pay type had an average number of absences of 6.1; males had 5.3. In this case, to find the

average number of absences, the number of absences in each category is totaled in the *CT* array, and the number of people in each category are counted in the *N* array. The average is then calculated by dividing each element in the *CT* array by the corresponding element in the *N* array. The *N* array is tested for zero before dividing to avoid a division by zero error.

	Gender	Pay Type	Education	Age Group	# of Days Absent
Employee 1					
2					
3					
.
55					

Figure 9.20a Cross-Tabulation Problem

Given Data	Required Results
Per employee: Gender (1 = F, 2 = M) Pay type (1 = S, 2 = H, 3 = C) Education (1 = N, 2 HS, 3 = C, 4 = B, 5 = G) Age group (1 = < 30; 2 = 30 to 50; 3 = > 50) # of days absent	Cross-tabulate for average number of days absent
Processing Required	
Calculation of average using cross-tabulation technique	
Solution Alternatives	
Must use cross-tabulation pointer technique	

Figure 9.20b Problem Analysis Chart

Interactivity (Structure) Chart

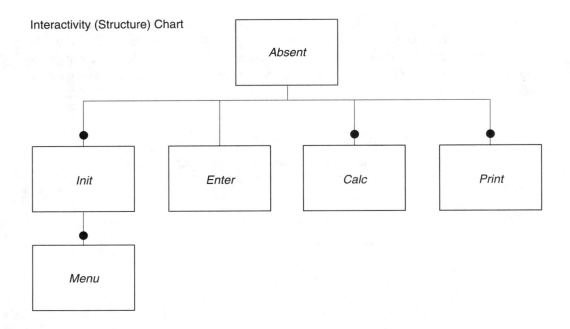

IPO Chart

Input	Processing	Module Reference	Output
For each employee	1. Set cross-tab array and counter array = 0	*Init*	Average # of days absent for any two: (cross-tabulation)
1. Gender	2. Enter data	*Enter*	1. Gender
2. Pay type	3. Print menu	*Menu*	2. Pay type
3. Education	4. Choose options	*Menu*	3. Education
4. Age group	5. Calculate cross-tabulation	*Calc*	4. Age
5. # of days absent	6. Print cross-tab array	*Print*	
	7 Repeat 3–7 until option 1 = 0		

Figure 9.20c Interactivity Chart and IPO Chart

Algorithm	Flowchart

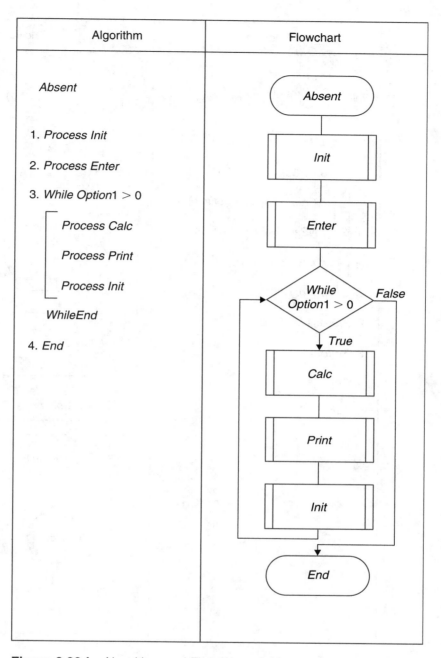

Figure 9.20d Algorithm and Flowchart of *Absent Control* Module for PIAT Cross-Tabulation Problem

Algorithm	Flowchart

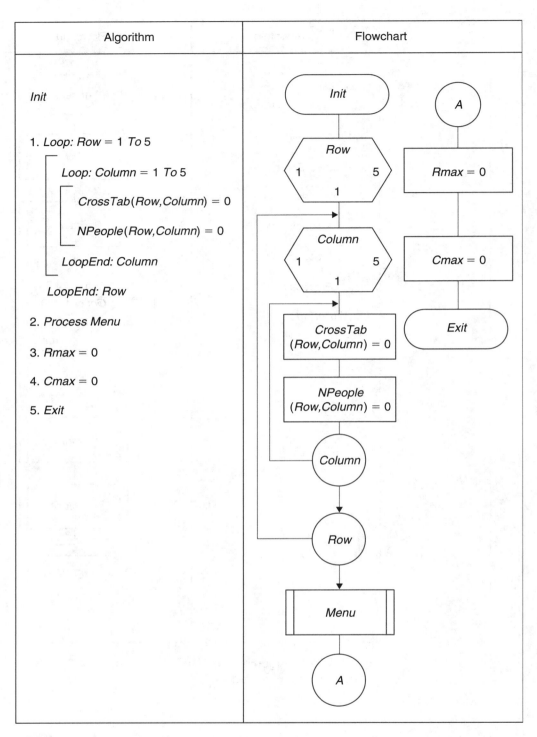

Init

1. *Loop: Row* = 1 *To* 5

 Loop: Column = 1 *To* 5

 CrossTab(*Row,Column*) = 0

 NPeople(*Row,Column*) = 0

 LoopEnd: Column

 LoopEnd: Row

2. *Process Menu*

3. *Rmax* = 0

4. *Cmax* = 0

5. *Exit*

Figure 9.20e Algorithm and Flowchart of *Init* Module for PIAT Cross-Tabulation Problem

Algorithm	Flowchart

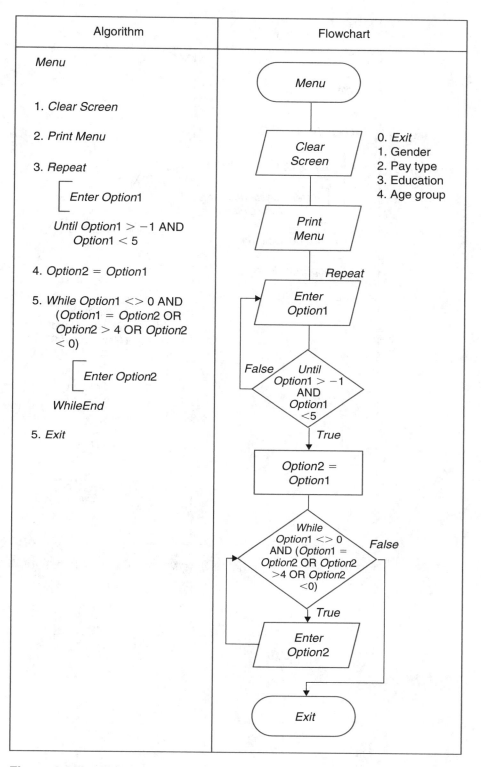

Algorithm side:

Menu

1. *Clear Screen*

2. *Print Menu*

3. *Repeat*

 *Enter Option*1

 *Until Option*1 > −1 AND
 *Option*1 < 5

4. *Option*2 = *Option*1

5. *While Option*1 <> 0 AND
 (*Option*1 = *Option*2 OR
 *Option*2 > 4 OR *Option*2
 < 0)

 *Enter Option*2

 WhileEnd

5. *Exit*

Flowchart side:

Menu

Clear Screen

0. *Exit*
1. Gender
2. Pay type
3. Education
4. Age group

Print Menu

Repeat

*Enter Option*1

False — *Until Option*1 > −1 AND *Option*1 < 5 — True

*Option*2 = *Option*1

*While Option*1 <> 0 AND (*Option*1 = *Option*2 OR *Option*2 > 4 OR *Option*2 < 0) — False / True

*Enter Option*2

Exit

Figure 9.20f Algorithm and Flowchart of *Menu* Module for PIAT Cross-Tabulation Problem

Algorithm	Flowchart
Enter 1. *Loop: Row* = 1 *To* 55 *Loop: Column* = 1 *To* 5 *Enter Questionnaire* (*Row,Column*) *LoopEnd: Column* *LoopEnd: Row* 2. *Exit*	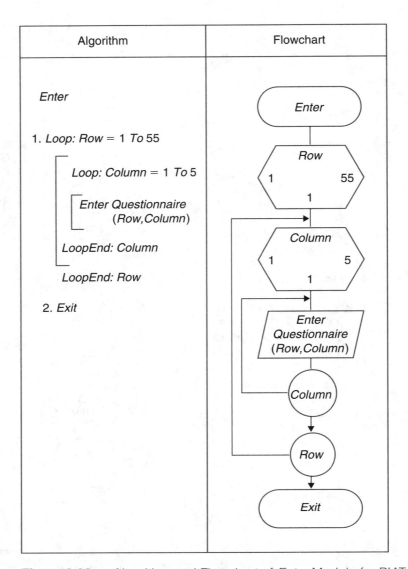

Figure 9.20g Algorithm and Flowchart of *Enter* Module for PIAT Cross-Tabulation Problem

Figure 9.20h Algorithm and Flowchart of *Calc* Module for PIAT Cross-Tabulation Problem

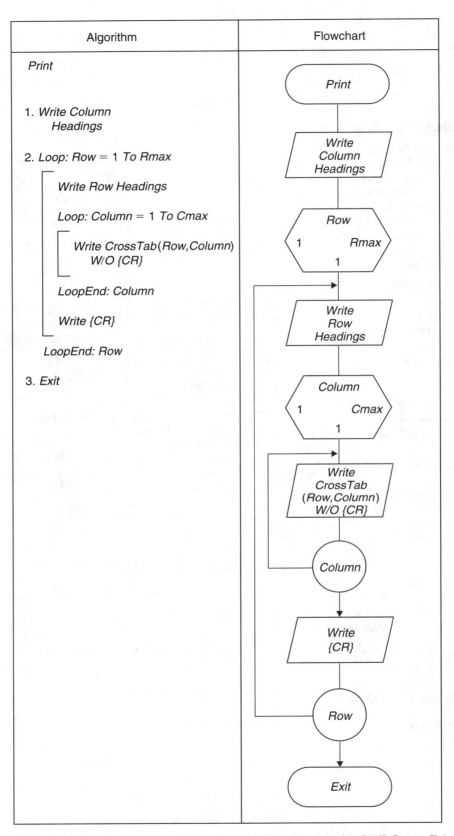

Algorithm	Flowchart

Algorithm

Print

1. *Write Column Headings*

2. *Loop: Row = 1 To Rmax*

 Write Row Headings

 Loop: Column = 1 To Cmax

 Write CrossTab(Row,Column) W/O {CR}

 LoopEnd: Column

 Write {CR}

 LoopEnd: Row

3. *Exit*

Figure 9.20i Algorithm and Flowchart of *Print* Module for PIAT Cross-Tabulation Problem

Summary

Arrays facilitate the processing of data that is needed more than once in the processing of a solution. Even though arrays are not difficult to learn, they are difficult to use well. Therefore, it is important that a student of programming learn how to use them in a solution. To use arrays, the student needs to learn to enter or load data into an array, to print an array, to sum the elements of an array, and to use an array to store data needed at a later point in the solution. There are three types of arrays: one-dimensional, two-dimensional, and multidimensional.

A technique that is important to the use of arrays is the pointer technique, wherein you use the value of an element in one array to point to the number of the element in another. It is used in frequency distributions and cross-tabulations.

New Terms

array	dynamic array	pointer technique
base-one system	multidimensional array	sequential search
base-zero system	one-dimensional array	static array
binary search	parallel arrays	two-dimensional array

Questions

1. Draw and name a one-dimensional array that would hold 10 temperatures. Number the elements.

2. Draw and name four parallel arrays that would hold the following data:

Store	Sales	Customers	Region
A24	5000	500	A
A26	3000	200	A
C30	6000	550	C
B44	4000	560	B

3. Draw and name a two-dimensional array that would hold the data for 10 homework scores for 15 students. Number the rows and the columns.

4. Can all of the data in question 2 be put into a two-dimensional array? Explain.

5. What is the pointer technique for finding data? Why is it used?

6. What are the problem requirements for using the pointer technique?

Problems

Complete the seven steps of solution development for the following problems.

1. Mr. Jones always gives True/False tests to his class. His tests always have 20 questions. The maximum class size is 35. He needs a program that will calculate the students' grades based on the best score.

 Grade

 A will range from the best score, to the best score minus 2.

 B will range from the best score minus 3, to the best score minus 4.

 C will range from the best score minus 5, to the best score minus 6.

 D will range from the best score minus 7, to the best score minus 8.

 F will be anything below the best score minus 8.

 Each student's ID and test answers will be entered. The output will be each student's ID, number correct, and grade, along with the single highest score for the class. Develop a solution for Mr. Jones's problem. Use four one-dimensional arrays—one for the correct scores and the other three for the needed output.

2. A restaurant manager wants to know how many employees are needed at the restaurant each hour of the day. The minimum number of employees needed at any hour is 3. After that, one additional employee is required for each 20 customers. The restaurant is open 24 hours a day. The manager has counted the number of customers each hour for 14 days. The manager will use the average number of customers for each hour over the 14 days to calculate the needed number of employees for each hour. Develop a solution to output the needed number of employees per hour. (There is no such thing as a partial employee.)

3. A company has 10 salespeople. The manager needs to know the average dollar amount of sales for each salesperson for a week, and the total dollar amount of sales for the store for each day and for the week. The store is open 7 days a week, and each salesperson gets 2 days off. The data are entered into a two-dimensional array with the days of the week as the columns and the salespeople as the rows. Develop a solution to output the needed information.

4. An instructor has 30 students in her class. Each student is identified by a number from 1 to 30. Grades are stored in a one-dimensional array. The instructor would like to enter a student number and have the student's test score printed on the monitor. Develop a solution to output the needed information.

5. An instructor has a class of 25 students. Each student is identified by a number from 1 to 25. All tests are stored in a two-dimensional array, with each column containing the grades for each test. The instructor would like to enter the student number and the test number and have the grade for that test printed on the monitor. Develop a solution to output the needed information.

6. The instructor in problem 5 would like to enter the last name of the student instead of the student number. Modify your solution to allow the instructor to enter the student name instead of the student number.

7. A university has four undergraduate class levels and a graduate school. There are 7 majors, although not all students have chosen a major. There are 1,200 students

attending the university. The administration would like to know how many students are in each level, and how many students have each major. They also would like to know how many of each class level have declared each major. Develop a solution to output the needed information.

8. A questionnaire was sent to a random selection of the alumni of a college. In all, 95 questionnaires were returned. The questionnaire requested the following items:

age

gender

marital status

college major

salary

The administration would like to know the average salary, given any two sets of items. Develop a solution to cross-tabulate the items and output the needed information. (Remember, the computer cannot divide by zero.)

9. **a.** The student names and the grades for four tests for Mr. Smith's class have been placed in parallel arrays. Mr. Smith would like to have one student's name and test scores printed. Develop a solution that will enter the student's name, search for the name in the same array, and then print the name and test scores. Use the sequential-search method.

b. What would have to change in the solution in problem 9a if we were to use a binary search instead of the sequential-search method?

c. Modify the solution in problem 9a to use a binary search instead of a sequential search.

10. Modify problem 4 in Chapter 8 (the Roman numeral problem) using arrays. Which method do you think is the most efficient for the programmer? Which method do you think is the most user-friendly?

11. The human resources manager of XYZ Corporation would like to analyze the following characteristics of company employees:
 a. the wages of women compared with those of men
 b. the total number of employees in each of the 12 departments
 c. the number of women and men in each of the 12 departments
 d. the average age of the women and men in each department

 Develop a solution for this problem.

12. John has a weather station in his house. He has been keeping track of the fastest wind speed for each day for two weeks. He would like to know the average wind speed over the two weeks, the days on which the highest wind speed and the lowest wind speed were recorded, and the difference between the highest wind speed recorded and each day's average wind speed.

13. Create a solution to print the number of times a pair of dice would be rolled before there would be a duplicate number. (*Hint:* Store the values of each roll in an array and check the values of the array each time the dice are rolled.)

14. Expand problem 13 to print the average number of rolls over *N* times. *N* is an input value.

WHAT'S WRONG WITH THIS?

Correct the following segments of algorithms:

1. $S = 1$

 While EmployeeNo< >0

 Enter EmployeeNo(s)

 $S = S + 1$

 WhileEnd

2. *Loop: Row = 1 To 5*

 Loop: Column = 1 To 3

 Print A(Column, Row)

 LoopEnd: Row

 LoopEnd: Column

3. *Loop: C = 1 To 100*

 Enter Name(EmployeeNumber)

 LoopEnd: C

Chapter 10

Sorting, Stacks, and Queues

Overview

Sorting Techniques

Stacks

Queues

Objectives

When you have finished this chapter, you should be able to:

1. Explain the different types of data structures used in a computer.
2. Use several sorting techniques.
3. Use stacks in a solution.
4. Use queues in a solution.

Data are stored in the computer in one of many logical ways in order to find needed values as fast as possible. The way data are stored is called the structure of data, hence the term *data structures*. You have already used several types of data structures in developing solutions for problems in this text. The simplest data structure is the single variable. This data structure was the first one you used. The single-variable data structure includes single values of the data types presented in Chapter 2. Other data structures you have used include strings and arrays. To review, a string is a type of array because it is a group of characters stored in a continuous fashion as in arrays. Many languages treat strings as arrays. An array consists of multiple values for one variable name. Data can be stored in one-dimensional, two-dimensional, or multidimensional arrays. The single variable and the array are types of data structures that are used as methods of storing data in the internal memory during the processing of the data. Methods of storing data on external memory sources are presented in Chapters 12 and 13. Sorting techniques,

stacks, and queues are presented in this chapter. Sorting places an array of values in order. There are many techniques to accomplish this. Three techniques are presented in this chapter. Stacks and queues are used to manipulate data in the computer and are important for the student to understand how they work.

Sorting Techniques

sorting

Most accessing techniques require data to be sorted. **Sorting** is the process of putting data in alphabetical or numeric order using one key field or a concatenation of two or more fields. Data are sorted according to the primary key. Once data are in order, they can be accessed by various means, including the sequential search and the binary search. These techniques were presented in Chapter 9.

There are many different techniques of sorting: The selection exchange sort, the bubble sort, and the shell sort. In this chapter we explain how techniques work, along with showing the algorithms and the flowcharts. Other popular sorting techniques include the quick sort and the heap sort. The best sorting method is determined by how large the array or file is and how close the file is to being in order. Ultimately the best sorting method is determined by the number of comparisons and switches that need to take place.

All sorting techniques require a comparison of two data items with a possibility of a switch. If the sort is in ascending order, the comparison would be to see if the primary key of data 1 is larger than the primary key of data 2. If it is, then data 1 is switched with data 2, and if not, they are left in the same position. The comparisons take place until data are in the required order.

Selection Sort

The first technique is the *selection exchange sort*. Figure 10.1 shows the switches made during each pass. The theory is to find the smallest value of the remaining values and switch with the value found in the first position of the remaining elements. During the first pass (first time through the outer loop) the smallest value (15) is switched with the first element (65). During the second pass the smallest of the remaining values (25) remained as the second element (25). During the third pass the smallest of the remaining values (34) remains as the third element since no element was found that was smaller. This continues until the last position is in the right order. See Figure 10.1 for all passes. Figure 10.2 shows the algorithm and the flowchart for the selection exchange sort.

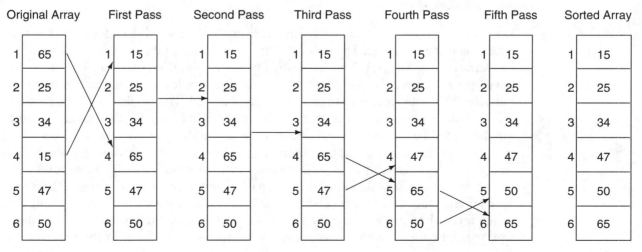

Figure 10.1 Selection Exchange Sort Technique

Algorithm	Flowchart

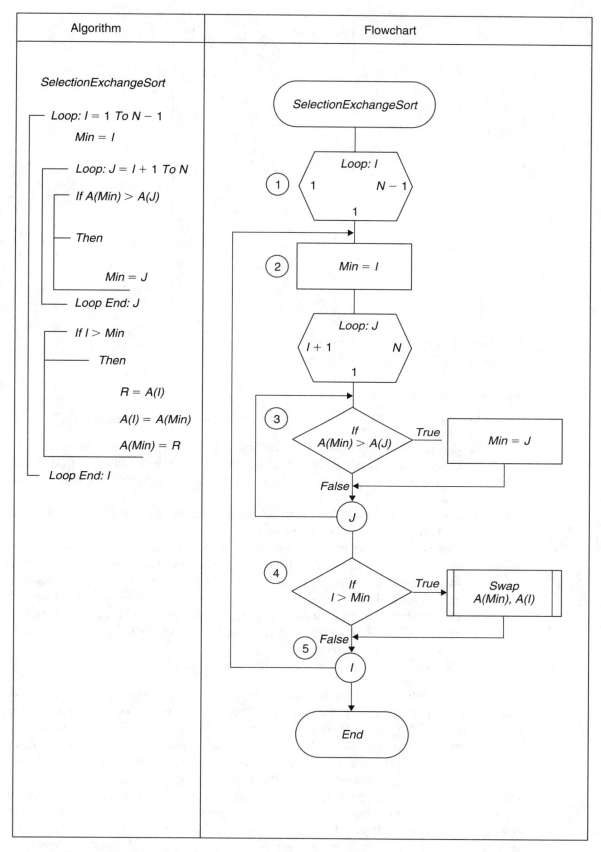

Figure 10.2a The Selection Exchange Sort

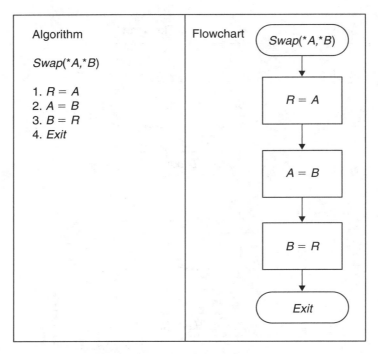

Figure 10.2b Algorithm and Flowchart for *Swap* Module

Notes on Figure 10.2a

The following notes explain the circled numbers on the flowchart of Figure 10.2a.

1. This loop is set up to start with the first element and continue to the second-to-last element. The last element will be in the correct order when the second-to-last element is in order, because there is nowhere else for the last element to be placed.

2. The initial start value for the minimum value is the value of the lowest element number of the unordered elements.

3. This is the comparison test. It tests to see if this value is less than the previously saved minimum value. If it is, then the element number of the minimum value is set equal to the present element number. If not, then the flow continues to loop back either to make another comparison or to drop out of the loop.

4. This test is to see if the minimum value is in an element other than the smallest element of this segment. If it is, then the two values are swapped; if not, then the elements remain the same.

5. The end of this loop increments the element number.

Bubble Sort

The next sorting technique we discuss is the *bubble sort*. Figure 10.3a shows the values of the array elements at the end of each iteration of the *J* loop. In Figure 10.3a, the first element (65) is compared to the second element (25). The first element is greater than the second and therefore they are exchanged. When *J* = 2, 65 is now the second element. The second element (65) is compared to the third element (34). The second element is greater than the third and therefore they are exchanged. The same is true for each of the values of *J*: Figure 10.3b shows the switches made in each pass using the bubble sort. The theory of the bubble sort is to compare each element with the next element. If the element is larger than the next element, the elements are switched. If not, they remain the same. After the first pass, the largest element has "bubbled"

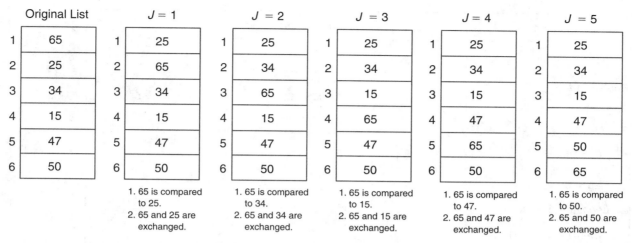

Figure 10.3a Example Pass, *I* = 1

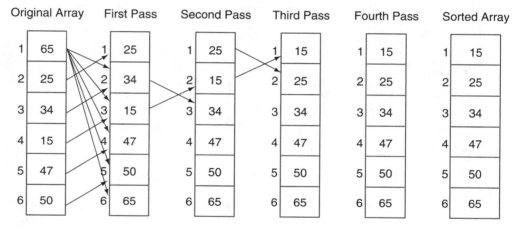

Figure 10.3b Bubble Sort

its way to the bottom. On the next pass elements 1 through $n - 1$ are considered because the nth element is the largest. The elements are again compared and the largest is bubbled down to the $n - 1$ element. A flag is set during each pass. If a switch has been made, another pass is made; if a switch has not been made, then data are in order and no more passes are made. During the second pass, only 15 and 34 need to be switched. All others are either in order or nearly in order. During the third pass 15 and 25 are switched. The value 15 now has bubbled to the top. During the fourth pass there are no switches; the flag has not been set, which indicates that the data are in order and no more passes need to be made. Figure 10.4 shows the algorithm and the flowchart for the bubble sort.

Notes on Figure 10.4

The following notes explain the circled numbers on the flowchart of Figure 10.4.

1. The flag is set equal to 1. This primes the loop so the test will pass the first time through.
2. The number of elements being compared is set equal to the number of elements minus 1. Since the comparison is always with one element and the next element, the last element does not need to be tested.

Algorithm	Flowchart

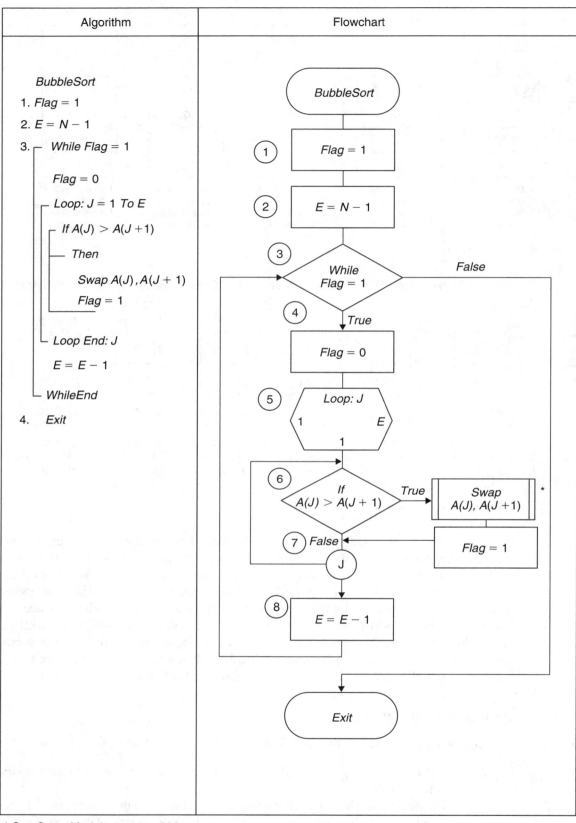

Algorithm column:

BubbleSort
1. *Flag = 1*
2. *E = N − 1*
3. ┌─ *While Flag = 1*

 Flag = 0

 ┌─ *Loop: J = 1 To E*

 ┌─ *If A(J) > A(J + 1)*

 ── *Then*

 Swap A(J), A(J + 1)

 Flag = 1

 └─ *Loop End: J*

 E = E − 1

└─ *WhileEnd*

4. *Exit*

Flowchart column:

BubbleSort

(1) *Flag = 1*

(2) *E = N − 1*

(3) *While Flag = 1* — *False*

(4) *True*

Flag = 0

(5) *Loop: J* — 1 — E — 1

(6) *If A(J) > A(J + 1)* — *True* — *Swap A(J), A(J + 1)* *

(7) *False* — *Flag = 1*

J

(8) *E = E − 1*

Exit

* See Swap Module on page 236

Figure 10.4 Algorithm and Flowchart for the Bubble Sort

3. The loop is set to continue as long as the flag is set equal to 1. This indicates that data are not in order.
4. The flag is set equal to zero. This says that data are in order until a switch is made and the flag is set equal to 1.
5. A loop is set up to compare the elements.
6. The comparison of the elements is made. When the present element is greater than the next element, the elements are switched and the flag is set equal to 1, indicating the data may not be in order yet.
7. The counter is incremented and the loop continues with the next element. If the elements have all been compared, the flow of the program drops out of the loop.
8. The number of elements to be compared is decreased by 1 because the last element of each loop is in the correct order.

Shell Sort

The last sort technique to be presented is the *shell sort*. Figure 10.5 shows the switches that have been made in each pass using the shell sort technique. The theory of the shell sort is to compare each element with another element in the data set using a gap to separate the elements. The gap during the first pass is the number of elements divided by 2. The truncated value is used. In Figure 10.5 the gap is 3 for the first pass since there are 6 elements. In the succeeding passes, the new gap is the old gap divided by 2. Again, the truncated value is used. In the second pass, the gap is 1 since the previous gap was 3. When two elements need to be switched, and there are elements a gap above the present element, then elements are compared upward until elements are reached that do not need switching. During the first pass the following comparisons are made:

1. *element 1 to element 4*—a switch is made (there are no elements a gap above element 1 so the next comparison is in order)
2. *element 2 to element 5*—no switches
3. *element 3 to element 6*—no switches

During the second pass the following comparisons are made:

1. *element 1 to element 2*—no switches
2. *element 2 to element 3*—no switches
3. *element 3 to element 4*—no switches

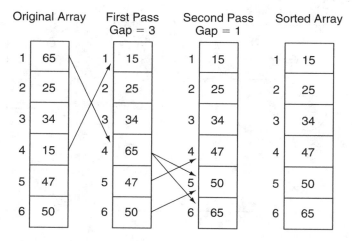

Figure 10.5 Shell Sort

4. *element 4 to element 5*—A switch is made and, because there are elements a gap above, the following elements are compared: the new value of element 4 to element 3—no switches; since no switch took place, the elements above the fourth element are assumed to be in order and the comparison continues in order.

5. *element 5 to element 6*—A switch is made, and other comparisons are made as above in 4.

At this time the data are in order. Figure 10.6 shows the algorithm and the flowchart for the shell sort.

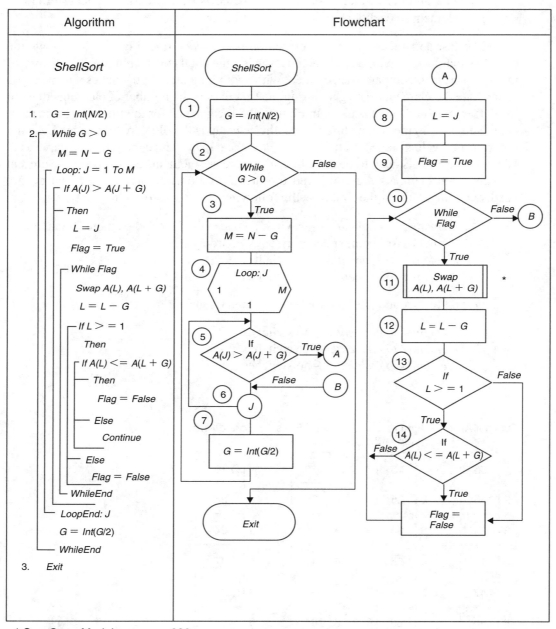

* See *Swap* Module on page 236

Figure 10.6 Algorithm and Flowchart for the Shell Sort

The following notes explain the circled numbers on the flowchart of Figure 10.6.

1. The gap is set to the truncated value of the number of elements divided by 2.
2. A loop is set up to continue while the gap is greater than zero.
3. The number of elements to be compared with another element is set equal to the number of elements minus the gap.
4. A loop is set up to start at the first element and continue to the element number set in note 3.
5. The comparison is made. If the element is greater than the element a gap below, then a switch needs to take place; if not, then the flow continues to the end of the loop.
6. The element number is incremented and the flow returns to the loop set up in note 4.
7. The gap is set equal to the truncated value of the last gap divided by 2. The flow then returns to the loop set in note 2.
8. *L* is set equal to the element number. This allows the comparisons with elements above the present element.
9. The *Flag* is set equal to *True* to prime the loop so flow will continue through the loop at least once.
10. A loop is set up to continue as long as *Flag* is *True*. *Flag* will be set equal to false when a switch is not necessary.
11. The switch is made.
12. *L* is set equal to the previous value of *L* minus the gap. This allows the checking to be made with elements above the present element.
13. This checks to see if there are any more elements to be compared.
14. If the elements need to be switched, the flow continues through the loop. If not, the *Flag* is set to *False* to stop the loop.

Stacks

stack

A **stack** is a list of numbers, such as an array of numbers, to which all additions are at one end and all deletions are at the same end. This is a last-in, first-out procedure. A stack is like a stack of plates: the last one added on the top is the first one to be used.

pushing the stack
popping the stack

When a value *(X)* is added to the stack, it is called **pushing the stack.** When a value *(X)* is used from the stack, it is called **popping the stack.** Once a number is used, it cannot be used again. The stack has a number, called the *stack pointer,* that points to the last value pushed and the next value to be popped. When the stack is pushed, the pointer is incremented and the value *(X)* being pushed is placed in the stack at the element number in the pointer. When the stack is popped, the value in the stack at the element number of the pointer is placed in *X,* and the pointer is decremented. Figure 10.7 shows a stack to which the following procedures have been implemented:

Push 3

Push 4

Push 7

Pop X

Pop X

Push 6

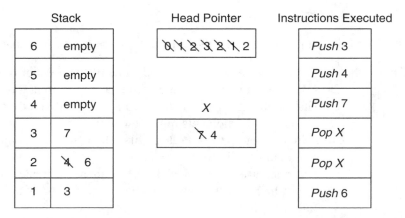

Stack		Head Pointer	Instructions Executed
6	empty	0̶ 1̶ 2̶ 3̶ 2̶ 1̶ 2	Push 3
5	empty		Push 4
4	empty	X	Push 7
3	7	7̶ 4	Pop X
2	4̶ 6		Pop X
1	3		Push 6

Figure 10.7 Example of a Stack That Has Been Pushed and Popped

Notes on Figure 10.8

Figure 10.8 shows the algorithm and flowchart to *push* the stack and to *pop* the stack. The following notes explain the circled numbers on the two flowcharts:

1. The *Error* flag is set to zero.
2. When the pointer is equal to the maximum number of elements in the stack, no more values can be pushed. An error message is printed, and the *Error* flag is set equal to 1.
3. When the pointer is not equal to the maximum number of elements, the pointer is incremented, and X is placed in the stack at the element number that is equal to the pointer.
4. The module is exited.
5. The *Error* flag is set to zero.
6. When the pointer is equal to zero, there are no values in the stack to be popped. An error message is printed, and the *Error* flag is set equal to 2.
7. When the pointer is greater than zero, X is set equal to the value of the element of the stack that has the element number of the pointer. The pointer is then decremented.
8. The module is exited.

Queues

Stacks manipulate data by the use of the *last-in, first-out (LIFO) principle.* Stacks act like a stack of plates: the last one on top of the stack is the first one you use. Queues manipulate data by the use of the *first-in, first-out (FIFO) principle.* Queues act like the checkout line in a grocery store—the first one in line is the first one to get served. Therefore, a **queue** is a list that adds data to one end and deletes data from the other end. (See Figure 10.9.)

queue

An array will serve as a queue, with two variables to act as pointers to the head and end of the queue. One method of implementing a queue is to always add to the bottom and delete from the top. After a deletion, the elements of the queue are all moved up one. However, this is time consuming and therefore not the best method. The method used in this text is a circular implementation of the queue. It adds to the bottom and deletes from the top until the queue has filled to the limit. At that time it starts adding to

Algorithm	Flowchart

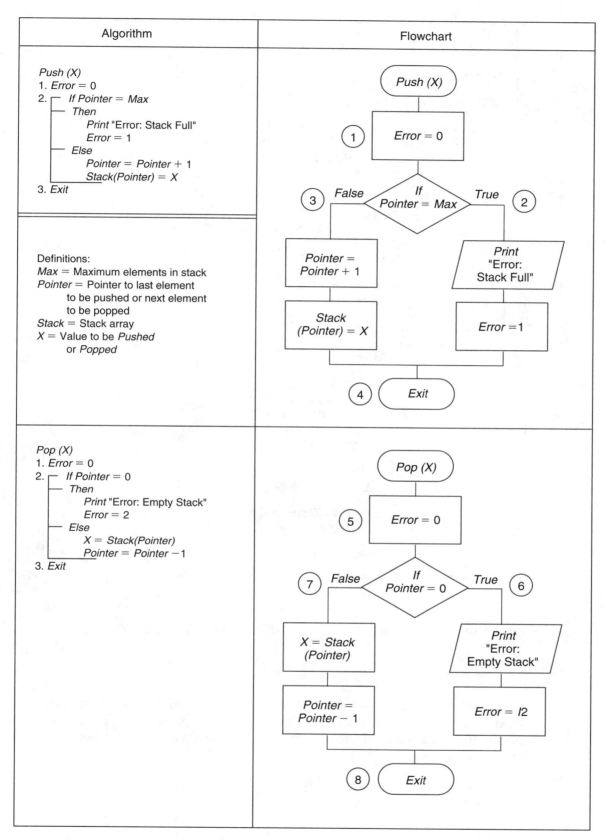

Push (X)
1. *Error* = 0
2. ⌐ *If Pointer = Max*
 ├ *Then*
 │ *Print* "Error: Stack Full"
 │ *Error* = 1
 ├ *Else*
 │ *Pointer = Pointer* + 1
 │ *Stack(Pointer)* = X
3. *Exit*

Definitions:
Max = Maximum elements in stack
Pointer = Pointer to last element
 to be pushed or next element
 to be popped
Stack = Stack array
X = Value to be *Pushed*
 or *Popped*

Pop (X)
1. *Error* = 0
2. ⌐ *If Pointer* = 0
 ├ *Then*
 │ *Print* "Error: Empty Stack"
 │ *Error* = 2
 ├ *Else*
 │ *X = Stack(Pointer)*
 │ *Pointer = Pointer* −1
3. *Exit*

Figure 10.8 Algorithm and Flowchart to Push and Pop a Stack

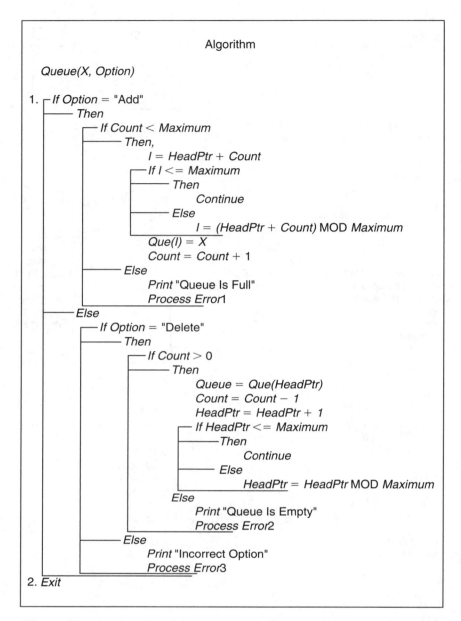

Figure 10.9a Algorithm for Additions and Deletions to a Queue

the top of the array, keeping track of where the head and the end of the queue are located. In this way elements are not moved from one place to another, as shown in Figure 10.9. The usage of linked lists (presented in Chapter 12) is another way to manipulate a queue.

Figure 10.9b Flowchart for Additions and Deletions to a Queue

Notes on Figure 10.9

Figure 10.9 shows the algorithm and flowchart of one method of how additions and deletions are made to a queue. The following notes explain the circled numbers on the flowchart. The module *Queue* has two parameters. The first is *X*, which is the value of the data to be added to the queue. *Option* is the flag to determine whether the user wants to add or delete data. If data are deleted, the value is returned in the name of the module, *Queue.*

1. Test to find out if data need to be added to the queue. When *Option* is equal to "Add," then the processing goes to circled 2.
2. Test to find out if the queue is full.
3. When the maximum length of the queue is equal to the number of values in the queue, the queue is full. Therefore, no more values may be added to the queue and an error occurs.
4. When the number of values in the queue is less than the maximum number allowed, then the element number where the new value is placed is set equal to the head pointer plus the number of values.
5. When the element number is greater than the maximum length of the queue, then the element number is recalculated. This allows the queue to wrap around, hence the circular implementation.
6. The new value is added to the queue and the count is increased by 1.
7. Test to find out if data needs to be deleted from the queue.
8. When *Option* equals something other than "Add" or "Delete," then there is an error.
9. Test to make sure *Count* is greater than zero.
10. When *Count* is less than zero, the *Queue* is empty. Therefore, data cannot be deleted from the queue and an error occurs.
11. The value is placed in the module name. Count is decremented and *HeadPtr* is incremented.
12. Test to find out if *HeadPtr* is greater than *Maximum* length of the queue.
13. If *HeadPtr* is greater than *Maximum* length, the value of *HeadPtr* is recalculated.
14. The module is exited.

Summary

Data are stored in many ways in both external and internal storage devices. These methods are called data structures. Internally, data are stored in single variables and arrays. Many times arrays need to be in order. This is accomplished through sorting techniques. The three techniques presented in this text are selection exchange sort, bubble sort, and shell sort. Stacks and queues are used to manipulate data. Algorithms for adding and deleting from stacks and queues have been presented in this chapter.

New Terms

popping the stack	queue	stack
pushing the stack	sorting	

Questions

1. What is a stack?
2. How does a stack differ from a queue?
3. Under what circumstances would you use a stack?

Problems

1. Identify the comparisons and the exchanges made to sort the following array using the selection exchange sort technique.

Number

23
45
13
5
56
74
10
30
65
40

2. Identify the comparisons and the exchanges made to sort the array found in problem 1 using the bubble sort technique.
3. Identify the comparisons and the exchanges made to sort the array found in problem 1 using the shell sort technique.
4. What would be the values found in a stack and the value of the stack pointer after the following executions:

Push 34

Push 54

Push 32

Pop X

Pop X

Push 10

Push 11

Pop X

5. What would be the values of a queue if the following were executed:

Add 34

Add 54

Add 32

Delete X

Delete X

Add 10

Add 11

Delete X

Chapter 11

File Concepts

Overview

Beginning File Concepts

Records as a Data Structure

Primary and Secondary Keys

Algorithm Instructions and Flowchart Symbols

Systems Flowcharts

Designing Records

Objectives

When you have finished this chapter, you should be able to:

1. Explain the concepts of records, fields, and files.
2. Explain the concept of a primer read.
3. Develop a systems flowchart.
4. Design an input record.

Most computer applications require processing of large amounts of data. Data cannot be held in the internal memory over a period of time because this memory is volatile. Data must be stored on an external storage source that is not volatile. This data is kept in files. Individual sets of data, called records, are then read into the computer to be processed or deleted, or new records are added to the files. Updating the files requires these records to be accessed. Records may be accessed sequentially, that is one after another, or randomly, that is to somehow choose the record to be processed. The computer can find the next record in the file or any record in which the record number has been identified. These records are another type of data structure. A record contains several pieces of data that can be manipulated at one time, which makes the finding, updating, and processing of data more efficient.

Beginning File Concepts

The basic concepts of data files include the following:

file

> *Files.* Data are stored in files. **Files** contain information pertinent to one application. Each file is divided into records. You might think of a file as a sort of table with the records listed vertically and the fields horizontally.

record

> *Records.* A **record** contains information pertaining to one entity in the file. Records are numbered from one to the maximum number of records in the file. Each record is divided into fields.

field

> *Fields.* A **field** contains one piece of datum. All records in a file have the same number of fields. Each corresponding field contains the same number of bytes, the same name, the same type of data, and the same format. That is, the first field in all records in a personnel file may contain the last name of an employee, the second field may contain the first name, the third field the employee's address, and so forth. The first field in all records is given attributes such as 25 byes, the field name of *LastName,* string data type, and so on. Each field has its own set of attributes. Only the field name must be a unique attribute.

Records as a Data Structure

The structure of a record is considered a data structure since a record is a way of storing data. The record is defined and given a name. It can then be referred to by the name or by its parts—the fields. It is defined by designating the fields and their attributes. Each field will have a name and can be used as an individual piece of data, or the record may be manipulated as a group of fields given the record name and number. The record name corresponds to the file, the file name, and the logical file number. There is only one record name per file. The individual records in the file are referred to by the record number. There can only be one record in the internal memory at a time.

Primary and Secondary Keys

key

A **key** is a value that is used in the solution either to arrange the file in order or to search through the file for a specific record. Each file has one or more key fields. A *key field* is the field in the record that is designated for the key. For example, the key field for a client file might be the field designated for the client number.

primary key

In order to find records, many techniques are used, including linked lists, binary tables, hashing, and others. Most of these techniques use a primary key to enable the program to find the needed record. The **primary key** is a field containing unique data for each record. Most techniques are ordered by the primary key. In that way a unique record may be found. The primary key may be an account number, a combination of last name and first name, the last name as long as there are no duplicates, or a computer-generated string value.

secondary key

Sometimes a record is accessed by a key other than the primary key. These other keys are called **secondary keys.** They may or may not be unique. In the case of the mailing list, a user may need a list of people living in a particular zip code area. In this case, the zip code would be a secondary key.

Algorithm Instructions and Flowchart Symbols

Several algorithm instructions and flowchart symbols have been covered so far in the text. In this chapter three more instructions will be added.

1. The *Open LFN* file name instruction tells the computer that the data in the file called *filename* is to be used, starting at the first record. *LFN* stands for

logical file number, a reference number to be used in the solution. It is used in the *Read* instruction and the *Close* instruction and refers to the file name in the *Open* instruction, which has the same logical file number. The *LFN* is used since there can be more than one file open at one time and the computer has to know which file to read from and which file to close. It is easier to use the *LFN* than to write the name of the file each time you want to reference it.

2. *Read (LFN) Record* copies the next record into the internal memory or into a small holding memory called a *buffer memory.* The use of the buffer memory speeds up the input processing.

3. *Close LFN* tells the computer that the file will not be used anymore. If a file is not closed, the data in the files may be lost. Once closed, the file may not be used again until it is reopened.

Table 11.1 includes all of the instructions and flowchart symbols covered so far.

Table 11.1 Algorithm Instructions and Flowchart Symbols *(continued on page 252)*

Algorithm Instruction	Flowchart Symbol	Definition (What the instruction tells the computer)
Start module name (module number)		Start processing a module.
Enter list of variables names		Enter data from a data block or from the keyboard into the following variable memory locations.
Variable = expression		Assign the value of the following expression to a variable location called the *assignment instruction*. A module may be processed as part of an expression, if there is a return value.
Write list of variable names		Write to the printer the values represented by the following variable names.
Print list of variable names		Print on the screen the values represented by the following variable names.
Process module name (list of parameters)		Execute the instructions in the named module and then return to execute the next instruction.
End/Exit		Stop the processing of the module. Processing ceases with the *End;* with the *Exit,* processing continues with the next instruction after the *Process.*

Algorithm Instruction	Flowchart Symbol	Definition (What the instruction tells the computer)
Return (variable)	(rounded rectangle)	Stop the processing of the module, place the value of the variable in the module name, and continue with the instruction continuing the module call.
If/Then/Else	(diamond)	When the condition is *True,* use one set of instructions; when the condition is *False,* use another set of instructions.
Continue	(rectangle) or no box	A placeholder. Does *no* processing and continues to next instruction.
Counter = Counter + 1 (*C = C + 1*)	(rectangle)	Increments the counter *C.*
Sum = Sum + Variable (*S = S + V*)	(rectangle)	Accumulates the values of the variable *V.*
While/WhileEnd	(diamond)	Repeat a set of instructions as long as a condition is *True.*
Repeat/Until	(diamond)	Repeat a set of instructions as long as a condition is *False.*
Loop: C = Begin To End *Step S* *LoopEnd : C*	(hexagon with *C*, *A*, *B*, *S*)	Repeat a set of instructions using a counter *C* that starts at *A(Begin)* and increments by *S(Step)* and *C* is greater than *B(End).*

Algorithm Instruction	Flowchart Symbol	Definition (What the instruction tells the computer)
CaseOf Variable *EndOfCase*	◇	Select a set of instructions to execute according to the value of the variable.
Open LFN, FN	▭	Tells the computer the data in the file named *FN* is needed starting with the first record. *(FN* is given a reference number called the *LFN).*
Read (LFN) *Record*	▱	Copy the next record into the internal memory from the opened file *LFN.*
Close LFN	▭	Tells the computer that the file corresponding to the *LFN* will not be used again.

Systems Flowcharts

systems flowchart

A **systems flowchart** indicates the flow of data throughout the entire computer system. This includes where the data are coming from (keyboard, disk drive, etc.), the name of the program to be processed, and where the information is to go (disk drive, tape drive, printer, etc.). Figure 11.1 includes some of the more common systems flowchart symbols. These include the keyboard, a disk drive, a tape drive, a printer, a program, and a monitor. Most of these symbols can be found on a flowchart template. Figure 11.2 shows an example of a systems flowchart. This chart shows that the data are read from the disk drive and processed by the report program. The results are printed on a printer and also written to the disk drive.

Designing Records

Designing Records

Recall that a file is composed of records. A record contains all of the data on a given subject, such as all of the employment and benefit information for one employee. Records are composed of individual items, called *fields*—for example, one employee's withholding status for income tax.

A programmer beginning to design a solution to a problem must first identify the data to be put in the files. It is important to design the record carefully to make sure all of the necessary data are included and the lengths of the fields are correct. The length of a field is measured by the number of character spaces an item in the field occupies when it is entered in the computer. For example, the length of the field for the field

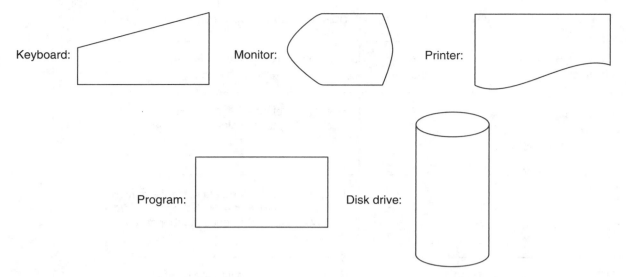

Figure 11.1 Systems Flowchart Symbols

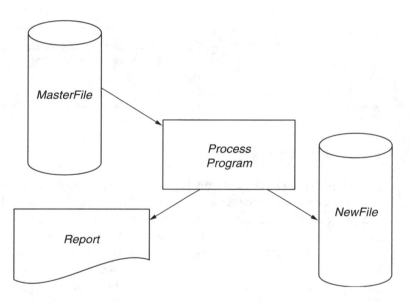

Figure 11.2 Example of a Systems Flowchart

name, *ZipCodeIn* (*in* for *input*), would be 10 characters long, allowing space in the field for a 9-digit code plus the underscore. The order of the fields is also important. When you fill out the Given Data section of the problem analysis chart, you will identify all of the data needed to process the file. Use the Record Data Dictionary and Record Layout (Appendix D, Figure D.6) to identify the name, length, data type, and so forth of each data field, and to design the record. These fields will become the record. Figure 11.3 shows the record data dictionary and the design of a record, the record layout, for a mailing list file. All records in a file will have the number of fields identified in the record data dictionary, so you design only one record.

When you are designing a record, there are many items to consider: the number of fields and their order, names, data types and lengths, and the total record length.

Record Data Dictionary

File Name: Mailing List

Field Number	Item Description	Field Name	Field Length	Data Type	# of Decimals	Comments
1	Last Name	LNameIn	15	C		
2	First Name	FNameIn	10	C		
3	Street Address	StAddressIn	20	C		
4	City	CityIn	20	C		
5	State	StateIn	2	C		
6	Zip Code	ZipCodeIn	10	C		
7	Telephone Number	TeleNoIn	12	C		

Record Layout

1 LNameIn 15	16 FNameIn 25	26 StAddressIn 45	46 CityIn 65	66 StateIn 67

68 ZipCodeIn 77	78 TeleNoIn 89			

Figure 11.3 Record Data Dictionary and Record Layout for a Mailing List File

1. The number of fields is the number of items you listed under the heading *Item Description* in the record data dictionary.
2. The order of the fields is determined by the order of importance of the data. Normally, the identifying fields will be first—those fields that will determine the order of the file, or the field that will be used to search for a specific record. Fields are also generally in the order of data entry, although this is not as important since the data-entry screen can be reordered.

 The problem will dictate the field used to order the file. If it is a mailing list, the field for ordering the file will be the zip code or the last name. The zip code field would be arranged numerically; the last name field, alphabetically. Also, the problem will dictate which fields will be used for a search. If the name of an individual is used to find the record, then the last name would be the search field. The fields used to order the file and the search fields are usually at the beginning of the record. The order of data entry would then be considered for the remaining fields.

3. The names of the fields should correspond to the item descriptions of the data. Part of the name should also indicate that it is input. The total hours worked might be written as *HoursIn,* or the rate of pay as *PayRateIn.* The field name is decided by the programmer. Any name is acceptable as long as it is an understandable name and can be read and interpreted easily by another programmer. The field name is used as a variable name in the solution.

4. The data type of each field is determined by the requirements of the solution. If the data type is numerical, then specify the number of decimal places. Field data types include numerical (numbers), character string (alphanumeric), and logical (*True* and *False*).

5. The length of the field is largely determined by the number of characters in the field. When the field is string character data, the length is determined by the longest piece of data that would be entered. For example, the length of the field *Salesperson name* would be at least as long as the longest name that would be entered into that field—such as Gullickson or Stanislovsky, at 10 and 12 characters long, respectively. String data are normally left justified in the field with the remainder of the field on the right filled in with blanks. If the programmer did not design enough space in the field and the data are longer than the field, then the computer will truncate the data on the right.

 When the data type is numerical, the length of the field must be large enough to accept the number of digits in the largest number that might be placed in the field. The length must include spaces for the decimal point and a negative sign. If the field is not large enough for the number, the computer will either return an error or truncate the number on the left. If the number is to be in scientific notation, four spaces must be included for the magnitude of the number, which is $E + nn$. The letter E stands for *times ten to the power of.* It is followed by a plus or minus sign and a two-digit number indicating the power of 10. Numbers are normally right justified in the field.

 When the data type is logical, normally the field length is one character—for T or F. If the date data type is used, the field length is predetermined, normally in the form of *MM/DD/YYYY.*

6. Records are normally stored in external memory in blocks or sections of a specific length. Normally the length of a block is 256 characters, but systems may differ. It is more efficient to transfer sections of data or blocks of data at one time than to transfer a character at a time from external memory to internal memory. The length of a block is determined by the operating system of the computer you are using, and therefore, the programmer has little or no control over this number. The total record length should be equal to or less than the number of characters in a block or else multiples of this number. That is, the total length of a record or block of records should be less than or equal to 256 or some multiple of 256. Planning record length this way saves space on the disk drive. If the length of a record is 260, for example, then each record will take two blocks of memory for storage. If the fields can be modified so the total length of the record is 256, which is only 4 characters less, the file will take half the space on the auxiliary storage device.

Summary

Concepts and terminology of record processing is an important aspect of applications on the computer. Most applications involve some type of file processing. Primary and secondary keys are used to find records that need to be processed. Good record design can increase the efficiency of the computer and therefore decrease time spent reading and writing to external storage devices.

New Terms

field	logical file number (LFN)	secondary key
file	primary key	systems flowchart
key	record	

Questions

1. What is the *LFN?* Why is it used?
2. Define a key and explain why it is used.

Problems

Design the input records and system flowcharts for the following problems:

1. The Eureka Lumber Company would like to calculate the gross pay for its employees. The input records should include the following: name, address, Social Security number, pay type (H = hourly, S = salary), pay rate, and hours worked.
2. A sales manager wants a program that lists all of the company's customers according to the salesperson assigned to each. The input file contains the following data: the customer's name, address, and telephone number, and the salesperson's name.
3. The Up-to-Date Department Store needs to convert its inventory from a manual system to a computerized system. The input record should include the following: the inventory number, the department number, the store number, the item description, the quantity, the wholesale price, the markup percentage, and the vendor.
4. A sales manager would like to be able to track the clients of each of his salespeople. He would like to know when each customer was last contacted, the outcome of the contact (not interested, sale made, call back later, no contact made), the sale amount if a sale was made, and the name and number of the salesperson.
5. Design the input record for a video/sound inventory for a TV or radio station. (CDs, DVDs, and VCRs are all used by the station.) How would this file be ordered?

Chapter 12

Linked Lists

Overview

Creating Linked Lists

Examples of Adding Data to/Deleting Data from Linked Lists

Algorithms and Flowcharts to Add, Delete, and Access Data in a Linked List

Objectives

When you have finished this chapter, you should be able to:

1. Develop a solution to a problem using a linked list technique.
2. Develop a solution to a problem using linked lists to access data.

Data are stored externally in files. In many applications these files hold large amounts of data. The problem now lies in how to update and access the needed data as fast as possible. The simplest way is sequentially—that is, to start at the beginning of the file and check each record until the correct record is found. Many times a file must be processed in order; therefore, the file must be accessed in order. The initial file should be in order; however, after adding and deleting records, the file has holes where the records were deleted and is unordered because of the addition of records. The problem now is how to add and delete records and still keep the file in order for processing. Using linked lists is one way of accessing an unordered file in an ordered manner. This chapter presents methods of creating the original file, adding records, deleting records, and processing the file using one or more linked lists.

Creating Linked Lists

linked list

A **linked list** is a file in which each record points to its successor, except for the last record, which has an end-of-list indicator. The method of pointing to the next record is a field, which contains the record number of the next record in order. This is called the

Rec. #	Key	Other Data	Link
1	5		2
2	10		3
3	17		4
4	25		5
5	30		6
6	35		0

ListPointer

1

EmptyPointer

0

0 indicates end of list.

Figure 12.1 Example of an Initially Created Linked List

linking field, since the value in this field links the records in proper order. Figure 12.1 shows a file that is a linked list. The file must contain a key field along with a corresponding link field. Notice that the link field of the first record points to the second record, which is the next to be processed. The link field of the second record points to the third record, which is the third record to be processed. The linking continues through the last record. The last record contains a zero, which indicates the last record in order.

Examples of Adding Data to/Deleting Data from Linked Lists

Changing Data in a Linked List

The advantage of a linked list is in the addition and deletion process. A file does not have to be physically rewritten to add and delete records. When a record is deleted, it is put into an empty list. The additions are placed in the records that have been deleted or at the end if there are no empty records. An empty records linked list is kept in the link field to locate the records that are available in which to place the additions.

If there are no empty records, the addition is placed at the bottom of the file. Figure 12.2 shows a file that has had additions and deletions. Notice the two linked lists—the data linked list is processed in the following order: 2, 1, 3, 7, 8, 6. The empty list is as follows: 4, 5. The data list starts at 2, which is designated by the *ListPointer.* The

Rec. #	Key	Other Data	Link
1	15		3
2	3		1
3	17		7
4	14		5
5	30		0
6	35		0
7	25		8
8	28		6

ListPointer

2

EmptyPointer

4

0 indicates end of list.

Figure 12.2 Example of a Linked List After Multiple Adds and Deletions

empty list starts at 4, which is designated by the empty pointer. The zero indicates the end of the list. Notice there is a zero in the link field for the end of each list. Figure 12.3 shows a file as records are added and deleted. Figure 12.3a shows the original file before any additions and deletions. Figure 12.3b shows the same file after all the following additions and deletions have been made. Each of the other illustrations in Figure 12.3 show one addition or deletion as indicated. The following additions and deletions are shown being completed:

1. Figure 12.3c: add 69
2. Figure 12.3d: delete 17
3. Figure 12.3e: delete 44
4. Figure 12.3f: add 37
5. Figure 12.3g: delete 29
6. Figure 12.3h: add 40
7. Figure 12.3i: add 90
8. Figure 12.3j: add 1
9. Figure 12.3k: add 16

Rec. #	Key	Other Data	Link
1	34		4
2	29		10
3	67		7
4	44		3
5	25		9
6	17		2
7	79		0
8	13		6
9	2		0
10	33		1

HeadPointer

8

EmptyPointer

5

Comment: Notice that records 5 and 9 are records that have been deleted in the past and are included in the empty list, even though there are data in the record. The used list skips these records.

Figure 12.3a Original File

Rec. #	Key	Other Data	Link
1	34		4
2	40		3
3	67		5
4	37		2
5	69		7
6	90		0
7	79		6
8	13		11
9	1		8
10	33		1
11	16		10

HeadPointer

9

EmptyPointer

0

Figure 12.3b File After the Additions and Deletions

Figure 12.3c Add 69

Figure 12.3d Delete 17

Figure 12.3e Delete 44

Figure 12.3f Add 37

Figure 12.3g Delete 29

Rec. #	Key	Other Data	Link
1 | 34 | | 4
2 | 2̶9̶ 40 | | 8̶ 3
3 | 67 | | 5
4 | 37 | | 3̶ 2
5 | 69 | | 7
6 | 17 | | 9
7 | 79 | | 0
8 | 13 | | 10
9 | 2 | | 0
10 | 33 | | 1

HeadPointer

8

EmptyPointer

2̶ 6

Figure 12.3h Add 40

Rec. #	Key	Other Data	Link
1	34		4
2	40		3
3	67		5
4	37		2
5	69		7
6	~~17~~ 90		~~0~~
7	79		~~6~~
8	13		10
9	2		0
10	33		1

HeadPointer

8

EmptyPointer

~~9~~

Figure 12.3i Add 90

Rec. #	Key	Other Data	Link
1	34		4
2	40		3
3	67		5
4	37		2
5	69		7
6	90		0
7	79		6
8	13		10
9	~~2~~ 1		~~9~~ 8
10	33		1

HeadPointer

~~8~~ 9

EmptyPointer

~~9~~ 0

Figure 12.3j Add 1

Rec. #	Key	Other Data	Link
1	34		4
2	40		3
3	67		5
4	37		2
5	69		7
6	90		0
7	79		6
8	13		~~10~~ 11
9	1		8
10	33		1
11	16		10

HeadPointer

9

EmptyPointer

0

Comment: In this case, since there were no more empty records, the new record was placed in an appended record.

Figure 12.3k Add 16

Algorithms and Flowcharts to Add, Delete, and Access Data in a Linked List

Figure 12.4 presents the algorithm and flowchart to create a linked list file and Figure 12.5 presents the interactivity chart and algorithms and flowcharts used to modify the linked list file. Follow the flowchart and algorithms in Figure 12.5b–k to see how the additions and deletions are accomplished as a computer program. In general, the steps to add and delete are as follows:

To add

1. Search to find where the new record will be logically inserted—if *NewRecord* > *ListRecord(R)*. (You need to remember the previous record number.)
2. Add *NewRecord* to the record number indicated by the *EmptyPointer* value.
3. Put the value of the *EmptyPointer* into the previous record link field of the previous record remembering the old value.
4. Put the value of the remembered old previous record link field (from step 3) into *NewRecord* link field remembering the old value.
5. Put the value of the remembered *NewRecord* link field (from step 4) into *EmptyPointer.*

To delete

1. Search to find the record to be deleted—if *DeleteRecord* = *ListRecord(R)*. (You will need to remember the previous record number.)
2. Put the value of the *EmptyPointer* into deleted record link field remembering the old value of the link field.
3. Put the remembered value of the old deleted record link field (from step 2) into previous record link field remembering the old value.
4. Put the remembered value of the old previous record link field (from step 3) into the *EmptyPointer.*

Remember these are general instructions. Refer to Figure 12.5b–k for the algorithms and flowcharts.

Notes on Figure 12.4

Figure 12.4 shows the algorithm and flowchart to create a linked list. The following notes explain the circled numbers for this figure.

1. Process a *Read* module, which opens the data file, enters all records for the file, and counts the number of records *(N)*. The file must have a key and an extra field for the link field.
2. The file is sorted in key order.
3. The *HeadPointer* is set to 1, since the first record would be the first record in order.
4. A loop is set up to process all records in order to add the correct link number in the link field. The loop starts with the first record and continues to the next to the last record, since the last record must have a zero to indicate the end of the list.
5. A record is read. The *Link* field is set equal to the record + 1, which would be the next record in order. The record is written to the file. The next record is then processed.
6. The last record is read. The *Link* field is set equal to zero. The record is written to the file.

Algorithm	Flowchart

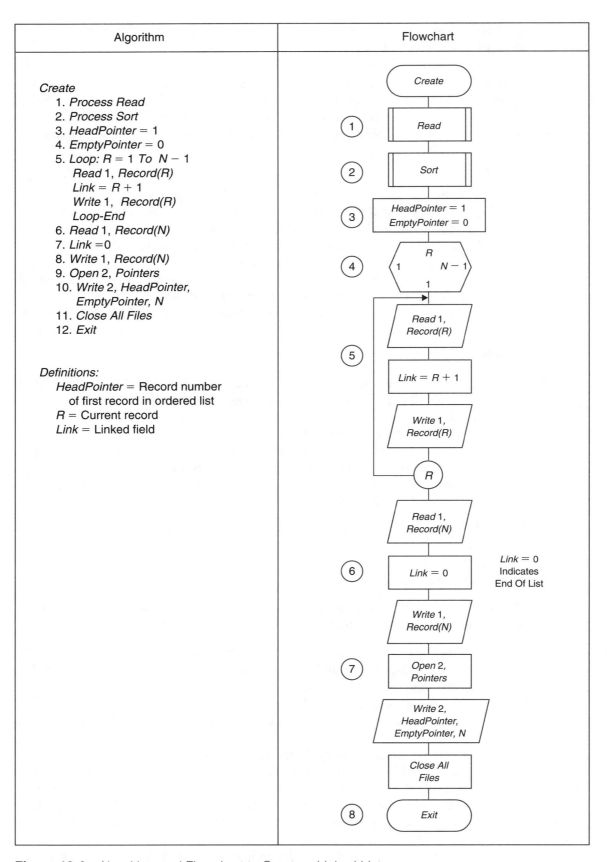

Create
 1. *Process Read*
 2. *Process Sort*
 3. *HeadPointer* = 1
 4. *EmptyPointer* = 0
 5. *Loop: R = 1 To N − 1*
 Read 1, *Record(R)*
 Link = R + 1
 Write 1, *Record(R)*
 Loop-End
 6. *Read* 1, *Record(N)*
 7. *Link =0*
 8. *Write* 1, *Record(N)*
 9. *Open* 2, *Pointers*
 10. *Write* 2, *HeadPointer,*
 EmptyPointer, N
 11. *Close All Files*
 12. *Exit*

Definitions:
 HeadPointer = Record number
 of first record in ordered list
 R = Current record
 Link = Linked field

Figure 12.4 Algorithm and Flowchart to Create a Linked List

7. The *Pointer* file is opened. The *HeadPointer, EmptyPointer,* and the number of records (*N*) is written to this file. All files are then closed.
8. The *Create* module is completed.

Notes on Figure 12.5

Figure 12.5 shows the interactivity (structure) chart, the algorithms, and the flowcharts for a program that processes and updates a file using a linked list technique. Figure 12.5a shows the structure chart for this program. The following are the notes explaining the circled numbers in Figure 12.5b–k.

1. The *Control* module for the LinkedList program.
2. Process the *Init* module.
3. This instruction primes the loop so the condition will be true the first time through the loop.
4. A loop is set up to continue to process or update the file until *Q* is entered for the choice in the *Menu* module.
5. The *Menu* module is processed, which prints the menu and allows the user to enter a value for *Choice.*
6. One of the modules is processed, according to the value of *Choice.*
7. The program is completed.
8. The *Init* module initializes values for the program.
9. The files are opened.
10. The values of *HeadPointer, EmptyPointer,* and *N* are read.
11. The *Pointer* file is closed, which ends the *Init* module.
12. The *Menu* module prints the menu and allows the user to enter a value for *Choice.*
13. The screen is cleared and the menu is printed on the screen.
14. A loop is set up to make sure a correct value is entered for *Choice.* When a correct value is entered the *Menu* module is completed.
15. The *Add* module allows the user to add a record to the linked list.
16. The new record number *(NR)* is set equal to the empty pointer. The data for a new record are entered through processing the *ReadNew* module.

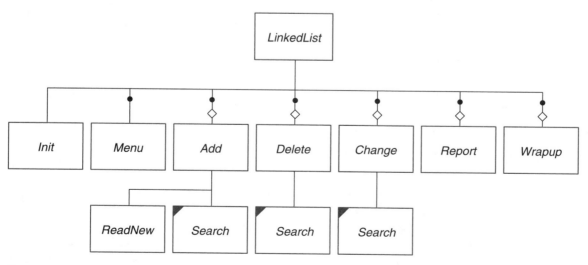

Figure 12.5a Interactivity Chart for Processing and Updating a Linked List

Algorithm	Flowchart

LinkedList
1. *Process Init*
2. *Choice* = "A"
3. *While Choice* < > "Q"
 Process Menu
 CaseOf Choice
 "A": *Process Add*
 "D": *Process Delete*
 "C": *Process Change*
 "R": *Process Report*
 "Q": *Process Quit*
 Case End
 While End
4. *End*

Definitions:
R = Present record
HeadPointer = First ordered record
EmptyPointer = First empty record
Choice = Menu selection
S = Error flag
 = 1: Record found
 = 2: Record not found
Link = Value of link field
Key = Value of key field
SKey = Search key
PR = Previous record

Figure 12.5b Algorithm and Flowchart of the *LinkedList* (*Control*) Module for Processing and Updating a Linked List

17. The search for the records that precede and succeed the new record is executed.
18. A test is made to see if there is a duplicate record. If there is, a message is printed and the *Add* module is exited.
19. If there is no duplicate record, a test is made to see if there is an empty record in which to place the new record. If there is no empty record, a record is appended to the end of the file. The number of records is incremented by 1

Algorithm	Flowchart

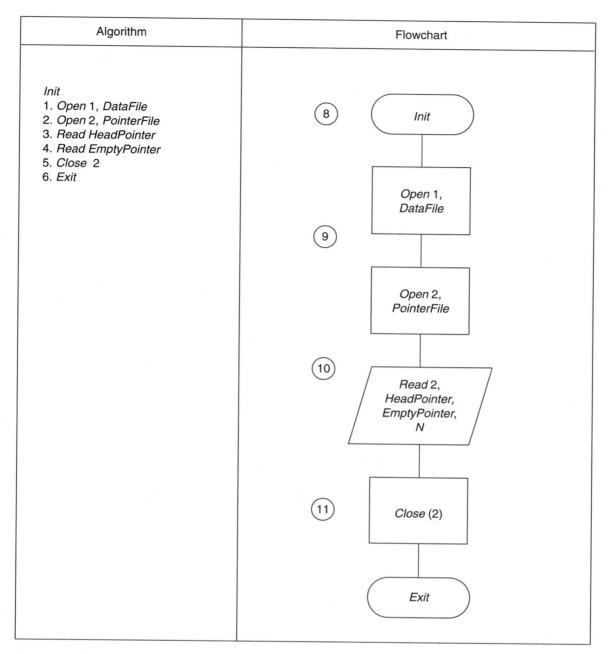

Init
1. *Open* 1, *DataFile*
2. *Open* 2, *PointerFile*
3. *Read HeadPointer*
4. *Read EmptyPointer*
5. *Close* 2
6. *Exit*

Figure 12.5c Algorithm and Flowchart of the *Init* Module for Processing and Updating a Linked List

and the new record number *(NR)* is set equal to the last record number, which is the total number of records.

20. If there is an empty record, the empty record is read and the *EmptyPointer* is set equal to the *Link* field value.
21. A test is made to see if the new record should be placed before the first record in order. If so, the *Link* field is set equal to the *HeadPointer,* the *HeadPointer* is set equal to the new record number *(NR),* and the record is written to the file.
22. If not, the link field of the previous record and the new record need to be updated. To do this, the new record is written to the file and the previous

Algorithm	Flowchart
Menu 1. *Clear Screen* 2. *Print Menu* 3. *Choice* = "Z" 4. *While Choice* <> "A" OR *Choice* <> "D" OR *Choice* <> "R" OR *Choice* <> "C" OR *Choice* <> "Q" *Enter Choice* *While End* 5. *Exit*	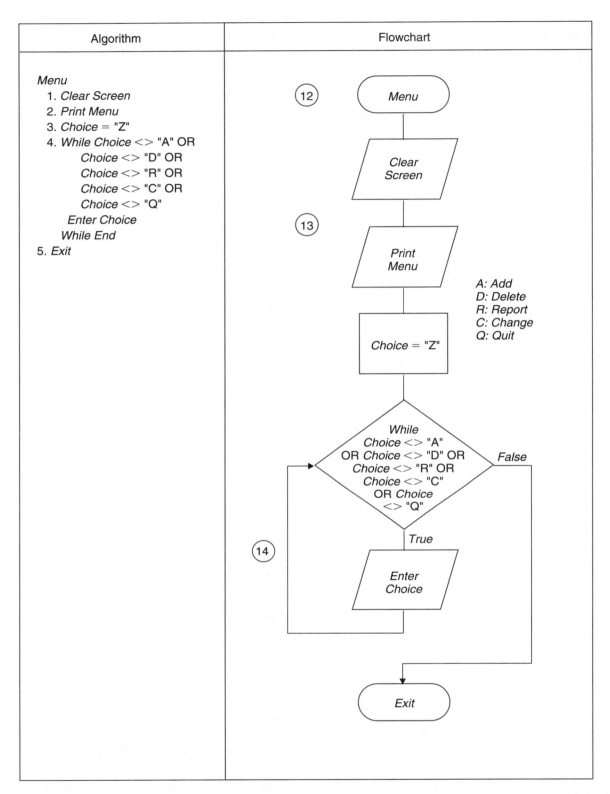

Figure 12.5d Algorithm and Flowchart of the *Menu* Module for Processing and Updating a Linked List

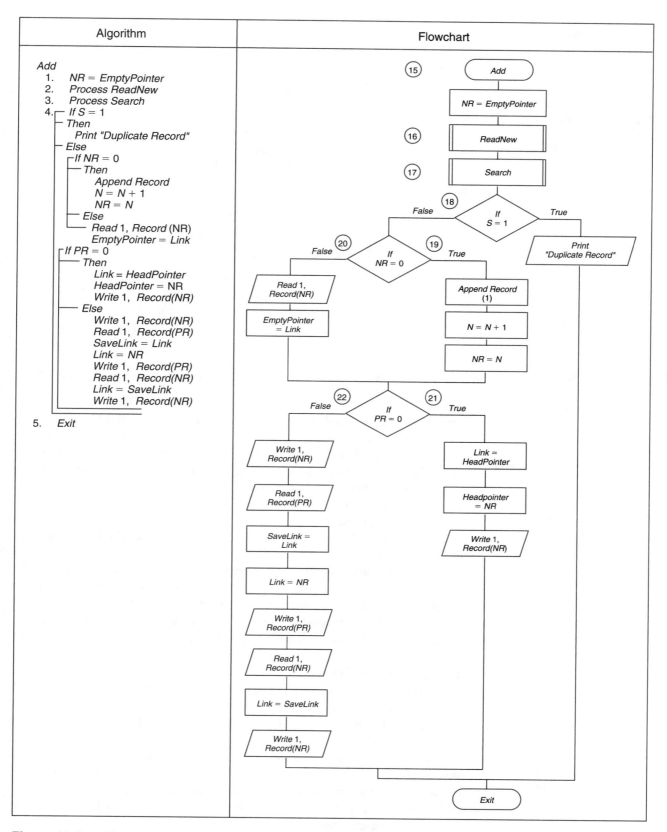

Algorithm	Flowchart

Algorithm

Add
1. *NR = EmptyPointer*
2. *Process ReadNew*
3. *Process Search*
4. *If S = 1*
 Then
 Print "Duplicate Record"
 Else
 If NR = 0
 Then
 Append Record
 N = N + 1
 NR = N
 Else
 Read 1, Record (NR)
 EmptyPointer = Link
 If PR = 0
 Then
 Link = HeadPointer
 HeadPointer = NR
 Write 1, Record(NR)
 Else
 Write 1, Record(NR)
 Read 1, Record(PR)
 SaveLink = Link
 Link = NR
 Write 1, Record(PR)
 Read 1, Record(NR)
 Link = SaveLink
 Write 1, Record(NR)
5. *Exit*

Figure 12.5e Algorithm and Flowchart of the *Add* Module for Processing and Updating a Linked List

Algorithm	Flowchart
ReadNew 1. *Read New Record Data* 2. *SKey = NRKey* 3. *Exit*	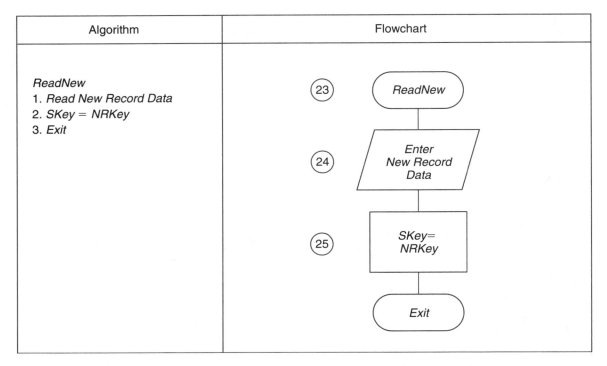

Figure 12.5f Algorithm and Flowchart of the *ReadNew* Module for Processing and Updating a Linked List

record is read. The *Link* field value is saved and the *Link* field is set equal to the new record number *(NR)*. The previous record is then written to the file and the new record is read. The Link field of the new record is set equal to the saved link value from the previous record and the new record is written to the file. This completes the Add module.

23. The *ReadNew* module enters data for the new record.
24. The new data are entered.
25. The search key *(SKey)* is set equal to the new record key. The *ReadNew* module is completed.
26. The *Search* module searches for a record using a search key value *(SKey)*.
27. The record number is set equal to the *HeadPointer*. The error flag *(S)* is set equal to zero, and the previous record number *(PR)* is set equal to zero.
28. A loop is set up to process the file until a record is found $(S = 1)$, or the key of the record is less than the search key $(S = 2)$, or the end of the list occurs $(S = 2)$.
29. The current record is read.
30. A test is made to see if the record has been found; if it has, *S* is set equal to 1 and the module is exited.
31. If the record has not been found, a test is made to see if the record key is less than the search key.
32. If it is not, *S* is set equal to 2 and the module is exited.
33. If it is, the record has not been found yet. The previous record *(PR)* is set equal to the present record number *(R),* and the end of the link is checked.
34. If the present record is at the end of the list, *S* is set equal to 2, *R* is set equal to zero, and the module is exited.
35. If present record is not at the end of the list, then the present record number *(R)* is set equal to the *Link* field value and the loop continues.

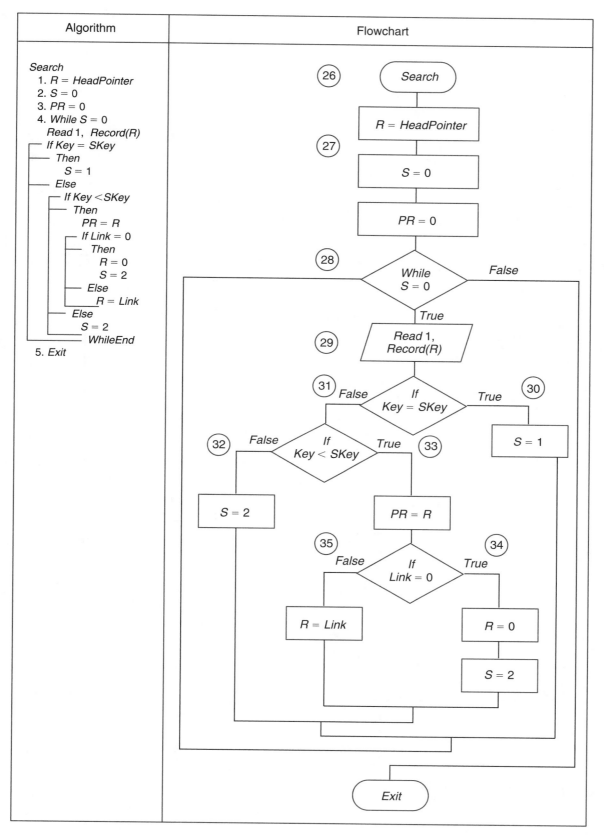

Figure 12.5g Algorithm and Flowchart of the *Search* Module for Processing and Updating a Linked List

Algorithm	Flowchart

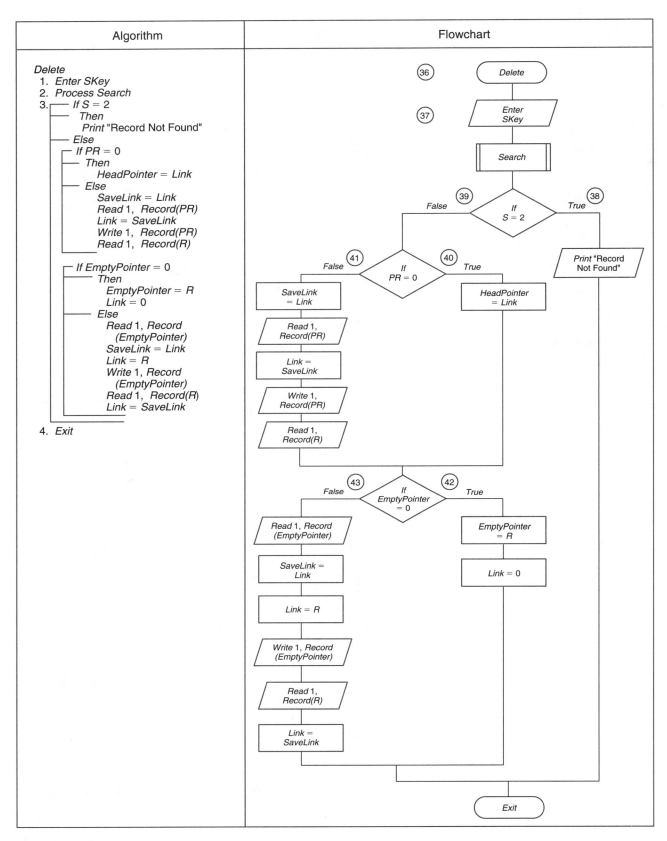

Delete
1. *Enter SKey*
2. *Process Search*
3. ┌─ *If S = 2*
 ├─ *Then*
 │ *Print "Record Not Found"*
 ├─ *Else*
 │ ┌─ *If PR = 0*
 │ ├─ *Then*
 │ │ *HeadPointer = Link*
 │ ├─ *Else*
 │ │ *SaveLink = Link*
 │ │ *Read 1, Record(PR)*
 │ │ *Link = SaveLink*
 │ │ *Write 1, Record(PR)*
 │ │ *Read 1, Record(R)*
 │ │
 │ ┌─ *If EmptyPointer = 0*
 │ ├─ *Then*
 │ │ *EmptyPointer = R*
 │ │ *Link = 0*
 │ ├─ *Else*
 │ │ *Read 1, Record*
 │ │ *(EmptyPointer)*
 │ │ *SaveLink = Link*
 │ │ *Link = R*
 │ │ *Write 1, Record*
 │ │ *(EmptyPointer)*
 │ │ *Read 1, Record(R)*
 │ └─ *Link = SaveLink*
4. *Exit*

Figure 12.5h Algorithm and Flowchart of the *Delete* Module for Processing and Updating a Linked List

Algorithm	Flowchart

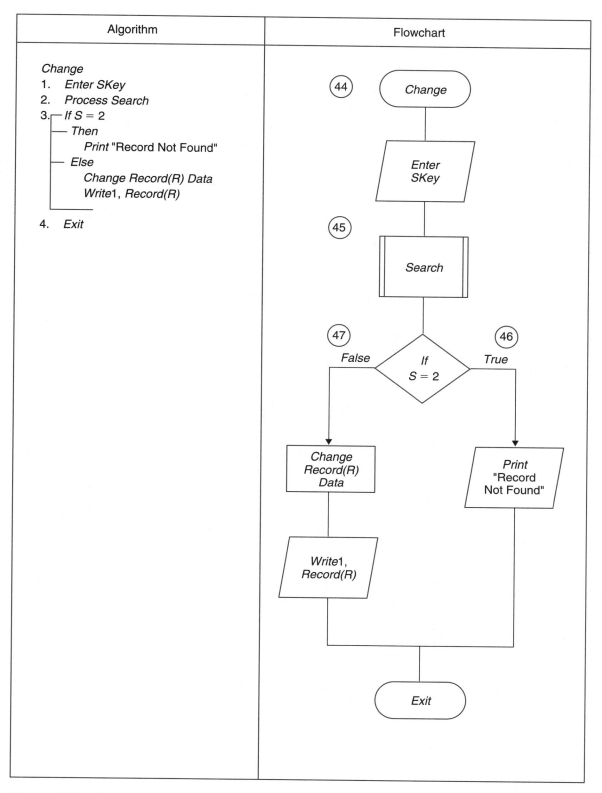

Change
1. *Enter SKey*
2. *Process Search*
3. *If S = 2*
 Then
 Print "Record Not Found"
 Else
 Change Record(R) Data
 *Write*1, *Record(R)*

4. *Exit*

Figure 12.5i Algorithm and Flowchart of the *Change* Module for Processing and Updating a Linked List

Algorithm	Flowchart

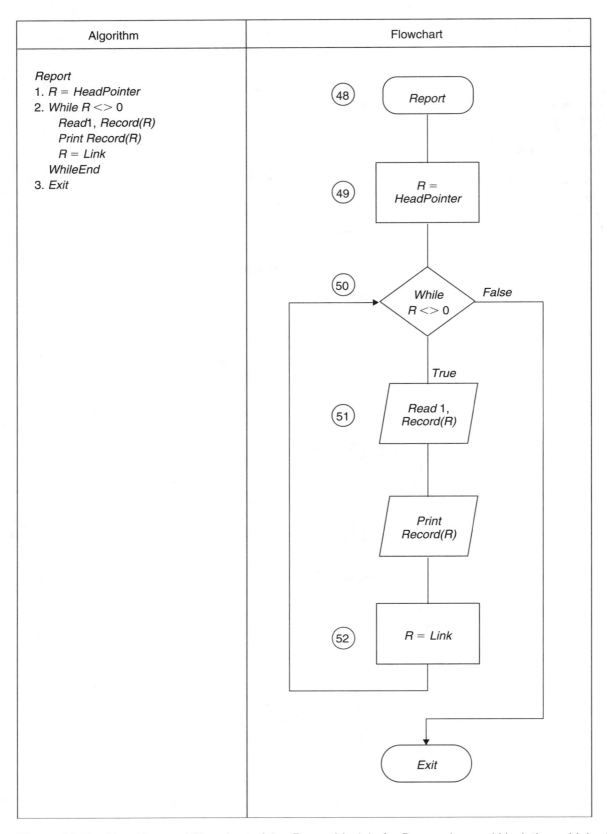

Report
1. *R = HeadPointer*
2. *While R <> 0*
 Read1, Record(R)
 Print Record(R)
 R = Link
 WhileEnd
3. *Exit*

Figure 12.5j Algorithm and Flowchart of the *Report* Module for Processing and Updating a Linked List

Algorithm	Flowchart
Wrapup 1. *Open* 2, *Pointers* 2. *Write* 2, *HeadPointer,* *EmptyPointer, N* 3. *Close All Files* 4. *Print* "Run Complete" 5. *Exit*	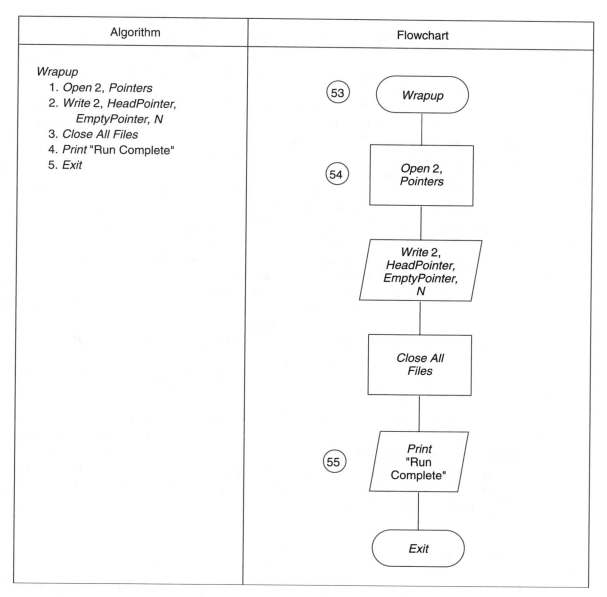

Figure 12.5k Algorithm and Flowchart of the *Wrapup* Module for Processing and Updating a Linked List

36. The *Delete* module allows the user to delete a record.
37. The search key of the record to be deleted is entered and the *Search* module is processed to find the correct record.
38. A test is made to see if the record was found. If it was not, an error message is printed, and the module is exited.
39. If a record was found, the link fields need to be updated. A test is made to see if the deleted record is the first record in the ordered list.
40. If it is, the *HeadPointer* is set equal to the *Link* field value.
41. If not, the *Link* field value is saved. The previous record is read. The *Link* field value is set equal to the saved link value. The previous record is written to the file, and the record to be deleted is read.
42. Next, the empty linked list needs to be updated. A test is made to see if the *EmptyPointer* is equal to zero. If it is, the *EmptyPointer* is set equal to the record number to be deleted and the *Link* field is set equal to zero.

43. If the *EmptyPointer* is not equal to zero, the *EmptyPointer* record is read. The *Link* field value is saved. The *Link* field is set equal to *R*. The *EmptyPointer* record is written to the file. The record to be deleted is read and the *Link* field is set equal to the saved link. The record to be deleted is written to the file. The module is exited.

44. The *Change* module allows the user to change data in a record.

45. A search key of the record to be changed is entered and the *Search* module is processed to find the correct record.

46. A test is made to see if the record was found. If it was not, an error message is printed, and the module is exited.

47. If the record was found, the data are changed, and the record is written to the file. The module is then exited.

48. The *Report* module processes a linked list in order.

49. The current record number is set equal to the *HeadPointer*.

50. A loop is set up to continue until the next record to be processed is zero.

51. The record is read, processed, and printed.

52. The current record is set equal to the *Link* field value and the loop continues until the value of the link field is zero.

53. The *Wrapup* module completes the program.

54. The *Pointer* file is opened. The values of the *HeadPointer, EmptyPointer,* and *N* are written to the *Pointer* file. All files are closed.

55. A message telling the user that the program run is complete is printed to the monitor. The module is exited.

The theory of linked lists can be expanded to include circularly linked lists, doubly linked lists, and multilinked lists. Circularly linked lists have no end. The last record is linked to the first record. This allows a search to continue from the last search, without starting at the first ordered record again. A doubly linked list has two linked fields. One is in ascending order, and the other is in descending order. Multilinked lists have multiple link fields, one for each way the file needs to be ordered.

Summary

Data files are kept in an external storage source. The use of linked lists is one method to add and delete records to a data file and still process the file in order. A linked list is a file in which each record has one or more fields in which is kept the pointer to its successor. In this way records may be deleted and new records added into the holes left by the deleted records or at the end of the file, and still the file will be processed in order.

New Terms

linked list

Questions

1. What is a linked list?
2. Does a linked list have to be in order? Explain your answer.

3. How does a circularly linked list differ from a singly linked list?

4. Under what circumstances would you use a linked list?

Problems

1. **a.** Using the following file and the name field, create the linked list in the Link #1 field. Designate the *EmptyPointer* and the *HeadPointer* for this link.

 b. Create a linked list for the debt in the Link #2 field. This will make the file into what is called a doubly linked file. Designate the *HeadPointer* for this link. Do you need another *EmptyPointer?* Explain your answer.

Rec. #	Name	Debt	Other Data	Link #1	Link #2
1	Dunlap	210			
2	Johnson	100			
3	White	125			
4	Green	275			
5	Smith	225			
6	Adams	25			
7	Black	400			
8	Cooper	50			
9	Bennet	350			
10	Olson	75			
11	Williams	175			
12	Nelson	200			
13	Holding	335			
14	Little	150			
15	Grey	250			
16	Brown	325			
17	Stone	300			
18	Smart	40			

2. Show the following updates on the file from problem 1:

Add:	Peterson	55
Delete:	Black	
Delete:	Adams	
Delete:	Stone	
Add:	Hudson	255
Add:	Neill	167

3. List the records that were compared when searching for Green. Use the file as updated in problem 2.

Answer problems 4–7 using the following data (add other data fields as desired):

1245	Hammer
1278	Screwdriver
1479	Saw
1098	Electric drill
3001	Electric saw
1174	Wrench
2023	Pliers
2488	Sander
5053	Sandpaper

4. Create a linked list using the inventory number for the order.

5. Add a linked list using the item description for the order.

6. Show the following additions to the file:
 a. 3423 Paint
 b. 3200 Paintbrush
 c. 6000 Drill press
 d. 1000 Nails

7. List the records that would be compared when searching for
 a. 3200 Paintbrush
 b. 2488 Sander

Chapter 13

Binary Trees

Overview

Creation of Binary Trees
Accessing Data in a Binary Tree
Traversal of Binary Trees

Objectives

When you have finished this chapter, you should be able to:

1. Explain how a binary tree is set up.
2. Develop a solution to a problem using a binary tree to search for data.

The use of binary trees is another method to update and access data files. Binary trees are more complicated to use; however, they tend to be faster when used with large amounts of data. They also are faster when a single record is often needed. Binary trees use two fields to indicate the next record to be accessed.

A tree structure uses a top-down or hierarchical structure for the data. The tree structure looks like an upside-down tree found in nature, with the root on top, the branches growing down, and the leaves at the bottom. A genealogy chart is an example of a tree structure. Each record is called a *node*. The top position is called the *root*. In Figure 13.1, the node with the key value of *G* is the root node. A node at a higher level in the tree is called the *parent*. Referring again to Figure 13.1, the node with the key value of *D* is the parent of the nodes with the key values of *B* and *F*. The nodes with the key values of *B* and *F* are called *children* since they are on a lower level in the tree. They are the children of *D*. The bottom nodes are called *leaf nodes*. A branch consists of the chain of nodes from the leaf to the root. A subtree consists of the chain of nodes from a node to the leaves.

Node
Root
Parent

Children
Leaf Node

Creating a Binary Tree
binary tree

A **binary tree** is a tree in which each node has, at the most, two children. Each record of the file has all of the regular data, including a key, plus two other fields. One holds the pointer to the left child node (called the *left node*) and the other holds the pointer to the right child node (called the *right node*). Figure 13.2 shows the data file that accompanies the tree diagram in Figure 13.1. Note that the root is midpoint at record 7. The left pointer for the root node is 4, and the right pointer is 11. These are shown as the children nodes of the root node in the tree diagram. The binary tree is in order when the left node is less than the current node and the right node is greater than the current node. Note on Figure 13.1 that this is always true.

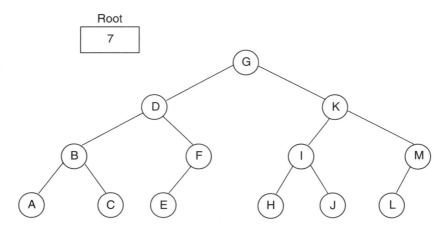

Figure 13.1 An Example of a Binary Tree

Record	Key	Data	Left Pointer	Right Pointer
1	A		*	*
2	B		1	3
3	C		*	*
4	D		2	6
5	E		*	*
6	F		5	*
7	G		4	11
8	H		*	*
9	I		8	10
10	J		*	*
11	K		9	13
12	L		*	*
13	M		12	*

Figure 13.2 File for Binary Tree in Figure 13.1

Notes on Figure 13.3

Figure 13.3 shows the algorithm and the flowchart to create a binary tree. The following notes explain the circled numbers on the flowchart for this procedure.

1. The *Create* module *creates* a data file with two pointer fields—the left pointer (pointer to the left node) and the right pointer (pointer to the right node).
2. Read the data for the file and count the number of records. Sort the file according to the key field.
3. Set the initial value of the lower bound (LB) to 1 and the upper bound (UB) to the number of records in the file (N).
4. Set the current node ($CNode$) to the whole number average of the lower bound and the upper bound. This is an integer division and therefore always rounds down.
5. The root node ($Root$) is set to the current node.
6. The node counter (C) is set equal to zero.
7. A loop is set up to continue to process the nodes as long as the node counter is less than the total records in the file.
8. The node counter is incremented.
9. The current node is read.
10. A test is made to see if the current node has a left child. If it does, the left pointer is set equal to the integer average of the lower bound and the current node minus 1. If it does not, the left pointer is set equal to zero, which indicates there are no more left nodes.
11. A test is made to see if the current node has a right child. If it does, the right pointer is set equal to the integer average of the upper bound and the current node plus 1. If it does not, the right pointer is set equal to zero, which indicates there are no more right nodes.
12. The pointers have values, and the record can now be written to the file.
13. The next node needs to be found.
14. When the left pointer is not equal to zero and the right pointer is not equal to zero, the new upper boundary is set equal to the current node minus one and the current node is set equal to the left pointer.
15. When the left pointer is not equal to zero and the right pointer is equal to zero, the values of the right pointer, the current node plus one, and the upper bound need to be saved by pushing the stack. The new upper boundary is equal to the current node minus one and the current node is set equal to the left pointer.
16. When the left pointer is equal to zero and the right pointer is not equal to zero, the lower bound needs to be set equal to the current node plus one and the current node is set equal to the right pointer.
17. When the left pointer is equal to zero and the right pointer is equal to zero and the stack pointer is equal to zero, all of the records in the file have been processed and the node counter is set equal to the total number of records in the file.
18. When the left pointer is equal to zero and the right pointer is equal to zero and the stack pointer is not equal to zero, the values of the upper bound, the lower bound, and the current node are popped from the stack.
19. The loop continues until the value of the node counter is greater than or equal to the number of records in the file.
20. The *Root* file is opened and the root record number is saved. All of the files are then closed.
21. The module is exited.

Algorithm	Flowchart

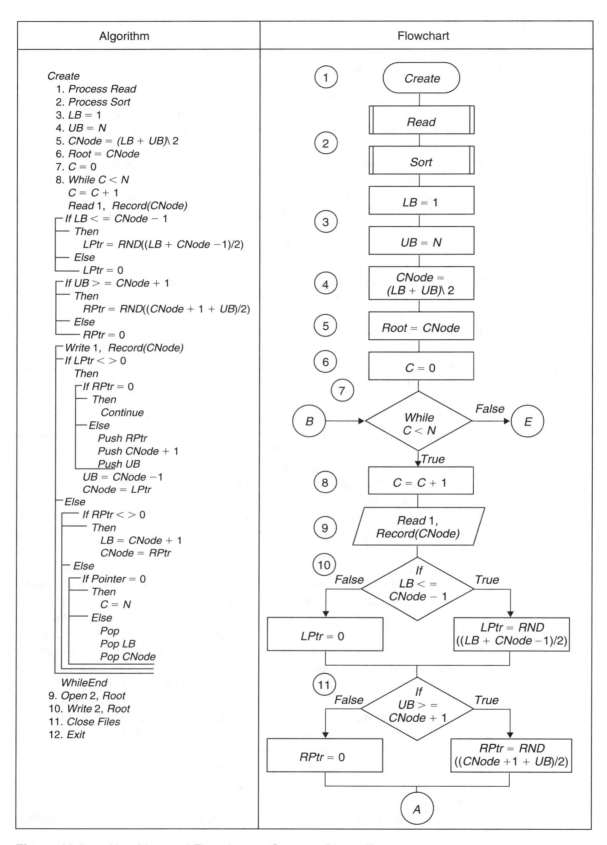

Figure 13.3a Algorithm and Flowchart to Create a Binary Tree

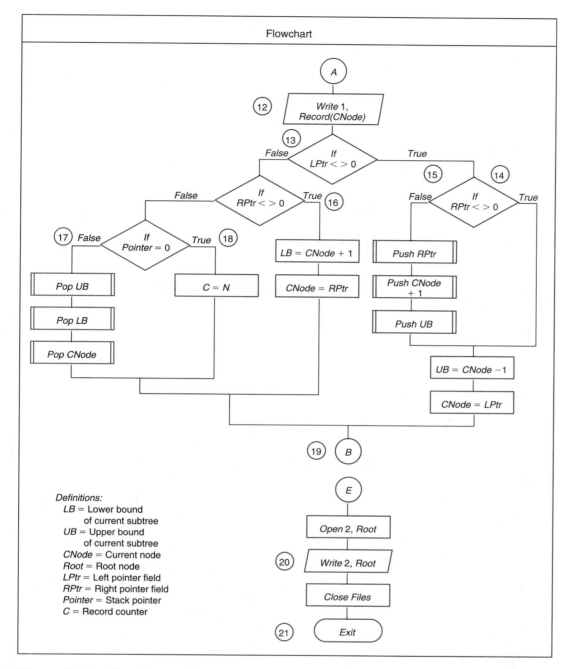

Figure 13.3b Flowchart to Create a Binary Tree

Figure 13.4 shows the tree diagram for the file found in Figure 13.5, which was created from the procedure in Figure 13.3.

Accessing Data in a Binary Tree

Accessing Data

One advantage of a tree structure is the search technique. Since all of the keys on the left of a node are less than the current node, and all of the keys on the right of a node are greater than the current node, the search can proceed down a branch, moving to the left and right according to the key. Using the file in Figure 13.5, the order of comparisons to

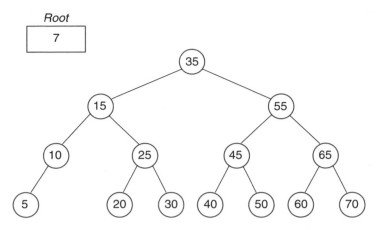

Figure 13.4 Binary Tree Created Using the Flowchart in Figure 13.3

Record	Key	Data	Left Pointer	Right Pointer
1	5		0	0
2	10		1	0
3	15		2	5
4	20		0	0
5	25		4	6
6	30		0	0
7	35		3	11
8	40		0	0
9	45		8	10
10	50		0	0
11	55		9	13
12	60		0	0
13	65		12	14
14	70		0	0

Figure 13.5 File for Binary Tree in Figure 13.3

find 30 would be 35, 15, 25, and 30. This would take four comparisons instead of six in a sequential search. To find the number 45, the order of comparisons would be 35, 55, and 45. This would take three comparisons instead of nine in a sequential search. As soon as the key value of the node equals the search key, the procedure stops.

Notes on Figure 13.6

Figure 13.6 shows the algorithm and the flowchart of the search module for a binary tree. The following are notes explaining the circled numbers in the flowchart of Figure 13.6.

 1. The *Search* module searches for a record given a search key.
 2. The current node (*CNode*) is set equal to the root node (*Root*).

Algorithm	Flowchart

Algorithm

Search
1. CNode = Root
2. PN = 0
3. S = 0
4. ┌ While S = 0
 Read 1, Record(CNode)
 ┌If Key = SKey
 ── Then
 S = 1
 ── Else
 ┌If Key < SKey
 ── Then
 CNode = LPtr
 ── Else
 CNode = RPtr
 ┌If CNode = 0
 ── Then
 S = 2
 ── Else
 Continue
 └
 WhileEnd

5. If S = 1
 Then
 Print Record Data
 Else
 Print "Record Not Found"

6. Exit

Definitions:
 CNode = Current node
 PN = Parent node
 S = Search flag
 1 = Record found
 2 = Record not found
 Key = Key of current record
 SKey = Search key
 RPtr = Pointer to right node

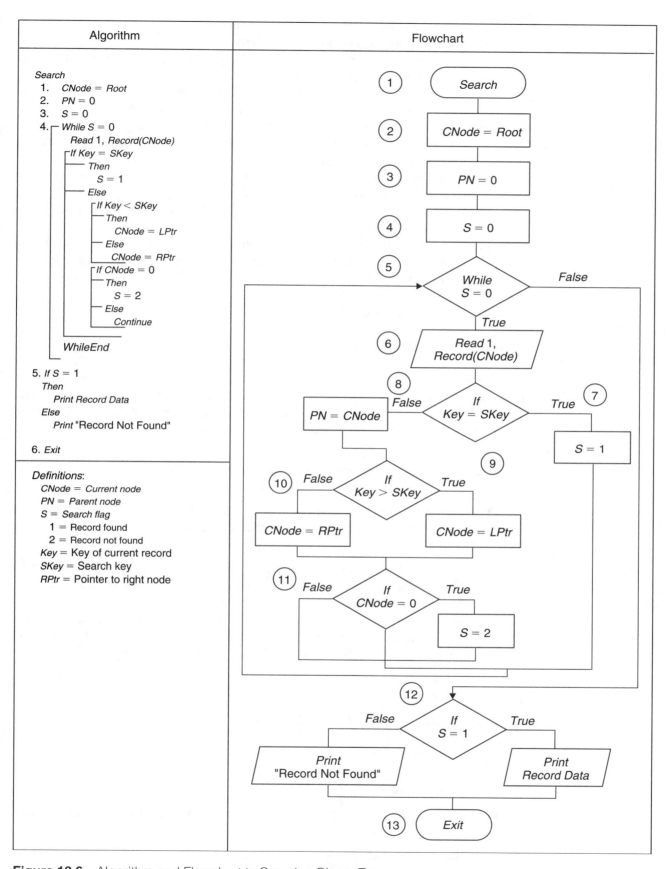

Figure 13.6 Algorithm and Flowchart to Search a Binary Tree

3. The parent node (*PN*) is initialized to zero.
4. The search flag (*S*) is initialized to zero.
5. A loop is set up to process the file as long as the search flag is equal to zero.
6. The current node record is read.
7. If the key of the current node is equal to the search key, the record has been found. The search flag is set equal to 1, indicating that the record has been found.
8. If the key of the current node is not equal to the search key, the parent node is set equal to the current node and a new current node is located. (The value of the parent node is required if you are adding or deleting records.)
9. If the key of the current node is less than the search key, then the next node to be compared is found at the left pointer.
10. If the key of the current node is greater than the search key, then the next node to be compared is found at the right pointer.
11. If the new current node is equal to zero, the record could not be found. The search flag is set equal to 2, indicating that the record could not be found.
12. If the search flag is 1, the record data are printed; if not, a message is printed stating that the record could not be found.
13. The module is exited.

Traversal of Binary Trees

traversal

Records in a file need to be processed. If a report is needed, this processing will most likely need to be in order. However, a binary tree can be processed in any of several orders. The processing of each node once in an orderly manner is called tree **traversal.** Every *traversal* algorithm faces three choices at each node:

1. Process the node.
2. Follow the left branch (follow the left node).
3. Follow the right branch (follow the right node).

Whichever of these three choices is taken, the other two must be completed at a later time. It is the order of these choices that specifies the traversal method. Three traversal methods are as follows:

Preorder

Inorder

Postorder

1. *Preorder.* The node is processed first, then the left branch, and then the right branch. This is abbreviated as *NLR* and represents the choices in 1, 2, 3 order.
2. *Inorder.* The left branch is processed first, then the node, and finally the right branch. This is abbreviated as *LNR* and represents the choices in 2, 1, 3 order.
3. *Postorder.* The left branch is processed first, then the right branch, and finally the node. This is abbreviated as *LRN* and represents the choices in 3, 2, 1 order.

The following list shows the order of the binary tree in Figure 13.1 when it is processed in each of the three methods:

1. *Preorder (NLR).* GDBACFEKIHJML
2. *Inorder (LNR).* ABCDEFGHIJKLM
3. *Postorder (LRN).* ACBEFDHJILMKG

Notes on Figure 13.7

Figure 13.7 shows the algorithm and the flowchart to process an inorder traversal of a binary tree. The following are notes for Figure 13.7:

1. The *Report* module processes the binary tree using an inorder traversal method.
2. The stack is initialized to zero.

Algorithm	Flowchart

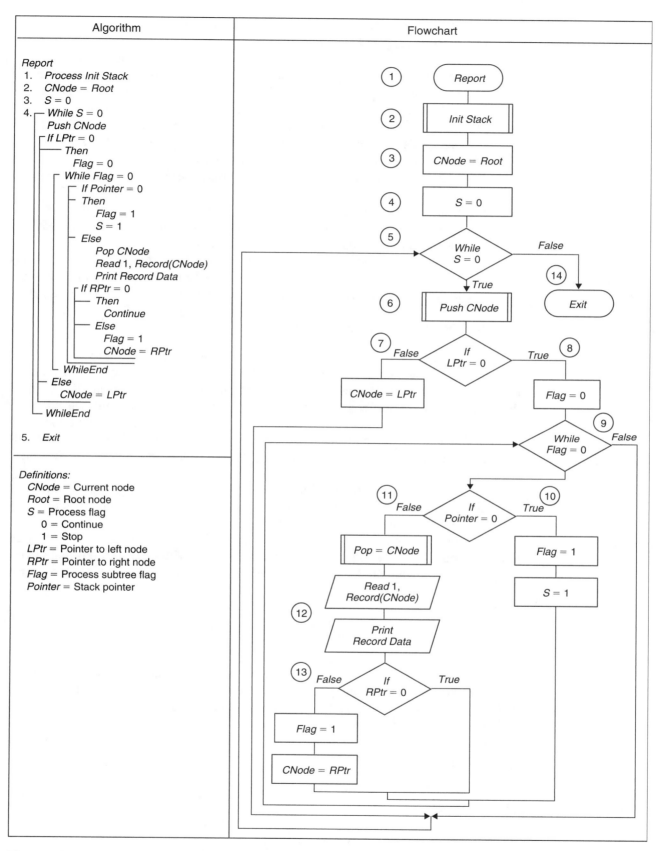

Algorithm (left column):

Report
1. *Process Init Stack*
2. *CNode = Root*
3. *S = 0*
4. ─ *While S = 0*
 Push CNode
 ┌ *If LPtr = 0*
 └── *Then*
 Flag = 0
 ┌── *While Flag = 0*
 ┌── *If Pointer = 0*
 ├── *Then*
 Flag = 1
 S = 1
 ├── *Else*
 Pop CNode
 Read 1, Record(CNode)
 Print Record Data
 ┌── *If RPtr = 0*
 ├── *Then*
 Continue
 └── *Else*
 Flag = 1
 CNode = RPtr
 └── *WhileEnd*
 ┌ *Else*
 CNode = LPtr
 └── *WhileEnd*

5. *Exit*

Definitions:
CNode = Current node
Root = Root node
S = Process flag
 0 = Continue
 1 = Stop
LPtr = Pointer to left node
RPtr = Pointer to right node
Flag = Process subtree flag
Pointer = Stack pointer

Figure 13.7 Algorithm and Flowchart to Process a Binary Tree in Order

3. The current node (*CNode*) is set equal to the root node.
4. The process flag is set equal to zero.
5. A loop is set up to process the file as long as the process flag is zero.
6. The current node is pushed into the stack. This is to keep track of where to return since the current node is the middle choice and needs to be processed.
7. If the left pointer is not zero, the current node is set equal to the left pointer.
8. If the left pointer is zero, either the end of the file is found, or a node is found that needs to be processed. A process branch flag is set equal to zero.
9. A loop is set up to process the nodes in the stack.
10. If the stack pointer is zero, all of the records have been processed. The process stack nodes flag (*Flag*) is set equal to 1 as is the process stack flag (*S*).
11. If the stack pointer is not zero, then a node needs to be processed.
12. The stack is popped with the current node. The current node data are read and the data are printed.
13. If the right pointer of the current node is zero, the next node to be processed is in the stack. If not, the right node needs to be processed. The process stack nodes flag is set equal to 1, and the current node is set equal to the right pointer.
14. The *Report* module is exited.

The binary tree of Figure 13.7 is balanced since there is no more than one node difference between the number of nodes on the right from the number of nodes on the left. When nodes are added and deleted, the tree tends to become unbalanced. The more the imbalance, the less effective the tree becomes. Therefore, the tree either needs to be balanced as the nodes are added or deleted, or the tree needs to be balanced periodically. There are standard techniques for these processes. Because of the complexities of balancing a binary tree, this text does not present the algorithms and flowcharts to update a binary tree.

More complex trees use multilinked tree structure techniques. In a multilinked tree structure, one node can have many children. This fact adds much complexity to the techniques of processing and updating these files.

hashing **Hashing** is another technique used with list. An algorithm for a formula is devised to find the correct record to retrieve. The major problem with this method is that of creating an algorithm that produces a unique record number, since two records cannot have the same record number.

Summary

Chapter 12 presented linked lists as a method to process data files. The use of binary trees is another method. A binary tree has two fields, one of which points to the left node and the other to the right node, that are used to process records. The method of traversal is determined by how the nodes need to be processed. The methods discussed in this chapter include preorder, inorder, and postorder. The use of multilinked trees is another method of processing data files.

New Terms

binary tree hashing traversal

Questions

1. What is a binary tree?
2. Does a binary tree have to be in order? Explain your answer.
3. Under what circumstances would you use a binary tree?

Problems

1. Using the master file found in problem 1, Chapter 12, develop the two pointer fields for a binary tree. Draw the tree diagram for this file.
2. List the records that were compared when searching for Green. (Use the tree developed in problem 1.)
3. Draw a binary tree using both the data in the table and the additions in problem 6 in Chapter 12.
4. Create a table for the binary tree in problem 3.
5. Using the binary tree created in problem 4, list the records that would be compared when searching for
 a. 3200 Paintbrush
 b. 2488 Sander

Unit Three

Supplementary Exercises

Develop a complete solution, including a data dictionary, to the following problems:

1. Have the computer deal four hands of 13 cards each. The deck should be randomly set up. Check to make sure there are no duplicate cards in the deck. You will need to use the random number generator and arrays.

2. Given a two-dimensional table, look up a value given a number corresponding to the first row and a number corresponding to the first column. Accept only values that are equal to the values found in the table (see Chapter 9—Table Look-up Technique).

 Example: *RowNumber* = 25 *ColNumber* = 100

 TABLE:

0	10	50	100	200	400
5	65	78	98	67	54
10	99	54	36	77	65
15	55	66	75	87	43
25	34	44	53	32	75
50	54	65	76	87	34

 THE ANSWER WOULD BE: 53

3. Modify the solution in problem 2 to accept values of *RowNumber* and *ColNumber* that are not exactly equal to one of the values found in the table.

4. The president of a college would like to know the age distribution of the students. Complete a solution using the frequency distribution technique to output the needed results.

5. Create a linked list of the following data. The data will be in ascending order by temperature.

Day	Temperature
Nov. 28	33
Nov. 29	38
Nov. 30	30
Dec. 1	43
Dec. 2	48
Dec. 3	42
Dec. 4	40

Delete all November readings and add:

Dec. 5	35
Dec. 6	33
Dec. 7	40

6. Create a binary tree using all data found in problem 5

UNIT FOUR

DATABASE MANAGEMENT SYSTEMS

Chapter 14

Database Management Systems

Overview

Why a DBMS?
DBMS Components
DBMS Models
Client–Server Model
DBMS Tasks

Objectives

When you have finished this chapter, you should be able to:

1. Define the components of a DBMS.
2. Understand why a DBMS is used.
3. Define the DBMS models.
4. Understand the tasks of a DBMS.
5. Understand the Client–Server model as it relates to DBMS.

One of the major requirements of a computer system is to manage large amounts of data efficiently. Today this is done for the most part through the use of database management systems. The major goal of a database management system (DBMS) is to gather large amounts of data and be able to process and update this data efficiently and by more than one person simultaneously. Another major goal of a database management system is to have the foundation of a future application already programmed. This includes the way the data is entered, stored, and accessed. From there a specific application can be built to suit the company or individual's needs.

Database Management Systems (DBMS) software is a data organizer. The primary function of a DBMS is to store large quantities of data, organize data, protect data integrity, and secure the data. This software is the key to many businesses. Business use of DBMS includes inventory management, client and sales tracking, financial management, and personnel management to name a few. Personal use of DBMS includes lists of address, CD collection, recipes collections, home inventory, and book collection, to name a few. A database management system in its simplest form usually consist of two parts, the "data" itself and the "client" to access the data. We see this access in daily life whenever we use the Internet, the browser being the "client" and the webpage being the server. There are, in fact, more "layers" involved when you access data via the Internet, but we will discuss that in Chapter 15. When a problem arises that requires the organization of large amounts of data, the primary software solution is the use of a DBMS.

Programming is necessary to use a DBMS efficiently. The language depends upon the database software in use. Structured Query Language (SQL) is rapidly becoming the standard language for accessing relational data industry wide. The modules that are necessary to develop depend upon the application and are tied to parts of the DBMS. It is important for a programmer to understand database theory because databases are the key to many Internet and business problems and because it takes programming to efficiently implement a database as a solution to a problem.

Why a DBMS?

The growth of businesses, along with their increased use of computers, has led to a significant increase in the demand for database management systems. The benefits of a DBMS include

1. *Centralization of data.* A DBMS allows the user to store all the data in an external storage device on a single computer instead of in many files on numerous computers at several locations. This reduces the number of times data has to be entered and updated, which reduces the possibility of errors. It also means that everyone working on the data can access up-to-date data simultaneously.
2. *Increased reliability of data.* It is important that data are reliable and as up to date as possible for everyone who needs to access the database. A company's reputation is in jeopardy if unreliable data are distributed.
3. *Decrease in redundancy of data.* A DBMS decreases the overlap of data. When several files contain the same data, then every file must be updated. With a DBMS, data are located in only one place.
4. *Simultaneous access of data.* A DBMS allows many people to access and update the same data simultaneously. This increases the productivity of individuals working with the database.
5. *Increased security of data.* A DBMS has security measures built in, so there is control over who may access and update specific data. Only a few appropriate people should have access to sensitive data. Also, only a few people should be allowed to change data in the database. A DBMS has passwords built in at different levels to increase the security of the data.
6. *Increased performance of data access.* A DBMS has the ability to allow fast access to the data through the use of indexing and built-in procedures that allow for extremely fast retrieval of large amount of preformatted and/or

summarized data. Without this performance, centralization of data in a geographically large organization would be difficult, and a distributed data model would be required, which has a number of reliability issues.

7. *Increased data integrity.* A DBMS has the ability to protect itself from "bad data" through the use of *transactions, constraints,* and *triggers,* which will be discussed in Chapter 15.

These are important reasons to implement a DBMS; however, because of these reasons, a DBMS becomes complex very quickly. Consequently, it is expensive to implement and maintain a DBMS.

DBMS Components

Entities
Attributes

A database is developed to store data. Just as the name implies, it stores data that needs to be retrieved at a later date. Items in the database that have one or more data values attached to them, such as an inventory item, an employee, a place, a thing, and so on, are called *entities.* Each entity has *attributes.* The attributes are data items that are required to be associated with the entity. For example, the attributes of a client entity might be last name, first name, street address, city, state, zip code, sales rep, and so forth. An entity set is a collection of related entities. An entity set may be inventory items, employees, clients, and so on.

field
record
table

This terminology is standard for database theory. However, you will find other terms used informally by the developers of specific DBMS. In this text we will refer to more informal names. An attribute is *a* **field.** An entity is *a* **record.** An entity set is *a* **table.** A database is a collection of related tables. For example, you might have a CD table. Each entity or record contains the attributes or fields about one CD. Each attribute or field contains one piece of data about the entity such as the name of the CD or its producer. Fields may contain entered numbers, text, images, hyperlinks, dates, or times, or may be results calculated using other fields.

property

Fields may contain entered numbers, text, images, hyperlinks, dates (datetime), or they may be the result of a calculation using other fields. These are called **properties** of the field, and a database designer will assign theses field properties carefully when creating the fields in a table. The importance of data design becomes apparent when you consider the potential for large amounts of data that will be collected over time. Many database languages reserve space for data not entered into a record, thus files sizes can bloat, causing space allocation issues as well as performance issues. More sophisticated database languages have the field *properties* to allow for dynamic space reservation, such that space is only used if needed. However, the designer has to know how to use these *properties* to attain the desired result. Some other property "gotchas:" consider a field to collect Social Security Number. Because we all know this is a number, we assume that the field would be a number. There are a few problems with this assumption. First, SSN is formatted as "999-99-9999," so to store this we would need to be a character field to accommodate the "-" entry, or you could save just the number part of the entry and then format the input and output to display the hyphens as needed. This would presumably work, but what if an SSN were 009-45-0345? If the field type was numeric, the database would drop off the leading zeros and store 9450345. Then, when you wanted to view this using a report of screen, the formatting would not know (necessarily) how to display the leading positions in the number. This would mean every report or screen designed to display SSN would have to know how to deal with the underlying data. If the data was stored as character data—i.e., "009-45-0345"—then no formatting

needs to be done, and it would be much simpler to design the screens and reports using this data. The tradeoff would be storage space required to store 11 characters versus a 9-decimal number. The designer would have to have the skill and knowledge to make these kinds of judgments when creating a database.

Other components besides tables are saved as part of a database. These include queries or views, constraints, triggers, defaults, stored procedures, and user-defined functions. Queries and view are predefined perspectives of the data that can be a single table or combinations of tables. **Constraints** are rules that the data must adhere to in order for the data to be saved. **Triggers** are built-in, user-defined routines that occur when data is manipulated, usually from a data insert, update, or delete action. Defaults are user-defined values when the record is created; the user doesn't have to enter this information. Stored procedures are code scripts with the database used to perform functions to the database. This code can be accessed from client software or from another stored procedure. User-defined functions are functions built into the database used by views and stored procedures for behaviors specific to the database.

Personal databases usually contain a reporting designer, a form design, and an interface scripting language for application automation. This type of database is typically used on a single computer for small database activities such as CD lists or small business management.

Larger database server systems separate the client functions from the database functions. This allows the database designer to create a database that "serves" data to a client through various types of data connections. It is the responsibility of the database and its designer to make sure the data is structured correctly and protected for data integrity and data security, whereas the client designer will focus on the user input (Forms) and output (Reports) interface. This is the basis for the "client-server" data access model.

constraint
trigger

DBMS Models

There are four basic types or models of database management systems: relational, hierarchical, network, and object-oriented databases.

relational database management system (RDBMS)

- **The Relational Database Management System (RDBMS)** is a system of tables with a common field that relates one table to another, thus the term *relational*. The RDBMS is less complex, costs less, accommodates smaller databases, and is used on smaller computers. This is the database you will probably use at home or in a small business. Chapter 15 presents problem solving using an RDBMS.

hierarchical database management system (DBMS)

- **The Hierarchical Database Management System (DBMS)** organizes data in a treelike structure according to record types. The relationship between records is parent–child (see Chapter 13).

network database management system (DBMS)

- **The Network Database Management System (DBMS)** is similar to the Hierarchical Database Management System with the exception that one record type (sometimes called tables) can relate to any number of other record types.

object-oriented database management system (DBMS)

- **Object-Oriented Database Management System (DBMS)** represent data in the form of objects as used in Object-Oriented Programming. As we will find out in Unit 5, Object-Oriented Programming (OOP), the database appears to the OOP designer as an object.

As wonderful as databases are, the drawbacks to the last three models are that they are complex and expensive. However, they can accommodate very large databases

that are required for large businesses with mainframe computer systems. They also require a team of individuals to maintain and update the database even after the database is in use.

Client Server Model

client server

The **client server** *model* started gaining acceptance in the 1980s. Its architecture was a vast improvement over its predecessor, mainframe architecture.

When using a mainframe system, the users interact with the mainframe host computer using terminals for key entry and display. All of the computing power is at the mainframe host computer. Limitations of mainframe architecture include: minimal support of graphical interfaces; no support of distributed computing, which could lead to distributed databases; and no shared computing power. The mainframe was typically a centralized host computer in one geographic location.

File sharing architecture is based on PC networking where files are downloaded from the main database and processed at the local PC. This strategy works when the shared usage is low and volume is low; however, in a real world environment file share architecture breaks down very quickly. Many personal database systems that attach to remote databases still need to process large amounts of data on the local PC using a form of file share architecture.

The client server model overcomes many of the issues with mainframe and file sharing architectures by sharing the workload between the server and the client, reducing the network traffic by providing a response for information instead of a complete file and by using Remote Procedure Calls (RPCs) or Standard Query Language (SQL) to communicate between the server and the client.

To understand the significance of the client server architecture as compared to the file share or mainframe architecture, consider a business database that handles client relations. This business has offices on the east and west coast of the United States. Each office has five customer service representatives. Using file share or mainframe architectures, each office would typically have a copy of the database at their location and on some regularity the database would be synced together (usually each night when the databases are not being used). This method presents many operational problems. First, how does an update of a client record that has been changed at the east coast office and the west coast office on the same day get reconciled? Secondly, how does each office get real time data without syncing more frequently? If a manager wants to run reports on the most current data how does she collect all the data together so the reports are accurate? As you can imagine the problems with this type of database architecture are significant and become more apparent as users and office locations increase.

Using client-server architecture the business gets the centralization of data and the distribution of client software while maintaining data access performance. This is accomplished by using store procedures on the server and remote procedure calls on the client to invoke the server to execute the procedure.

Consider the same business described above that has a central database using a database server to send data to the appropriate requestor in real time. This would include managing record locking and updates and deletions so that users would be receiving the most up-to-date information. The record locking would prevent simultaneous updates to records. All of this can be accomplished with acceptable performance due to the ability of the server to send only the data needed for each client instead of complete files.

The following is an example of a remote procedure call and a store procedure used to receive the call. Notice the data parameter that is sent in the call is used to filter the record set returned by the call.

Remote procedure call example:

```
GetNewPersonnel '01/01/2008'
```

Stored Procedure Example: This example returns a set of records from the table tbl_Personnel where the LastUpdate field has a date greater than or equal to the date passed in via the remote procedure call. In the previous RPC example the date of '01/01/2008' was passed to the GetNewPersonnel stored procedure so only the record with the LastUpdate field greater than or equal to '01/01/2008' would be returned.

```
CREATE PROCEDURE GetNewPersonnel
@LastDate Datetime,

AS
        Select*
        from tbl_Personnel where tbl_Personnel.LastUpdate
        >= @LastDate
```

From this example you can see that only a limited amount of records would be returned to the requesting client. The client server interaction would then minimize the amount of network traffic which greatly enhances software performance.

In addition to selecting data from a database server, the client-server model can add, update and delete database information. All of this functionality is typically part of a database **transaction.** The transaction usually has a begin-commit or begin-rollback cycle depending on the outcome of the transaction. An example of a transaction is a patient medical chart that is sent as a set of patient data records to the server as a batch update. If the connection is lost while sending the records the transaction will rollback so that incomplete patient information does not become available at the server. This is imperative so that medical personnel don't misinterpret incomplete information when caring for a patient. If all of the records reach the server then the transaction is committed and the data becomes available at the server.

transaction

The client-server model has allowed for the centralization of data without the sacrifice of high performance data access from multiple geographic locations. This technology, along with higher internet networking speeds, has greatly enhanced the usability of database servers in business enterprises.

DBMS Tasks

A DBMS must perform many tasks. These are available in all databases; however, some may require programming in more complex systems.

1. *Designing and creating a database.* This is part of the planning stage of implementing a DBMS. A good design aids in the easy use of the DBMS. A bad design can decrease productivity, increase frustrations, and will probably have to go back to be redesigned. Once the design is done, then the database can be created through the use of the DBMS. Data then must be entered into the database. This may be a time-consuming effort.
2. *Entering data.* Once the database is created and tested, data must be entered. This may be a huge task depending on the complexity of the database, and it may require months of planning and data entry.

3. *Maintaining data.* After the data is entered, it must be maintained—that is, the user must have the ability to add, delete, and change data. A company is dynamic and data changes constantly; therefore, the database must be updated often.

4. *Accessing of data.* The user must also have the ability to access any data electronically or on a printed copy. This may be through the use of a computer monitor or through printed reports. A database is not of much use if you cannot access the data.

5. *Selecting data.* Most of the time only specific data is needed; therefore, employees must have the ability to access selected records and fields. This is accomplished through the use of a query function. The query function allows the user to select needed records and fields by putting the needed data into a new table for output use. When data are updated, these tables are also updated automatically.

6. *Sorting records.* Most reports required the data to be in some kind of order. This is accomplished by sorting the records by one field or a combination of fields. The records may be ordered alphabetically or numerically and in ascending or descending order.

7. *Securing data.* It is very important that data is secure. A DBMS has built-in security mechanisms that can be implemented to ensure the integrity of the data.

8. *Producing reports.* One of the most important tasks to the user is that reports on data need to be developed and produced. The ultimate goal of a DBMS is for people to access and report information.

9. *Using a language to make the database a "turnkey" system.* A large database requires many people to use it in a company. These users normally are not familiar with the inner workings of the DBMS they are using. Therefore, the developer of the database must make the application as user-friendly as possible. This is done through the use of a programming language. Some RDBMSs use Visual Basic (VB). Larger systems use Structural Query Language (SQL) or Extensible Markup Language (XML) to build databases that are accessible not only to local employees but also to Internet users. Many businesses sell through the Internet and therefore must make the database of items they are selling available to the public. Also, the database must allow buyers to add their own data such as name, address, telephone number, and so forth. These languages have instructions that increase the productivity of the programmer in developing the project.

These tasks are important functions of a DBMS and are used by the programmer and the user to develop a good solution to a problem.

Summary

Database management systems are used to manage large amounts of data in businesses as well as at home. They allow the user to enter, delete, update, and access data. Security issues are part of the development of an application using a DBMS. There are several DBMS types or models: relational, hierarchical, network, and object-oriented. Each uses a different method of storing and retrieving data. A DBMS has various tasks to perform, including queries, sorting, defaults, triggering, and stored procedures (scripts) as well as securing, maintaining, and accessing the data.

New Terms

client server

constraint

Database Management
System (DBMS)

field

Hierarchical Database
Management System
(DBMS)

Network Database
Management System
(DBMS)

Object-Oriented Database
Management System
(DBMS)

property

record

Relational Database
Management System
(RDBMS)

table

transactions

trigger

Questions

1. Why would a company or a home user want to use a DBMS?

2. List and explain the DBMS models.

3. Why is each of the various tasks important to the application developer and to the user of a DBMS?

Chapter 15

Relational Database Management Systems

Overview

Objectives

When you have finished this chapter, you should be able to:

1. Understand the parts of a relational database created in an RDBMS.
2. Normalize relational database tables.
3. Create the schema for a relational database.
4. Design queries for a relational database.
5. Design forms for a relational database.
6. Design reports for a relational database.
7. Plan a relational database for a specific problem.

A Relational Database Management System (RDBMS) is a type of DBMS. The RDBMS uses a common field that relates one table to another, hence the name Relational DBMS. This type of database is usually used by smaller computers and is the one you normally will find on microcomputers. This chapter presents problem-solving techniques for building applications using an RDBMS.

Tables, Records, and Fields

table
record
field

Data are organized into one or more tables or entity sets. A **table** is a group of related records or entities. Each record is an entity in the table. A **record** is a group of related fields or attributes. Each **field** or attribute is a specific piece of data pertaining to the record. Each record in the table includes fields that are created in the design of the table. Each record is given a number. Each field is given a name. This name is the same for all records. Each table, query, report, and form is also given a name. You should name each according to what data they contain. The database is given a file name.

Let's examine an example of a database for a CD collection where only the CD names, producers, and dates of publication will be organized (see Figure 15.1). The database will be called *CD Collection*. There will be only one table called *CDs*. Each record, a horizontal row of data, will contain data in four separate areas, called fields: ID Number, Name, Producer, and Date. These fields and their descriptions as follows:

Field Description	Field Name
ID Number	ID Number
Name of CD	Name
The producer	Producer
Date of publication	Date

Records are numbered starting with one. Individual fields have the same number of characters in every record. For example, if 25 characters have been specified for the field called Name, then every record has a maximum of 25 characters to enter the name of the CD.

Database File Name: *CD Collection*

Table Name: *CDs*

Fields: → ID Number Name Producer Date

	ID Number	Name	Producer	Date
Record 1	500	Winds	XYZ Corp	2000
Record 2	502	Whale Song	XYZ Corp	2001
Record 3	503	Songs of Ireland	ECL Publishers	2003
⋮				
Record N				

Figure 15.1 CDs Table

You may have a derived field also called a computed field. The data in this type of field is derived, or computed from, other fields. For example, the retail cost may be computed from the wholesale cost and the percentage markup.

Tables are holders of data to be organized and printed. In the planning stages of a database, it is important that all data required for the printed reports are part of one of the tables. Therefore, when you are developing a solution to a problem requiring a database, you should identify the information required for the reports. This sounds backwards; however, you need to know where you are going in order to know how to start. When you have your reports planned, then you may define your tables. The third step is to plan how to get from the data to the report. Remember: Plan your output, then your input, and finally your processing.

Primary, Secondary, and Foreign Keys

primary key

One field may be designated as a **primary key.** A primary key field contains unique data, that is, data that will not be repeated in the same field of another record. For example, the CD ID number (ID Number) would be a primary key in the *CDs* table. It is used in many projects to designate an identification number or an account number. You do not have to designate a primary key field. Many tables do not have a field that is unique. If you designate a field as a primary key, the RDBMS will not allow you to enter a value that is repeated from another record.

Secondary keys are not necessarily unique. They are primarily used to search for a specific record when you do not know the primary key. For example, in the CD example you may not know the ID number (ID Number), but you may know the name of the CD (Name). Therefore, you could search on the CD name.

foreign key

A **foreign key** is a relational field to another table. The foreign key is a primary key in another table and determines the relationship between the tables. For example, you may have information about the producers of the CD in the second table. The producer's identification number would be the primary key in the *Producers* table. In order to find the producer information for a CD you need to have the producers identification number in the *CDs* table also. This would be a foreign key in the *CDs* table whereas it is a primary key in the *Producers* table. The field name is the same in the two tables (see Figure 15.2).

Normalizing Tables

For most problems, data should be separated into multiple but related tables. Let's revisit the *CD Collection* database. This time there are more fields required, including the name, artist, and time length of each track on each CD. The address information for the publisher is also required. Figure 15.3 shows a single list of attributes, or fields, for a table if all data were to go into one table. This table has several problems. First, how many fields should be reserved for the music selections? Each CD has a different number of selections. Another problem arises when data is repeated in many records, such as the publishers' addresses. This repetition creates possible errors in entry as well as in table maintenance. Therefore, database tables should be normalized. **Normalizing**

normalizing

tables is separating data into multiple, related tables to increase efficiency as much as possible when entering, using, and updating data.

Other problems that may occur in database design are null data and data redundancy. Null data have no value, as all value is absent. Primary keys cannot contain null data. A null data field is not a blank field because a blank field contains spaces, which are characters. Null values should be eliminated if at all possible.

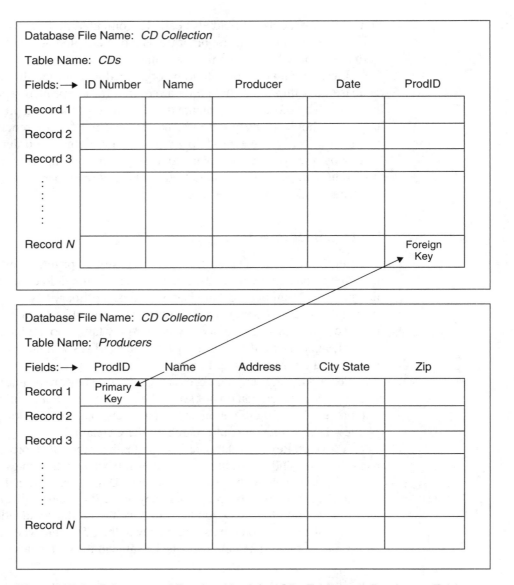

Figure 15.2 Primary and Foreign Keys for *CDs* Table and *Producers* Table

Multiple values within a field occur when there is more than one value required for one field. Data repetition occurs when data is repeated in multiple records. Lost data occurs when pertinent data is deleted when a record is deleted. These three problems lead to three types of anomalies.

1. The insertion anomaly occurs when you cannot add a record because there is more than one value required for one field and the number of values for this field differ in each record, such as in the case of the music selections. If the number of values for a field is the same for all records, the solution is to make multiple fields. However, as in the case of the music selections, there is a different number of values for each record. Therefore, you cannot designate different fields for each value because you do not know the number of values. This creates what is called an *unflat table,* a table that requires a different number of fields for each record. An unflat table is not allowed in an RDBMS. The solution is to create another table with a relational field tying the new table to the old table.

	CD Name	Selection	Artist	Producer	Date	Time	Address	City	State	Zipcode	Telephone
Record 1											
Record 2											
Record 3											
⋮											
Record N											

Attributes or Fields
CD Name
Selection
Artist
Producer
Date
Time
Address
City
State
Zipcode
Telephone

Figure 15.3 Attributes of the *CDs* Table

2. The update anomaly occurs when the same data must be changed in more than one record, as in the case of the publishers' addresses. Because there are considerably fewer publishers than CDs, there are many records to update when the address of a publisher changes. The solution is to create a table for the information on the publishers with a relational field tying the new table to the old table.

3. The deletion anomaly occurs when there is a loss of critical data when you delete a record. In the case of the CD collection, assume the publishers' information were to be kept in the original table. If only one CD had a specific publisher and that CD was deleted, you would lose the address information for that publisher. In contrast, if the address information is in a separate publisher information table, even if there were no CDs by that publisher in your collection, the address information would still remain in the publisher information table.

Normalization takes care of these problems. The first normalization takes care of unflat tables, or the insertion problem. The second normalization takes care of repeated data, or the update problem. The third normalization takes care of key data as a nonkey field of the file, or the deletion problem.

When you are normalizing a table, the first step is to create a list of fields or attributes required for the output reports. See Figure 15.4 for the original field list, the list after the first normalization, and the list after the second normalization. There is no need

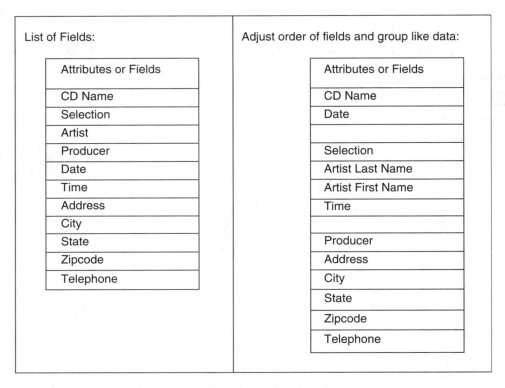

Figure 15.4a *Normalization of CDs Table Original Data*

for a third normalization. The original table shows all fields. Notice the fields that hold multiple data are simply named to represent the data, in this case Selections, Artist, and Time. The list is then divided into separate fields, such as the *Artist* into Artist first name and Artist last name, and grouped together like fields, in this case the CD data, the Selection data, and the Producers' data.

The next step is to develop the first normalized form of your database. You will create a new table with one field that is identical to a field in the original table in order to show the relationship between the two tables; in this case, CDID. This is the CD identification number. The field in the *Selections* table is the foreign key and the field in the *CD Collections* table is the primary key. This is because the primary key must be unique and there are many records in the *Selections* table compared to one record in the *CD Collections* table. The steps to complete the first normalization are as follows:

1. Move related fields that have more than one value to the new table. In this case move the fields associated with the selections to the new table, named *Selections.*
2. Add the foreign key to the new table and a field with the same name as a primary key to the original table. In this case add the foreign key of fk_CDID to the *Selections* table and the primary key of CDID to the *CDs* table.

This will produce a new table and a modified table (see Figure 15.4b).

The next step is to develop the second normalized form of your database. You will be creating a third table with one field that is identical to a field in the original table to show the relation between the two tables, in this case PRODID (see Figure 15.4c). The steps to complete the second normalization are as follows:

1. Move the related fields that are in more than one record to a new table. In this case move the fields associated with the producers to the *Producers* table.

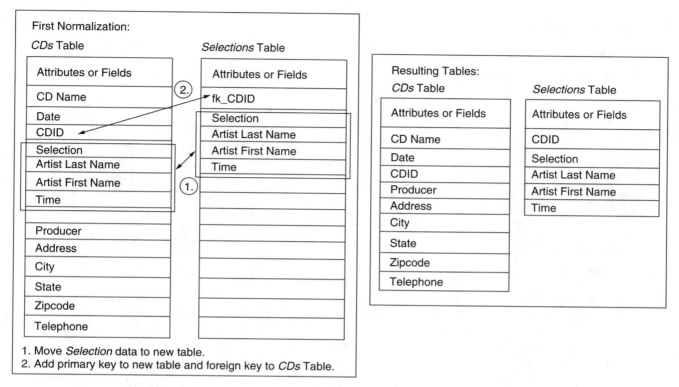

First Normalization:

CDs Table

Attributes or Fields
CD Name
Date
CDID
Selection
Artist Last Name
Artist First Name
Time
Producer
Address
City
State
Zipcode
Telephone

Selections Table

2.

Attributes or Fields
fk_CDID
Selection
Artist Last Name
Artist First Name
Time

1.

Resulting Tables:

CDs Table

Attributes or Fields
CD Name
Date
CDID
Producer
Address
City
State
Zipcode
Telephone

Selections Table

Attributes or Fields
CDID
Selection
Artist Last Name
Artist First Name
Time

1. Move *Selection* data to new table.
2. Add primary key to new table and foreign key to *CDs* Table.

Figure 15.4b First Normalization

2. Add a field in the new table that will be a primary key and the same named field in the modified table as a foreign key. In this case add the primary key of PRODID to the *Producers* table and the foreign key of fk_PRODID to the *CDs* table.

There are now three tables.

The last step, if required, is to develop the third normalized form of your database. You would be creating a fourth table with one field that is identical to a field in the original table to show the relation between the two tables. Data to be moved from the first table are not necessarily repeated in multiple records but are data that you want to save even if the record is deleted. To complete the third normalization, create a new relation field in both tables and move the required data to the new table. In our *CD Collection* database case, there are no data that require a third normalization.

You now should have your tables in the most efficient form possible. If any of the normalizations require more than one new table, you would need to repeat the steps for that normalization. Complete all required new tables in each normalization before continuing on to the next normalization. You will rarely use all three normalizations for a solution to a problem; however, you should examine the original table for the possibility of all three.

Entity Relation Model (ERM)

entity relation model (ERM)

An **Entity Relation Model** is a model of the data that provides the designer with three main semantic concepts: entities, relationships, and attributes. Entities are distinct objects in the enterprise, relationships are the interaction of the entities, and attribute describe the entities and relationships. When designing using an E-R model, the entities

Second Normalization:

CDs Table		Producers Table		Selections Table

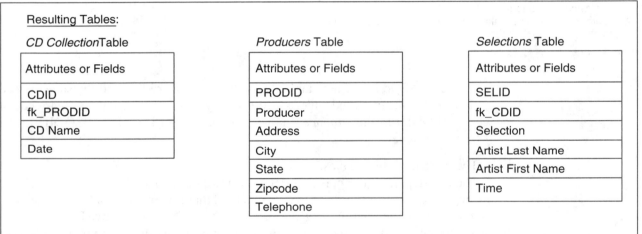

1. Move *Producer* fields to *Producers* Table.
2. Add primary key of PRODID to *Producers* table and foreign key of PRODID to *CDs* table.

Figure 15.4c Second Normalization and Final Tables

and relationships become tables, and the attributes become the fields within the tables. By creating the E-R model in the early stages of database design, the designer can describe the enterprise model and flush out any problems with the data design before moving to far into the database creation stage.

Consider our previous CD example. From our original table we derived three entities—*Publishers*, *CDs*, and *Selection*—and two relationships—Publishers to CDs and CDs to Selections. Figure 15.5 describes these entities and their relationships using an E-R model.

Once an E-R model has been created, the table structure becomes apparent. Figure 15.6 shows the tables used to implement the entities in the E-R model. As you can see, the *Selections* table has a foreign key to the *CDs* table (fk_CDID), and the *CDs* table has a foreign key to the *Producers* table (fk_PRODID).

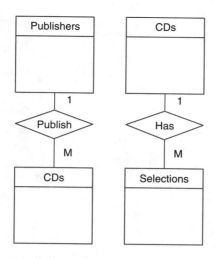

Figure 15.5 Entity Relation Model.

Figure 15.6 Entity Relation Model and Schema

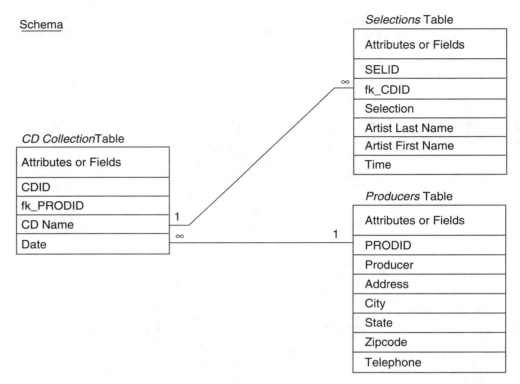

Schema

Figure 15.7 Schema of the *CD Collection* Database

Schema

schema

The **schema** of your database shows the relationships among the tables (see Figure 15.7). Start with the normalized list of attributes for each table. Then draw a line between the tables connecting the relational fields. Add a one or an infinity sign (∞) on each end of the line to indicate the following:

1. One (1) to one (1) indicates that one record in one table relates to one record in another table. A one (1) appears on both ends of the line.
2. One (1) to many (∞) indicates that one record in the table on the one (1) side references to many records in the table on the infinity (∞) side. A one (1) is placed on the end of the line pointing to the table that references to one record and a many sign is placed on the other end.
3. Many to many (∞) indicates that there are many records in one table that are related to many records in the other table. An infinity sign (∞) appears on both ends of the line.

Figure 15.7 shows the schema for the *CD Collection* database example. Notice that there are three tables, including the *CDs* table, the *Selections* table, and the *Producers* table.

Creating Tables

Data are entered into the tables through forms or a data view listing. The form shows one record on the monitor at a time. The data view shows multiple records, but only as many fields as will fit on the monitor. You must scroll for additional fields. Tables must

be created by designating the fields and their defining characteristics. Each field in a table has field characteristics, including the field name, the data type, the description of the field, the number of characters in the field (called the field size), the number of decimal places for numbers, format, input mask, and default value.

The name of the field should be long enough to readily identify the contents. However, it should be short enough so that the exact name can be remembered easily, and the field header in the form or in the data view does not take up too much space. The field description describes the contents of the field. The field size is the maximum number of characters any entry will require. If the field contains a name, the field size may be 20 characters if all records have names fewer than 21 characters. The computer will not allow you to enter more characters than the size of the field. If you have a name that is longer than 20 characters, you must increase the size of the field by changing the design of the table.

SQL databases have standard database types with varying attributes depending on the type. Character fields consist of alphanumeric data and the number of allowed characters is specified. *Varchar(x)* or *nvarchar(x)*, where x is the number of allowed characters, is a data type used by SQL RDBMS. *nvarchar* differs from *varchar* in that it can be used for multilingual data storage; however it takes twice as much space to store that data. Numeric data consist of many different storage formats including *integer*, *smallint*, *tinyint*, *real*, *float*, and *decimal*, to name a few. There is also date information called *datetime* or *smalldatetime*, which hold data information to very precise levels—*datetime* to 3.33 milliseconds. Bit or boolean fields hold a single bit (0 or 1) and are usually used to indicate a yes or no data point. Memo or Text fields are used to hold more data that standard character fields (*nvarchar*, *varchar*, etc)—these fields do not have a field size and are variable length by design. These are used for large amounts of text data that have no pattern to the information—for instance, a medical narrative about a patient's condition. Binary data can hold any object's data type. These are used to store pictures, audio files, video files, or any other binary data type. A database designer must take into consideration the data types provided by the database being used when designing the tables needed for an application. Speed, functionality, and storage requirements depend greatly on the data types used by the designer.

Each data type has attributes that need to be specified when creating them. Character data needs the field length; decimal data needs the number of decimal places, for example. Other data types have no size attribute. For instance, integers are fixed in size as described in Figure 15.8.

Some RDBMS systems contain other attributes such as input mask, format, and text alignment. These attributes pertain mainly to the client interface and not the data type. They help the client interface designer when composing forms and reports by automatically enforcing these attributes. For instance, an input mask can specify the parentheses and dashes in a phone number and enforce the data entry to be numeric. A sample input mask for a phone number would be "(999) 999-9999" where the "9" indicates the numeric entries. Conversely, the format attribute would determine how that data would be displayed either in a form or a report.

RDBMS also may contain default values and validation rule attributes. These attributes help to protect the data from bad data entry. For instance, if you are documenting patient information about diastolic blood pressure, a validation rule would protect from values less than 0 and greater than 500. A more complex validation may protect for a male patient's condition entered as pregnant. Each RDBMS offers varying levels of sophistication of data validation at the database design level for data protection. Default value attribute is used to populate a field at creation time. For instance,

Data Types	Description
bigint	Integer data from -2^{63} through $2^{63} - 1$
int	Integer data from -2^{31} through $2^{31} - 1$
smallint	Integer data from -2^{15} through $2^{15} - 1$
tinyint	Integer data from 0 through 255
bit	Integer data with either a 1 or 0 value
decimal	Numeric data from $-10^{38} + 1$ through $10^{38} - 1$
numeric	Numeric data from $-10^{38} + 1$ through $10^{38} - 1$
money	Monetary data values from -2^{63} through $2^{63} - 1$
smallmoney	Monetary data values from $-214,748.3648$ through $+214,748.3647$
float	Floating precision number data from $-1.79E + 308$ through $1.79E + 308$
real	Floating precision number data from $-3.40E + 38$ through $3.40E + 38$
datetime	Date and time data from January 1, 1753, through December 31, 9999, with an accuracy of 3.33 milliseconds
smalldatetime	Date and time data from January 1, 1900, through June 6, 2079, with an accuracy of one minute
char	Fixed-length character data with a maximum length of 8,000 characters
varchar	Variable-length data with a maximum of 8,000 characters
text	Variable-length data with a maximum length of $2^{31} - 1$ characters
nchar	Fixed-length Unicode data with a maximum length of 4,000 characters
nvarchar	Variable-length Unicode data with a maximum length of 4,000 characters
ntext	Variable-length Unicode data with a maximum length of $2^{30} - 1$ characters
binary	Fixed-length binary data with a maximum length of 8,000 bytes

Figure 15.8 Database Data Types

when most of the clients for a business are in California, then a default value for the State Field would be set to CA. The feature decreases the number of keystrokes in the data entry process, which inherently reduces the possibility of bad data.

Queries

query

query table

Queries are the way to select fields and/or records to be processed. The result of a query is a **query table** that contains the selected data items required for an output report. When a query is made, you set up a query design that will select the required items from a specified table. Figure 15.9 shows an example of a query made on the *CDs* table. Notice that the field names are in the top row, the table name is in the second row, the selected fields are in the third row, and the criteria "date > 1990" is in the fourth row. The fifth row is not used. This query will create a query table with records from the *CDs* table that have been published after 1990. You may then print this new query table through the use of reports.

The query table is defined by using five rows of information. The first row contains the table name where the data for each field are found. The second row contains an *X,* which specifies the sort field for the new query table. The third row specifies the fields that should be included in the new table. The fourth and fifth rows specify the criteria for selecting records. All ANDs are in the same row, and the OR is in the fifth row.

Field Name:	Name	Artist	Producer	Date
Table:	*CDs*	*CDs*	*CDs*	*CDs*
Sort:	X			
Show:	X	X	X	X
Criteria:				> 1990
OR:				

Figure 15.9 Example of a Query

You will use relational operators to specify the criteria. Figure 15.10 shows examples of criteria. Example 1 shows one criterion: Cost is less than 25. Using this criteria, the new query table will include all records in which the cost is less than 25. Example 2 shows two criteria that both must be true in order to include a record in the function calculations. Notice that the criteria are on the same row. This is similar to the AND operator. The resulting table will include all records where the value of Cost is less than 25 and Quantity is less than 10. Example 3 also shows two criteria, but only one of these criteria must be true in order to include a record in the function calculations. Notice that the criteria are on separate rows. This is similar to the OR operator. The resulting table will include all records with Cost less than 25 or Quantity less than 10. Example 4 shows three criteria using both the AND and the OR logic. In this case, in order for the record to be included, the Cost must be greater than or equal to 10 and the Quantity must be less than 5, or the Cost must be less than 10. The resulting table will include all records in which the Cost is less than 10 and all records in which the Cost is greater than or equal to 10 and the Quantity is less than 5. In the fourth row notice the AND operator and in the fifth row the OR operator. When you want your selection to be based on two or more criteria and they all have to be met, then you place each criterion in the fourth row under the associated field name. When only one of the criteria must be met, then you place each criterion on different rows. Be very careful when you start mixing ANDs and ORs to ensure you are asking for the correct records to be selected. Check your resulting table carefully as well. If you identify more or fewer records than you had expected from the query, then you need to correct the design of the query.

The types of queries you will perform are determined by the project. You may want special sums, averages, or special updates. Just about any application that is used with and RDBMS requires some type of query.

Queries are developed through the use of an interface to the powerful Structural Query Language (SQL). SQL exists to facilitate the retrieval of selected data needed for processing. You may program your own methods of retrieving needed data by learning to use SQL. Many RDBMSs allow the users extensive use of SQL. This tends to decrease the user friendliness of the application for the developer while increasing its flexibility. The final results should create a database that is user friendly for the end user. This is the job of the programmer. Other RDBMS types use a programming language such as Visual

Example 1:

Field Name	Item	Cost	Quantity
Table			
Sort	X		
Show	X	X	X
Criteria		< 25	
OR			

Example 2:

Field Name	Item	Cost	Quantity
Table			
Sort	X		
Show	X	X	X
Criteria		< 25	< 10
OR			

Example 3:

Field Name	Item	Cost	Quantity
Table			
Sort	X		
Show	X	X	X
Criteria		< 25	
OR			< 10

Example 4:

Field Name	Item	Cost	Quantity
Table			
Sort	X		
Show	X	X	X
Criteria		>= 10	< 5
OR		< 10	

Figure 15.10 Example of Criteria Ranges for Database Functions

Basic to develop interfaces between the user and the database. The four logic structures are used to attach scripts or modules that contain short sets of instructions for interactive devices such as buttons or check boxes. An interactive screen may be developed to aid the user in the updating and processing of the tables in a database. The developer of a database must know programming to be able to develop these scripts or modules.

Interface Design

Most solutions to business problems are designed to be accessed through an interface. A form with buttons is set up as an interface to automate the use of the database. This form is sometimes called a switchboard because it switches from one activity to another

through the use of buttons. Chapters 16 and 17 present information on the design and implementation of interfaces. These interfaces are developed through the use of a programming language.

Form Design

form

Forms allow the user to see all or some of the fields of a record on the monitor. The table is transversed through the use of buttons to go to the next, the previous, the last, or the first record. Derived fields may be added. Fields may be placed and moved to any location on the monitor. The data may be viewed or updated. New records may be added. Each field is labeled and has an input box that holds the data.

The form must be designed well to ensure the end user's productivity. Fields should be located on the form for easy reading and entering of data. If a source document is being used, the fields should be located on the monitor in the same order as on the source document. Key information should be located in one area. The form should be pleasant to look at and read, and pertinent information should be easy to locate. Add graphics only to enhance the locating and reading of data. Remember that users of this form will be viewing it day after day. You want them to enjoy looking it.

Reports

report

Reports are really the reason you have completed everything else. **Reports** are printed documents of the records in a specific database or query table. You may choose any or all of the fields to be included in your report. In the case of the *CD Collection* database example, the report may include only the CD names and artists. You may sort them in any way you please. You may sort them by CD names, artists, date, or publisher depending upon the requirements of the problem. To design a report, you need to specify the report headings, the footers, the headers, the contents of each column, the width of the column, the format of the data, the column headings, the sorting criteria for the data, and the subtotals that will be calculated. You also may specify images to be imported on the document and other line art as required by the specifications of the problem.

You may specify the column width as greater than, equal to, or less than the field length. If the data do not fit into the column they will word wrap within the column. To avoid this, try to make the columns at least as wide as the field length. You do need to stay within the width of the paper on which you are creating the report. The number of characters across the page is dependent upon the font type, the number of characters, and the font size that you are using. Try to specify extra space for each column. You may have as many columns as you desire; however, the data must fit into the columns on the printed page.

Planning a Solution Using an RDBMS

This section presents forms to help you plan the development of databases. The first form allows you to list the required reports and the required data for each report. You should start with a list of reports and the corresponding data for the reports because this is how you will know what data is needed for the database. See Figure 15.11 for the report list form.

List of Required Reports:

Report Name	Data to Be Included in Report

Figure 15.11 Lists of Required Reports Form

Original Table:		First Normalization New Table(s)		Second Normalization New Table(s)		Third Normalization New Table(s)	
Item	Field Name	Item	Field Name	Item	Field Name	Item	Field Name

Figure 15.12 RDBMS Table Development Form

The next step is to list all of the data and create the field names. Figure 15.12 presents a form for entering the data items and field names. When you finish listing the data items and field names, you will need to normalize the original table to separate the data items into related tables. After you have normalized the database, then create the schema. Figure 15.13 presents a form for developing the schema. Figure 15.14 presents a form for designing each table. In this step, the fields and their attributes are specified. You will need one of these forms for each table. After your tables are designed, you would design each of your database forms. You would designate the background, the fields that will be on the form, and their layout. Figure 15.15 presents a form to help design each form. Notice the place for the algorithms and flowcharts for your scripts that are attached to the form.

The next step is to design your queries. Figure 15.16 presents a form to help you. The last step is to design your reports. You would specify margins, headers, footers, report headings, column contents, column widths, and anything else that you want to specify for a report. See Figure 15.17 for a report layout form.

The last step is to develop your modules (macros or scripts). Use the algorithm and flowchart form to develop each module. Indicate on the algorithm and flowchart form the database form to which it is attached. An example of the form is found in Figure 15.18.

Figure 15.13 Schema Form

Table Name:_____

Field Name	Description	Data Type	Field Length	No. of Decimals	Format	Input Mask	Default Value

Figure 15.14 Field Characteristics for One Table

Background:_____
Table:_____

```
┌─────────────────────────────────────────────────────────────────┐
│                                                                   │
│                                                                   │
│                                                                   │
│                                                                   │
│                                                                   │
│                                                                   │
│                                                                   │
│                                                                   │
│                                                                   │
└─────────────────────────────────────────────────────────────────┘
```

Figure 15.15 Form Design

Table Name:_____

Field Name:							
Table:							
Sort:							
Show:							
Criteria:							
OR:							

Figure 15.16 Query Design Form

Example RDBMS: Home Inventory

Problem: John has just purchased homeowner's insurance. His insurance agent has indicated that in case of a disaster he should have an inventory of everything he owns. He has just purchased a new computer with an RDBMS installed on it. John would like to use this for his inventory. He would like to keep the following information on his possessions:

1. Item
2. Original cost
3. Room where it is located
4. Information about the store where the item was purchased
5. Appraised value of jewelry, artwork, and antiques
6. Appraiser's name, address, and phone number

Report Layout:

Report Name: _____

 Table or Query Name:_____

Margins:

 Top: _____ Top Printer: _____

 Bottom: _____ Bottom Printer: _____

 Left: _____ Left Printer: _____

 Right: _____ Right Printer: _____

 Header: _____ Top Printer: _____

 Footer: _____ Bottom Printer: _____

Paper Size: _____Orientation: _____Color/B&W: _____

Sort By: _____

Subtotals on Following Fields: _____

Images to Be Imported:

File	Description	Use	Location

Header Contents:

Footer Contents:

Report Heading:

Column Heading					
Field Name					
Column Width					

Figure 15.17 Report Layout Form

John would like the following reports:

1. An alphabetical listing of the items and all associated data
2. A list of the stores
3. A list of the appraisers
4. A form for the monitor to view each item
5. A list of items worth more than $500

Figure 15.19 presents the planning forms for this example.

| Macro Name: _____ | |
| Attach to Form: _____ | |
Algorithm:	Flowchart:

Figure 15.18 Algorithm and Flowchart Form for Database Module

Report Name	Data to Be Included in Report
Inventory	item, original value, room, appraised value,
	store information, appraiser information
Stores	store information
Appraisers	appraiser information
Items Over 500	item, original value, appraised value
Form to Show One Item:	
Inventory	item, original value, room, appraised value,
	store, appraiser information

Figure 15.19a List of Reports

This example involves an inventory for a household. This is a typical problem that arises for personal use of RDBMS. There are four reports and one screen form that are required. After normalization, there are three tables: *Inventory, Store,* and *Appraiser.* The schema is developed next. There are three tables with a relationship between the *Inventory* table and the other two tables of many records to one record. There are many inventory items that were purchased at the same store and that had the same appraiser.

Original Table:		First Normalization New Table(s)		Second Normalization New Table(s)		Third Normalization New Table(s)	
Item	Field Name	Item	Field Name	Item	Field Name	Item	Field Name
Item	Item	None		Table 2:		None	
Room	Room			Store Purchased	Store		
Original Value	Value			Store Address	SAddress		
Appraised Value	AppValue			Store City	SCity		
Store Purchased	Store			Store State	SState		
Store Address	SAddress			Store Zipcode	SZipcode		
Store City	SCity			Store Phone	SPhone		
Store State	SState						
Store Zipcode	SZipcode						
Store Phone	SPhone			Table 3:			
Appraiser	Appraiser			Appraiser	Appraiser		
App. Address	AAddress			App. Address	AAddress		
App. City	ACity			App. City	ACity		
App. State	AState			App. State	AState		
App. Zipcode	AZipcode			App. Zipcode	AZipcode		
App. Phone	APhone			App. Phone	APhone		
Rel. Field	fk_SID						
Rel. Field	fk_AID						

Figure 15.19b Table Development

input mask

The fields and their characteristics for each table were developed next. Notice the **input masks** on the telephone numbers. The screen form for one inventory item was developed. The items were placed on the screen in the best viewing order. Report Four required a query to select all items that cost or were appraised at more than $500. The reports then were planned. Report One lists the inventory and requires the *Stores* and *Appraisers* tables. Report Two lists the store information from the *Stores* table. Report Three lists the appraiser's information from the *Appraisers* table. Report Four uses the query table to list the items that cost or were appraised at more than $500.

Databases must be maintained. This is a continuous and complex job that many times is handled by a person called the database administrator or database manager. The more complex the database, the bigger the need for a single person responsible for maintaining it. Even at home, the database must be maintained. It is best to have one person in charge of that maintenance.

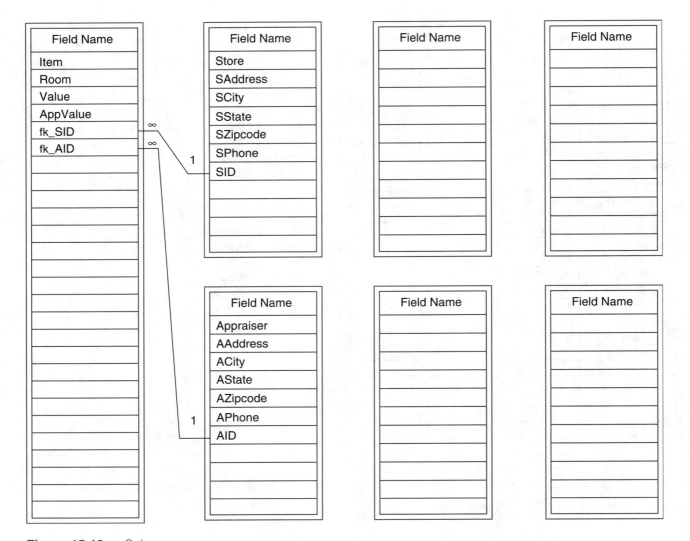

Field Name
Item
Room
Value
AppValue
fk_SID
fk_AID

Field Name
Store
SAddress
SCity
SState
SZipcode
SPhone
SID

Field Name

Field Name

Field Name
Appraiser
AAddress
ACity
AState
AZipcode
APhone
AID

Field Name

Field Name

Figure 15.19c Schema

Field Name	Description	Data Type	Field Length	# of Decimals	Format	Input Mask	Default Value
Table: *Inventory*							
Item	Inventory Item	Text	10				
Room	Location	Text	10				
Value	Original Value	Number	10	2			
AppValue	Appraised Value	Number	10	2			
fk_SID	Rel. Field	Text	5				
fk_AID	Rel. Field	Text	5				
Table: *Stores*							
SID	Rel. Field	Text	5				
Store	Store Name	Text	10				
SAddress	Store Address	Text	15				
SCity	Store City	Text	10				
SState	Store State	Text	3				
SZipcode	Store Zip Code	Text	10				
SPhone	Store Phone	Text	15			(xxx) xxx-xxxx	
Table: *Appraisers*							
AID	Rel. Field	Text	5				
Appraiser	Appraiser Name	Text	10				
AAddress	App. Address	Text	15				
ACity	App. City	Text	10				
AState	App. State	Text	3				
AZipcode	App. Zip Code	Text	10				
APhone	App. Phone	Text	15			(xxx) xxx-xxxx	

Figure 15.19d Table Characteristics

Background:__Default____
Table:__Inventory/Store/Appraisers____

Item Name: | Item |

Room Where Located: | Room |

Original Value: | Value | Store Where Purchased: | Store |

Appraised Value: | AppValue | Appraiser: | Appraiser |

Figure 15.19e Form Design

Table Name:___Inventory_____

Field Name:	Item	Room	Value	AppValue	SID	AID	
Table:	*Inventory*	*Inventory*	*Inventory*	*Inventory*	*Inventory*	*Inventory*	
Sort:							
Show:	X	X	X	X			
Criteria:			> 500				
OR:				> 500			

Figure 15.19f Queries

Summary

Relational Database Management Systems (RDBMSs) are data organizers. They allow the end user to enter data, organize them, and print reports. Databases created through the use of an RDBMS have multiple parts, including tables that hold all the data, forms that display data, queries that select data, reports that output organized data, and macros that help automate the database.

Tables are designed through analysis of the reports required. The data are then normalized into tables for the most efficient entry, use, and update of the database. A table is a group of related records. A record contains fields of individual pieces of data. The database schema shows the relationship between tables.

When designing a database, all the parts are designed individually, many times by different specialists with different areas of expertise. The team of designers is usually led by a systems analyst who has the oversight of the entire system. The database itself is designed by a database designer whose expertise is in data normalization and optimization. The user interface is designed by a GUI designer who gives great attention to consistent look and feel as well as human interface guidelines. Report designers work on consistent layout as well as expertise in statistical analysis. Together this team creates the building blocks that become the final application.

RDBMSs have become a primary resource of businesses. RDBMSs in a large-scale enterprise represent a major capital investment in the design, maintenance, and upgrading of functionality. It is extremely important to design the database using the discipline described in this chapter. The tools will allow designers to take a very complex system and break it down into smaller parts that become easier to understand and maintain.

New Terms

Entity Relation Model (ERM)

field

foreign key

form

input mask

normalizing

primary key

query

query table

record

report

schema

table

Questions

1. Name and explain the parts of a database.
2. What is a primary key?
3. When would you use a primary key?
4. Why would you not use a primary key? Give an example.
5. What is a foreign key?
6. Why is a database table normalized?
7. Explain the process of normalizing your database table.
8. Explain a schema. Give an example of each of the types of table relationships.
9. Name and describe four attributes of a field. Include examples of each attribute in your answer.
10. Explain a query.
11. In example 15.7, how would you change the query to reflect the following:
 a. Include in the report only the name, the artist, and the producer.
 b. Include only CDs by Tom Smith in the report.
 c. Include only Tom Smith CDs that were produced after 1985.
 d. Include all CDs that were produced after 1995 and all by Tom Smith.
 e. Include all CDs that were produced after 1995 and all Tom Smith CDs that were produced after 1985.

Problems

1. Bill owns a hardware store. He has a special catalog for customers that have indicated they would like to receive one. He has their names, addresses, and favorite department. He would like to have mailing labels printed for these customers. Bill also would like to have a list organized by favorite departments so he can add specials about the most popular departments. Plan an RDBMS that solves this problem.

2. Susan has an audiotape collection that she wants to catalog. She would like to create the following reports:
 a. An alphabetical listing of the names of the tapes and associated information (artist and favorite listening place)
 b. An alphabetical listing of the artists and their tapes
 c. A listing of the tapes organized by where she most likes to listen to them (the car, bedroom, family room, while walking or outside)
 d. A listing of all music selections and the tape on which each is found

 Plan an RDBMS for this problem.

3. You are the secretary of the Computer Club. You want to computerize the club's membership list. You have the name, address, telephone number, and e-mail address of each member. You also would like to add the committee name to which each member is assigned and when the committee meets. You want to create a report listing all members' information such as their names and e-mail addresses, a form that lists all information for each member, and mailing labels. Plan an RDBMS for this problem.

4. The New Plays Repertory Theater would like to computerize its ticket sales. The theater seats 500 people, offers seven plays each year, and sells season tickets and

single-night tickets. The season tickets are all for performances at the same time during the week. Each play has 20 performances. The theater keeps a customer list of those people who buy tickets in order to send play information for advertising purposes.

The reports they would like to create are:

a. A listing of available seats
b. A listing of all plays and the actors in the plays
c. A listing of customers
d. Labels printed for all customers
e. A listing of season ticket holders

Plan an RDBMS for this problem.

5. You are planning a trip to France. You are compiling a lot of research on lodging, restaurants, and things to do in the cities you are interested in visiting. The data is beginning to overwhelm you. Therefore, you would like to organize it on the computer. The reports you would like include:

a. A listing of all lodgings and associated information
b. A listing of all restaurants and associated information
c. A listing of all activities and associated information
d. A listing of each city with the lodging, restaurants, and activities associated with it

Plan an RDBMS for this problem.

6. Sam is the sales manager at the regional office of XYZ Gadgets, Inc. He needs to prepare an annual report that includes:

a. A listing of salespeople and their territory, sales, and number of clients
b. A listing of all clients
c. A listing of territories and the total number of , salespeople, and clients associated with each territory
d. A listing of the total sales per month

Plan an RDBMS for this problem.

UNIT FIVE

OBJECT-ORIENTED PROGRAMMING

Chapter 16

Concepts of Object-Oriented Programming

Overview

Object-Oriented Programming
 Classes
 Inheritance
 Objects
 Functions

Graphical User Interface (GUI)

Event-Driven Object-Oriented Programming
 Events
 User-Defined Events
 Interactivity

Objectives

When you have finished this chapter, you should be able to:

1. Determine the difference between a procedural solution and an object-oriented solution.
2. Use object-oriented concepts in the design of a solution to a problem.
3. Recognize when it is appropriate to use inheritance when designing classes.

Computer hardware and software have constantly become more and more complex as new innovations in computer science and technology have evolved. The graphical user interface (GUI) as well as Internet browser technologies are prime examples of this rapid change. As a result of these innovations, more and more people with varying skill levels have become users of computers in the workplace and the home. Expectations for performance as well as user-friendliness have grown along with the innovations.

Software designers look for new strategies in programming in order to exploit the rapidly changing functionality and innovation in computer technology; one of these strategies is object-oriented programming (OOP).

Object-oriented programming (OOP) has become the standard programming methodology for software engineers and developers. It is a different way of approaching a solution to a problem. OOP methodology may be used to create procedural-type programs, but more importantly, it lends itself to use with a GUI. Because the GUI is an interactive user interface that uses icons and menus, a nonlinear approach to programming is required. This is because the user has the option to choose any one of many things to do—save a document, print a document, insert a picture, change attributes of a document, and so on. Object-oriented programming allows a programmer to develop a nonlinear approach to a solution. When working with OOP instead of thinking about the various processes or the procedures of how to solve the problem, one looks at parts of the problem in terms of data: the properties of data, the attributes of data, how data work together, and how to develop functions that describe how data behave. You will still work with modules; however, the modules will be related to the data parts and not the procedural parts of the solution. The result is a nonprocedural and a nonlinear solution to a problem.

This chapter will introduce new concepts and terms used in object-oriented programming. The chapter is divided into two parts. The first part will present concepts and terms used in object-oriented programming such as C++ or Visual Basic.net. The second part will present concepts and terms used in event-driven object-oriented languages such as Visual Basic.net and Lingo. Both are driven by data objects, messages, and events sent to the modules to complete the required processing, but the basic problem-solving is different.

Object-Oriented Programming

Program design using object-oriented programming languages, for example C++, allows the programmer to look at the solution in terms of data parts instead of procedures. Consider a library book checkout system. In a procedural program, you would design the program with the procedures in mind:

- Input of the data—book name, book number, date, client, and so on
- Checking out the book
- Checking in the book
- Printout of all outstanding books
- Printout of all books
- Add, delete, and update book information

In an object-oriented program, you would design the program with the data parts in mind:

- Books
- Clients

Each part then would be assigned responsibilities:

- Books
 - Properties
 - ID of the book
 - Author of the book
 - Title of the book

- Methods
 - Check in the book
 - Check out the book
 - Add, edit, or delete a book
- Clients
 - Properties
 - ID of the client.
 - Name, address, etc. of the client
 - Methods
 - List of books checked out
 - History of client activity
 - Add, edit, or delete client data

There may be other data parts and other responsibilities, but you should be able to see the difference in the strategy of the solution. In order to complete the responsibilities, each part needs to interact with other parts. Now let's put some common names to the ideas presented.

Classes

class

A **class** is a collection of like items or objects. The class defines the members (objects) in the class. A class also defines the "portholes" for the rest of the program to manipulate the class or read the current state of the class. When you create a class, you are essentially creating a new data type. Accounts in a bank would be a class; cars in a car dealership would be a class. In our library problem, the classes are *Books* and *Clients*. Associated with each class is a set of properties, structures, functions, and/or behaviors. The *Books* class contains the property definitions that define objects of that class: an ID code, location in the library, and so on. In addition, the class defines operations (functions) that can manipulate class objects such as the ability to check in and out, and so forth. The *Clients* class would have the properties of client name, client address, client ID code, and others. An object is an instance of its class. For example, *Tom Sawyer* by Mark Twain is a book object, which belongs to the *Books* class. Figure 16.1 shows a diagram of the *Books* class. Superclasses may be created in which all subclasses have *inherited* characteristics. This relationship is called **inheritance.** Inheritance allows designer to reuse code from superclass to subclass in the same way the book object is part of the book class. The book class would contain attributes about all books, for example, title and ID, while the book object would contain the specifics about a particular book, for example, Title: *Tom Sawyer*, ID: *TS1983838*. If our library example were to be expanded to include magazines, tapes, CDs, and other media types, we would create a superclass of library items. Each subclass adds characteristics and therefore becomes more specific. Another example might be the superclass of mammals that have specific characteristics that define a mammal. Humans are a subclass of the superclass of mammals and have inherited all the characteristics of the superclass of mammals, but have more characteristics that distinguish a human from another mammal. Figure 16.2 shows a diagram of the *Mammals* class, its members (objects, for example, *Humans, Marsupials,* etc.) that are subclasses of the *Mammals* class, and the members or objects of the *Humans* class. Notice that there are classes (*Humans, Marsupials,* etc.) that are members of another class (*Mammals*). This makes the *Humans* class, the *Marsupials* class, and others, subclasses of *Mammals*.

inheritance

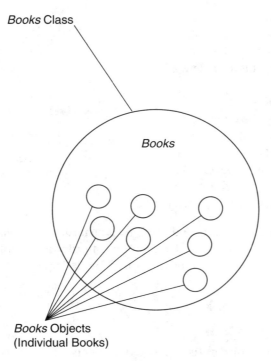

Books Class

Books

Books Objects
(Individual Books)

Figure 16.1 Example of the *Books* Class and Its Objects (instance of a class)

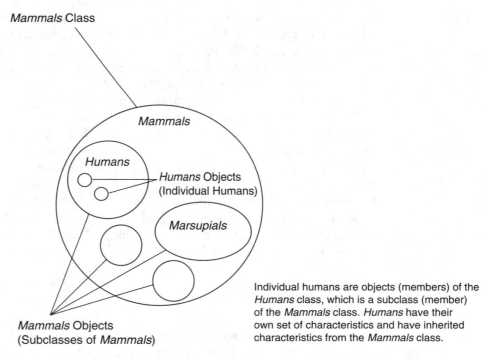

Mammals Class

Mammals

Humans

Humans Objects
(Individual Humans)

Marsupials

Mammals Objects
(Subclasses of *Mammals*)

Individual humans are objects (members) of the *Humans* class, which is a subclass (member) of the *Mammals* class. *Humans* have their own set of characteristics and have inherited characteristics from the *Mammals* class.

Figure 16.2 Example of the Mammals Class, Its Objects, Which Are Subclasses, and the Objects of the Subclasses

The class also defines operations to manipulate class objects. These will be defined through the use of functions. The functions will be executed whenever they are called within a program. The function call includes the object and any data (parameters) required by the function. A function may be executed often in a single execution of the program and never used in another. For example, you may print several times when using a word processor on one occasion and never at another time. It is left to the user to decide what functions are needed during the running of the application and it is left up to the programmer to make sure all needed functions are part of the program. In our library checkout system, functions defined in the *Books* class will define how to mark that the book is checked out, how the book is marked as checked in, how to update book data, how to add and delete books, and how to list the book's attributes. Functions defined in the *Clients* class will define how to list all the books checked out for each client, how to print client data, how to update client data, how to add and delete clients, and so forth. These are all of the things that can be done with a specific book (*Books* object) or a specific client (*Clients* object).

Inheritance

Inheritance was introduced in the previous section on classes. Inheritance is an important part of OOP because it greatly reduces the amount of programming needed to accomplish many common tasks. For instance, consider the creation of a form used to enter client or book data. A form is merely a built-in object in Visual Basic—it has standard properties and methods, but in our solution we will add a new standard function *close*—to a form. In Figure 16.3 we build such a form with the button and underlying code to close a form. The programmer would never use this form directly; instead, another form would inherit from this form.

The two form examples in Figures 16.4 and 16.5 are inherited from the *inheritance form* (base form) below. Notice the Close button at the bottom. All of the other fields and labels are unique to the newly created forms, whereas the Close button is not. Many forms can be created using this base form. If the developer needs to add common functionality to all of the forms, she only needs to add it to the base form and all other forms will inherit the new functionality. The beauty of this is the reduced time to modify multiple

Figure 16.3 Example of an Inheritance Form

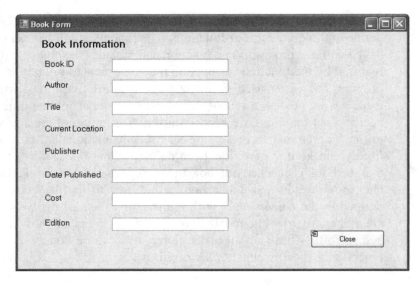

Figure 16.4 Example of an Inherited *Book* Form

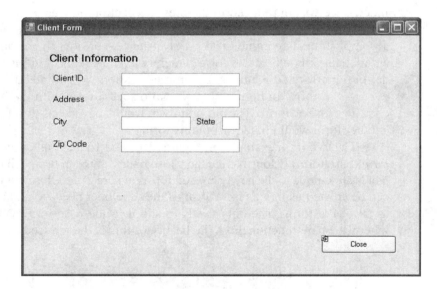

Figure 16.5 Example of an Inherited *Client* Form

forms as well as reduced redundancy in code, which reduces the possibility of bug introduction. In turn, this speeds the development process.

When the Close button is pressed or clicked, the underlying code in the base form will execute the *event* closing the form that this button has inherited. There is no need to constantly rewrite form close code for each form in your application.

Objects

An instance of an object is paramount to understanding why OOP is so important. In regular structural programming we tend to think in terms of linear programming: An event happens (like a form button is pushed) and something happens as a result. In OOP we begin to think in terms of "I need one of these objects to do some work," so we create

an instance of the object and let it work for us. The beauty is we can create multiple instances of the same object to do the same kind of work with different circumstances (variable setting). The instance will keep track of its own stack of variables independent of other instances of the same class. Then when we are done with the object we can destroy it, which removes it from memory.

object
instance of a class

An **object** is an **instance** (member) **of a class**. In our library checkout system example, each book would be an object of the *Books* class, and each client would be an object of the *Clients* class. An object consists of one or more data values that define the object. An object may be a graphic, a person, a device, a magazine, a book, a tape, a video clip, a sound clip, or some other data value, depending upon the class of which it is a member. It is what you, as a programmer, work with in the same manner as you work with a specific record in a file.

Once an object instance has done the work needed, it can be destroyed, which allows for memory to be freed, greatly enhancing the performance of the system. Procedural programs typically completely load the entire program, which takes up all the resources that the program needs to complete the task; whereas in OOP, objects can be instantiated and destroyed so computer systems can perform much more complex operation with smaller impact on the system resources.

Functions

Developing the solutions for each function follows exactly the same steps you have been using for procedural programming, since each individual function is a procedural module. Each function is cohesive, and data are coupled in the same manner as was done in procedural programming. While an object-oriented solution may be set up as procedural in nature, the power of object-oriented programming is in the way the program is controlled. In object-oriented programming, the user has almost complete control of the execution and the execution is controlled mainly through the use of icons, menus, and a pointing device. When an icon or a menu item is selected, the function for that item is executed. You may print a document at any time, not just when the document is completed. You may calculate at any time, even if there are no data. You may change your data at any time, before or after the calculation, not just at the beginning of the program. All this is possible when using object-oriented programming methods and a graphical user interface.

As a programmer, part of your job is to identify the classes and objects, and their attributes and functions. It also is your job to design the various interface screens and menus. Many functions are activated through the use of a menu. Because the solution is no longer procedural, that is, executed from the start of the solution to the last and controlled by the computer, it is your job to make the solution as user-friendly as possible, allowing the user to execute functions whenever necessary. It also is your job to make sure the user does not execute a function at the wrong time, which would produce destroyed data or garbage. You may want to develop safety windows that allow the user to back out of a function if he entered it at the wrong time. This nonprocedural approach takes a different type of analysis and thought process. Once you are at the function level and designing the instructions within the function, the logic structures are the same as in a procedural solution.

Graphical User Interface (GUI)

graphical user
interface (GUI)

A **graphical user interface (GUI)** is a computer screen designed for easy interaction between the user and the computer. Each item on the screen is an object with related responsibilities. A GUI may be designed using a language such as C++ or an event-driven

language such as Visual Basic or Lingo. Chapter 17 presents information on interface design. The graphical user interface is now the standard user interface.

Event-Driven Object-Oriented Programming

Event-driven object-oriented languages have many built-in capabilities to assist in the development of a GUI. Part of the language includes a relatively easy way to add and design interactivity tools, such as buttons, menus, input boxes, and so on, along with a relatively easy method of adding scripts to these tools. Examples of these types of languages are Visual Basic.Net and C# (C Sharp). These languages have been developed for object-oriented programming much like C++, the original object-oriented language. These languages are easier to learn than an object-oriented language such as C++; however, they are not as flexible in the development of a solution to a problem.

event-driven object-oriented programming

Event-driven object-oriented programming uses actions or events to trigger the execution of a set of instructions called a script. A script is another name for a module. The GUI is designed so that each item on the screen is an object with assigned properties. There are no programmer-defined classes. The object may be in the form of a button, a graphic, a user input box, an output box, a pull-down menu, a text box, a video clip, a sound clip, or anything else that has been placed on the screen. The properties of these objects may be such things as location on the screen, the name of the object, color, text formats, color palette used, designation of editable text, size, speed of video or sound, and so on. A script may be attached to each object. There is an overall program script that designates any actions that refer to the entire application, such as initializations, beeps of the mouse, or designating global variables (called public variables). Once the application starts, the user has complete control over the order of processing through the use of events, the GUI, a pointing device, and a keyboard.

multiple-thread

Many languages now support **multiple-thread** events. This is the concept of more than one process of code operating at the same time, or asynchronously. Programmers use these techniques to perform lightweight system tasks or timed events using a system time to refresh an object status. For example, a user is filling out a form on the screen that has certain fields that are required based on the values in other fields. The programmer may want to display the field list of required fields as a sidebar on the form. In order for the sidebar to refresh as the user types, the programmer can invoke a timed thread to run every five seconds. The thread would examine the fields the user has filled in and update the sidebar display appropriately. The alternative would be to invoke the update after every *AfterUpdate* event for each field.

Events

event

An **event** is something that happens in the computer. Some typical events are the following:

on mousedown	*on change*
on mouseup	*before update*
on keydown	*after update*
on keyup	

Each language has its own set of events. The only time the script for an event is executed is when the event happens. When a button is clicked, a set of instructions attached to the clicked object is executed when the mouse button goes down. A different set of instructions

may be executed when the mouse button comes up. When a specific key is depressed or released, another set of instructions may be executed. In this case, the computer saves the value of the key. The programmer may use this information in the script. The program is executed through the use of events, many of which are directed by the user.

User-Defined Events

user-defined event

Many programming languages have the capability of implementing **user-defined events.** So in addition to the built-in events described above, a programmer can create an event and then raise it when needed. This is especially helpful when objects need to communicate to other objects without depending on them. For example: let's suppose we created an object call *BookProcess* whose purpose was to read book data from a large data file and process the data one record at a time. Within the looping structure of the read function in the object we raise an event called *BroadcastProgress*. When we raise the event, we pass three variables—one that represents the percentage of completion, one that is the record count, and the last the current title of the book being processed. The code might look something like this:

```
Public Class clsBookProcess

    'Create the event
    Public Event BroadcastProgress(ByVal intPercentComplete As
    Int16, ByVal intCount As Int16, ByVal strTitle As String)

    Public Sub ProcessBook()
       Dim dr as datarow
        'Get the total count of books
        'tblBook is the table of books being processed
        'BookId and Title are fields in the table
       Dim intTotalCounter as Integer = tblBooks.Count
       Dim intCounter as integer = 0
       Dim intPercentageComplete as Int
       For each dr in tblBooks.Rows
               'Read the data
               'Do some work to read the data from tblBooks
               (Not shown)

               'PercentComplete is calculated
               intPercentageComplete = Cint((intcounter /
               intTotlaCounter) * 100)

               'Raise the event here
               RaiseEvent BroadcastProgress(intPercentageComplete,
               dr("BookID"), dr("Title"))
        Next
     End Sub
End Class
```

The form in Figure 16.6 would have code in it to handle the event *BroadcastProgress*. In effect, the form is listening to the object doing the processing of the book data and displaying it to a user so the user can follow the progress of the work being done. That code would look like the following:

The object gets created:

```
Dim WithEvents BookProcess As New clsBookProcess
```

Figure 16.6 Progress Form

The subfunction handles (listens to) *BroadcastProgress*:

```
Private Sub ListenToBookProcess(ByVal intPercentComplete As
Int, ByVal intCount As Int, ByVal strTitle As String) Handles
BookProcess. BroadcastProgress

    Me.ProgressBar.Value = intPercentComplete
    Me.BookTitle.Text = "Working on record " &
    intCount.ToString & " " & strTitle

End Sub

Private Sub Button1_Click(ByVal sender As System.Object,
ByVal e As System.EventArgs) Handles Button1.Click
    BookProcess.processbook()
End Sub
End Class
```

Now let's suppose that you have this same object running the same code in the middle of the night automatically from a completely different program. The *Progress Form* in this new program doesn't exist. So when the code runs, the *BroadcastProgress* event occurs but *Progress Form* is not listening. For an OOP language this is no problem. The object is broadcasting that it has done the work, but unless another object is listening, nothing happens. There is no dependency between the *Progress Form* and the *BookProcess* object—the two objects are not coupled, yet they can interact using user-defined events.

Interactivity

interactivity

When using event-driven languages, **interactivity** exists between screens or between the user and the computer. Each screen becomes an entity to be designed and programmed. Interaction may cause something to happen on the screen, take the user to a new or a modified screen, stop the program from running, or create a printed document. This interaction produces a nonlinear application. For example, let's look at a problem to calculate the interest of an amount of money over several years. The user has to input the amount, the interest, and the number of years. In a procedural solution, the program

specifies the order in which the user enters the data and changes may or may not be allowed without starting over. In an event-driven object-oriented solution, there would be three user input boxes on the screen. The user may input the data in any order and change any of the data as necessary. The calculation does not take place until the user requests the answer through the use of a button—an event.

navigational tools Interactivity requires that **navigational tools** be built into the program. These tools include hot spots, hot objects, time, and different types of buttons such as a back button, a forward button, a jump button, a menu button, a quit button, and so on. It is very important to plan navigation carefully. The user needs to navigate through the program with ease and with as little frustration as possible and must be able to quit at any time.

Summary

Object-oriented programming requires a different approach to developing a solution to a problem. The programmer must look at the data parts and the events of the problem and not the processes of the problem. New terminology is used with object-oriented programming. A class is a group of items with designated attributes and functions. An object is an instance of the class. Subclasses and objects inherit the properties of the class of which it is a member. Classes must interact with each other to obtain needed data for functions to complete the responsibilities of the class. Inheritance is the relationship between a superclass and a subclass. It allows designers create common functionality in a superclass that a subclass can use. Event-driven object-oriented programming uses screen objects that are assigned properties and scripts. User-defined events expand the event-driven functions, beyond the built-in events, to allow designer to have events execute as a result of any given action. Interaction between screens is accomplished by events that happen when the program is executed.

New Terms

class	inheritance	object
event	instance of a class	object-oriented
event-driven object-oriented programming	interactivity	programming (OOP)
	multiple-thread	user-defined event
graphical user interface (GUI)	navigational tools	

Questions

1. What is the relationship between a class and an object in object-oriented programming?
2. What is the difference between a procedural solution and an object-oriented solution to a problem?
3. What is a GUI?
4. Why is a GUI important to the development of solutions to problems today?
5. What is an example of an event?
6. What is the difference between an event and a user-defined event?
7. Describe how a class would inherit functionality from another class.

Problems

1. Explain what classes you would use in the solutions to the following problems:
 a. A restaurant wants a scheduling system for its employees. The software will allow the restaurant owner to schedule employees for up to 40 hours in a seven-day week. The restaurant is open from 6:00 AM to 10:00 PM. The system should include a check-in and a check-out system for the employees, a printout of employees' work hours, and the ability to change hours if necessary.
 b. A college computer lab manager wants a system to check in and check out students using the lab. The system should include the ability to check a student in and out of the lab, to check lab materials in and out, to keep track of students' hours, and to track all materials that are checked out. The system should also have the ability to determine if a computer is open before allowing the student to check in.

Chapter 17

Object-Oriented Program Design

Overview

Designing an Object-Oriented Application
Interface Design
Designing an Event-Driven Object-Oriented Application

Objectives

When you have finished this chapter, you should be able to:

1. Understand how to "think" in object-orientation.
2. Recognize when and how to apply inheritance to class.
3. Determine the classes, properties, and functions for an object-oriented solution.
4. Design an object-oriented programming solution.
5. Design a functional, user-friendly user interface.
6. Design the storyboards for an event-driven object-oriented solution.
7. Determine the objects and the scripts needed for an event-driven object-oriented solution.

Designing object-oriented applications requires somewhat different tools and problem-solving strategies. Modules and interactivity take on a different meaning within an application. New tools need to be explored. These tools have not been standardized as much as the procedural tools that were introduced at the beginning of this text. The tools presented in this chapter include the output and input requirements chart; the user interface screen design chart; the class, properties, and functions chart; the attributes of class properties chart; an interactivity diagram; storyboards; the object dictionary; and the interactivity chart for an event-driven object-oriented program.

Many people use Unified Modeling Language (UML) to design a solution using a object-oriented language. An overview of UML is presented in Appendix B. You may want to use that approach rather than the approach presented in this chapter. It consists of the development of several diagrams describing the solution. Both methods present ways of helping you design the most efficient solution to complex problems. Remember that these methods help you design the overall view of the solution and the way the final program is executed. Each individual function uses the four logic structures and the various data structures presented in Chapters 4–13.

Designing an Object-Oriented Application

When working with object-oriented languages such as C++, C#, or VB.Net, there are certain design rules and steps you need to follow. In order to think in object orientation, you must understand the concepts of object orientation—specifically, the treating of class objects like "black boxes" of code with "portholes" that other objects can use to ask for information or have processes performed. In other words, all of the properties and functions within the objects are declared as *private* or *public*. The *public* functions in an object can use the *private* function within the object; this ensures encapsulation of the code specific to the object's purpose. These public functions and properties are the "portholes" into the object. None of the private functions or properties are accessible from other objects.

Second, applying inheritance to object creation, a designer must consider all of the objects needed in the application and how those objects group together. A class would be created that would provide an instance of variables and functions common to all of the objects in the group. This class is called a super class. All of the objects in the group would inherit from this newly created super class. The objects in the group would be a subclass of the super class. The super class and subclass are related in a generalization to specialization relationship: the super class being the generalized functions and properties while the subclass is the specialized functions and properties. The following is a VB.Net example of a super class, subclass, and the instantiation and calling code from a form. Figure 17.1 shows the screen display.

```
Public Class clsSuperClass
    'Declare a private variable for storing a string
    Private m_strWordToDisplay As String

    'Let an outside object change the private varible
    'This is a propery of the super class for setting the words
    to print
```

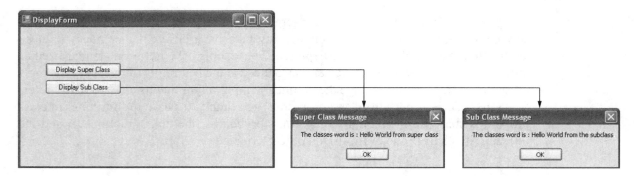

Figure 17.1 *Displayform* Example and Resulting Messages

```vb
    'This changes the private variable m_strWordToDisplay
    Public Property WordToDisplay() As String
        Get
        'Here is where the current value can be examined by an
        outside object
            Return m_strWordToDisplay
        End Get
        Set(ByVal value As String)
        'Here is where the variable is changed.
            m_strWordToDisplay = value
        End Set
    End Property

    Public Sub DisplaySuperClassWord()
        'Display a message
        MsgBox("The classes word is : " & m_strWordToDisplay)
    End Sub
End Class

Public Class clsSubClass
    Inherits clsSuperClass
    'Here is the private variable for a sub class.
    'Let set the default to "Hello World from the subclass".
    Private m_strWordToDisplay As String = "Hello World from the
    subclass"

    Public Sub DisplaySubClassWord()
        'Display a message
        MsgBox("The classes word is : " & m_strWordToDisplay)
    End Sub
End Class

Public Class DisplayForm
    'instantiate the sub class
    Dim m_subclass As New clsSubClass

    Private Sub btnDisplaySuperClass_Click(ByVal sender As
    System.Object, ByVal e As
System.EventArgs) Handles btnDisplaySuperClass.Click

        'Set the superclass WordToDisplay property
        m_subclass.WordToDisplay = "Hello World from super
        class"

        'Run the inherited DisplaySuperClassWord function from
        the subclass
        m_subclass.DisplaySuperClassWord()
    End Sub

    Private Sub btnDisplaySubClass_Click(ByVal sender As
    System.Object, ByVal e As
System.EventArgs) Handles btnDisplaySubClass.Click
        'Run the function in the sub class to display the word
        m_subclass.DisplaySubClassWord()
    End Sub
End Class
```

Notice that the super class is never instantiated in the form; instead, it is automatically instantiated when the subclass, *clsSubClass*, is created. The public function *DisplaySuperClassWord()* is available because it has been inherited. So when the event *btnDisplaySuperClass_Click* is executed by the users clicking the button, the message box appears with "Hello World from super class" in the text.

There are potentially multiple layers of the super class–subclass–subclass depending on the complexity of the object generalization and specialization. As you start to design your application, object-oriented thinking will help in the class structure hierarchy as you will begin to understand how and where to locate functions within the classes. This discipline will reduce code redundancy because common functions and variables will reside in a super class for inheritance.

When working with an object-oriented language such as C++, there are certain steps you need to take in the basic design of the application. These steps are as follows:

1. Determine the requirements of the program in terms of input, output, and needed data requirements. This is accomplished by discussing requirements with users, a knowledge base of the current system in place (if any), and research.
2. Determine the classes, including the properties and their attributes, and functions of each class. This includes data classes, built-in classes such as forms and reports, and any other utility classes needed to build the application. Once these classes are determined, an inheritance hierarchy can be created.
3. Determine the interactivity between classes and between the functions within the class. This defines the public functions and properties, "portholes," within the class.
4. Determine the instructions to accomplish each function.

A more detailed explanation of these steps follows, including a description of the tools designed to help develop each step.

Step 1: Determine the requirements of the program in terms of output and needed data requirements. From the given information, you will need to determine first what the output requirements are and design the user interface. Until you know what output is required and what the interface screens will look like, it is impossible to continue with an object-oriented solution. The output requirements will determine needed data to execute the program. The first part of this step is to use the *output and input requirements chart* to list all output requirements and all input values along with how they will be formatted when entered. Figure 17.2a shows a blank output and input requirements chart. Figure 17.2b shows this chart as it might be filled in for the library checkout system

Output Requirements	Input Requirements	Input Format

Figure 17.2a The Output and Input Requirements Chart

Output Requirements	Input Requirements	Input Format
List of Books	Book Data:	Screen for adding/deleting
Individual Book Data	ISBN	String, 15 characters, file
Change data—check in and check out books	Library Number	String, 15 characters, file
	Name	String, 25 characters, file
Add and Delete Books	Author(s)	String, 30 characters, file
List of Clients	Publisher	String, 15 characters, file
	Year of Publication	Date, 10 characters, file
	Area Location in Library	String, 10 characters, file
	Checked In or Out	Logical, 1 character, screen, file
	Client ID Checked Out To	String, 5 characters, screen, file
	Client Data:	Screen for adding/deleting
	Client ID	String, 5 characters, file
	Name	String, 25 characters, file
	Address	String, 25 characters, file
	City	String, 15 characters, file
	State	String, 2 characters, file
	Zip Code	String, 10 characters, file
	Telephone	String, 15 characters, file
	Books Checked Out: Library number and ISBN	Multiple entries (maximum 10) String, 15 characters, screen, file String, 15 characters, screen, file

Figure 17.2b The Output and Input Requirements Chart for the Library Checkout System

introduced in Chapter 16. The output and input requirements chart is similar to the problem analysis chart introduced earlier; however, with OOP you are not concerned with the processing as much as you are with the data and overall functions associated with the data. This chart is divided into three parts. In the first column, you should list the output requirements. From the output, determine the input required and list these items

in the second column. In the third column, list how you will enter the input values—in an input box, as a result of a query, or some other method, along with any other information about the data.

screen The next part of this step is to design the user interface screen(s). A **screen** is the image on the monitor. You will need to place all labels, input fields, output fields, and any graphics, text, and other formatting that will enhance the aesthetics of the screen(s). You may need to design a control panel or use buttons or hot spots or your output may look very similar to that of a procedural solution. Figure 17.3a shows a form you can use to draw a thumbnail sketch of the design. Figure 17.3b shows one idea of how a library checkout system screen might look. You may have designed the screen with a very different look. Design concept of user interfaces will be discussed later in this chapter. Without knowing anything about these design concepts, how would you change the thumbnail sketch to improve readability, ease of use, and aesthetics?

Step 2: Determine the classes of data. The second step that takes place in the design of the object-oriented programming solution of a problem is to break the data into classes. Figure 17.4a shows the *class, properties, and functions chart* used to define the classes along with the properties and functions for each class. When determining classes, remember to look for common functionality between classes. This may indicate the potential for a super class. The boxes in the first column are used to list each class as defined by the developer. Each box should contain one class name. The boxes in the second column are used to list the properties of class in the first column. There will be one or more properties for each class. The third column is used to list the functions for each class. Figure 17.4b illustrates a class, properties, and functions chart for the library checkout system. Notice that the two classes are *Books* and *Clients*. The properties are the data that are required for each *Books* object or each *Clients* object. The functions are a list of things that each object is required to accomplish. One of the functions of the

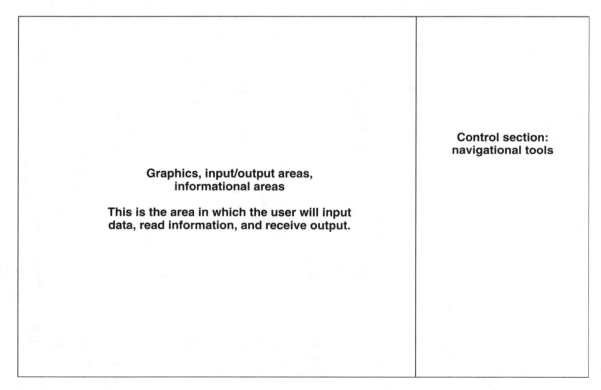

Figure 17.3a The User Interface Screen Design Chart

Figure 17.3b The User Interface Screen Design Chart for the Library Checkout System

Class	Properties	Functions

Figure 17.4a The Class, Properties, and Functions Chart

Class	Properties	Functions
Books	Library ID Number Name Author ISBN Number Publisher Year of Publication Checked Out Client Checked Out To Area in Library	Check out book Check in book List each book data Add and delete books Update book data
Clients	Client ID Name Address City State Zip Code Telephone Books Checked Out	Add and delete books checked out Add and delete client Update client List client data

Figure 17.4b Example of a Class, Properties, and Functions Chart for the Library Checkout System

Books class is to be able to add or delete a *Books* object. Another is to be able to register as part of the properties of the *Books* class regardless of whether an object is checked out. Can you think of other properties or functions that are needed for this system? The properties and functions define the class. Can you think of common functionality that the *Books* object and the *Clients* object share that might become a super class?

Each property has attributes, such as the data type, the string length, and so on. Figure 17.5a shows the *attributes of class properties chart*. An attributes of class properties chart is created for each class. On the chart the class is listed at the top and the properties are listed on the left. The attributes for each property are listed in the area to the right of the properties. Figure 17.5b shows the library checkout *Books* class attributes of class properties chart.

Step 3: Determine the interactivity between the classes and between the functions within classes. Interactivity will occur within the functions of the class and also between the classes. When a client is checking out a book, the *Clients* class function of book checkout is executed. During this process, the *Books* class function of updating data must be executed. The classes are interacting with each other. When the *Books* class function of listing the *Books'* object's properties and the book is checked out, the *Books* class must interact with the *Clients* class to obtain information about who has checked out the book. Also, the functions within the class may interact with each other. In the process of the function of book checkout in the *Clients* class, the *Clients'* object's properties must be updated. Figure 17.6a shows a generic *interactivity chart for an object-oriented solution* to a problem. Notice that each of the classes is separate. The functions that define each class may interact within that class or they may interact directly with a function from another class. If a function from class 1 needs to interact with a function from class 2, the function from class 1 may directly access the class 2 function. If a

Class: _____

Property	Attributes

Figure 17.5a The Attributes of Class Properties Chart

Class: _____*Books* Class_____

Property	Attributes
Library ID Number	String, 15 characters, file (screen to add or delete or change)
Name	String, 15 characters, file (screen to add or delete or change)
Author	String, 25 characters, file (screen to add or delete or change)
ISBN Number	String, 30 characters, file (screen to add or delete or change)
Publisher	String, 15 characters, file (screen to add or delete or change)
Year of Publication	Date, 10 characters, file (screen to add or delete or change)
Checked Out	String, 10 characters, file (changed from client input)
Client Checked Out To	Logical, 1 character, screen, file (changed from client input)
Area in Library	String, 5 characters, screen, file (screen to add or delete or change)

Figure 17.5b Example of an Attributes of Class Properties for the Books Class

function from class 1 needs to interact with a function from class 2, then the function within class 2 must be declared as public so the "porthole" is open from class 1 to interact with class 2. Figure 17.6b shows the interactivity chart for the library checkout system. Notice the functions for each class that will need to be public so that each class can interact.

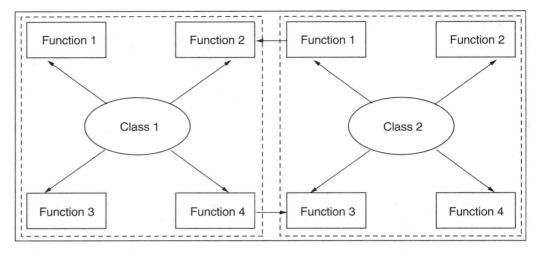

Figure 17.6a Interactivity Diagram for an Object-Oriented Solution to a Problem

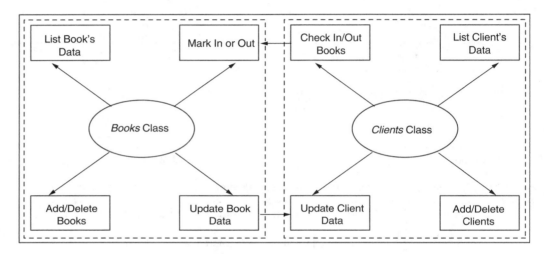

Figure 17.6b Interactivity Diagram for the Library Checkout System

Step 4: Determine the instructions to accomplish each function. Determining instructions to accomplish each function is the last step in the design of an object-oriented application. These instructions are similar to the instructions presented in Units One, Two, and Three of this text. Each language may have some specialized instructions. However, the four logic structures will be used in the same manner as in a procedural solution. The instructions for each function are small sets of procedural instructions. Each function is a cohesive module. The same rules hold true when using coupling methods such as global variables, parameters, and return values just as with the procedural approach to solution design.

Interface Design

A graphical user interface (GUI) is usually developed when using a language such as C++, and it must be developed when using an event-driven object-oriented language such as Visual Basic or Lingo. The success of an application many times depends on the GUI design. There are five very basic rules you must follow when developing an interface design.

Rule 1: Never lose sight of the purpose or the message. The problem should have a purpose. Never lose sight of that purpose. Interface screens should be designed with this purpose in mind. The use of appropriate artwork, video clips, and sound clips ensures the enhancement of the message. If an appropriate object cannot be found, leave it out. If you are designing an interface that introduces Alaska and you can find only palm trees, leave out the trees. Consider finding something else that is appropriate, such as a bear or a seal.

Rule 2: Keep it simple. With so many choices of clip art, photoclips, video clips, and other artwork available, it is easy to overdo the amount of material on the screen. The message is always the key to a successful application. If the message is lost in the glitz of other material on the screen, the application is a failure. Text should be kept at a minimum. People will not read a lot of text on a screen, even in a scroll bar text box. To increase readability, spread the text over several screens instead of cramming everything on one screen. In our complex world, many times simplicity is a welcomed format.

Rule 3: Be consistent. Consistent does not mean constant. Screens should have the same look and feel throughout the application, but should not be boring. Subtle changes can be very attractive and eye catching. Different screens should use the same or look-alike fonts. A *font* is the typeface of the text. Fonts vary greatly in appearance. There are formal fonts, informal fonts, text fonts, title fonts, and so on. You want to choose your font carefully in conjunction with the purpose of the application. You would not want to use a different set of fonts on each screen or within the same screen. The user will get frustrated. Also, be consistent with colors. Develop a color scheme and use it throughout the application. Change the colors only when the change enhances the message.

Rule 4: Design the navigation with the user in mind. A program must be easy to navigate. The width and breadth of the menus must be taken into consideration. A "breadcrumb" system can be used to show the user where she is within the system and allow her to retreat to previous screens. The ability to get back to the Main Menu or Home as well as Exit should be available from any screen within the system.

Rule 5: Understand when you can break the rules. Rules can be broken, but only for good reasons. If you break one of the first three rules, make sure the message has been enhanced and interest in the topic has been increased.

These rules allow the designer to create a functional, user-friendly interface. This is important, as a user will be more satisfied with a well-designed interface.

The application should have a visual style that is consistent with the purpose of the project. If the project is formal, the style should be formal. The fonts should be traditional fonts, the artwork should be serious and in conjunction with the theme of the project. If the project is informal, then more fun fonts can be used and the artwork can include some cartoons. However, even in the most formal project, a moment of levity many times is appreciated.

Each screen needs to be designed using the following elements: backgrounds, windows, navigational tools such as buttons and hot spots, input and output boxes, graphics, text, video, sound, and animation. The background of each screen should be similar to all other screens. Again, subtle changes add interest. Navigational tools should be placed in the same area on the screen. Navigational tools do not need to be buttons. Leaves on a tree, fish in a pond, rocks on the beach, houses on a street all can be navigational tools. Buttons tend to be boring. Try to create new types of navigational tools. User input areas need to be large enough for the user to see and in a convenient and logical place on the screen to enter the data. The same holds true for the output. Text should be limited to a few lines per screen or placed in a scrolled text box with a contrasting

background for easy reading. Graphics, video, and sound should be added with caution and only to enhance the message or purpose of the screen. Any materials that have a copyright can only be used if you have permission of the author. These items should add interest or should add information to data already presented.

A well-designed interface is pleasant to look at, functional, and provides easy access to all of the functions of the program. A well-designed interface allows the user to navigate through the program in a nonlinear mode and should include the ability to quit the program at any time.

Designing an Event-Driven Object-Oriented Application

The steps to create an event-driven object-oriented project are as follows:

Step 1: Define the audience and the environment.
Step 2: Create the storyboards.
Step 3: Define all objects.
Step 4: Define the interactivity between screens.
Step 5: Define the scripts.

Step 1: Define the audience and the environment. In addition to the problem definition as part of the problem-solving steps as described in Chapter 1, the audience and the environment in which the project will be viewed must also be defined. The audience needs to be defined in terms of size, age, and knowledge. In general, the larger the audience, the fewer objects on the screen. More text and more objects can be placed on the screen if the viewer is sitting directly in front of the monitor as opposed to a situation in which the viewer is part of a 500-person audience. Terminology and graphics differ according to age and knowledge of the subject. Buzz words may be used if the audience is knowledgeable, but should not be used for an audience with minimal subject knowledge. The environment in which the project will be viewed is also important to analyze. Questions that need to be answered include What hardware and software will be used? What types of equipment are required? and What is the viewing area? Audience and environment analysis can make the difference between a successful project and one that is unsuccessful. The audience using the library checkout system would be the librarian on duty. She would know about the library and about the system; therefore, the interface can be simple, and buzz words may be used. Only one person at a time will be using the system; therefore, more information may be placed on the screen. The environment will be the library; therefore, the equipment needs to be quiet—no sound and a very quiet printer if needed. The system needs to be networked to the main computer files and needs to be dedicated to the library checkout system during all hours that the library is open.

storyboard

Step 2: Create the storyboards. **Storyboards** define what is placed on the screens and the order of development of the screens. Figure 17.7a presents an example storyboard. Figure 17.7b shows a storyboard for the main screen in the library checkout system. In the box, the developer sketches the objects to be placed on the screen. Fine detail is not necessary, but all objects should be placed in enough detail so the programmer can use this document as a plan to start the computerization of the application. The lines allow for notes on the screen such as interactivity guidelines, object sources, animation effects, and so on. Each storyboard should have a reference number. Storyboards allow the developer to organize data, objects, and ideas.

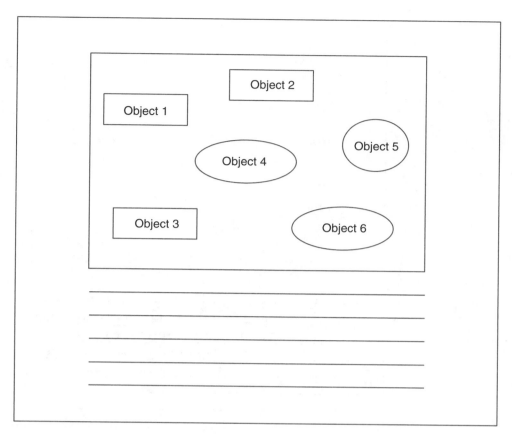

Figure 17.7a The Storyboard

Step 3: Define all objects. Screens are made up of objects. These objects may be developed in the software package, or they may be imported from another source. Just as we needed a data dictionary when using a procedural language, we need an object dictionary for event-driven object-oriented languages. Figure 17.8a (also found in Appendix D) shows an object dictionary form. Figure 17.8b shows an example object dictionary for the library checkout system. Data that pertain to the object need to be placed in the object dictionary. This includes the name of the object, the source and/or file name, the file type and extension, the screens in which it appears, whether the object is a hyper-object, input object, or output object, and whether there is a script attached to it. The name of the object identifies it as an object and can later be referred to by the name. This is similar to naming constants. The source and/or file name column identifies where the object was created or obtained. The object may be created within the program, or it may be obtained from a CD-ROM; created in another package such as a paint package, or an animation package; or imported from a digital camera, an audiotape, or from many other sources. The name of the file is necessary so the file may be located. The file type and extension column defines the type file, such as a bitmapped file or a data file. The file extension defines the format file. The next column lists the storyboards or screens in which the object is found. The last two columns are check columns. The first indicates if this object is a hyper-object, an input object, or an output object, indicated by an *H, I,* or *O.* The last column indicates if there is a script attached to the object. A yes or a check mark indicates a script. The programmer can refer to this list when creating the screens on the computer. This will save time in trying to locate objects.

Figure 17.7b A Storyboard for the Library Checkout System

Object Name	Source/File Name	File Type/Extension	Screen Number(s)	H/I/O*	Script

* H = Hyper, I = Input, O = Output

Figure 17.8a Object Dictionary Form

Step 4: Define the interactivity between screens. The next step is to design the interactivity between the screens. Figure 17.9a shows an interactivity chart for an event-driven object-oriented solution to a problem. Figure 17.9b shows an example interactivity chart for the main screen in the library checkout system. An interactivity chart starts with the storyboard. There will be an interactivity chart for each screen. The storyboard is the center of the interactivity chart. Surrounding the storyboard are rectangles indicating the scripts and to which object each is attached. If a script calls another script, the interactivity between these scripts is shown (see Figure 17.9a). The interactivity diagram will not show the scripts that are separate from the interactivity, such as a script that clicks the mouse when a mouse button is pushed.

Object Name	Source/File Name	File Type/Extension	Screen Number(s)	H/I/O*	Script
Client ID			Main	I	Y
Book ID			Main	I	Y
Client Data			Main	O	N
Book Data			Main	O	N
Check In Button			Main	H	Y
Check Out Button			Main	H	Y
Add/Delete Client Button			All	H	Y
Add/Delete Client Button			All	H	Y
List Books Button			All	H	Y
List Clients Button			All	H	Y
Next Book Button			All	H	Y
Next Client Button			All	H	Y
Exit Button			All	H	Y
Man/Newspaper Graphic	ManReading	BMP	All		N
Background	Library Picture	TIF	All		N

* H = Hyper, I = Input, O = Output

Figure 17.8b Sample Object Dictionary for the Library Checkout System

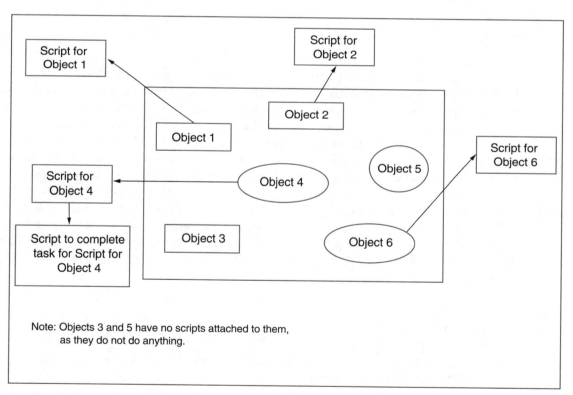

Figure 17.9a Interactivity Chart for an Event-Driven Object-Oriented Solution

Step 5: Define the script. Scripts are short sets of instructions written in the language used by the application, i.e., C++, C#, VB.Net. These scripts are procedural in nature and will either return a result or perform a process. The logic structures presented in earlier chapters in this text hold true for these scripts. Variables within the object's

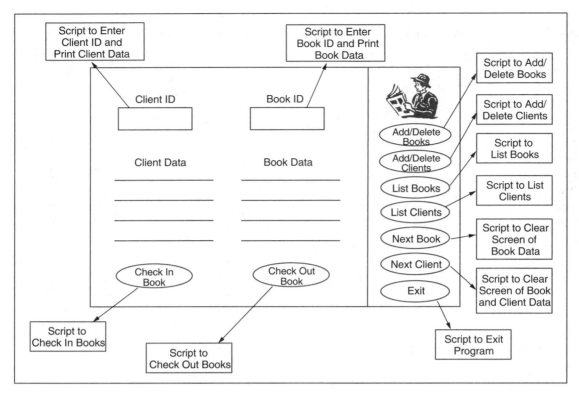

Figure 17.9b Example Interactivity Chart for the Library Checkout System

scripts are not made public to external objects; instead, properties are used to set object level variables. If data is needed from one object to another the return of a public function or property must be public in order for the external object to access the data.

Object-oriented programming has become the standard practice for newly created software applications. It has been recognized in the industry as the best way to handle large complex application requirements because it breaks down the solution into many smaller subsets that can be managed by *objects* within the application. Much like people having different specific jobs in an organization, objects also perform different tasks with an application. Procedural programming is still prevalent in many industries and still has its place within object-oriented design; however, it is no longer the standard method of application development. Students should learn "object-oriented" thinking with encapsulated procedural design. With this knowledge an application can easily be created to solve any problem at hand.

Summary

There are several steps a programmer should follow when designing an object-oriented program. They include the following:

1. Define the classes.
2. Define the responsibilities for each class.
3. Determine the interactivity between the classes.
4. Determine the instructions to accomplish each responsibility.

Most programs today use a graphic user interface so the user can easily guide the program. A user interface needs to be functional, nice to look at, and easy to use. When designing an event-driven object-oriented program, follow these five steps:

Step 1. Define the audience and the environment.
Step 2. Create the storyboards.
Step 3. Define all objects.
Step 4. Define the interactivity between screens.
Step 5. Define the scripts.

Tools introduced in this chapter include the output and input requirements chart; user interface screen design chart; class, properties, and functions chart; attributes of class properties chart; interactivity diagram; storyboard; object dictionary; and interactivity chart for an event-driven object-oriented program. A well-designed program allows for better efficiency in programming and maintenance.

New Terms

screen storyboard

Questions

1. What is the purpose of the following charts?
 a. output and input requirements chart
 b. user interface screen design chart
 c. class, properties, and functions chart
 d. attributes for class properties chart
 e. interactivity chart for an object-oriented programming solution
 f. storyboard
 g. object dictionary
 h. interactivity chart for an event-driven object-oriented programming solution
2. What are the steps to design an object-oriented solution to a problem?
3. What are the steps to design an event-driven object-oriented solution to a problem?
4. What are the rules to design a user interface?

Problems

1. Design a solution to the following problems using the four steps to design an object-oriented solution.
 a. A restaurant wants a scheduling system for its employees. The software will allow the restaurant owner to schedule employees for up to 40 hours in a seven-day week. The restaurant is open from 6:00 AM to 10:00 PM. The system should include a check-in and a check-out system for the employees, a printout of employees' work hours, and the ability to change hours if necessary.

b. A college computer lab manager wants a system to check in and check out students using the lab. The system should include the ability to check a student in and out of the lab, to check lab materials in and out, to keep track of students' hours, and to track all materials that are checked out. The system should also have the ability to determine if a computer is open before allowing the student to check in.

2. Design a solution to each of the problems in problem 1 using the five steps to design an event-driven object-oriented solution.

Unit Five

Supplementary Exercises

1. Design a solution to the following problems using the five steps to design an object-oriented solution.
 a. A retail store wants an inventory system to track inventory in and out of the warehouse. The system should allow inventory to come into and out of the warehouse from outside the store and from within the store. It should allow a numbering system and have the ability to reorder items as needed.
 b. A catalog company wants to have a customer ordering system. This system should allow clients to phone in an order, have the computer process the order, update the inventory, and print out an order form that is also electronically sent to the warehouse.

2. Design a solution to each of the problems in problem 1 using the five steps to design an event-driven object-oriented solution.

UNIT SIX

INTRODUCTION TO GAME DEVELOPMENT

Chapter 18

Introduction to Concepts
of Game Development Using
Object-Oriented Programming

Overview

Game Development
Planning the Game
 Game Resources
Steps to Develop a Simple Game

Objectives

When you have finished this chapter, you should be able to:

1. Understand the terminology used in game development.
2. Understand the game development process.

The electronic game industry has grown tremendously in the last ten years. Games are types of computer software designed to be interactive—with the user making decisions using the mouse, the keyboard, or joysticks—and have a story line with goals and rewards for the user. Games include educational games, games for fun, casino slot machine games, and games for advertising, to name some categories. Many students plan to make the game development industry a career.

For the most part, game development uses object-oriented programming techniques and special languages developed especially for the industry. This chapter will present the basic concepts of game development using object-oriented programming techniques. However, many people are requesting that games process at a faster rate. The industry is responding to this request by programming games in assembly language. This takes a greater amount of time and is far more tedious to develop; however, the product does run faster. Chapter 19 will present an introduction to basic concepts of assembly language programming.

Game Development

Game development can be fun. It is also a lot of work. Planning is essential and may take more time than the development of the game. You probably will be developing the game with many other people, so the planning will be done as a group. As one of the team, you need to be a team player, be able to compromise, and understand that good group interaction will produce the best game. You also need to understand that members of the group will have various talents—some may be artists, others programmers, and others leaders.

Planning the Game

The game developer needs to plan the game before starting to develop it. There are many things to keep in mind during the planning process. Sketching helps in the planning stage and the development of the game since then you can start to visualize the finished product.

1. Players or users are an important consideration when developing computer games, which game developers need to keep in mind. The intended audience will affect the plan of the game. Considerations include the age of the users, the reason to use the game, and the experience of the players.

2. Games need a story line. The story line may be simple—such as a catching a rabbit before it jumps in a hole—or very complex. You should start with a simple game then proceed slowly to the complex. Write down the story line, explaining what will happen in the game from start to finish, including a timeline showing what will happen during the execution of the game.

3. Players need to make decisions during the execution of the game. You should include in your plan the types of decisions you want the user to make, keeping in mind that the player needs to be in control, without frustration, given the audience for which the game is written.

4. Games need resources. These resources will be explained in the next section of this chapter; however, they include such things as the background, the objects, and the actions or events. Include with these resources the way they look, including the textures and the 3-D effect you might want.

5. Games should have a goal, which is how the user finishes the game. This might be as simple as catching the rabbit or as complex as obtaining a number of treasures. The goal should include how the user will accomplish this task. Goals should be attainable for the audience for which the game is written.

6. Users expect rewards as the game progresses. This may include points of some kind or stockpiling treasures, and it may include a list of top point players. Again, keep the audience in mind when planning your rewards: A preschooler may not understand the concept of points.

Once your plan is completed to the best of your ability, then it is time to start the development of the game on the computer.

Game development software uses object-oriented programming techniques. Most of the things presented in this chapter are an extension of Chapters 16 and 17. We will not be creating a game, only describing the process and the terms used in the game development industry.

Game Resources

Parts of the Environment

- **Objects:** Objects are the entities of the game. This includes all of the parts that you will eventually see on the screen.
- **Environment:** **Environments** are where the objects live.
- **Sprites:** **Sprites** are animated images used to represent the objects. They allow the object to do something according to the program of the sprite, such as walk or bounce.
- **Sounds:** **Sounds** are the music or other sounds that act as a background or as effects. In our modern world sound is necessary in anything on screen, whether it is a game, an advertisement, or a movie.
- **Backgrounds:** **Backgrounds** are the images used to give the environment dimension and substance.
- **Events:** Events are the interaction between the player and the game.
- **Instances:** Instances are the objects in the environment. You may have more than one instance of an object, such as more than one ball; however, you may have different sprites attached to the different instances.

room

sprite

sound

background

When developing a game, you need an environment to define the setting and a background so the environment has definition. You need to place instances of objects so you can define the program, such as the grass, the rabbit, a ball, or a wall. Each object needs a sprite, or animated image, so it can viewed on the screen. Events are defined to make the object do something or change an action.

Other Types of Resources

script

- Scripts: **Scripts** are a set of instructions given to an object or a sprite. These instructions use the four logic structures to develop the program.
- Timelines: Timelines specify when something will happen.

Steps to Develop a Simple Game

The ultimate goal of game development is the completed game, and the process to get there has many steps. The final product needs to be a good game that will sell well and be enjoyed by users. In this section we will describe the steps to develop a simple game. The development of a more complex game is similar but expanded.

1. Plan your game carefully. When you are finished planning, your game should go together smoothly. You may spend more time planning the game than developing it.
2. Use game development software to complete your game. Many resources are included in the software, which will eliminate developing some of the resources on your own. This saves time and energy. When you do create your own resources, you will want to keep them so you can use them at another time.
3. Create the resources not found in the game development software. These will include the objects, the sprites, and the music or sounds. You will need to define the events for your objects.

4. Create your environment.
5. Give your environment a background. Specify the textures and any images that will be permanent.
6. Add instances of your object to the environment.
7. Test your game by running the program. Run it first in the debug mode, which will allow you to correct the program as you go. Then run it normally and have fun with it.
8. If you are in industry, the next step is to market the product.

Summary

Electronic game development has become a very big industry in the computer world in the last ten years. Game development uses object-oriented programming techniques. There are also high-level languages for the purpose of developing games. New terminology has been introduced, such as sprites, scripts, environments, backgrounds, and so on. Planning is essential to the development of good games. When developing a large game, a team of people will be the developer since companies need to get the game to market as soon as possible.

New Terms

background	script	sprite
environment	sound	

Questions

1. What are the steps to develop a good game?
2. What are some requirements for a person to work as part of a team to develop a game?

Problems

1. Using a game that you enjoy playing, answer the following questions:
 a. What is name of the game?
 b. What is its goal?
 c. What are the objects?
 d. What do the objects do?
 e. What does the environment look like?
 f. What types of interaction between the player and the computer does this game use? What type of input devices do you use to play the game?
 g. Sketch the environment, including the background.
 h. Add the objects and sketch in what they will do.
 i. What are the rewards that you receive in this game?
2. Answer the following questions about a simple game you would like to develop:
 a. What simple game would you like to develop?
 b. What is the goal?

c. What are the objects?
d. What would you like the objects to do?
e. What does the environment look like?
f. What types of interaction between the player and the computer would you like to see? What type of input devices would you use?
g. Sketch the environment including the background.
h. Add an object and sketch in what it will do.
i. What are the rewards that you would like to implement?

Chapter 19

Introduction to Assembly Language

Overview

Assembly Language Versus High-Level Languages

Assembly Language Concepts

Some Basic Assembly Language Instructions

Assembly Language Equivalents to the Four Logic Structures

Objectives

When you have finished this chapter, you should be able to:

1. Know the difference between developing a solution in assembly language and high level languages.
2. Recognize some basic assembly language instructions.
3. Develop short solutions using assembly language.

Game players have requested that the games run faster. To accommodate this request, the game development industry has responded by using assembly language to develop games for the advanced user. This requires specially trained programmers, takes more time hence costs more money to develop, and is far more tedious for the developer. However, as long as the developer has enough financing to complete the development, the product should make a profit because it will run faster as requested by users. This chapter will present the basic concepts of assembly language.

Assembly Language Versus High-Level Languages

machine language

assembly language

The computer works with zeros and ones, called **machine language.** All programming languages must be translated into these zeros and ones in order for the computer to process a program. The next step up from machine language is **assembly language.** Assembly language is a direct translation from normally a three-letter assembly language instruction to a machine language instruction. Once the translation is complete, assembly language is as fast as if it were written in machine language. The next level up is high-level languages. The rest of this book is written with high-level languages in mind. There are two ways a high-level language is translated into machine language. One is a compiler, which takes the high-level language and changes it permanently into machine language. After the change has taken place, the machine language instructions are executed. These machine language instructions are used until the program is compiled again. The problem with a compiler is that the translation is not always the most efficient; however, it is cheaper to use because it takes less time to program a solution to a problem. Languages such as C++ use a compiler. The second way is an interpreter. Basic requires an interpreter. In this case, each high-level language instruction is changed temporarily as the program is executed. Each time the program is executed, the translation takes place again. Again, the translation is not necessarily the most efficient. Therefore, if speed is required, efficiency is also required, hence the use of assembly language is a better selection.

Assembly Language Concepts

accumulator

register

Assembly language requires the use of individual instructions. In a high-level language, the equation $A = B + C$ is one instruction. In assembly language, this equation requires three instructions. You need to load the accumulator with B, add C, and then store the result in A. The **accumulator** is where any calculations take place. The high-level language is easier to write and read; however, with assembly language the programmer has more control of the efficiency of the solution. Along with the accumulator, the computer uses **registers** to keep numbers that it may use now or later, saving the time to read and write to memory. Registers are high-speed temporary holding areas built into the computer to hold instructions and data needed for the current processing.

Every machine has different machine language codes and uses different registers. The new computers have a very complex set of assembly language instructions. If you do any assembly language programming, the first thing you must do is to find out the instructions that your machine uses. This set is found in your computer manual, online, or through the maker of your computer. After you have a list of the instructions, study them very carefully in order to develop the most efficient program. This chapter will present some generic assembly language instructions for you to try out.

Some Basic Assembly Language Instructions

Assembly language instructions are formatted with an instruction followed by a parameter, which may be an address or a number, depending upon the instruction. Most assembly languages today can use two parameters; however, in this chapter we will keep it simple and use only one. The instructions we will be using are as following. The names of some of these instructions are probably not the same as in your instruction set, but you will be able to begin to understand how to use instructions at this level of computer execution.

Instruction	Description
LDA X	Load the accumulator with the value found in the address named X
LDN N	Load the accumulator with the value of N
ADD X	Add the value found in the address named X to the value found in the accumulator
ADN N	Add the value of N to the value found in the accumulator
SUB X	Subtract the value found in the address named X from the value found in the accumulator
SBN N	Subtract the value of N from the value found in the accumulator
MUL X	Multiply the value found in the address named X by the value found in the accumulator
MLN N	Multiply the value of N by the value found in the accumulator
DIV X	Divide the value found in the address named X by the value found in the accumulator
DVN N	Divide the value of N by the value found in the accumulator
STO X	Store the value of the accumulator into address X
JMP X	Jump to instruction number X
JPZ X	Jump to instruction number X when the accumulator is zero
JPN X	Jump to instruction number X when the accumulator is negative
JPP X	Jump to instruction number X when the accumulator is positive
RD X	Store a value from the keyboard into the address X

These are just a few assembly language instructions that we will use in the next section. The number of instructions varies. The more you know about the set of assembly language instructions for your computer, the more efficient your program can be.

Assembly Language Equivalents to the Four Logic Structures

You have studied the four logic structures in this book. Let's look as the equivalent assembly language instructions.

Sequential Logic Structure

To calculate $A = B + C + D$, the assembly language instructions are

```
. . . . . . . . . . .
10      LDA   B
11      ADD   C
12      ADD   D
13      STO   A
. . . . . . . . .
```

Decision Logic Structure

For the decision instruction:

$$If \; A \; = \; B$$
$$Then$$
$$C \; = \; A \; + \; B$$
$$Else$$
$$C \; = \; A \; - \; B$$

The assembly language equivalent is:

```
. . . . . . . . . .
24        LDA    A
25        SUB    B
26        JMZ    31
27        LDA    A
28        SUB    B
29        STO    C
30        JMP    34
31        LDA    A
32        ADD    B
33        STO    C
34        . . . . . . . .
```

Loop Logic Structure

For the loop logic structure:

$$A \; = \; 5$$
$$B \; = \; 10$$
$$While \; A \; < \; B$$
$$Enter \; D$$
$$J \; = \; J \; + \; D$$
$$A \; = \; A \; - \; 1$$
$$WhileEnd$$

The assembly language instructions would be:

```
. . . . . . . . . .
10        LDN    5
11        STO    A
12        LDN    10
13        STO    B
14        SUB    A
15        JPZ    25
16        RD     J
17        LDA    D
18        ADD    J
19        STO    D
20        LDA    A
21        ADN    1
22        STO    A
23        LDA    B
24        JMP    14
25        . . . . . . . .
```

Case Logic Structure

This would be the same as the decision logic structure, as both are equivalent with the exception that one is easier to write and read depending upon the application.

The four logic structures are presented here. You can expand on these examples for other problems. This chapter gives you a brief introduction to assembly language. If you are interested in learning more, you might want to take an assembly language class.

Summary

Assembly language is used when efficiency is more important than time or money. It is the next step up from machine language and is hard to use and to read. However, with the increased needs of the game development industry, speed is the primary goal of the programs. Every computer has its own set of assembly language instructions. In this chapter the instructions are generic. The equivalent assembly language instructions for the four logic structures are presented.

New Terms

accumulator machine language

assembly language register

Questions

1. Compare machine language to assembly language.
2. Compare assembly language to high-level languages.
3. Find the assembly language instruction set for your computer.
 a. How do the equivalent instructions for your computer compare to what you found in this chapter?
 b. How many instructions are in your instruction set?
 c. Are there terms that you have not heard of before? If so, what are they?
4. Why or why would you not want to program in assembly language?
5. What instructions would you like to have in an assembly language set?

Problems

1. Develop a set of assembly language instructions that are equivalent to the *Repeat/Until* instruction.
2. Develop a set of assembly language instructions that are equivalent to the *Automatic Loop* instruction.
3. Develop a set of assembly language instructions that store the largest of three numbers, A, B, and C, into D.

UNIT SEVEN

FILE PROCESSING

Chapter 20

Sequential-Access File Applications

Overview

Processing Sequential-Access Files

The Primer *Read*

Designing Output Reports

Headings and Line Counters

Control-Breaks

Multiple Control-Breaks

Using Indicators for Program Control

Error Handling

Null Files

Objectives

When you have finished this chapter, you should be able to:

1. Design an output record.
2. Develop a solution to process a sequential-access file.
3. Explain the concept of page control, including headings and page breaks.
4. Explain the concept of control breaks.
5. Explain the concept of indicators.
6. Explain the concept of error handling.

Most business computer applications require some type of file processing. In many such cases reports are generated for managers. These reports greatly aid the company's managers in making decisions for the present and future well-being of the company. Therefore, the design of these reports should be well thought out. Some rules for good report design

are presented in this chapter. This chapter presents techniques of processing sequential files for business applications. Such techniques include page breaks, page headings, control-breaks, multiple control-breaks, indicators, error handling, and null files.

The solution to be developed in this chapter is for the following problem:

Problem: The vice president in charge of sales for a company needs to know the company's total sales during the last period. The sales are made by individual sales-people. The output needed is a list of all individual sales and the total sales for the company. Figure 20.1 illustrates the record data dictionary and the record layout for this problem.

Record Data Dictionary

File Name: Sales

Field Number	Item Description	Field Name	Field Length	Data Type	# of Decimals	Comments
1	Sales Date	Date	8	String		MM/DD/YY
2	Salesperson #	SN	3	String		
3	District #	DN	3	String		
4	Region #	RN	3	String		
5	Salesperson Name	SName	20	String		Last name first
6	Customer Name	CName	20	String		Last name first
7	Customer Street	CStreet	10	String		
8	Customer City	CCity	8	String		
9	Customer State	CState	2	String		
10	Customer Zip Code	CZipCode	10	String		
11	Customer Phone	CPhone	14	String		(xxx)-xxx-xxxx
12	Sales Amount	Sales	10	Real	2	

Record Layout

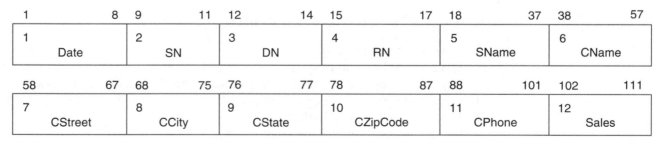

Figure 20.1 Record Data Dictionary and Record Layout for Company Sales Problem

Processing Sequential-Access Files

Processing
Sequential Files

To process the records in a file by sequential access, either the *While/WhileEnd* or the *Repeat/Until* loop is used. The processing is very similar with both of these loop structures. The *While/WhileEnd* loop logic structure will be used throughout this chapter and Chapter 21.

endoffile (EOF)

When the user enters file data, a whole record is copied either into the computer's working memory or into a buffer memory. In sequential-access record processing, after a record is read into memory, it is processed and then the next record is read. This sequence continues until the computer encounters the **EndOfFile (EOF)** marker, at which time the processing stops. The *EOF* marker is a signal to the computer indicating that there are no more records in the file. When the *EndofFile* marker is encountered, a status flag, or indicator, is set internally in the computer. This indicator is then tested as a logical data type function. The function name is EOF(LFN). The value of the *EOF(LFN)* function is *False* until the *EndofFile* marker is encountered. At this time the value of the *EOF(LFN)* becomes *True*. When the *EOF(LFN)* function has a value of *True,* all processing of records must stop. The *EndofFile* is encountered during the *Read* instruction. The user should not do any processing after the *EOF* because there are no more records to be processed. If the *EOF* marker is processed as a record, the computer will either return an error, or the last record will be processed twice since no new data replaced the old. Therefore, within the loop, the *Read* cannot be the first module to be processed. It must be processed just before the processing of the condition of the *EOF(LFN);* therefore, it has to be the last module processed in the loop. This is the case when the *Read* statement actually sets the *EOF* status flag at the time of the execution of the *Read.* However, some languages look ahead for the *EOF.* In this case, during the execution of the *Read,* the last record to be processed would be read and the status flag set at the same time. When the language uses the look-ahead method of finding the *EOF,* the primer *Read* is not used, and the *Read* statement is the first statement in the loop. This book will present file processing using the primer *Read.*

The Primer *Read*

Primer *Read*

Since the *Read* must be the last module processed, the computer needs data to process the first time through the loop. Therefore, there has to be a *Read* before the loop begins. This *Read* is called the *primer Read.* It primes the loop with data just as a pump is primed with water. Without this primer *Read* there would be no data to process the first time through the loop. If the *Read* were at the beginning of the loop, the *EOF(LFN)* would be processed as a record.

Figure 20.2 shows the *Control* module algorithm and flowchart for record processing. Notice the primer *Read* just before the loop. Also, notice the use of the logical *EOF* function. The condition to be processed is *Not EOF(LFN).* The resultant of this condition is *True* when the value of the function *EOF(LFN)* is *False,* or when the end-of-file flag has not been encountered. This is because *Not False* is *True.* When the *EndofFile* marker is encountered, the value of the function is *True.* The resultant of the condition, therefore, is *False* since *Not True* is *False.* The loop condition is read as *While Not End of File.* The three modules processed in the loop are the *Calc,* the *Print,* and the *Read* modules. An alternative method is to incorporate these three modules into one module called the *Proc* module. The *Proc* module would then process these three modules. In some languages this method is preferred because of the syntax of the loop structure.

Algorithm	Flowchart

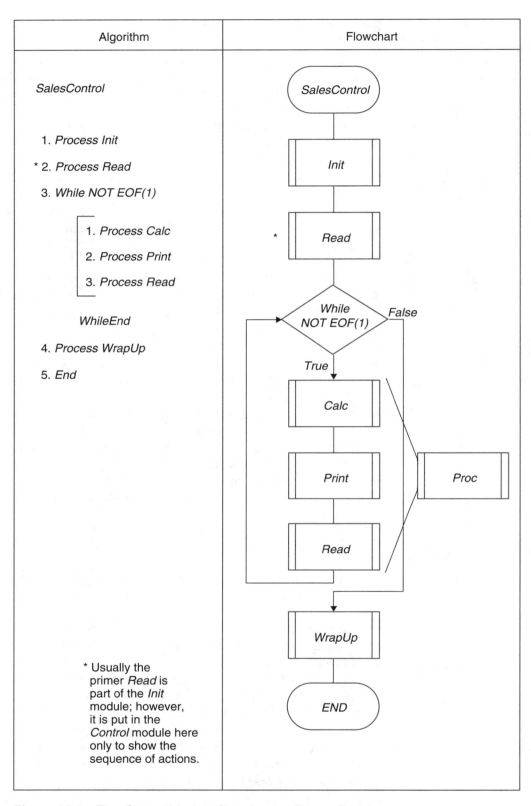

SalesControl

1. *Process Init*

* 2. *Process Read*

3. *While NOT EOF(1)*

 1. *Process Calc*

 2. *Process Print*

 3. *Process Read*

 WhileEnd

4. *Process WrapUp*

5. *End*

* Usually the primer *Read* is part of the *Init* module; however, it is put in the *Control* module here only to show the sequence of actions.

Figure 20.2 The *Control* Module Showing the Primer *Read*

Designing Output Reports

Output Reports

Output reports should be designed with the user in mind. When you are working on a problem solution, you record the information needed on the report in the Required Results section of the problem analysis chart. Where to place specific information within a report depends on the user's needs. The report should be designed so that the user can glean all the information needed in a matter of minutes. The basic rule for developing good reports is to plan to print only the information relevant to the person using the report. Any very important information should be highlighted in some way, so it is easily spotted. Time is valuable, and the computer is a productivity tool. The report should increase the productivity of the person for whom it was designed.

Within the report there are different types of lines. Heading lines are found at the top of the report or at the top of each page. The information found in these lines includes such items as company name, date and time of the execution of the program, programmer name, column headings, page number, manager's name, and the like. Detail lines print the specific information for each record in the file. Summary lines print information about groups of like records; summary lines are printed during a control-break and at the end of the report. Exception lines indicate an error in the data of the record. Exception lines can be either printed as part of the report or as a separate report called an *exceptions report*.

Report headings can also include relevant information about the company, such as its address, the division, the department and so on; the name of the report; the date; and any other pertinent information, such as the name of the person who will be using the report, the programmer, and so on, which is listed only once on the report. Print this report heading either on a page by itself or on the top of the first page. On the first page, as on all succeeding pages, print the column headings. Number all pages at the top, except for the first page with report headings. Using the Screen Design and Printer Design forms (Figures D.7 and D.8 in Appendix D), you can design output reports. The design of reports should be accomplished with the help and approval of the user.

The computer screen has 80 columns and from 24 to 26 rows. All of it can be used for input and output and for communication with the user. The screen design form can be used to design whatever has to be placed on the screen. Generally, the input and all inquiries and communication with the user are printed on the screen. Reports are generally written to the printer. Printers use paper that is normally 66 lines long and anywhere from 80 to 144 characters wide, although other paper sizes can be used. The printer form can be used to design the output reports.

Headings and Line Counters

page break

To implement the report design, the programmer designs a few new modules. One is the *ReportHeadings* module, which writes the report heading. Another module writes the column headings. A third processes what needs to be done when one page is full and another page is to begin, referred to as a **page break**. This is called a *PageBreak* module.

The first thing to do is to incorporate each of these modules into the structure chart. The *ReportHeadings* and the primer *Read* are processed by the *Init* module. The *PageBreak* module is executed by the *Print* module since it is part of the printing process (see Figure 20.3).

In the *Init* module, the page number needs to be initialized to one and the report headings processed. Figure 20.4b shows the algorithm and the flowchart of the *Init*

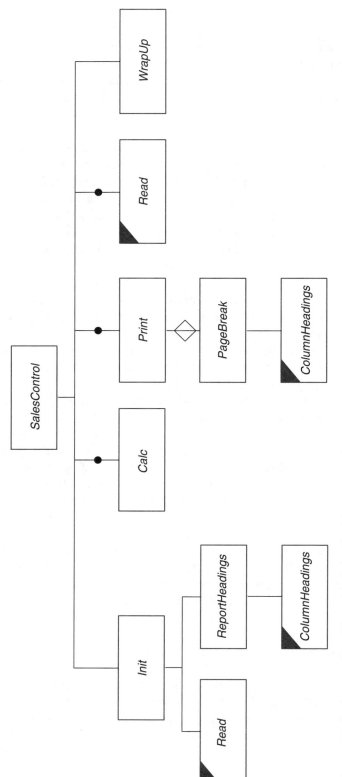

Figure 20.3 Interactivity Chart for Sales Problem

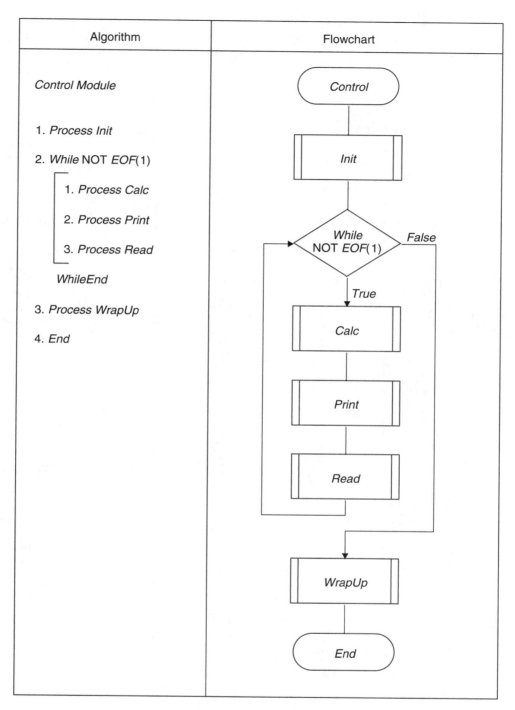

Algorithm	Flowchart
Control Module 1. *Process Init* 2. *While* NOT *EOF*(1) 1. *Process Calc* 2. *Process Print* 3. *Process Read* *WhileEnd* 3. *Process WrapUp* 4. *End*	*Control* → *Init* → *While NOT EOF*(1) — False True → *Calc* → *Print* → *Read* → *WrapUp* → *End*

Figure 20.4a Algorithm and Flowchart of *Control* Module for Sales Problem

module. The sales file is opened first. Then the sales total is set equal to zero, the maximum line count (the number of lines to the bottom margin) is set equal to 60, and the page number is set equal to 1. Next, the primer *Read* is processed, and finally, the report headings are written to the printer.

In the *Print* module, the line count has to be tested to see if the end of the page is encountered. If it is, then the *PageBreak* module is executed. Figure 20.4e shows the

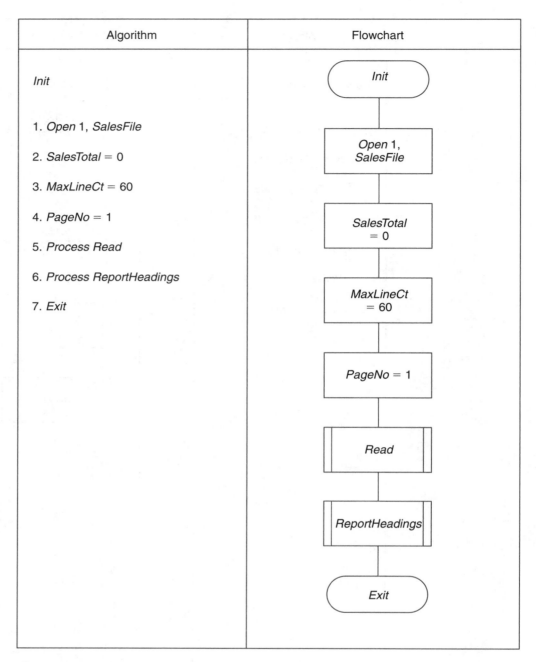

Algorithm	Flowchart
Init 1. *Open* 1, *SalesFile* 2. *SalesTotal* = 0 3. *MaxLineCt* = 60 4. *PageNo* = 1 5. *Process Read* 6. *Process ReportHeadings* 7. *Exit*	

Figure 20.4b Algorithm and Flowchart of *Init* Module for Sales Problem

algorithm and the flowchart of the *Print* module. Every time a line is written to the printer, it is counted in the line counter *(LineCt)*. In the *Print* module, before anything can be written to the printer, the line count must be compared to the maximum line count. When the line count is greater than or equal to the maximum line count, then the page break must be processed before the record is written to the printer. If it is not, the record is written to the printer and one is added to the line count.

Each of the additional modules—the *ReportHeadings,* the *PageHeadings,* the *ColumnHeadings,* and the *PageBreak*—must be developed. The *ReportHeadings* module gets the data from the system, prints the lines of the report heading, including the

Algorithm	Flowchart

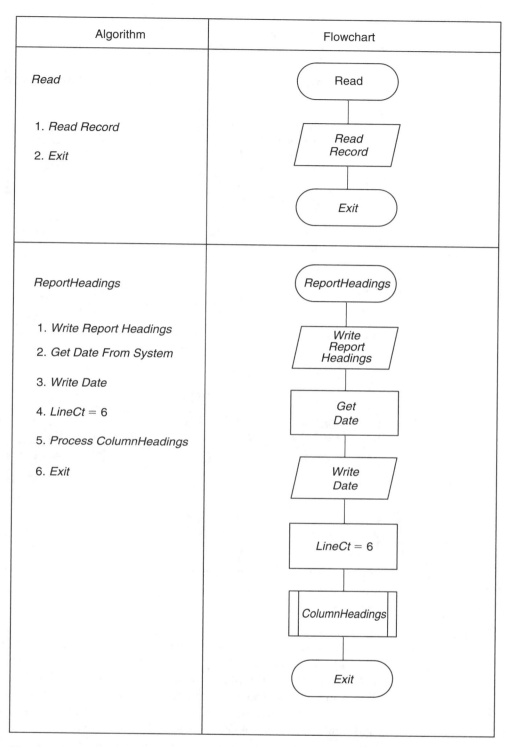

Read

1. *Read Record*
2. *Exit*

ReportHeadings

1. *Write Report Headings*
2. *Get Date From System*
3. *Write Date*
4. *LineCt* = 6
5. *Process ColumnHeadings*
6. *Exit*

Figure 20.4c Algorithms and Flowcharts of *Read* and *ReportHeadings* Modules for Sales Problem

Algorithm	Flowchart
ColumnHeadings 1. *Write Column Headings* (Including line space before and after) 2. *LineCt = LineCt* + 3 3. *Exit*	ColumnHeadings → Write Column Headings → LineCt = LineCt + 3 → Exit
Calc 1. *SalesTotal = SalesTotal + Sales* 2. *Exit*	Calc → SalesTotal = SalesTotal + Sales → Exit

Figure 20.4d Algorithms and Flowcharts of *ColumnHeadings* and *Calc* Modules for Sales Problem

column headings, and initializes the line counter to the number of lines already used by the *ReportHeadings*. See Figure 20.4c to see the order of processing. Notice that the report headings are written first, and then the system date is retrieved and printed, the line count is initialized to 6, and the column headings are written to the printer.

The page break adds one to the page counter, prints the lines of the page headings, and reinitializes the line counter to the number of lines used by the page headings. The *PageBreak* module also ejects the page, writes the *PageHeadings,* and processes the *ColumnHeadings* module. The *PageBreak* module is shown in Figure 20.4f. Notice that the page is ejected first. Next, the page number is incremented, and then the page headings, which include the page number, are written. The line count is set to the number of lines used by the page headings. Finally, the column headings are written.

The *ColumnHeadings* module prints the column headings and increments the line counter by the number of lines the column headings use (see Figure 20.4d). Be sure to

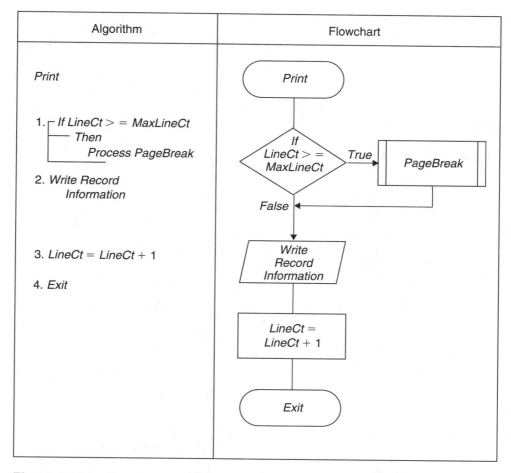

Algorithm	Flowchart
Print	
1. If LineCt > = MaxLineCt Then Process PageBreak	
2. Write Record Information	
3. LineCt = LineCt + 1	
4. Exit	

Figure 20.4e Algorithm and Flowchart of *Print* Module for Sales Problem

include the spacer lines in the total line count. Spacer lines are lines in which nothing is printed. These lines allow extra white space for readability.

Keep in mind the function of each module as you analyze what is processed in it. Figure 20.4a–g shows all the algorithms and flowcharts for the sales problem, including the headings and the page breaks.

Control-Breaks

control-breaks

Control-breaks are used to give subtotals for a group of similar records. For example, the requirements for a report might be to list all sales, with totals for each salesperson and a grand total for the company. The processing must temporarily break and write each salesperson's total to the printer before proceeding to the next salesperson.

In order to design a program that processes control-breaks, designate one field, such as salesperson's number, as the control field. The file must be previously sorted using this field. The file must be in order of the salesperson's number so that each salesperson's records will be together in the file. If the file has not been sorted by salesperson's number, then the control-break cannot work; that is, the program will not process totals for each salesperson, much less compile the necessary information for each.

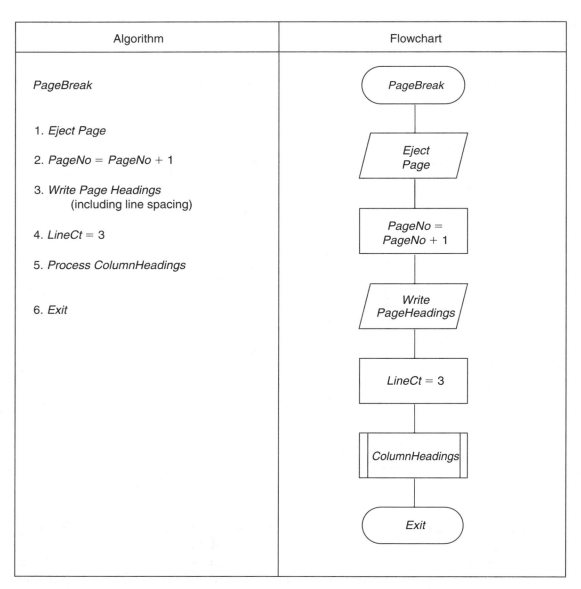

Algorithm	Flowchart
PageBreak 1. *Eject Page* 2. *PageNo = PageNo + 1* 3. *Write Page Headings* (including line spacing) 4. *LineCt = 3* 5. *Process ColumnHeadings* 6. *Exit*	*PageBreak* → *Eject Page* → *PageNo = PageNo + 1* → *Write PageHeadings* → *LineCt = 3* → *ColumnHeadings* → *Exit*

Figure 20.4f Algorithm and Flowchart of *PageBreak* Module for Sales Problem

Keep the value of the control field of the first record, or the first record after the control-break occurs, in a holding variable memory location. This holding variable contains the first value of the control field of each group of records. In the example in Figure 20.5, the holding variable would be where the initial value of each salesperson's number is kept. The variable name used in the example is *SNHold,* meaning *salesperson number hold value.* The value of the field is the same for all records for a salesperson; therefore, only the first value has to be kept. The salesperson's number does not change until a new salesperson is encountered. At that time the control-break is processed and the hold value is assigned a new value. The value of the control field of each record is compared to the hold value, and when they are no longer equal, the control-break occurs.

The *ControlBreak* module processes all instructions that the computer has to follow each time the value of the control field changes. The instructions for the sales example stated previously in this chapter would include the following: Print the subtotals, add the subtotals to the total for the company, set each subtotal to zero, and set the hold

Algorithm	Flowchart

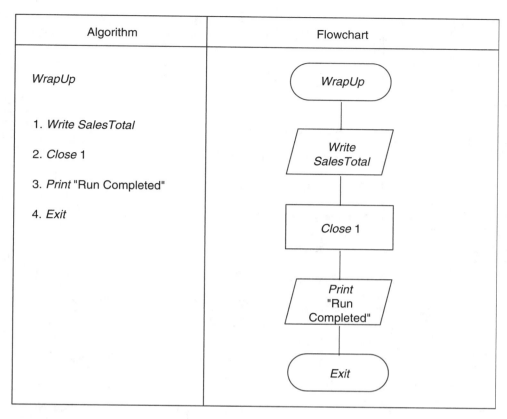

WrapUp

1. *Write SalesTotal*

2. *Close* 1

3. *Print* "Run Completed"

4. *Exit*

Figure 20.4g Algorithm and Flowchart of *WrapUp* Module for Sales Problem

value to the value of the new control field. In Figure 20.5, the control break is illustrated. The salesperson's total is written to the printer. Next, the line count is incremented by the number of lines it took to write the totals, including the spacer lines. Next, the salesperson's total is added to the company total. Finally, the salesperson's total is set back to zero, and the salesperson's hold value (*SNHold*) is set equal to the new salesperson's number.

The *ControlBreak* is the only new module required to process control-breaks. However, you must make changes in other modules. In the *Init* module, set the totals to zero and the hold value to the value of the control field for the first record. In the *Calc* module, test for the *ControlBreak*. That is, test the present value of the control field against its hold value. When the two values are not equal, the *ControlBreak* module will be processed. In the *WrapUp* module, the control-break will be executed to process the totals for the last value of the control field.

Notice in Figure 20.5a, the two changes in the *Init* module are to set the salesperson's total to zero, and the salesperson's hold value (*SNHold*) to the first person's number. In the *Calc* module (Figure 20.5b) the hold value is compared to the current salesperson number. When they are not equal, the record is the first record for the next salesperson and, therefore, the control-break has to be processed. The other change in the *Calc* module is that the salesperson's total is accumulated instead of the company's total. The company's total is accumulated in the *ControlBreak* module using the salesperson's total. The last change is in the *WrapUp* module in Figure 20.5d. The last salesperson's total must be written to the printer, and the company total must be updated before the completion of the processing; therefore, the control-break must be processed as the first instruction in the *WrapUp* module.

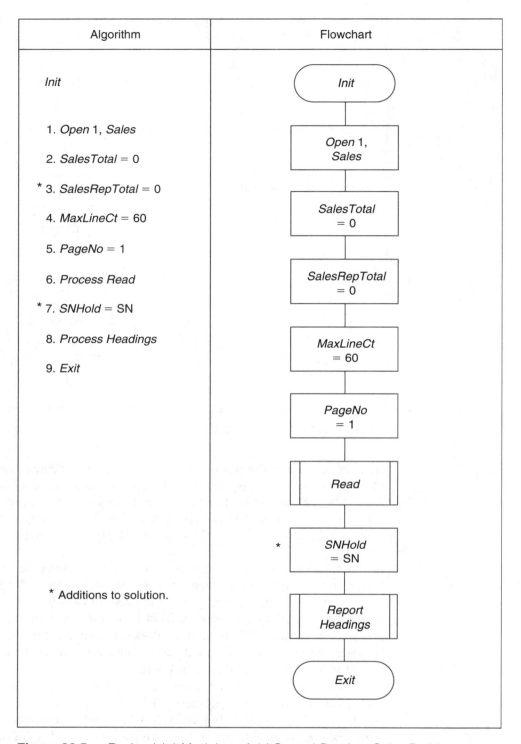

Algorithm	Flowchart
Init	
1. *Open* 1, *Sales*	
2. *SalesTotal* = 0	
* 3. *SalesRepTotal* = 0	
4. *MaxLineCt* = 60	
5. *PageNo* = 1	
6. *Process Read*	
* 7. *SNHold* = SN	
8. *Process Headings*	
9. *Exit*	
* Additions to solution.	

Figure 20.5a Revised *Init* Module to Add Control-Break to Sales Problem

Figure 20.5 shows all of the changes needed in the solution to the sales problem in order to include the subtotal for each salesperson. A single asterisk indicates where additional instructions were placed. The double asterisk indicates instructions that were changed.

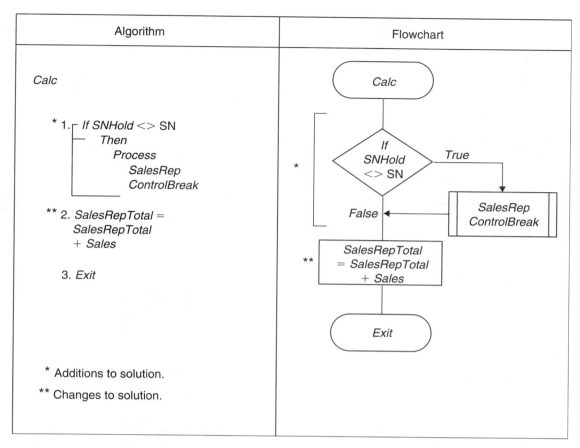

Algorithm	Flowchart
Calc	

Algorithm side:

Calc

* 1. If SNHold <> SN
 Then
 Process
 SalesRep
 ControlBreak

** 2. SalesRepTotal =
 SalesRepTotal
 + Sales

3. Exit

* Additions to solution.

** Changes to solution.

Figure 20.5b Revised *Calc* Module to Add Control-Break to Sales Problem

Multiple Control-Breaks

multiple control-breaks **Multiple control-breaks** involve subtotals on more than one field. For example, the requirements of a problem might be to find the total sales for each region, for each district within each region, and for each salesperson within each district. In this case there would be three control fields—region, district, and salesperson. The file must be sorted using a concatenation of the fields on which there will be a control-break, starting with the field that encompasses the largest grouping, and ending with the field that encompasses the smallest grouping. This file would be sorted the following way: regions in order within the company; districts in order within each region; salespersons in order within each district. The programmer would sort the file on the concatenation (the combining of strings by placing the first in front of the second) of the three fields, with the largest area of sales first, the second largest second, and the smallest third. In this case, the file would be ordered by region + district + salesperson.

All instructions processed in a single control-break also would be executed in each of the control-breaks in a multiple control-break. In the *Init* module, the programmer initializes all three totals to zero, and sets the hold values for all three control fields to the value of the first control field. In the *Calc* module, all control fields are tested, moving from largest to smallest. The programmer designs a *ControlBreak* module for each control field, with the first instruction a process block for the next smaller group.

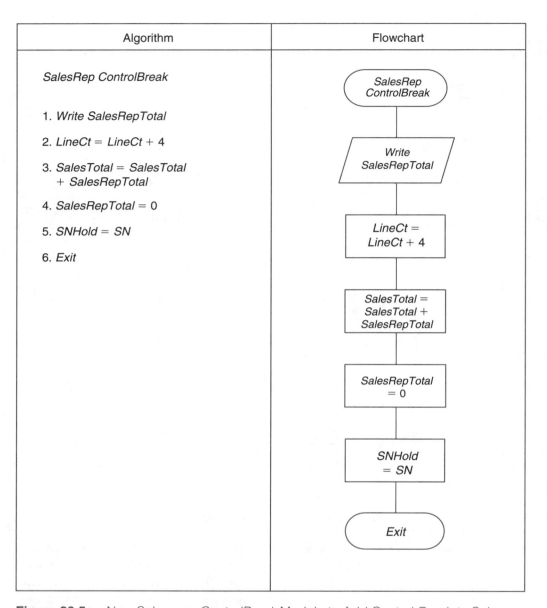

Algorithm	Flowchart
SalesRep ControlBreak 1. *Write SalesRepTotal* 2. *LineCt = LineCt + 4* 3. *SalesTotal = SalesTotal + SalesRepTotal* 4. *SalesRepTotal = 0* 5. *SNHold = SN* 6. *Exit*	

Figure 20.5c New Salesman *ControlBreak* Module to Add Control-Break to Sales Problem

Again, using the sales file as an example, whenever the region changes, the district and the salesperson fields also must change. This sweeping change occurs because there is no overlap of districts between regions, or of salespersons between districts. The programmer sets up the solution so that the largest group is processed, which then processes the next largest group, and so forth, until the smallest group has been processed. Figure 20.6 shows the interactivity chart of the multiple control break for the sales file discussed in this section.

Figure 20.7 shows the algorithms and flowcharts of a multiple control break for the sales problem illustrated throughout this chapter. *SNHold, DNHold,* and *RNHold* are the hold values for the salesperson, the district, and the region, respectively. *SN, DN,* and *RN* are the current values of the salesperson's number, the district number, and the region number, respectively. Here again, the single asterisk indicates where additional instructions were placed. The double asterisk indicates instructions that were changed.

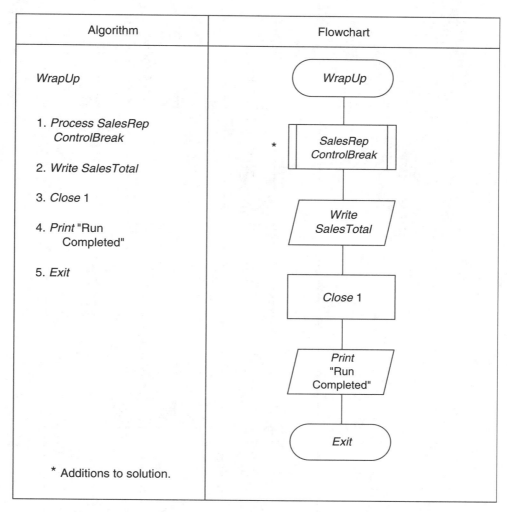

Algorithm	Flowchart
WrapUp 1. *Process SalesRep ControlBreak* 2. *Write SalesTotal* 3. *Close* 1 4. *Print* "Run Completed" 5. *Exit* * Additions to solution.	*WrapUp* * *SalesRep ControlBreak* *Write SalesTotal* *Close* 1 *Print* "Run Completed" *Exit*

Figure 20.5d Revised *WrapUp* Module to Add Control-Break to Sales Problem

Using Indicators for Program Control

Indicators

As in other types of processing, programmers can use indicators in record processing to change the normal course of processing. A printed date of purchase or sales may be required at the beginning of each page of a report and each time the date changes, but not with every record. The value of the control field may be printed only when it changes and at the start of a new page. Indicators are used to signal the computer regarding when to print the date or the value of the control field. Indicators also are used in data validation. Data validation is done by checking the data to see that it is correct or within proper range limits. When the computer finds an error, an indicator is set to *True* to indicate that there has been an error. A programmer can then use this error indicator to signal the computer not to process the record that contains an error.

The sales example can be modified to show how a programmer can use an indicator to print the date of sales at the top of each page, as well as when the date of sales changes. The programmer sets an indicator to *True* in both the *PageBreak* module and the *Read* Module to indicate when the date is to be printed. In the *Print* module, the indicator is tested; when it is on, the date of sales is printed. When it is off, the date of

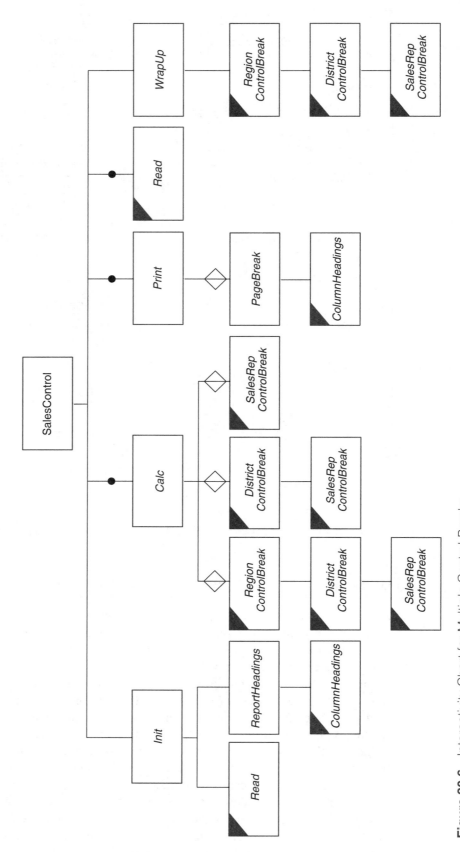

Figure 20.6 Interactivity Chart for Multiple Control-Breaks

Algorithm	Flowchart

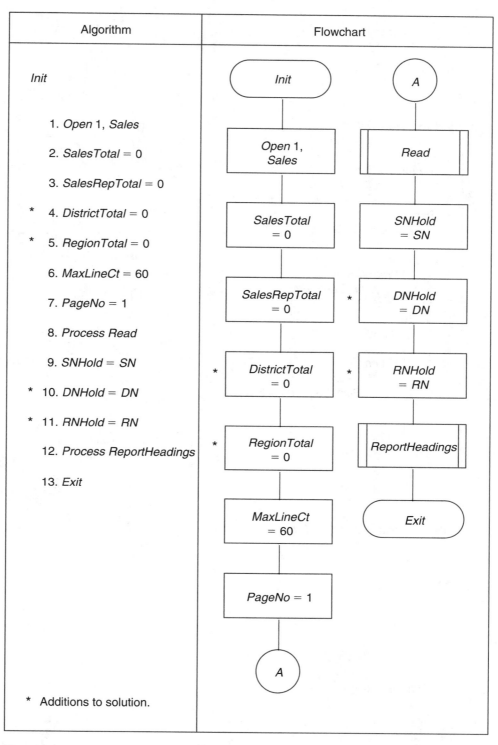

Init

 1. *Open* 1, *Sales*

 2. *SalesTotal* = 0

 3. *SalesRepTotal* = 0

* 4. *DistrictTotal* = 0

* 5. *RegionTotal* = 0

 6. *MaxLineCt* = 60

 7. *PageNo* = 1

 8. *Process Read*

 9. *SNHold* = *SN*

* 10. *DNHold* = *DN*

* 11. *RNHold* = *RN*

 12. *Process ReportHeadings*

 13. *Exit*

* Additions to solution.

Figure 20.7a Revised *Init* Module to Add Multiple Control-Breaks to Sales Problem

Algorithm	Flowchart

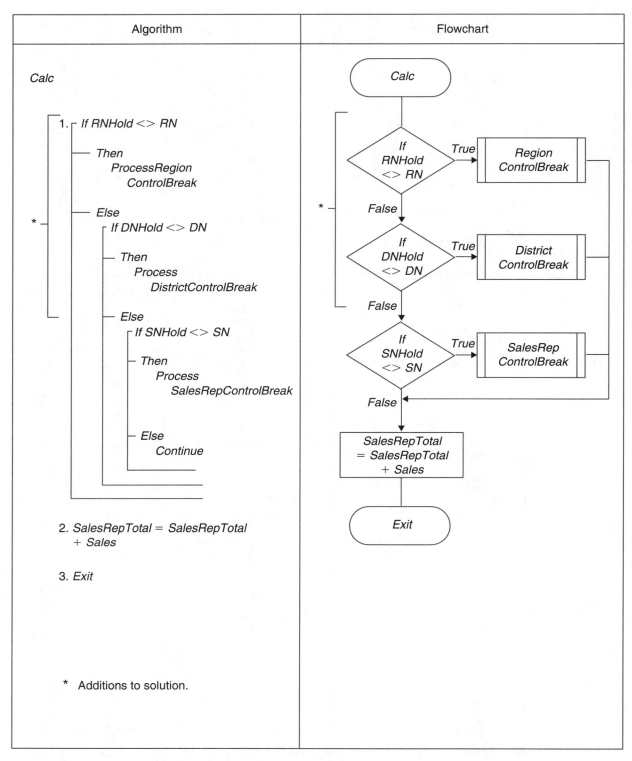

Calc

1. If RNHold <> RN
 Then
 ProcessRegion
 ControlBreak
 Else
 If DNHold <> DN
 Then
 Process
 DistrictControlBreak
 Else
 If SNHold <> SN
 Then
 Process
 SalesRepControlBreak
 Else
 Continue

2. SalesRepTotal = SalesRepTotal
 + Sales

3. Exit

* Additions to solution.

Figure 20.7b Revised *Calc* Module to Add Multiple Control-Breaks to Sales Problem

Algorithm	Flowchart
Region ControlBreak 1. *Process DistrictControlBreak* 2. *Write RegionTotal* 3. *LineCt = LineCt + 4* 4. *SalesTotal = SalesTotal + RegionTotal* 5. *RegionTotal = 0* 6. *RNHold = RN* 7. *Exit* * New module.	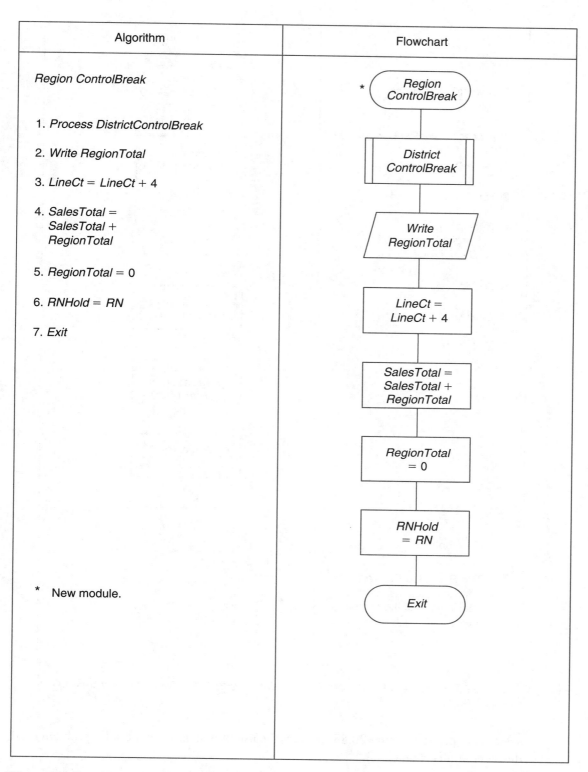

Figure 20.7c New *Region ControlBreak* Module to Add Multiple Control-Breaks to Sales Problem

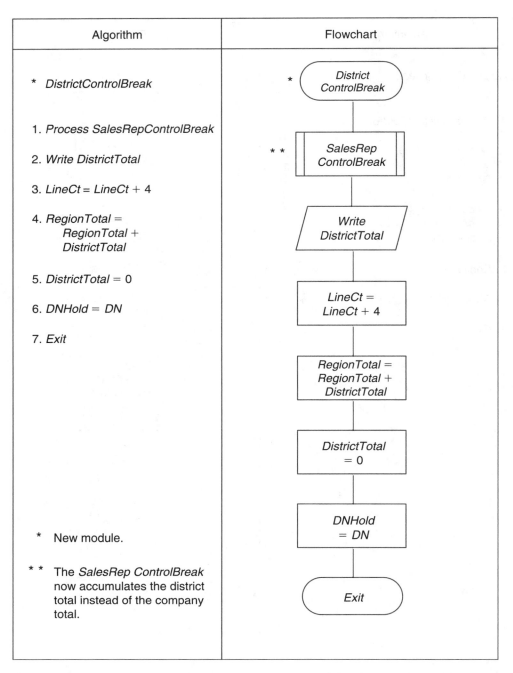

Algorithm	Flowchart
* *DistrictControlBreak* 1. *Process SalesRepControlBreak* 2. *Write DistrictTotal* 3. *LineCt = LineCt* + 4 4. *RegionTotal =* *RegionTotal +* *DistrictTotal* 5. *DistrictTotal* = 0 6. *DNHold = DN* 7. *Exit* * New module. * * The *SalesRep ControlBreak* now accumulates the district total instead of the company total.	

Figure 20.7d New *District ControlBreak* Module to Add Multiple Control-Breaks to Sales Problem

sales is not printed. Figure 20.8 illustrates the use of indicators in the sales problem used throughout this chapter.

Error Handling

Error Handling

For data validation (finding errors in the data records), you need a new module to be processed from the *Read* module. Data validation is accomplished through the decision structure. Usually, straight-through logic is used because all data error conditions have

Algorithm	Flowchart
*SalesRep ControlBreak 1. Write SalesRepTotal 2. LineCt = LineCt + 4 3. DistrictTotal = DistrictTotal + SalesRepTotal 4. SalesRepTotal = 0 5. SNHold = SN 6. Exit * This module is new.	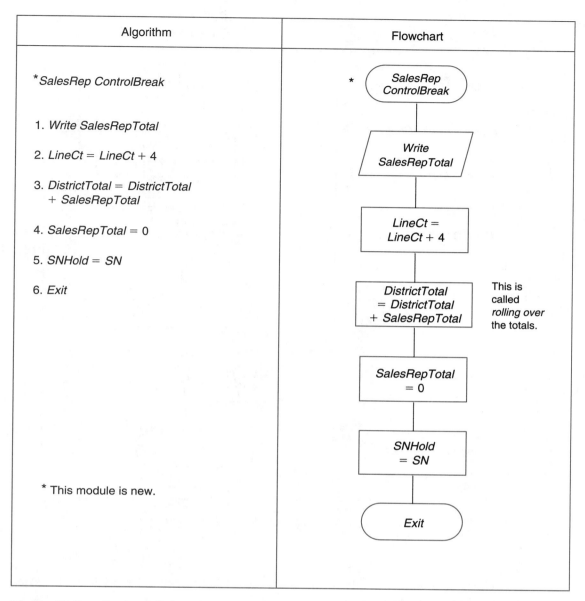

Figure 20.7e Revised *Salesman ControlBreak* Module to Add Multiple Control-Breaks to Sales Problem

to be processed in order for the computer to find all errors in the record. The conditions for data validation are provided to the programmer by the problem. When the computer finds an error while processing the *Error Validation* module, a message is written to an error report, the error indicator is set equal to *True,* and the processing of the *Data Validation* module or *Error* module is continued. If any errors are found, the record with errors is not processed, and the next record is read. This results in two reports—the regular report, which excludes the records with errors, and the error report (sometimes called an exceptions report), which includes them. For example, a *Data Validation* or *Error* module might check to see that the amount of a check is less than a given amount, or that an account number is all numbers, or that a name is all letters.

After the computer reads the record in the *Read* module, it should process the *Error* module. In the programming, use a loop structure to read until a good record or an

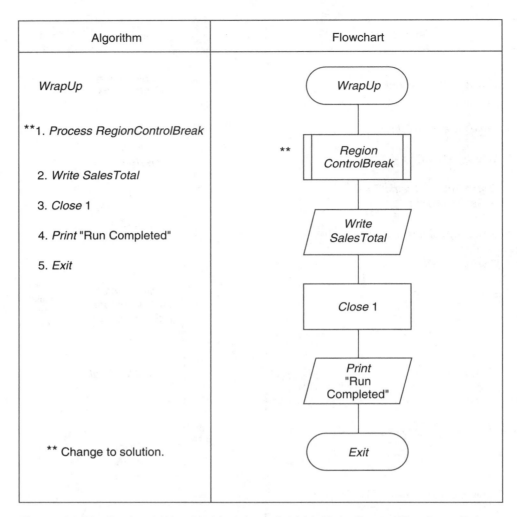

Algorithm	Flowchart
WrapUp ****1.** *Process RegionControlBreak* 2. *Write SalesTotal* 3. *Close* 1 4. *Print* "Run Completed" 5. *Exit* ****** Change to solution.	*WrapUp* → *Region ControlBreak* (**) → *Write SalesTotal* → *Close* 1 → *Print "Run Completed"* → *Exit*

Figure 20.7f Revised *WrapUp* Module to Add Multiple Control-Breaks to Sales Problem

End-OfFile is found. Examples of the *Read* module and the *Error* module for the sales problem are found in Figure 20.9.

Often a large portion of the processing of a record is data validation. It is an important part of record processing because it helps eliminate problematic and costly errors.

Null Files

null file

Another problem that arises when you are working with files is how to deal with the **null file,** or empty file. If a file is empty the computer prints an error message on the screen and processing halts. See Figure 20.10 to see the changes a programmer makes in the *Init* and the *WrapUp* modules to accommodate a null file. The *Init* module is designed so a null file indicator is set to *True,* an error message is printed, and all processing is skipped, except to close the files in the *WrapUp* module if an *EndOfFile* is encountered after the primer *Read.*

Algorithm	Flowchart

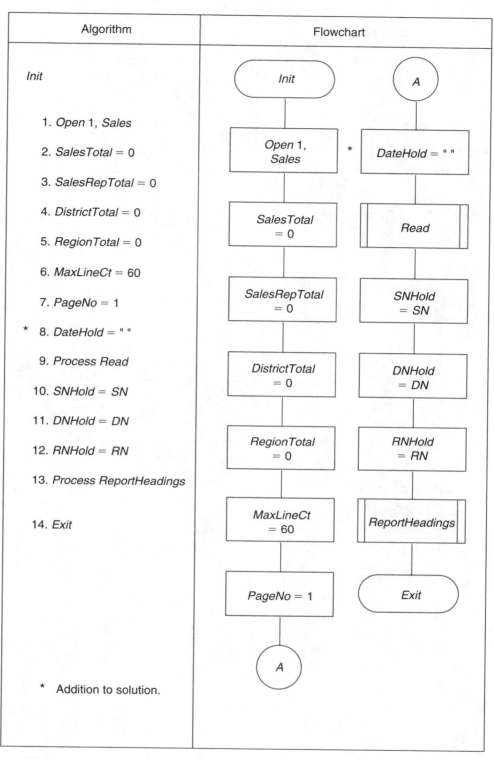

Init

 1. *Open* 1, *Sales*

 2. *SalesTotal* = 0

 3. *SalesRepTotal* = 0

 4. *DistrictTotal* = 0

 5. *RegionTotal* = 0

 6. *MaxLineCt* = 60

 7. *PageNo* = 1

* 8. *DateHold* = " "

 9. *Process Read*

 10. *SNHold* = *SN*

 11. *DNHold* = *DN*

 12. *RNHold* = *RN*

 13. *Process ReportHeadings*

 14. *Exit*

 * Addition to solution.

Figure 20.8a Modified *Init* Module to Add the Indicator to the Sales Problem

Algorithm	Flowchart
Read 1. *Read Record* * 2. ⎡ *If DateHold <> Date* AND NOT *EOF*(1) ⎯ *Then* *DateIndicator = True* *DateHold = Date* ⎯ *Else* *Continue* 3. *Exit* * Additions to solution.	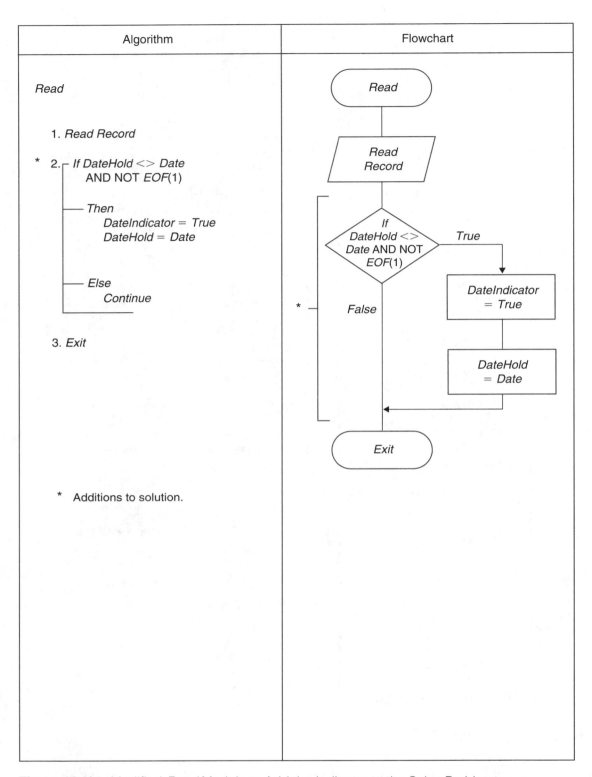

Figure 20.8b Modified *Read* Module to Add the Indicator to the Sales Problem

Algorithm	Flowchart
Print 1. ┌ *If LineCt >= MaxLineCt* ├── *Then* *Process PageBreak* * 2. ┌ *If Date Indicator* ├── *Then* *Write Date* W/O *{CR}* *DateIndicator* *= False* 3. *Write Record Information* 4. *LineCt = LineCt + 1* 5. *Exit* * Additions to solution.	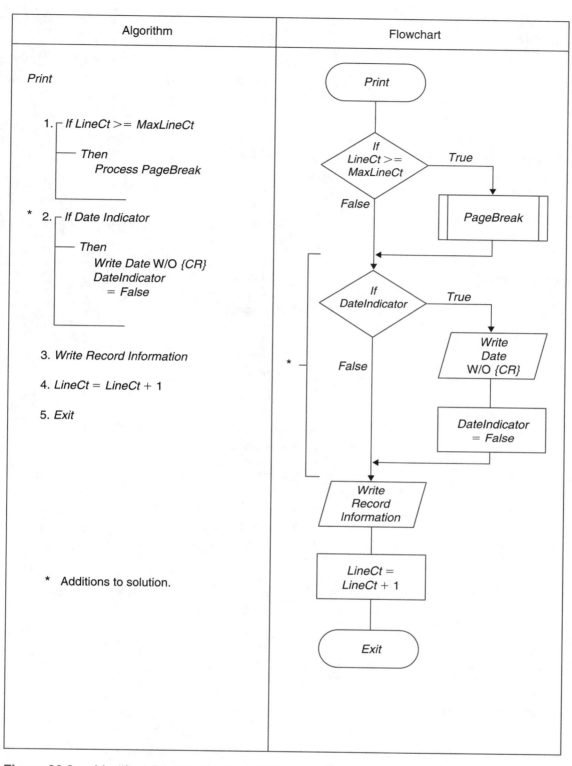

Figure 20.8c Modified *Print* Module to Add the Indicator to the Sales Problem

Algorithm	Flowchart
PageBreak 1. *EjectPage* 2. *PageNo = PageNo* + 1 3. *Write PageHeadings* 4. *LineCt* = 3 * 5. *DateIndicator = True* 6. *Process ColumnHeadings* 7. *Exit* * Additions to solution.	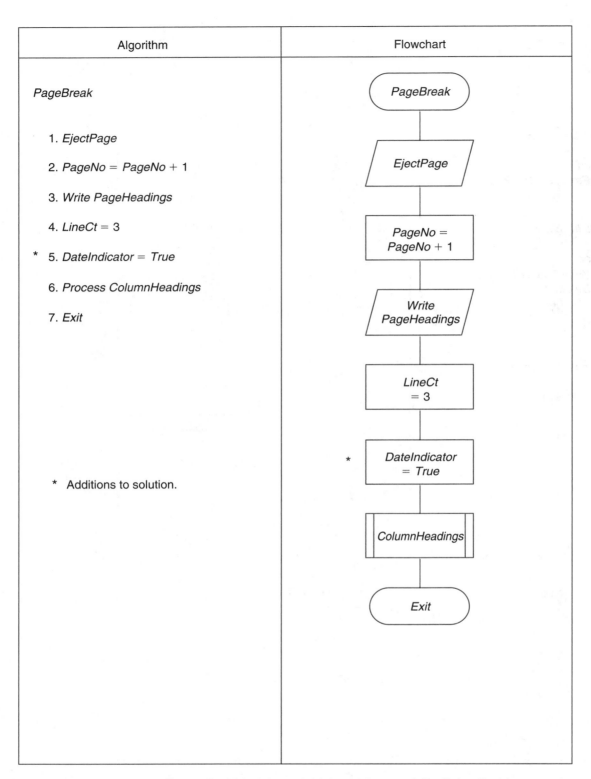

Figure 20.8d Modified *PageBreak* Module to Add the Indicator to the Sales Problem

Algorithm	Flowchart

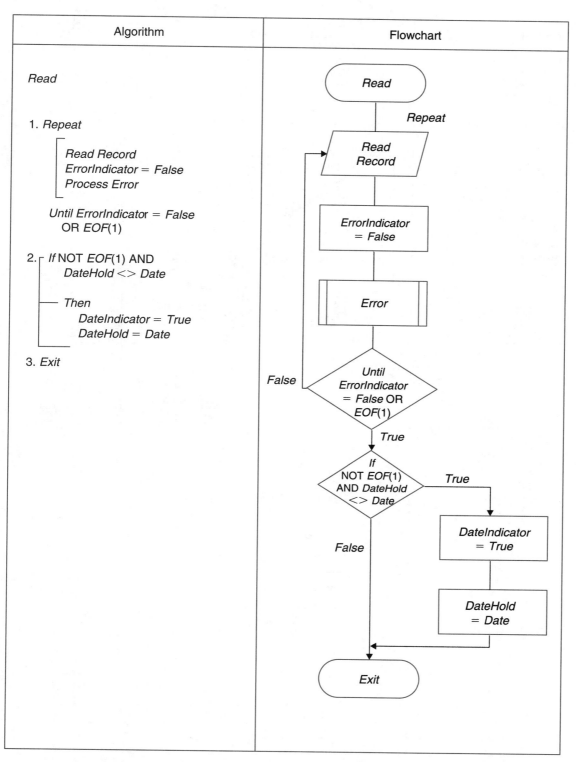

Read

1. *Repeat*

 Read Record
 ErrorIndicator = False
 Process Error

 Until ErrorIndicator = False
 OR EOF(1)

2. *If* NOT *EOF*(1) AND
 DateHold <> Date

 — *Then*
 DateIndicator = True
 DateHold = Date

3. *Exit*

Figure 20.9a Modified *Read* Module to Add Data Error Handling to the Sales Problem

Algorithm	Flowchart
Error 1. ┌ *If* NOT *EOF*(1) ├─ *Then* ┌ *If* \<Data\> *Invalid* ├─ *Then* * ErrorIndicator* = *True* *Write Error* *Message* 2. *Exit* * Repeat for each error check.	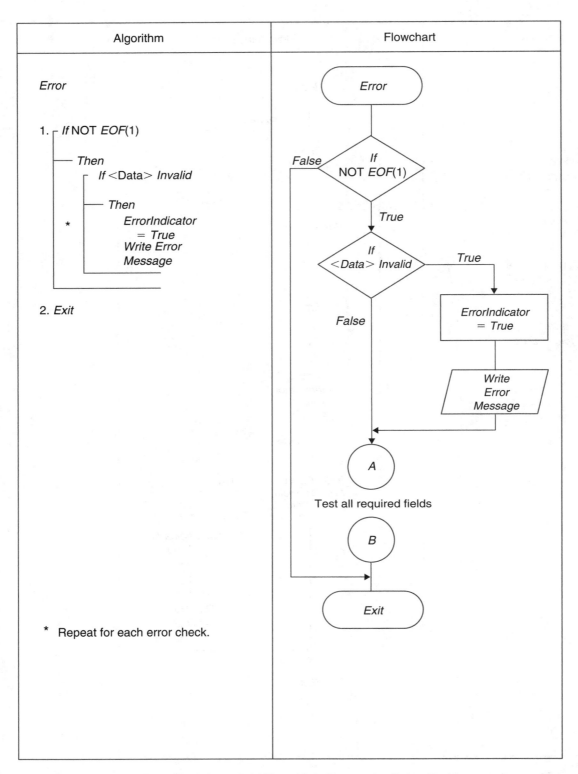

Figure 20.9b New *Error* Module to Add Error Handling to the Sales Problem

Algorithm	Flowchart

Init

1. *Open* 1, *Sales*

2. *SalesTotal* = 0

3. *SalesRepTotal* = 0

4. *DistrictTotal* = 0

5. *RegionTotal* = 0

6. *MaxLineCt* = 60

7. *PageNo* = 1

8. *DateHold* = " "

9. *Process Read*

10. ┌ *If EOF*(1)

 ├── *Then*
 　　Print Error
 　　　　Message

 　　NullIndicator
 　　= *True*

 ├── *Else*
 　　SNHold = *SN*
 　　DNHold = *DN*
 　　RNHold = *RN*
 　　Process ReportHeadings

11. *Exit*

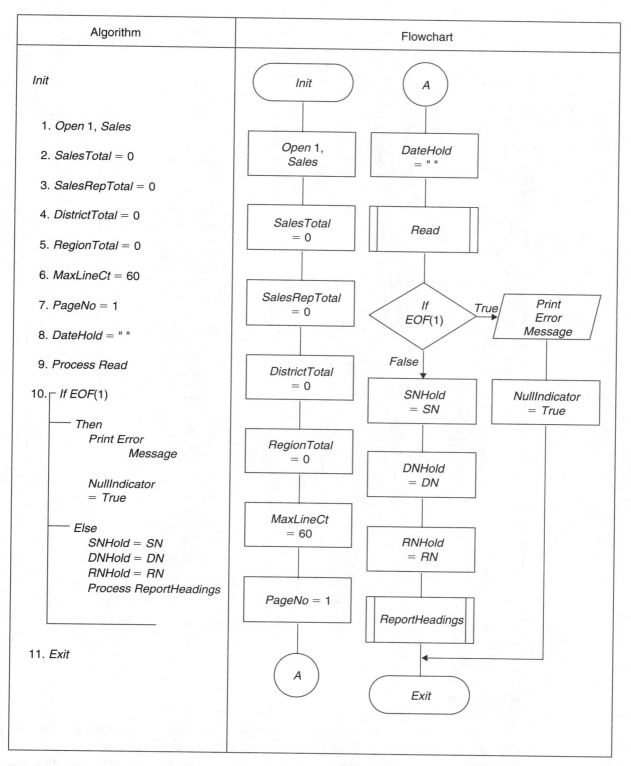

Figure 20.10a Modified *Init* Module to Handle a Null File in the Sales Problem

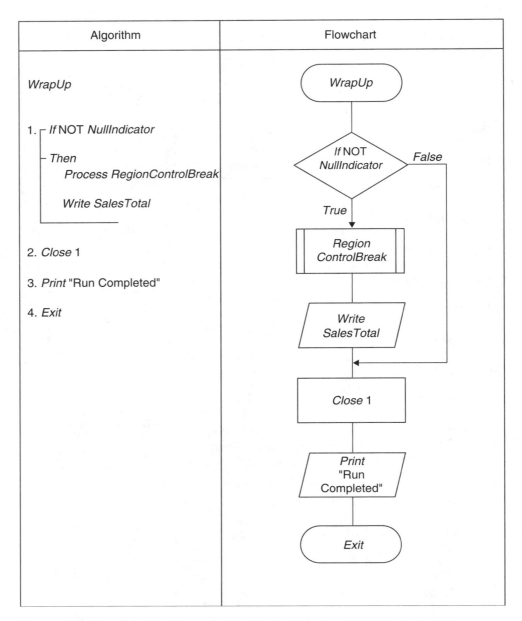

Algorithm	Flowchart
WrapUp 1. ⌐ *If* NOT *NullIndicator* ⌐ *Then* *Process RegionControlBreak* *Write SalesTotal* 2. *Close* 1 3. *Print* "Run Completed" 4. *Exit*	

Figure 20.10b Modified *WrapUp* Module to Handle a Null File in the Sales
Problem

Summary

The concepts of record processing, including control-breaks, indicators, and data validation, are important to both programming and applications. Control-breaks are important because many business reports call for subtotals or other intermediate results, such as the number of customers a salesperson contacted or the number of items in an inventory.

A good programmer designs output reports with the user in mind. Report headings, data placement, and general organization are very important.

A programmer handles data errors, null files, or changes in processing with the use of indicators. A finished solution should be as correct and as foolproof as possible. Data-entry errors are made often. Even if 99% of entry records are correct, that means there is still one error in every 100 entries. With thousands of pieces of data entered daily, there are many errors. Indicators are used anytime the programmer needs to indicate to the computer that another set of instructions is to be used.

For computer users in business, sequential-access processing techniques such as those covered in this chapter are keys to productivity.

New Terms

control-break	multiple control-break	page break
EndOfFile (EOF)	null file	

Questions

1. Name the items to consider when designing a record. Explain each.
2. What is a page break?
3. What are control-breaks?
4. What is a null file?
5. Why is it important to consider a null file when processing files?

Problems

Using the input records and systems flowcharts developed in Chapter 11, develop a solution for the following problems. Your solution should include a problem analysis chart, an IPO chart, a data dictionary, an interactivity chart, algorithms and flowcharts for each module, and an output report design.

1. Develop a solution to calculate the gross pay for the employees of a company. The input records should include the following: name, address, Social Security number, pay type (H = hourly, S = salary), rate of pay, and hours worked. The output report should include all input data plus the gross pay.

2. A sales manager wants a program that lists all of the company's customers according to the salesperson assigned to each. She would also like the number of the salesperson's customers to be totaled at the end of the list. The name of the salesperson should be printed only at the top of the page or when the processing encounters a new salesperson. The input file contains the following data: the customer's name, address, telephone number, and the salesperson's name.

3. Develop a solution for an inventory problem. The input record should include the following: the inventory number, the department number, the store number, the item description, the quantity, the wholesale price, the markup percentage, and the vendor. The output report should include the input data, plus the retail price, the total value of the item in stock (quantity * price), and the total wholesale and retail values of the stock for each department and for each store. The company totals should be printed at the end of the report.

4. A sales manager would like to be able to track the clients of each of his salespeople. He would like to know when each customer was last contacted, the outcome of the contact (not interested, sale made, call back later, no contact made), the sale amount if a sale was made, and the name and number of the salesperson. He would like the list of clients to be in chronological order according to the last contact time by salesperson. He would also like a total of sales per day per salesperson. Develop the solution to the manager's problem. In what order should the file be sorted?

What would you have to do if the manager also wanted a client list in alphabetical order?

Chapter 21

Sequential-Access File Updating

Overview

Creating Files
The Master File
Transaction Files
Activity Files
Backup Files
Updating the Master File Using a Transaction File
Putting It All Together
A Useful Alternative Method

Objectives

When you have finished this chapter, you should be able to:

1. Design a solution to update sequential files.
2. Explain the use of a master file.
3. Explain the use of a transaction file.
4. Explain the use of an activity file.
5. Explain the use of a backup file.

Businesses are dynamic, and so are their data-processing requirements. Therefore, the data files used in business must be easily updated. Chapter 20 explained how to process a sequential-access file, including data validation, but it did not explain how to update one. This chapter explains and illustrates the technique for updating a sequential file using a transaction file.

Updating a file means adding, deleting, or changing records to keep the information in the file current.

1. *Adding records.* When new data are generated, new records have to be added to a file. When a new employee starts work, data about that person must be added to the personnel file; when a sale has been made, the data from the sales receipt must be added to the sales file, and so on.

2. *Deleting records.* There must be a way to delete obsolete data from a file. When a record is deleted, the user chooses one of several options about what to do with it. These options include:
 a. The record may be discarded, never to be seen again.
 b. The record may be placed in an archival file, so that the information can be retrieved at a later date, if needed.
 c. The record may be placed in an activity file to show when it was deleted.

3. *Changing records.* Data in a record must be changed from time to time for a variety of reasons. The data may be incorrect, or they may have changed. When data have changed, the date and the changes themselves can go into an activity file for future inquiries.

Files can be processed in two ways. The first method is **batch processing,** in which data collected over a period of time are processed all at once without human intervention. This is the most efficient for the computer because it doesn't have to wait for a person to respond. However, it is not as efficient for people since they have to wait until a batch run is made. Because of the relatively long batch turnaround time, data that are currently being used are frequently not up to date. The more efficient type of pro-

cessing for people is **interactive processing**, in which data are entered and updated at the same time. In this case, the data in the file are as current as the data being entered at any given time. The person communicating with the computer is interacting with it through commands or menus.

Since sequential files are processed in order, it is inefficient to update them interactively. Therefore, sequential files are best updated by batch processing. All of the changes are put into a transaction file, which is a separate file that is periodically used to update all the files at one time. This update may be done daily, weekly, or as often as company policies require.

Creating Files

You have to create a file before you can use it. That is, you have to design the structure of the file and communicate it to the computer. This structure includes the layout of the record and the kind of file—sequential or random access. The files discussed in this chapter, as well as all other files, are designed by the methods described in Chapter 11. Use the Record Data Dictionary and Layout Form (Appendix D, Figure D.6) to design the structure of the record. When you create a file, you designate the fields of each record and specify the attributes of each field, such as the name of the field, the length of the field, the data type, and the number of decimals for numeric data. All records have different data but the same attributes. Then you put together the record layout to specify the way the record will look.

When you create a new file from an old one, all previous data in the file are destroyed. Therefore, create a new file over an old one only when it is necessary, and when you wish to delete the information in the old file.

The Master File

master file

The **master file** is the file in which all the data needed for processing are kept current. Common types of master files include inventory files, payroll files, and mailing list files. The files used in the sequential-access solutions in Chapter 20 are master data files. The data are arranged in order of processing, and they are kept in the same order during processing and after the updates are completed. In this chapter, the terms *old master file* and *new master file* are used. The former means the master file before the update, and the latter expression refers to the master file after the update.

Transaction Files

transaction file

Transaction files contain all the data needed to update the master file. You construct a transaction file by entering records that contain new data for the master file. The entries are made as new data arise and then are sorted according to the requirements of the master file. The records in the transaction file must be in the same order as that in the master file since they will be used to update the master file records sequentially. That is, if the master file is sorted in account number order, then the transaction file must be sorted in account number order. Or if the master file is sorted according to the last name, then the transaction file must be sorted accordingly.

Activity Files

activity files

All completed file updates are listed in an **activity file** (audit trail file). Each time a user executes the update program, he will append the activity file (add new entries to the end of the file) to show what has happened to the master file. The activity file is the only file in a company from which the records are never deleted. It is important because it is the only file that can tell auditors what has happened to any particular record.

Backup Files

backup file

Backup files contain the records as they were before the last file update. It is important to keep backup files in case something happens to the current master file. Machine or human errors that destroy part or all of a file are fairly common occurrences. If the current master file is destroyed, the user can copy the backup file into the old master file, rerun the update program with the last transaction file, and then start the processing again. There are two ways to make a backup file: One is to rename the old master file (containing the data that existed before the most recent update) as a backup; the other is to copy a file—old, new, master, transaction, or activity—onto another auxiliary storage medium, either disk or tape.

Updating the Master File
Using a Transaction File

Figure 21.1 shows a generalized systems flowchart to update a sequential-access file. Figure 21.2 shows a specific solution for updating a file. You design an update solution by using the loop structure and the decision structure. Be cautious to avoid common programming errors, such as allowing the addition of a record with a key field that

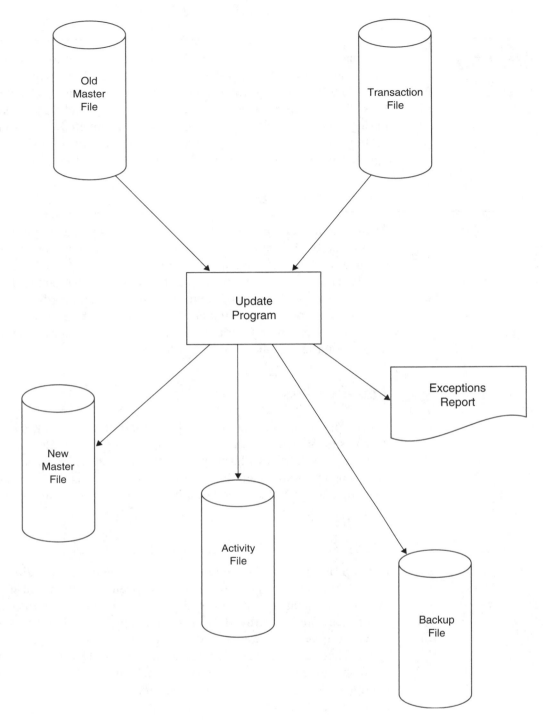

Figure 21.1 Systems Flowchart to Update a Sequential-Access File

already exists. The key field, remember, is the field that has a unique piece of data that is used to order the master file and the transaction file. This error can be caused by incorrectly entering a key in the transaction file. Entering an incorrect key can cause another error: trying to delete or change a nonexistent record. Therefore, part of the solution should contain checks so that any transaction records containing such errors are not used to update the master file but instead are written to an error output report. Check

UpdateFile

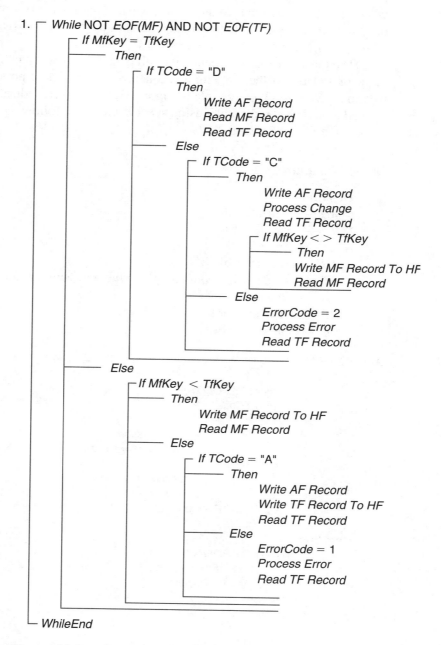

1. While NOT *EOF(MF)* AND NOT *EOF(TF)*
 If *MfKey = TfKey*
 Then
 If *TCode = "D"*
 Then
 Write AF Record
 Read MF Record
 Read TF Record
 Else
 If *TCode = "C"*
 Then
 Write AF Record
 Process Change
 Read TF Record
 If *MfKey < > TfKey*
 Then
 Write MF Record To HF
 Read MF Record
 Else
 ErrorCode = 2
 Process Error
 Read TF Record
 Else
 If *MfKey < TfKey*
 Then
 Write MF Record To HF
 Read MF Record
 Else
 If *TCode = "A"*
 Then
 Write AF Record
 Write TF Record To HF
 Read TF Record
 Else
 ErrorCode = 1
 Process Error
 Read TF Record
 WhileEnd

Figure 21.2a Sequential-File Updating Through a Transaction File—Algorithm

data for errors by using an *If/Then/Else* instruction. When an error is found, that transaction record will not be processed but will be written to the error output record. See Chapter 20 for more information about error checks.

Note: An alternative solution to the problem of updating a sequential file is presented in the final section of this chapter and illustrated in Figure 21.4. See the discussion there.

After the data in a transaction record have been used to update the file, a new transaction record is read into internal memory. Likewise, after a master file record has been updated, or found to have no changes, a new master file record is read into internal

memory. Through the use of transaction codes—codes that indicate to the computer what type of transaction is to take place, whether adding the record, deleting the record, or changing the record—and the comparison of the transaction record to the master file record, the file is updated record by record.

The master file might contain payroll data, inventory data, or sales data. The technique of updating is the same for all sequential files and does not depend on the type of data in a given file. The example in Figure 21.2, therefore, indicates the type of files to be read in and used rather than using specific data. The following notes explain each of the steps in Figure 21.2a–d.

Notes for Figure 21.2

Definitions
- *MF*—old master file
- *TF*—transaction file
- *AF*—activity file
- *HF*—new master file
- *TCode*—transaction code (a field in the transaction record)
 "A"—add a record
 "D"—delete a record
 "C"—change a record

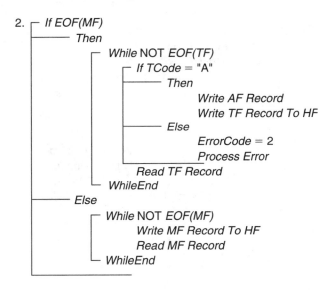

```
2.  ┌─ If EOF(MF)
    ├──── Then
    │       ┌─ While NOT EOF(TF)
    │       │    ┌─ If TCode = "A"
    │       │    ├──── Then
    │       │    │        Write AF Record
    │       │    │        Write TF Record To HF
    │       │    └──── Else
    │       │             ErrorCode = 2
    │       │             Process Error
    │       │    Read TF Record
    │       └─ WhileEnd
    ├──── Else
    │       ┌─ While NOT EOF(MF)
    │       │    Write MF Record To HF
    │       │    Read MF Record
    │       └─ WhileEnd
    └─
```

3. *Close Files (MF, TF, HF, AF)*

4. *Replace Backup File With MF*

5. *Replace MF With HF*

6. *Exit*

Figure 21.2b Sequential-File Updating Through a Transaction File—Algorithm

Flowchart

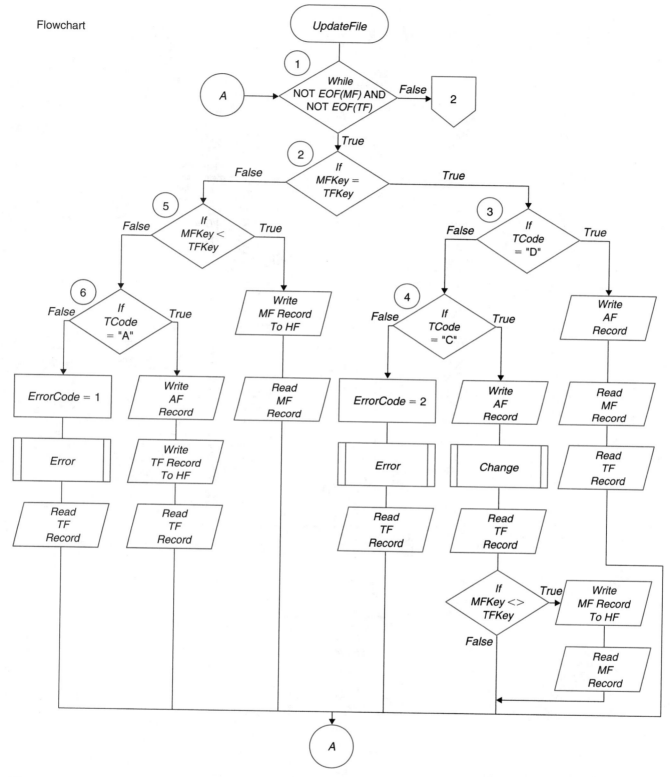

Figure 21.2c Sequential-File Updating Through a Transaction File—Flowchart

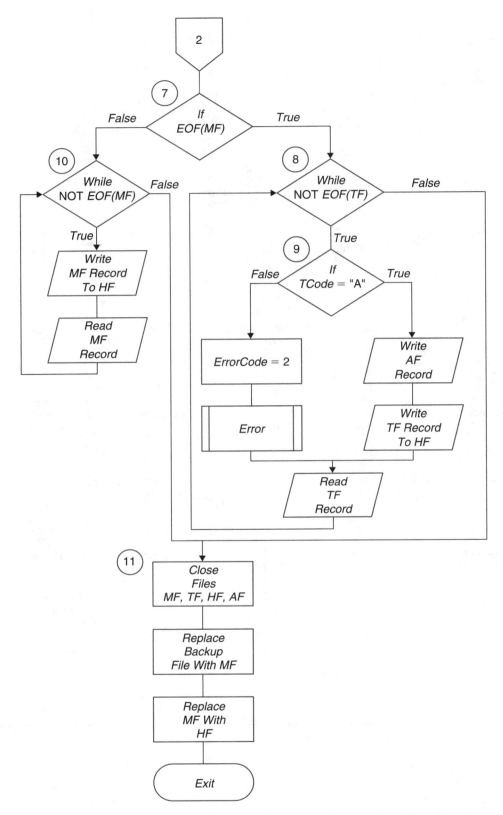

Figure 21.2d Sequential-File Updating Through a Transaction File—Flowchart

- *MfKey*—master file key field
- *TfKey*—transaction key field
- *ErrorCode*—code that indicates an error has been found: A 1 indicates an attempt to change or delete a nonexistent record; a 2 indicates that a record with a duplicate key is being added.

The numbers of the notes correspond to the circled numbers in the flowchart.

1. This loop continues as long as there are records in both the old master file and the transaction file. When the *EndOfFile (EOF)* of either file is reached, the processing continues at 7.
2. When the old master file key field is equal to the transaction file key field, the only two processes that occur are changing or deleting records. When the two fields are not equal, either the old master file record is to remain the same, or the transaction file record is added to the master file. There may be many records that will not have any updates made to them.
3. When the transaction code is equal to "D," then the information is written to the activity file, and another master file record and another transaction file record are read. Since the record was not written to the new master file, it has been deleted.
4. When the transaction code is equal to "C," then the information is written to the activity file, the master record is changed internally in the computer's memory (not in external memory), and then the changed master file record is written to the new master file. Another transaction file record is then read.

 This transaction file key is checked against the current master file key. If they are equal, processing continues without reading in another master file record. If they are not equal, then no more updating needs to be done to the current master file record, and another one is read.
5. If the transaction file and master file keys are equal and the transaction code does not equal either "D" or "C," then there is an error in the transaction record. When an error occurs, an error message is written to an error report, and another transaction record is read.
6. When the master file key is less than the transaction file key, then nothing has to be done to that record. The master file record is written to the new master file, and another master file record is read.
7. When the master file key is greater than the transaction file key, then the transaction file should be added to the master file. When the transaction code is equal to an "A," then the information is written to the activity file, the transaction record is written to the new master file, and another transaction record is read. If the master file key is greater than the transaction file key and the transaction code does not equal "A," then there is an error in the transaction record. An error message is then written to the error report, and another transaction record is read.
8. When an *EOF* occurs in either the old master file or the transaction file, the preceding loop stops, and the program processes the remaining records on the file that has not encountered an *EOF*. That is, if the *EOF* is encountered on the old master file, then the remaining transaction file records are processed; if the *EOF* is encountered on the transaction file, then the remaining old master file records are processed.
9. The transaction file records are processed until the *EOF* on the transaction file has been reached.

10. The remaining records on the transaction file must be records to be added to the master file. When the transaction code is equal to "A," then the information is written to the activity file, the transaction record is written to the new master file, and another transaction file record is read. If the transaction code is not equal to "A," then there is an error in the transaction file record. When an error occurs, an error message is written to the error report, and another transaction file record is read.

11. The master file records are processed until the *EOF* on the old master file is encountered. Since there are no more transactions to be done on the master file, these records are simply written to the new master file and a new record is read.

12. After the *EOF* has been encountered on both the old master file and the transaction file, all files are closed. Then the data in the backup file are replaced with the data in the old master file, and the data in the old master file are replaced with the data in the new master file. It is then ready to be used for the next update processing.

Putting It All Together

Example

Figure 21.3 demonstrates a complete solution for an update to an inventory file. The *Control* module (Figure 21.3b) is very simple: The *Init* is processed, then the *Update* module, and finally the *WrapUp* module. The *Init* module of Figure 21.3c opens the four files and reads the first record in the old master file (the inventory file) and the transaction file.

The *Update* module (Figure 21.3d) contains three loops. The first loop continues as long as there are records in both files. Either the second or third loop completes the process of updating the inventory file. In the first loop, one module *(Equal)* is processed when the transaction file key *(TInvNo)* is equal to the master file key *(InvNo)* for the current record; another module *(NotEqual)* is processed when they are not equal. In the second loop, when the end-of-file has been reached for the old master file, the remaining transaction records should all be add records and are added in the *Add* module. If the transaction code is not equal to "A," then the *Error* module is processed. In the third loop, the *EndOfFile* for the transaction file has been reached and there are no more updates to the master file. The remaining master file records are copied to the new master file in the *NoChange* module. Either the second or third loop is processed, not both.

In the *Equal* module (Figure 21.3e), the processes that can take place are to change the record (transaction code = "C") or to delete the record (transaction code = "D"). If the transaction code equals anything else, it is an error, and the *Error1* module is processed. In the *NotEqual* module, when the master file key is less than the transaction file key, there are no updates to that master file record. When it is not less than the transaction file key, then the transaction code should be an "A" and the transaction record is added to the master file. If it is not an "A," then there is an error, and the *Error2* module is processed.

The *NoChange* module (Figure 21.3f) writes the data to the new master file and reads the next record from the old master file. The *Add* module writes the transaction record to the activity file and the new master file and then reads the next record from the transaction file.

The *Error2* module (Figure 21.3g) writes an error message to the output error report and reads the next transaction file record. If there is an error in the transaction file, that record should not be processed. The *Delete* module (Figure 21.3h) writes the transaction file record to the activity file and reads the next record from the old master file and the transaction file. The *Error1* module writes an error message to the output error report and reads the next transaction file record.

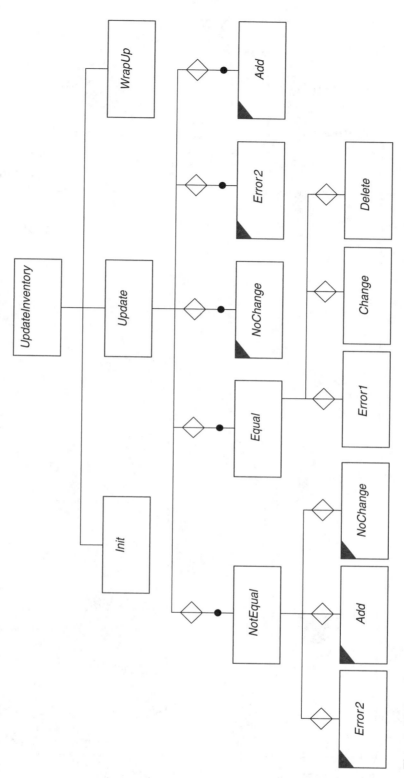

Figure 21.3a Interactivity Chart for Inventory Problem

Algorithm	Flowchart

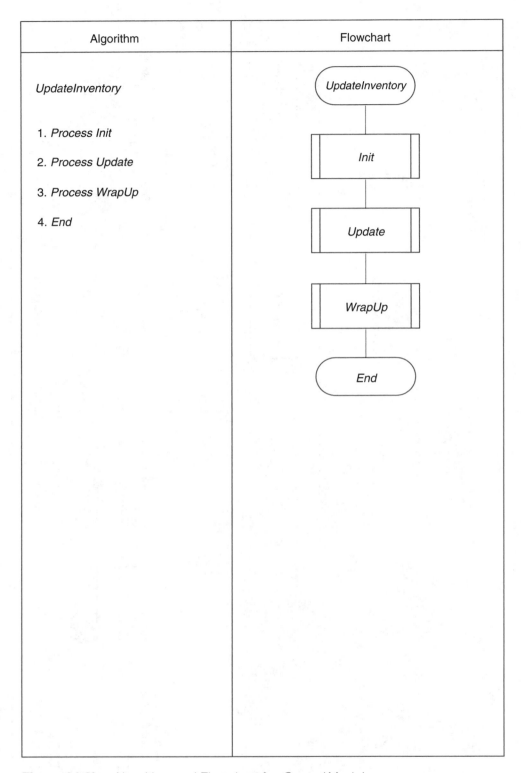

Figure 21.3b Algorithm and Flowchart for *Control* Module

Algorithm	Flowchart
Init 1. *Open* 1, *Inventory For Input* 2. *Open* 2, *Transaction For Input* 3. *Open* 3, *Activity For Append* 4. *Open* 4, *Temporary For Output* 5. *Read*(1) *Record* 6. *Read*(2) *Record* 7. *Exit*	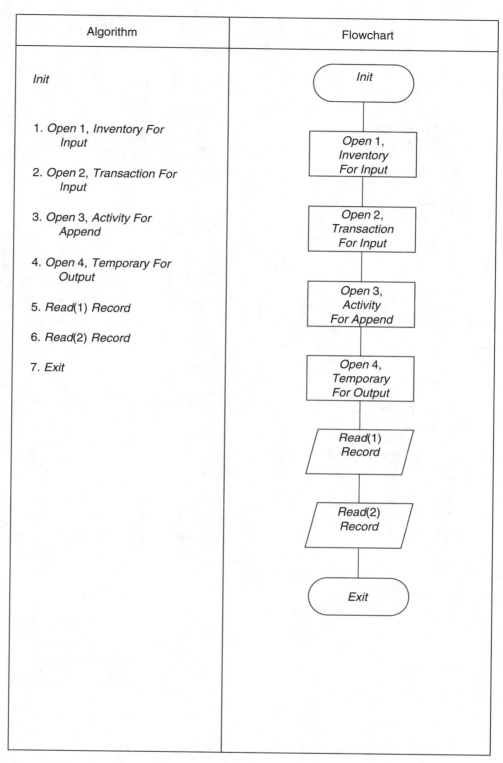

Figure 21.3c Algorithm and Flowchart for *Init* Module

Algorithm	Flowchart

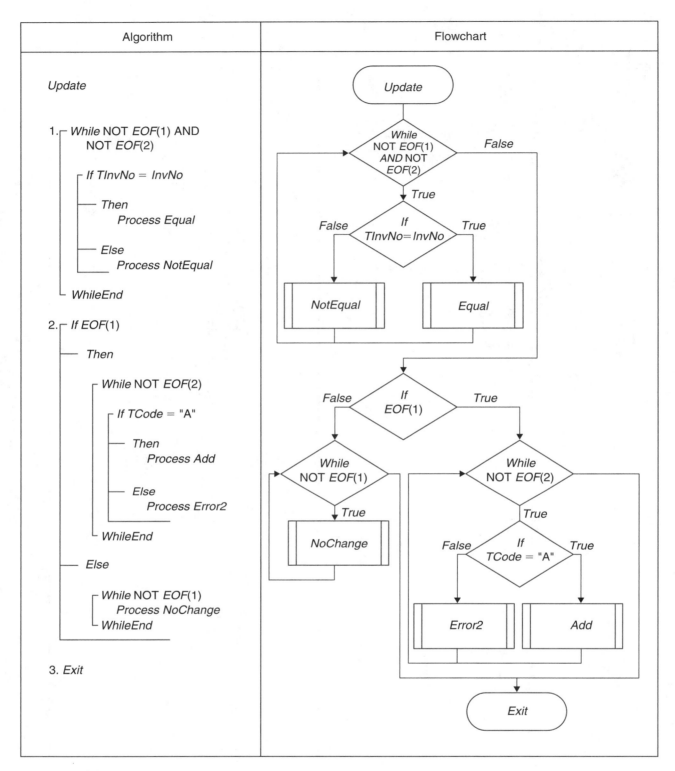

Update

1. ┌ *While* NOT *EOF*(1) AND
 NOT *EOF*(2)

 ┌ *If TInvNo = InvNo*

 ├── *Then*
 Process Equal

 └── *Else*
 Process NotEqual

 └ *WhileEnd*

2. ┌ *If EOF*(1)

 ├── *Then*

 ┌ *While* NOT *EOF*(2)

 ├ *If TCode* = "A"

 ├── *Then*
 Process Add

 ├── *Else*
 Process Error2

 └ *WhileEnd*

 ├── *Else*

 ┌ *While* NOT *EOF*(1)
 │ *Process NoChange*
 └ *WhileEnd*

3. *Exit*

Figure 21.3d Algorithm and Flowchart for *Update* Module

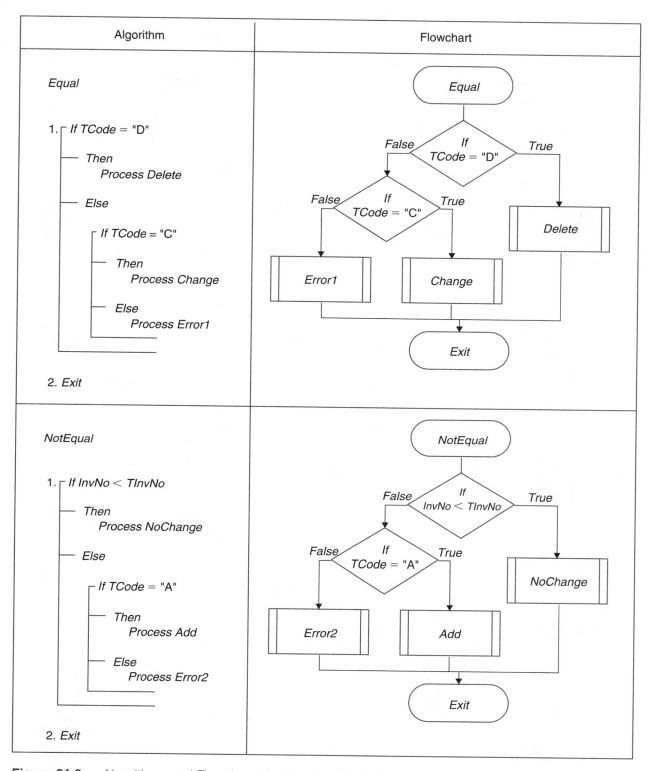

Algorithm	Flowchart
Equal 1. ⌐ *If TCode = "D"* — *Then* *Process Delete* — *Else* ⌐ *If TCode = "C"* — *Then* *Process Change* — *Else* *Process Error1* 2. *Exit*	
NotEqual 1. ⌐ *If InvNo < TInvNo* — *Then* *Process NoChange* — *Else* ⌐ *If TCode = "A"* — *Then* *Process Add* — *Else* *Process Error2* 2. *Exit*	

Figure 21.3e Algorithms and Flowcharts for *Equal* and *NotEqual* Modules

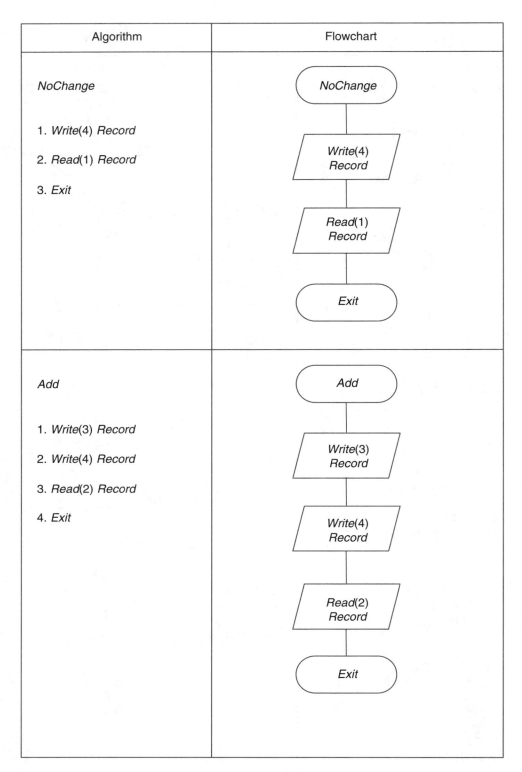

Algorithm	Flowchart
NoChange 1. *Write*(4) *Record* 2. *Read*(1) *Record* 3. *Exit*	
Add 1. *Write*(3) *Record* 2. *Write*(4) *Record* 3. *Read*(2) *Record* 4. *Exit*	

Figure 21.3f Algorithms and Flowcharts for *NoChange* and *Add* Modules

Algorithm	Flowchart
Error2 1. *Write Error Message* *(Nonexistent InvNo)* 2. *Read(2) Record* 3. *Exit*	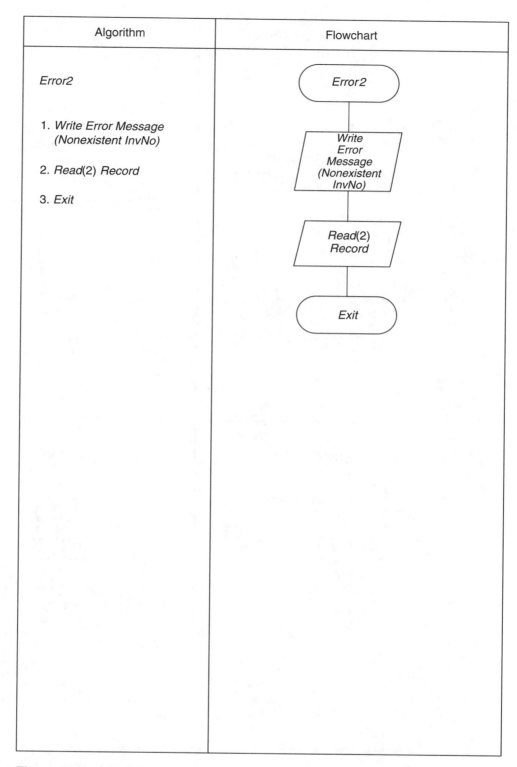

Figure 21.3g Algorithm and Flowchart for *Error2* Module

Algorithm	Flowchart

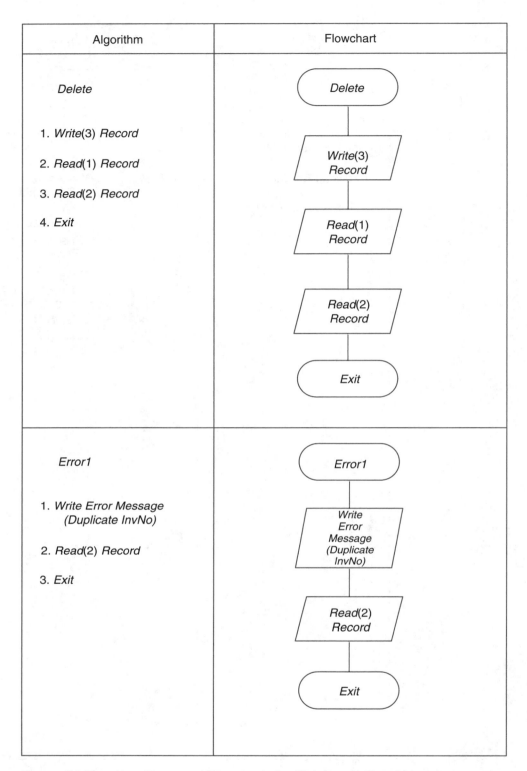

Delete

1. *Write*(3) *Record*

2. *Read*(1) *Record*

3. *Read*(2) *Record*

4. *Exit*

Error1

1. *Write Error Message (Duplicate InvNo)*

2. *Read*(2) *Record*

3. *Exit*

Figure 21.3h Algorithms and Flowcharts for *Delete* and *Error1* Modules

 The *Change* module (Figure 21.3i) is the most involved in that each field must be checked to see if the data in that field need to be changed. In this solution, (transaction code = "*D*") or " " (a null field—a field with nothing in it) indicates there is to be no change in that field. First, the transaction record is written to the activity file. Then the master file record is changed. The updated master file record is written to the

Algorithm	Flowchart

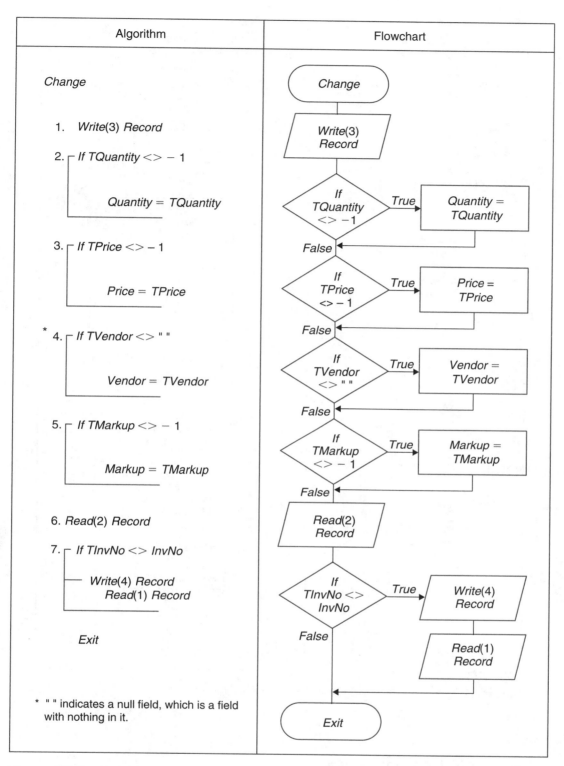

Change

1. *Write(3) Record*

2. ⌐ *If TQuantity <> − 1*

 Quantity = TQuantity

3. ⌐ *If TPrice <> − 1*

 Price = TPrice

* 4. ⌐ *If TVendor <> " "*

 Vendor = TVendor

5. ⌐ *If TMarkup <> − 1*

 Markup = TMarkup

6. *Read(2) Record*

7. ⌐ *If TInvNo <> InvNo*

 — *Write(4) Record*
 Read(1) Record

 Exit

* " " indicates a null field, which is a field with nothing in it.

Figure 21.3i Algorithm and Flowchart for *Change* Module

new master file. The next transaction file record is read and checked to see if it is still equal to the master file record. If it is equal, there are more changes to be made to the master file record; if not, the next master file record is read.

In the *WrapUp* module (Figure 21.3j), the files are closed, the old master file is renamed as the backup file, the new master file is renamed as the inventory file, and a message is printed to the screen that the run is completed.

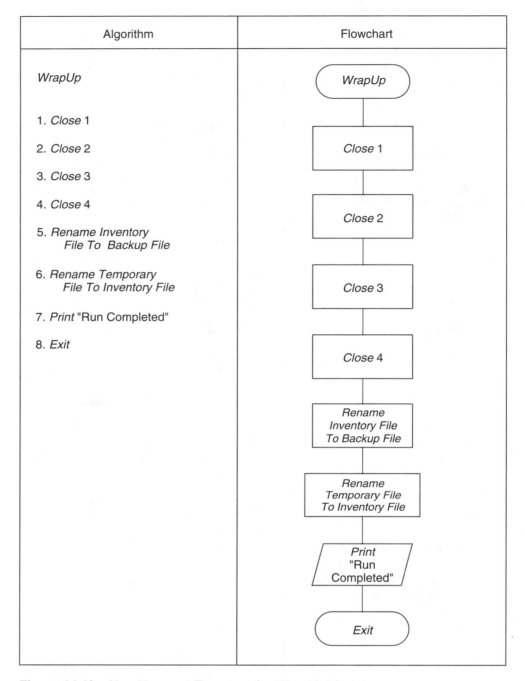

Algorithm	Flowchart
WrapUp 1. *Close* 1 2. *Close* 2 3. *Close* 3 4. *Close* 4 5. *Rename Inventory File To Backup File* 6. *Rename Temporary File To Inventory File* 7. *Print* "Run Completed" 8. *Exit*	

Figure 21.3j Algorithm and Flowchart for *WrapUp* Module

A Useful Alternative Method

Alternative Method

Figure 21.4 shows an alternative solution to the sequential file update problem. The main difference between the alternative solutions is how the update is driven. In the other examples in this chapter, the update is driven by the key. All updates, including adding records, changing records, and deleting records, are completed at the same time in key order. In the alternate method, the update is driven by the type of update; that is,

```
1. Open TF, AF
2. Read TF Record
3. HCode = TCode
4. While NOT EOF(TF)
      Open MF, HF
      Read MF Record
      While NOT EOF(MF) AND NOT EOF(TF) AND TCode = HCode
            If TCode = "A"
                  Then
                        If MfKey = TfKey
                              Then
                                    Process Error1
                                    Read TF Record
                              Else
                                    If MfKey < TfKey
                                          Then
                                                Write MF Record To HF
                                                Read MF Record
                                          Else
                                                Write AF Record
                                                Write TF Record To HF
                                                Read TF Record
                  Else
                        If TCode = "D"
                              Then
                                    If MfKey =
                                          Then
                                                Write AF Record
                                                Read MF Record
                                                Read TF Record
                                          Else
                                                If MfKey < TfKey
                                                      Then
                                                            Write MF Record To HF
                                                            Read MF Record
                                                      Else
                                                            Process Error2
                                                            Read TF Record
                              Else
                                    If MfKey = TfKey
                                          Then
                                                Write AF Record
                                                Process Change
                                                Write MF Record To HF
                                                Read TF Record
                                                If MfKey <> TfKey
                                                      Then
                                                            Read MF Record
                                                      Else
                                                            Continue
                                          Else
                                                If MfKey < TfKey
                                                      Then
                                                            Write MF Record To HF
                                                            Read MF Record
                                                      Else
                                                            Process Errors
                                                            Read TF Record
      WhileEnd
      While NOT EOF(MF)
            Write MF Record To HF
            Read MF Record
      WhileEnd
      Close File (MF, HF)
      Replace Backup File With MF
      Replace MF With HF
      WhileEnd
5. Close File (TF, AF)
6. Exit
```

Figure 21.4a Algorithm for Alternative Method of Sequential-Access File Update

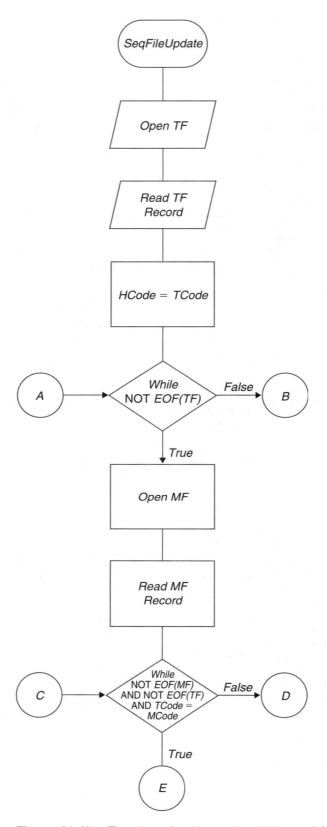

Figure 21.4b Flowchart for Alternative Method of Sequential-Access File Update

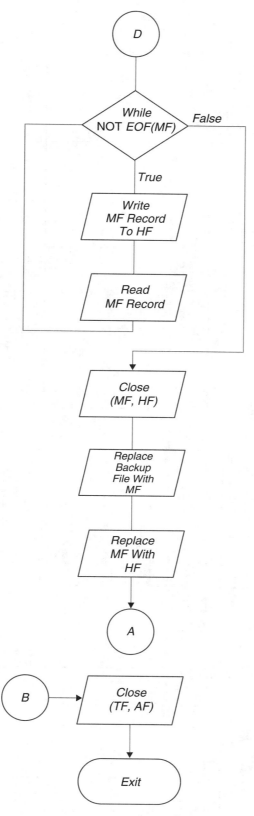

Figure 21.4c Flowchart for Alternative Method of Sequential-Access File Update

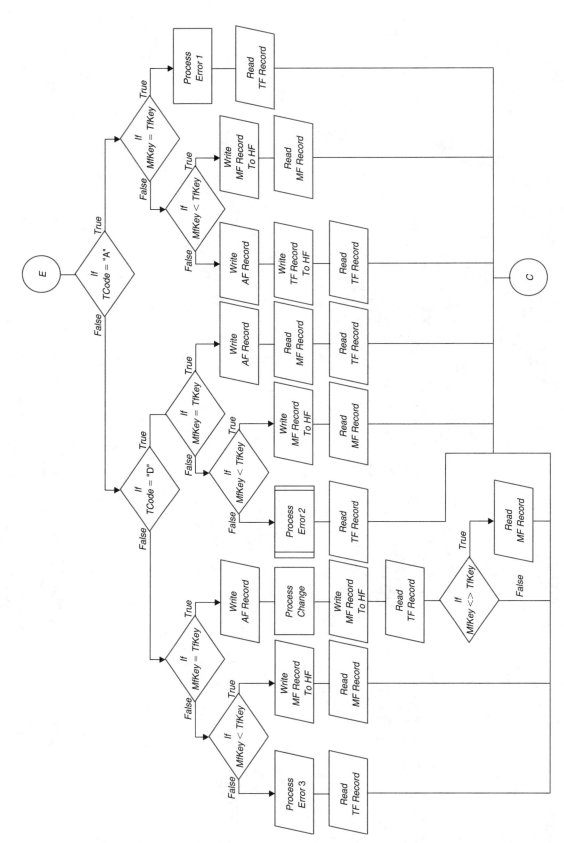

Figure 21.4d Flowchart for Alternative Method of Sequential-Access File Update

all adds are completed at one time, as are the deletions and changes. When using the alternative method, the transaction file must be sorted using the transaction code as the primary key and the primary key of the master file as the secondary key.

Summary

File updating is an essential part of working with files. The process of updating files includes adding, deleting, and changing records. Computer users use batch processing to update sequential files since random processing of sequential records is time-consuming on the computer. Updating a sequential file involves the following files: a transaction file, which contains all the updates; an activity file, which contains a record of all processes completed on the file; a backup file, which is the master file before the last update; a new master file, the updated master file; and, of course, the old master file, which contains the records to be updated. Sequential file updating involves updating the master file with the additions, deletions, and changes listed in the transaction file. After an update is completed, a new transaction file is created, and after a period of time, the user processes the master and the transaction files together again.

New Terms

activity file	batch processing	master file
backup file	interactive processing	transaction file

Questions

1. What processes are included in updating a file?
2. State the functions of the following files:
 a. old master file
 b. transaction file
 c. activity file
 d. new master file
 e. backup file

Problems

1. Develop a solution and data dictionary to update a client file given the following master and transaction file records. (The master file is in client number order.)

Master File Record

client #	name	telephone	address	city-state	zip code	last call	amount of last order

Transaction File Record

client #	tcode	name	telephone	address	city-state	zip code	last call	amount of last order

2. Develop a solution and data dictionary to update a book file for a library. After each update is complete, the librarian would like a copy of all new listings. Design the master file record and the transaction file record. The data in the master file record should include:
 a. reference number
 b. author
 c. title
 d. publisher
 e. ISBN
 f. copyright date
 g. number of copies
 h. subject

3. Develop a solution to update the file used in problem 1 in Chapter 20, on page 413.

4. Develop a solution to update the file used in problem 3 in Chapter 20, on page 413

Unit Seven

Supplementary Exercises

Develop a complete solution, including a data dictionary, for the following problems:

1. The financial director of a private school would like a tracking system for the students at the school.

 a. Design the file. The information on the student includes: name, home address and telephone, age, sex, class status, parent's name (one parent), dormitory room, tuition, room fees, board fees, book fees, computer fees, miscellaneous fees, date of payment on each charge.

 b. Design the reports needed:
 Student directory
 Charges
 Outstanding fees
 List of students by dormitory
 List of students by class

 c. Develop a solution using sequential-access files to output the needed reports.

 d. Develop an update program.

Appendix A

Otto the Robot

You may be able to understand your own knowledge base and the knowledge base of others around you without much trouble. You also may be able to modify your solutions to everyday problems according to these knowledge bases. These knowledge bases are very broad and varied. However, when you are working with a computer, the knowledge base is defined for you and tends to be limited. You may not use any other instructions, actions, or formats. The rules, called syntax, are defined for you. To better understand this concept, we will move from our everyday problems to a robot called Otto.

Otto the robot has a very limited knowledge base. Otto can sit, stand, add, subtract, and check some of his systems, among other things. His language or knowledge base is defined by 15 actions. You must define your solutions to Otto's problems within the limitations of this knowledge base.

Assumptions

There are usually certain assumptions that need to be made when solving problems, such as a common language. Other assumptions we will make regarding Otto are as follows:

1. Otto always starts from a sitting position with his hands and arms by his side.
2. Otto must always end his maneuvers in a sitting position. This means you have to tell him to sit down at the end of your solution.

Simple Actions

Let's start with a few simple actions in Otto's knowledge base.

Action 1: Stand up. Otto will stand up from his chair to an upright position.

Action 2: Sit down. Otto will sit down. You must make sure the chair is behind him or he will sit on the floor.

Action 3: Take step. Otto will take one step forward.

Action 4: Turn right. Otto will turn right 90 degrees.

Problem

With these four actions in Otto's knowledge base, let's solve the following problem: Write a set of numbered step-by-step instructions to make Otto walk three steps forward and then return and sit in his chair. Use the six problem-solving steps presented in Chapter 1 to develop the solution.

1. Identify the problem: Make Otto stand up, walk three steps forward, turn around, walk to his chair, then turn around and sit down.
2. Understand the problem: Do you understand what he is to do? Otto's knowledge base is limited to his four actions.
3. Alternative solutions:
 1. Stand up, walk three steps forward, turn right 180 degrees and go back to chair, and sit down.
 2. Stand up, walk three steps forward, turn left 180 degrees and go back to chair, and sit down.
4. Select the best solution: Solution number one is the best since Otto can only turn right.
5. Plan the solution by listing the set of instructions (Solution 1):
 1. stand up
 2. take step
 3. take step
 4. take step
 5. turn right
 6. turn right
 7. take step
 8. take step
 9. take step
 10. turn right
 11. turn right
 12. sit down
6. Test solution. Have someone test this solution to see if it works.

There are many instructions in this solution.

Repeat Action

Let's add another action that will allow us to repeat the same action several times. This will be the fifth action in Otto's knowledge base.

Action 5: Repeat—[Action] *x* times, where *x* is a given number such as 3, 6, 8, and so on.

Now, let's rewrite the instructions in problem-solving Step 5 (Solution 2):

1. stand up (same as Instruction 1 in Solution 1)
2. repeat [take step] 3 times (same as Instructions 2–4 in Solution 1)
3. repeat [turn right] 2 times (same as Instructions 5–6 in Solution 1)

4. repeat [take step] 3 times (same as Instructions 7–9 in Solution 1)
5. repeat [turn right] 2 times (same as Instructions 10–11 in Solution 1)
6. sit down (same as Instruction 12 in Solution 1)

We now have 6 numbered instructions that complete the same task as the 12 numbered instructions did in Solution 1. Will Otto react differently? No, he will do exactly the same thing. He will stand up, walk three steps forward, turn 180 degrees to the right, walk back, turn 180 degrees to the right, and sit down. The actual number of actions he takes is the same. The only difference is that to move forward he will take three steps with only one instruction instead of requiring three instructions. We can decrease the number of instructions even further (Solution 3):

1. stand up
2. repeat [[[take step] 3 times, [turn right] 2 times] 2 times]
3. sit down

Note: The double set of brackets used above reflect a technique called *nesting*. Just as you might put one basket inside another basket (nested), you are placing repeated instructions inside another repeated instruction. The inside set of brackets contain instructions that are executed before the outer set of bracketed instructions.

The number of actual steps and turns Otto takes is the same. You need to decide which set of instructions is easiest for you to read and write, and the easiest to understand by someone else.

Now let's add some more actions to Otto's knowledge base.

Arm Actions

Action 6: Raise arms. Raises arms to a forward position perpendicular to his body.

Action 7: Lower arms. Lowers arms to a position at the side of his body.

Arithmetic Actions

Otto has one memory location that may be changed by one of the following instructions. This memory location always starts at zero when the execution of the instruction set begins.

Action 8: Add one. Adds one to the memory location.

Action 9: Subtract one. Subtracts one from the memory location.

Action 10: Set number to zero. Sets memory location to zero.

Conditional Actions

One thing a computer needs is the ability to make a decision given certain data. With Otto, these tests use his memory location and sensory devices in his fingertips. Otto can determine when his memory location is zero. He can determine if his hands are touching

something. He can determine if his hands are touching a door because the door has a different sensory return than anything else. These actions include three tests:

Action 11: Test—Is the number in your memory zero?

Yes, then: (one action for yes answer)

No, else: (one action for no answer)

Action 12: Test—Are you touching anything?

Yes, then: (one action for yes answer)

No, else: (one action for no answer)

Action 13: Test—Are you touching a door?

Yes, then: (one action for yes answer)

No, else: (one action for no answer)

An example of one of these tests would be (let's say this is Instruction 15):

15. Test: Is the number in your memory zero?

Yes, then: Turn right

No: Take step

Many times there are several actions that need to take place for the yes actions and/or the no actions, or the action requires jumping to another instruction either after or before the present instruction. This necessitates a new transfer action.

Transfer Action

Action 14: Goto *i*, where *i* is an instruction number, either one or more actions before or one or more actions after the present instruction. An example would be:

8. Goto 5 or

12. Goto 15

An example of a conditional action using the Goto *i* action is:

18. Take step.

19. Subtract one.

20. Test: Is your memory zero?

Yes, then: Goto 21

No, then: Goto 18

21. Repeat [turn right] 2 times

22. (Continue with other actions)

One More Action

You will need one more action to complete the exercises at the end of this appendix.

Action 15: Open door. Opens a door; the door will close after Otto walks through it. There are 15 actions in Otto's knowledge base. Remember that you must use these actions and no other ones. Also, remember that each instruction must be

written in the proper form as this is the extent of Otto's knowledge. For example, you must write:

Repeat [take step] 3 times,

And *not:*

Take 3 steps or

Repeat 3 times take step

Remember that Otto executes the instructions in the order you give them. When you use the Goto *i* action, he will execute instruction *i* next and then continue at that point with the execution. Let's review the 15 actions:

Action 1: Stand up. Otto will stand up from his chair in an upright position.

Action 2: Sit down. Otto will sit down. You must make sure the chair is behind him or he will sit on the floor.

Action 3: Take step. Otto will take one step forward.

Action 4: Turn right. Otto will turn right 90 degrees.

Action 5: Repeat—[Action] *x* times, where *x* is a given number such as 3, 6, 8, and so on.

Action 6: Raise arms. Raises arms to a forward position perpendicular to his body.

Action 7: Lower arms. Lowers arms to a position at the side of his body.

Action 8: Add one. Adds one to the memory location.

Action 9: Subtract one. Subtracts one from the memory location.

Action 10: Set memory location to zero.

Action 11: Test—Is the number in your memory zero?

Yes, then: (one action for yes answer)

No, else: (one action for no answer)

Action 12: Test—Are you touching anything?

Yes, then: (one action for yes answer)

No, else: (one action for no answer)

Action 13: Test—Are you touching a door?

Yes, then: (one action for yes answer)

No, else: (one action for no answer)

Action 14: Goto *i*, where *i* is an instruction number, either before or after the present instruction.

Action 15: Open door. Opens a door; the door will close after Otto walks through it.

Otto is set up to help you organize your solutions in a logical order and to realize that the computer cannot read your mind. You must give it a complete set of instructions. One of the most frustrating things when working with a computer is that it does exactly what it is instructed to do, not what you thought you instructed it to do.

Problems

1. How would you make Otto turn left?

2. The following three sets of instructions for Otto are incorrect. Find the problem(s) and correct the solution.

a.
 1. Stand up
 2. Take step
 3. Add 1 to memory
 4. Goto 2
 5. Sit down
b.
 1. Stand up
 2. Repeat [take step] 3 times
 3. If touching something
 Yes, then: goto 4
 No, else: goto 2
 4. Turn right 2 times
 5. Goto 2
 6. Sit down
c.
 1. Stand up
 2. Take 2 steps
 3. Turn
 4. Take 3 steps
 5. Turn
 6. Take 3 steps
 7. Turn
 8. Take 3 steps
 9. Turn
 10. Take 1 step
 11. Sit down

Using Otto's 15 actions, write a set of step-by-step instructions to have Otto complete problems 3 through 8. An Otto simulator is available at the Instructor Resource Center. Ask your instructor to make this simulator available to you to check your solutions.

3. Direct Otto to walk in a square that is three steps on each side. All turns are to be right-hand turns. How many solutions are there to this problem?

4. Direct Otto to walk in a square that is three steps on each side. All turns are to be left-hand turns.

5. Direct Otto to walk to a wall that is an unknown whole number of steps (no partial steps) in front of Otto, and then walk back and sit down in his chair. The back of the chair is taller than Otto and can be touched by Otto's raised hands, when Otto is directly in front of his chair.

6. Direct Otto to walk to a wall that is an unknown whole number of steps (no partial steps) in front of Otto, and then walk back and sit down in his chair. The back of the chair is shorter than Otto's raised hands when Otto is directly in front of his chair. Therefore, Otto's hands cannot touch the back of the chair.

7. Write *one* set of instructions that will direct Otto through any maze with its entrance and exit on the same side (see Figure A.1). The maze has no dead ends and no intersections. From Otto's starting position, the entrance is two steps forward. When Otto is facing the entrance, the exit is three steps to his right. Figure A.1 shows three example mazes for you to test your solution. Do not make separate solutions for each maze. Your solutions should allow Otto to walk through any mazes such as those shown in Figure A.1. Test your solution with a maze that you designed.

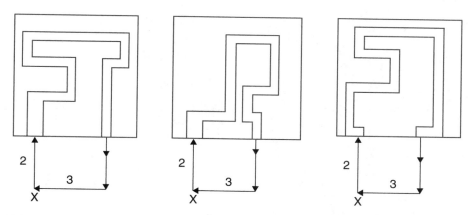

Figure A.1 Example Mazes for Problem 7

8. Modify your solution in Problem 7 to accommodate a change in the place of the exit. Your solution should allow for the exit to be any place on the perimeter of the maze. Figure A.2 shows three example mazes for you to test your solution. Again, do not write separate solutions for each maze. Your solution should allow Otto to walk back to his chair from any exit, such as those in Figure A.2. Test your solution with a maze that you designed.

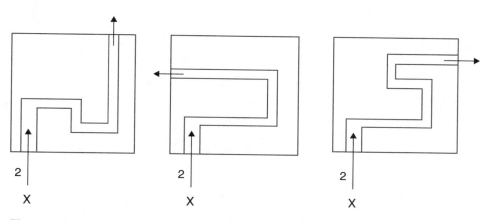

Figure A.2 Example Mazes for Problem 8

9. How would you modify Otto's knowledge base so you are able to write a solution for the following tasks? Specify the modifications and then write the set of instructions for each of the tasks.
 a. Direct Otto to walk in a triangle that has three steps on each side.
 b. Direct Otto to walk to a table and pick up a book.
 c. Modify your instruction set in problem 5 (to walk to the wall and back) to have Otto detect an object in his path.

10. Design your own robot actions. What actions do you think are important for your robot? What type of problems could your robot solve?

Appendix B

Overview of UML
(Unified Modeling Language)

Unified Modeling Language (UML) is used to create a logical model of your solution. It uses various diagrams to describe the entire system. These diagrams help produce a model of the problem and lead to a better understanding of the requirements of a problem. Through a better understanding of a problem, a better solution can be developed using an object-oriented language. UML is increasingly being used in the programming industry to design and communicate a solution to a problem. This appendix presents an overview of the various diagrams and terminology that accompanies them.

The five diagrams defined in this appendix are use case diagrams, class diagrams, sequence diagrams, state chart diagrams, and activity diagrams.

Use Case Diagrams

Use case diagrams describe how a system functions from the user's standpoint. They present who may use what part of the system. There are basically two parts of a use case diagram: the actor and the use case. The actor represents the users of the system, including human and nonhuman entities. The use case describes the services required by the actor. It is represented by an oval with the service or function written inside. Communication is indicated by lines connecting the actor and the use case. The series of use cases required for this part of the solution are encased in a rectangle with the name of the system in the top part of the rectangle. See Figure B.1.

The actors in Figure B.2 are the librarian and the client. The case uses are to add books, delete books, add clients, delete clients, list books, list clients, check out books, and check in books. There may be others, but these are some of the functions of the system. The client may access only the check-in and check-out case uses. The librarian may access all case uses. The assistant librarian can access everything except adding or deleting books and clients.

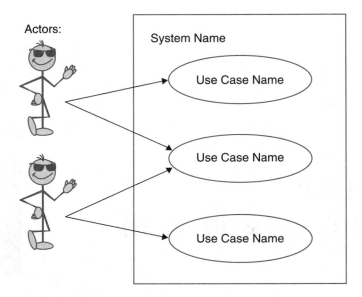

Figure B.1 Use Case Diagram

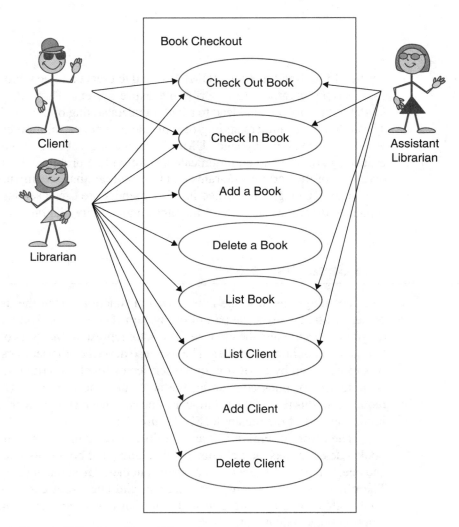

Figure B.2 Use Case Diagram

Class Diagrams

Class diagrams graphically describe how a class functions. Basically, they describe the data structure of the solution. They describe the class, their attributes, and their operations. The simplest form is:

Class Name
Attributes
Operations

See Figure B.3 for a class diagram of the *Books* class. The *Books* class includes all books. The attributes for the *Books* class include library ID number, the name of the book, its author, its ISBN, its publisher, year of its publication, whether it is checked out, the client to whom the book is checked out, and where in the library the book is located. The functions that involve the *Books* class include checking out a book, checking in a book, listing all books, adding books, deleting books, and updating data on individual books.

Sequence Diagrams

Sequencing diagrams graphically present the interactivity between objects. The interactions are represented as messages in the diagram. The diagram shows the actions by the user and the subsequent actions that result between objects. See Figure B.4. Notice that the user interacts with the system by sending a message of what is to be accomplished to an object. The object may then send another message to another object to accomplish another task. The series may include any number of messages. The number of objects that are performing tasks and interacting with other objects also may be unlimited. See Figure B.5 for a sequence diagram of starting a car. The user sends a message to the ignition by turning the key. The ignition then sends a message to the engine to start. The user sends a message to the engine to accelerate or not by pressing

Books Class
Library ID number Name Author ISBN Publisher Year of publication Checked out Client checked out to Area in library
Check out book Check in book List each book data Add book Delete book Update book data

Figure B.3 Class Diagram of *Books* Class

Figure B.4 Sequence Diagram

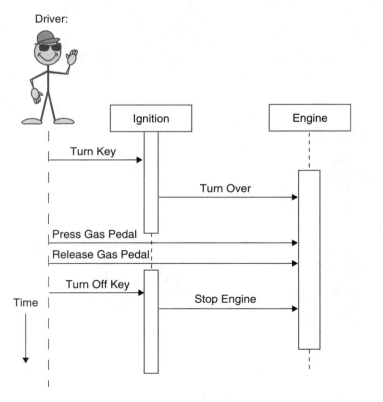

Figure B.5 Sequence Diagram for Starting and Turning Off a Car Engine

or releasing the gas pedal. The user sends a message to the ignition to turn off the engine by turning the key. The ignition then sends a message to the engine to stop running. This diagram is simplified. You may add brakes, gears, and so forth to this diagram.

Statechart Diagrams

A statechart diagram describes what happens to a given value of an object as it proceeds through the system. See Figure B.6. An event is an activity that sends a message that causes something to happen. The action is the set of tasks or instructions that is the response to the event.

Activity Diagrams

An activity diagram describes the flow of activities. This type of diagram is similar to a data flow chart. It specifies what happens and when. The major difference is in the symbols used. Because you are representing general activities and not specific instructions, all activities use a flattened ellipse. See Figure B.7. You may add decision structures as necessary. The flow may be from top down or may be from left to right as in Figure B.8.

These UML diagrams illustrate how you can design and develop a solution using an object-oriented language. When you write the various functions, modules, or scripts, you will use the four logic structures presented in Chapters 4–8.

Figure B.6 Statechart Diagram

Figure B.7 Activity Diagram

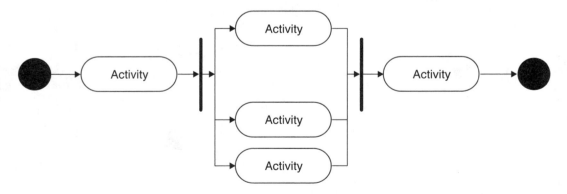

Figure B.8 Horizontal Activity Diagram

Appendix C

ASCII and EBCDIC Codes for Data Representation

Character	EBCDIC Code Binary Code	Decimal Value
0	1111 0000	240
1	1111 0001	241
2	1111 0010	242
3	1111 0011	243
4	1111 0100	244
5	1111 0101	245
6	1111 0110	246
7	1111 0111	247
8	1111 1000	248
9	1111 1001	249
Space	0100 0000	64
.	0100 1011	75
<	0100 1100	76
(0100 1101	77
+	0100 1110	78
&	0101 0000	80
!	0101 1010	90
$	0101 1011	91
*	0101 1100	92
)	0101 1101	93
;	0101 1110	94
,	0110 1011	107
%	0110 1100	108
_	0110 1101	109
>	0110 1110	110
?	0110 1111	111
:	0111 1010	122
#	0111 1011	123
@	0111 1100	124
'	0111 1101	125
=	0111 1110	126
"	0111 1111	127

Character	EBCDIC Code Binary Code	Decimal Value
A	1100 0001	193
B	1100 0010	194
C	1100 0011	195
D	1100 0100	196
E	1100 0101	197
F	1100 0110	198
G	1100 0111	199
H	1100 1000	200
I	1100 1001	201
J	1101 0001	209
K	1101 0010	210
L	1101 0011	211
M	1101 0100	212
N	1101 0101	213
O	1101 0110	214
P	1101 0111	215
Q	1101 1000	216
R	1101 1001	217
S	1110 0010	226
T	1110 0011	227
U	1110 0100	228
V	1110 0101	229
W	1110 0110	230
X	1110 0111	231
Y	1110 1000	232
Z	1110 1001	233
a	1000 0001	129
b	1000 0010	130
c	1000 0011	131
d	1000 0100	132
e	1000 0101	133
f	1000 0110	134
g	1000 0111	135
h	1000 1000	136
i	1000 1001	137
j	1001 0001	145
k	1001 0010	146
l	1001 0011	147
m	1001 0100	148
n	1001 0101	149
o	1001 0110	150
p	1001 0111	151
q	1001 1000	152
r	1001 1001	153
s	1010 0010	162
t	1010 0011	163
u	1010 0100	164
v	1010 0101	165
w	1010 0110	166
x	1010 0111	167
y	1010 1000	168
z	1010 1001	169

Figure C.1 EBCDIC Codes

ASCII in Mnemonic	Binary Code	Decimal Code	Octal Code	Hex Code	Remark
NUL	00 00 00 00	0	000	00	Null, tape feed.
SOH	00 00 00 01	1	001	01	Start of heading; also SOM, start of message.
STX	00 00 00 10	2	002	02	Start of text; also EOA, end of address.
ETX	00 00 00 11	3	003	03	End of text; also EOM, end of message.
EOT	00 00 01 00	4	004	04	End of transmission (End); shut off TWX machines.
ENQ	00 00 01 01	5	005	05	Inquiry (Inqry); also WRU.
ACK	00 00 01 10	6	006	06	Acknowledge; also RU.
BEL	00 00 01 11	7	007	07	Ring the bell.
BS	00 00 10 00	8	010	08	Backspace; also FEO, format effector.
HT	00 00 10 01	9	011	09	Horizontal tab.
LF	00 00 10 10	10	012	0A	Line feed or line space (New line); advance paper to next line.
VT	00 00 10 11	11	013	0B	Vertical tab (VTAB).
FF	00 00 11 00	12	014	0C	Form feed to top of next page (Page).
CR	00 00 11 01	13	015	0D	Carriage return to beginning line.
SO	00 00 11 10	14	016	0E	Shift out; changes ribbon color to red.
SI	00 00 11 11	15	017	0F	Shift in; changes ribbon color to black.
DLE	00 01 00 00	16	020	10	Data line escape.
DC1	00 01 00 01	17	021	11	Device control 1; turns on transmitter (reader).
DC2	00 01 00 10	18	022	12	Device control 2; turns on punch or auxiliary.
DC3	00 01 00 11	19	023	13	Device control 3; turns off transmitter (reader).
DC4	00 01 01 00	20	024	14	Device control 4; turns off punch or auxiliary.
NAK	00 01 01 01	21	025	15	Negative acknowledge; also ERR, error.
SYN	00 01 01 10	22	026	16	Synchronous file (SYNC).
ETB	00 01 01 11	23	027	17	End of transmission block; also LEM, logical end of medium.
CAN	00 01 10 00	24	030	18	Cancel (Cancl).
EM	00 01 10 01	25	031	19	End of medium.
SUB	00 01 10 10	26	032	1A	Substitute.
ESC	00 01 10 11	27	033	1B	Escape.
FS	00 01 11 00	28	034	1C	File separator.
GS	00 01 11 01	29	035	1D	Group separator.
RS	00 01 11 10	30	036	1E	Record separator.
US	00 01 11 11	31	037	1F	Unit separator.
Space	00 10 00 00	32	040	20	
!	00 10 00 01	33	041	21	
"	00 10 00 10	34	042	22	
#	00 10 00 11	35	043	23	
$	00 10 01 00	36	044	24	
%	00 10 01 01	37	045	25	
&	00 10 01 10	38	046	26	
'	00 10 01 11	39	047	27	Apostrophe.
(00 10 10 00	40	050	28	
)	00 10 10 01	41	051	29	
*	00 10 10 10	42	052	2A	
+	00 10 10 11	43	053	2B	
,	00 10 11 00	44	054	2C	
-	00 10 11 01	45	055	2D	Hyphen.
.	00 10 11 10	46	056	2E	
/	00 10 11 11	47	057	2F	

Figure C.2 ASCII Codes *(continued on pages 459–460)*

ASCII in Mnemonic	Binary Code	Decimal Code	Octal Code	Hex Code	Remark
0	00 11 00 00	48	060	30	
1	00 11 00 01	49	061	31	
2	00 11 00 10	50	062	32	
3	00 11 00 11	51	063	33	
4	00 11 01 00	52	064	34	
5	00 11 01 01	53	065	35	
6	00 11 01 10	54	066	36	
7	00 11 01 11	55	067	37	
8	00 11 10 00	56	070	38	
9	00 11 10 01	57	071	39	
:	00 11 10 10	58	072	3A	
;	00 11 10 11	59	073	3B	
<	00 11 11 00	60	074	3C	
=	00 11 11 01	61	075	3D	
>	00 11 11 10	62	076	3E	
?	00 11 11 11	63	077	3F	
@	01 00 00 00	64	100	40	
A	01 00 00 01	65	101	41	
B	01 00 00 10	66	102	42	
C	01 00 00 11	67	103	43	
D	01 00 01 00	68	104	44	
E	01 00 01 01	69	105	45	
F	01 00 01 10	70	106	46	
G	01 00 01 11	71	107	47	
H	01 00 10 00	72	110	48	
I	01 00 10 01	73	111	49	
J	01 00 10 10	74	112	4A	
K	01 00 10 11	75	113	4B	
L	01 00 11 00	76	114	4C	
M	01 00 11 01	77	115	4D	
N	01 00 11 10	78	116	4E	
O	01 00 11 11	79	117	4F	
P	01 01 00 00	80	120	50	
Q	01 01 00 01	81	121	51	
R	01 01 00 10	82	122	52	
S	01 01 00 11	83	123	53	
T	01 01 01 00	84	124	54	
U	01 01 01 01	85	125	55	
V	01 01 01 10	86	126	56	
W	01 01 01 11	87	127	57	
X	01 01 10 00	88	130	58	
Y	01 01 10 01	89	131	59	
Z	01 01 10 10	90	132	5A	
[01 01 10 11	91	133	5B	
]	01 01 11 00	92	134	5C	
]	01 01 11 01	93	135	5D	
^	01 01 11 10	94	136	5E	
−	01 01 11 11	95	137	5F	Underline.

Figure C.2 (continued from page 458)

ASCII in Mnemonic	Binary Code	Decimal Code	Octal Code	Hex Code	Remark	
'	01 10 00 00	96	140	60	Accent grave.	
a	01 10 00 01	97	141	61		
b	01 10 00 10	98	142	62		
c	01 10 00 11	99	143	63		
d	01 10 01 00	100	144	64		
e	01 10 01 01	101	145	65		
f	01 10 01 10	102	146	66		
g	01 10 01 11	103	147	67		
h	01 10 10 00	104	150	68		
i	01 10 10 01	105	151	69		
j	01 10 10 10	106	152	6A		
k	01 10 10 11	107	153	6B		
l	01 10 11 00	108	154	6C		
m	01 10 11 01	109	155	6D		
n	01 10 11 10	110	156	6E		
o	01 10 11 11	111	157	6F		
p	01 11 00 00	112	160	70		
q	01 11 00 01	113	161	71		
r	01 11 00 10	114	162	72		
s	01 11 00 11	115	163	73		
t	01 11 01 00	116	164	74		
u	01 11 01 01	117	165	75		
v	01 11 01 10	118	166	76		
w	01 11 01 11	119	167	77		
x	01 11 10 00	120	170	78		
y	01 11 10 01	121	171	79		
z	01 11 10 10	122	172	7A		
{	01 11 10 11	123	173	7B		
		01 11 11 00	124	174	7C	Alt mode.
}	01 11 11 01	125	175	7D		
~	01 11 11 10	126	176	7E		
DEL	01 11 11 11	127	177	7F	Delete, rub out.	

Figure C.2 (continued from page 459)

Appendix D

Forms to Use in Problem Solving

Given Data	Required Results
Required Processing	**Solution Alternatives**

Figure D.1 Problem Analysis Chart

Figure D.2 The Interactivity Chart

Input	Processing	Module Reference	Output

Figure D.3 The IPO Chart

Algorithm	Flowchart

Figure D.4 Algorithm and Flowchart *(continued on page 465)*

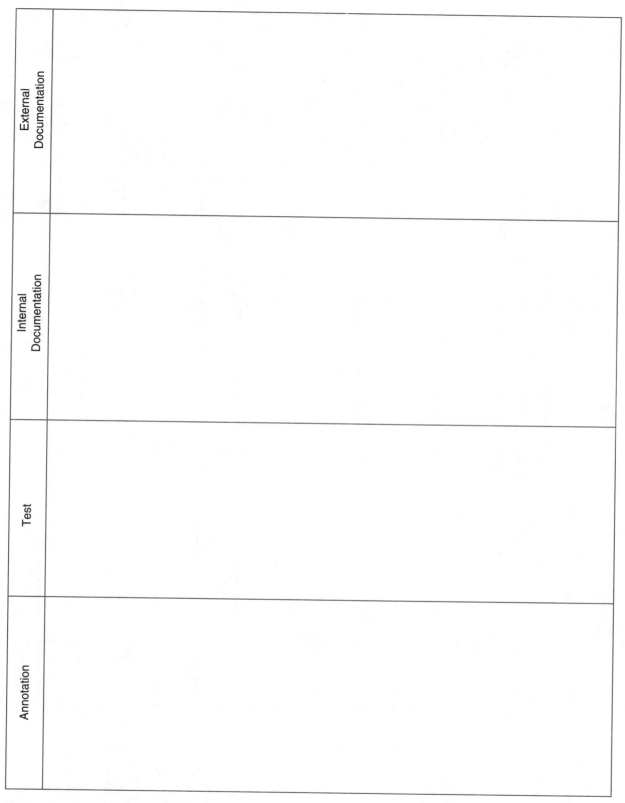

Figure D.4 *(continued from page 464)*

Item	Variable Name	Data Type	Module	Scope	Pseudonyms/Module	Error Checks

Figure D.5 Data Dictionary

Record Data Dictionary

Field	Item Description	Field Name	Field Length	Data Type	Number of Decimals	Comments

Record Layout

Figure D.6 Record Data Dictionary and Record Layout

Figure D.7 Screen Design

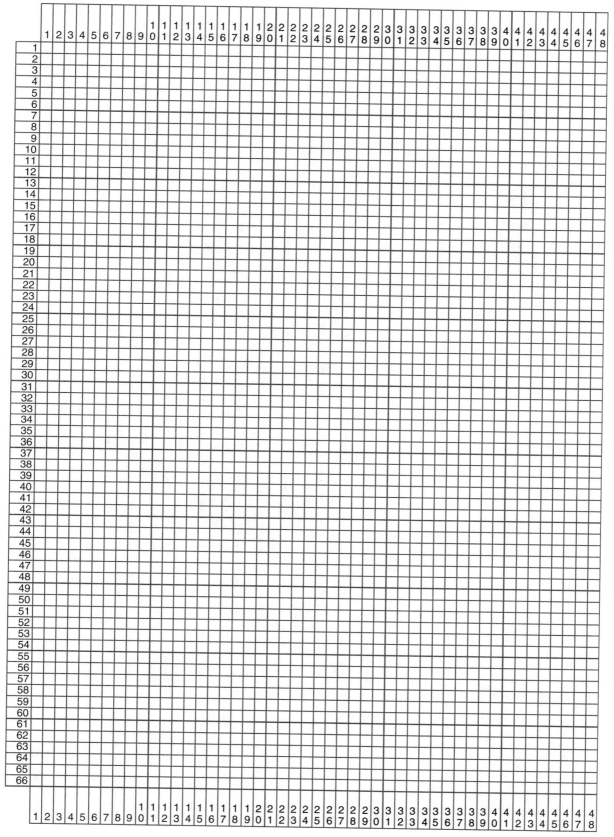

Figure D.8 The Print Chart *(continued on pages 470–471)*

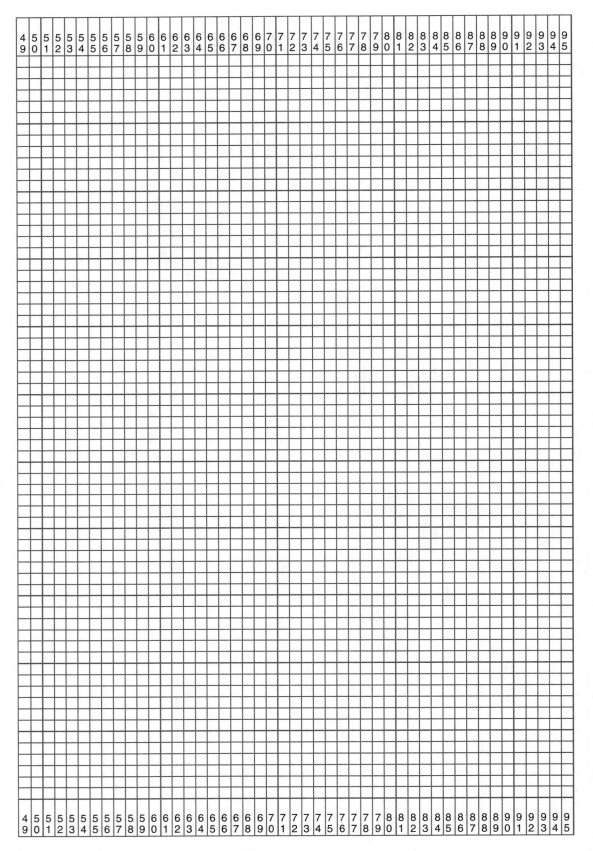

Figure D.8 *(continued from page 469)*

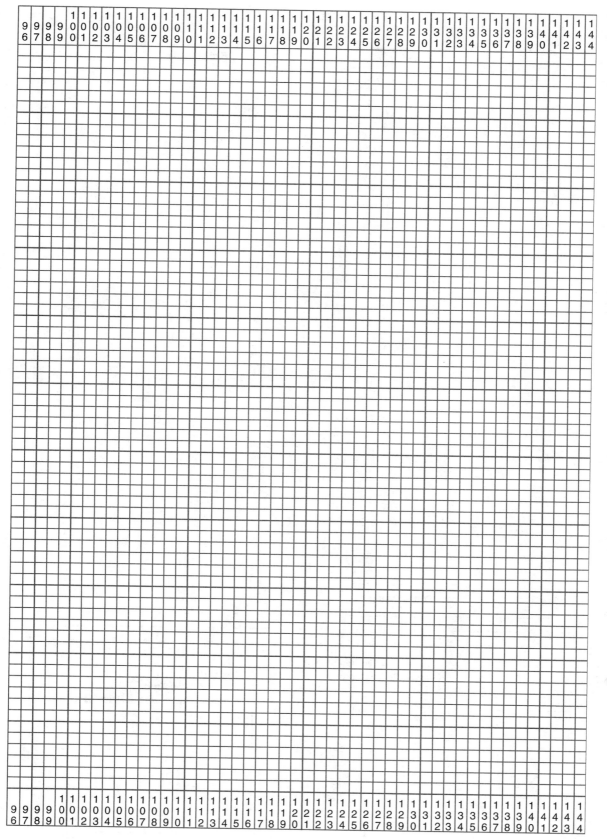

Figure D.8 (continued from page 470)

Header: _____

Left Margin: _____ Top Margin: _____ Right Margin: _____

Tabs:

Bottom Margin: _____

Footer: _____

| Paper Size: _____
Page Orientation: _____
Justification: _____ | Other Information
Graphics to Be Used: | Reminders:
 Mark Guidelines
 Mark Page Number Placement |

Figure D.9 Page Planning Guide for Word Processing

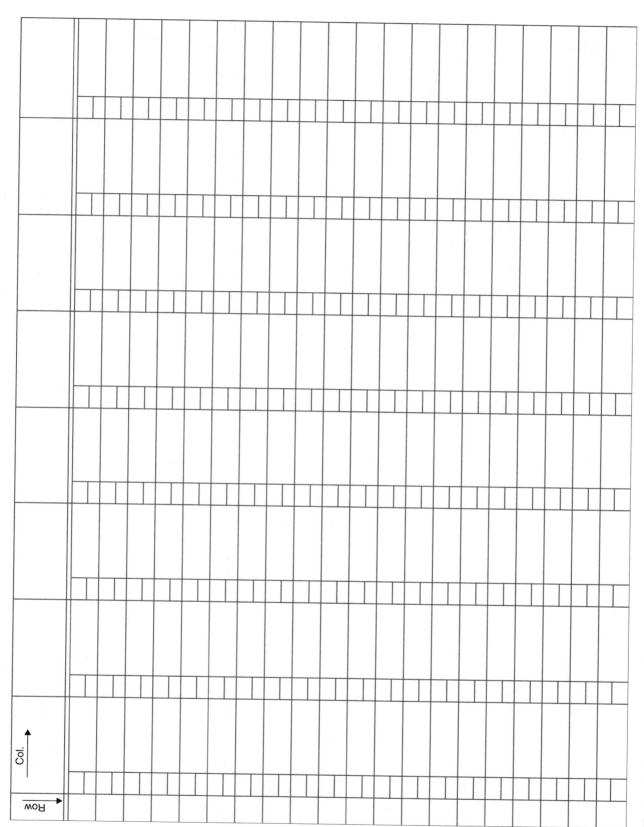

Col.

Row

Figure D.10 Spreadsheet Planning Guide

Output Requirements	Input Requirements	Input Format

Figure D.11 Output and Input Requirements Chart

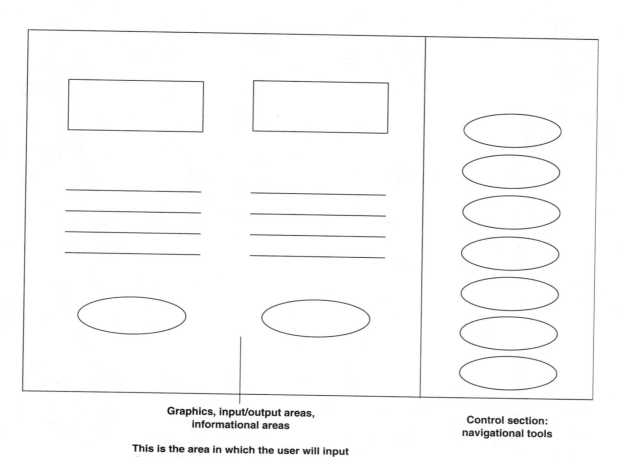

**Graphics, input/output areas,
informational areas**

**This is the area in which the user will input
data, read information, and receive output.**

**Control section:
navigational tools**

Figure D.12 The User Interface Screen Design Chart

Class	Properties	Functions

Figure D.13 Class, Properties, and Functions Chart

Class: _____

Property	Attributes

Figure D.14 Attributes of a Class Properties Chart

Figure D.15 Storyboard

Object Name	Source/File Name	File Type/Extension	Screen Number(s)	H/I/O*	Script

*H = Hyper, I = Input, O = Output

Figure D.16 Object Dictionary

Appendix E

Other Problem-Solving Tools

Problem-solving techniques using six basic tools have been presented throughout this book. There are other tools for problem solving that have not been presented. Among these tools are Nassi-Schneiderman charts and Warnier-Orr diagrams. Since these tools are replacement tools for the algorithm and flowcharts, they were not presented earlier in this text.

Both Nassi-Schneiderman charts (N-S) and Warnier-Orr diagrams are used to create structured solutions. Many people prefer one of these tools to flowcharts. Whichever tool is chosen, the use is the same. You should plan the solution, complete the problem-solving process, and end with a solution that is well done.

Nassi-Schneiderman Charts

Nassi-Schneiderman charts are sometimes called structured flowcharts. They are also referred to as N-S charts. These charts consist of a stack of rectangles one on top of the other and put together without flowlines. Processing flow always runs from the top to the bottom of the stack of rectangles. Figure E.1 shows the four logic structures as they would appear in an N-S chart. Note the similarity to algorithms as presented in this book. Figure E.3 shows an example problem comparing a Warnier-Orr diagram to an N-S chart. N-S charts fit better on one page. However, since there is no means to continue to the next page and there is no way to indicate a *GoTo*, the modules are required to be short and cohesive.

Warnier-Orr Diagrams

The theory behind Warnier-Orr diagrams is similar to an interactivity chart. The differences are:

1. The Warnier-Orr diagrams are sideways.
2. There are no rectangles.
3. They use a pseudocode for the instructions.

Sequential Logic Structure

1. Instruction
2. Instruction
3. Instruction
4. Instruction

Decision Logic Structure

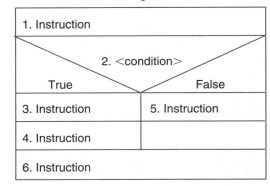

1. Instruction	
2. <condition>	
True	False
3. Instruction	5. Instruction
4. Instruction	
6. Instruction	

Loop Logic Structure

1. Instruction	
2. While <condition>	
	3. Instruction
	4. Instruction
	5. Instruction
	WhileEnd
6. Instruction	

Case Logic Structure

1. Instruction	
2. Case of <variable>	
= const1:	3. Instruction
= const2:	4. Instruction
= const3:	5. Instruction
otherwise:	6. Instruction
7. Instruction	

Figure E.1 The Four Structures Using Nassi-Schneiderman Charts

A Warnier-Orr diagram consists of a series of left braces, pseudocodelike instructions, and a few special symbols. The symbols include:

{	The brace is used to enclose a zero logically related set of instructions.
(0,1)	A set of instructions is executed zero or one time. This is the notation for the decision and the case structure.
(0, *n*) or *n*	A set of instructions is executed zero to *n* times. This is the notation for the *While/WhileEnd* loop structure.
(1, *n*)	A set of instructions is executed one to *n* times. This is the notation for *Repeat/Until* structure.
Blank or 1	A set of instructions is executed one time.
+	Exclusive OR. This is used with the (0,1) notation to show a selection.

Figure E.2 shows the four structures as written with Warnier-Orr diagrams. Notice the processes are broken up into modules just as in the structure chart. Most flowcharting templates have the Warnier-Orr bracket on one side. Figure E.3 shows the same problem developed using a Warnier-Orr diagram and a Nassi-Schneiderman chart.

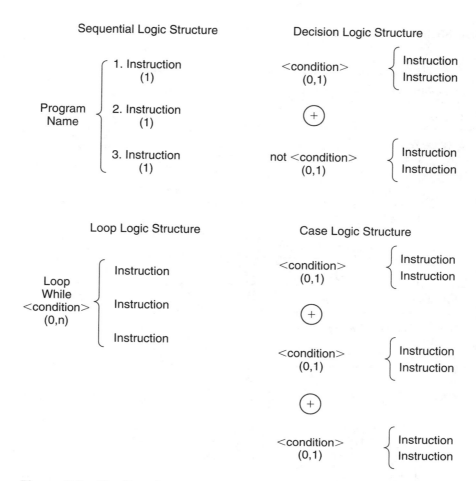

Figure E.2 The Four Structures Using Warnier-Orr Diagrams

Nassi-Schneiderman Charts

Warnier-Orr Diagrams

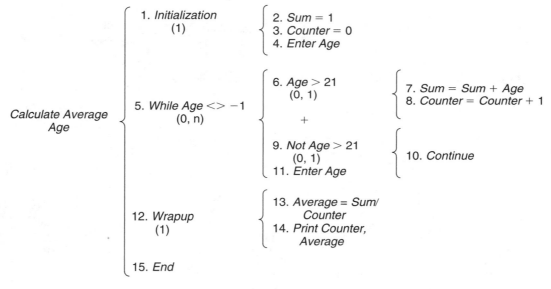

Figure E.3 Comparison of a Nassi-Schneiderman Chart and a Warnier-Orr Diagram

Appendix F

Other Functions

Mathematical Functions:

Int(x)	Returns the integer part of *x*
MOD(x, y)	Returns the whole number remainder of *x/y*
Round(x, n)	Returns the number *x* rounded to *n* decimal places
Sqrt(x)	Returns the square root of *x*

Other Functions:

If(condition, x, y)	Returns *x* if condition is true, *y* if false
Choose(x, v0, v1, v2, v3, ...)	Returns the value of the expression in the *x*th position in the list $v_0 - v_n$
VLookup(x, range, column)	Looks up the value *x* in the table at *range* (range where the table is located) and then returns the value found in *column* (column number in the table starting with the left-most column as zero)
Date(year, month, day)	The Julian calendar date of *year, month, day*
Now	The Julian calendar date of today

Financial Functions:

CTerm(int, fv, pv)	Returns the number of periods for the investment of *pv* to grow to *fv,* earning the rate of *int*
Ddb(cost, salvage, life, period)	Returns the double-declining depreciation of an asset, during *period,* given *cost, salvage value,* and the *life* of the asset
Fv(pmt, int, term)	Returns the future value of *term* number of payments, earning *int* rate
Irr(guess, range)	Returns the internal rate of return of the cash flows in *range,* with a guess needed for calculating purposes
Npv(int, range)	Returns the net present value of a series of cash flows in *range,* discounted at *int* rate
Pmt(prin, int, term)	Returns the payment needed to pay off the loan of *prin,* at the *int* interest rate, over *term* number of periods
Pv(pmt, int, term)	Returns the present value of *term* number of *pmt* payments, discounted at the *int* interest rate

Rate(fv, pv, term)	Returns the rate needed for *pv* to grow to *fv* over *term* number of periods
Sln(cost, salvage, life)	Returns the straight-line depreciation of an asset, given *cost, salvage value,* and the *life* of the asset
Syd(cost, salvage, life, period)	Returns the sum-of-the-years digits depreciation of an asset, during *period,* given *cost, salvage value,* and the *life* of the asset
Term(pmt, int, fv)	Returns the term needed for periodic payments of *pmt* to grow to *fv* with an interest rate of *int*

Statistical Functions:

Avg(range)	Returns the average of the values in *range*
Count(range)	Returns the number of values in *range*
CountIf(range, condition)	Returns the number of *x* values in the range
Max(range)	Returns the highest value in *range*
Min(range)	Returns the lowest value in *range*
Std(range)	Returns the standard deviation of the values in *range*
Sum(range)	Returns the summation of the values in *range*
Var(range)	Returns the variance of the values in *range*

Glossary

Accumulating Keeping a running total by adding a current value in the form of a variable to a previous sum to find the current total. The instruction for accumulating is *Sum = Sum + Variable.*

Accumulator Where calculations take place.

Activity file A file containing all of the updates to a master file.

Algorithmic solution A sequence of instructions to solve a problem. A computer programmer writes a solution in the form of an algorithm before coding it into a computer language.

Algorithm A solution to a problem that can be solved through a sequence of instructions.

Annotated flowchart A flowchart with explanations written beside the symbols.

Array Sometimes called a subscripted variable; a block of memory locations in the internal memory that is assigned to one variable name. Arrays may be one-dimensional, two-dimensional, or multidimensional.

Assembly language A three-letter representation of a machine language instruction.

Automatic-counter loop One of three types of loop instructions. The automatic-counter loop enables the computer to repeat a set of instructions by using a variable as a counter that starts at a beginning number that is incremented by a given number each time the program executes the set of instructions. The loop stops when the counter is larger than a given ending number.

Background The images used to give the rooms dimension and substance.

Backup file A file containing a master file as it was before the last update.

Base-one system A computer system in which array element numbers begin with one rather than zero.

Base-zero system A computer system in which element numbers begin with zero rather than one.

Batch processing Running successive sets of data through a program all at one time without human intervention.

Binary search A technique used to search for a single element in an array or a single record in a file.

Binary tree A list that has been created to have two linked fields—one to the right and one to the left to form a tree structure.

Breadcrumbs or breadcrumb trails A navigation system whose purpose is to give users a way to keep track of their location within programs or documents.

Bug An error in a computer program.

Calculation **module** A *Process* module that does arithmetic calculations and accumulates, counts, or manipulates numeric data in some way.

Case logic structure One of the four logic structures for organizing the instructions to the computer that make up a program. The case structure allows the computer to select one set of instructions from among many, through data given by the user or calculated in the solution.

Cell The intersection of a row and a column in a spreadsheet.

Cell protection A command used with spreadsheet packages to prevent the movement of the cursor into a cell.

Character data The data set of the character data type; it includes all symbols available on a computer.

Class A class is part of a solution of an object-oriented solution to a problem. A class models the properties or characteristics of a set of objects.

Client-server The term that refers to a relationship between two computers; one acting as the client making requests of another program, while the server is fulfilling the request of the client(s).

Codes Character data input by a user to direct the flow of processing, such as in the coded options in a record.

Cohesion Relates to the functional independence of the module and to the performance of a single task within the module.

Command An instruction to the computer in a productivity package or an operating system. Normally, a command is not part of a program.

Concatenation Adding one piece of string data to another by placing the second piece immediately after the first.

Constant A value in a program that cannot change during processing.

Constraint Used by database to enforce referential integrity between two tables.

Control-break A break in processing to print subtotals, or number of items, controlled by one field in a file.

Control **module** The module controlling the processing of all of the subtasks in a solution.

Coupling Techniques used to pass data from one module to another. Coupling techniques include the use of global variables, parameters, and return values.

Data Unorganized facts.

Data type The kind of data of a variable or a constant. The three basic data types are numeric, character, and logical.

Data Validation **module** Module that Checks data to make sure it is correct

Database Management System (DBMS) Software that stores large quantities of data, organizes data, and prints reports.

Debugging The process of correcting errors in a computer program.

Decision logic structure One of the four logic structures for organizing the instructions to the computer that make up a program. The decision structure selects one of two sets of instructions according to the resultant of a condition.

Decision table A programming aid to writing decision instructions for the computer; it consists of a rectangular grid divided into four parts, which specifies all possible actions the computer could take for each possible set of conditions.

Default value A value of a variable that is built into a program and that the computer automatically uses unless the value is changed by the user.

Desktop publisher More versatile than a word-processing program. As a page layout program, the user can take text from a word processor and graphics from a graphics program and combine them into a professional-quality document.

Drag and drop Drag and drop is the ability to select a portion of a document and move it to another part of the document or to another document.

Dynamic array An array in which the maximum number of elements can change during processing.

EndOfFile (EOF) The marker in a computer solution indicating that there are no more records to be processed.

Entity Relation Model (ERM) A model of the data that provides the designer with three main semantic concepts: entities, relationships, and attributes.

Equation A variable that is assigned the value of an expression, another variable, or a constant, as in $A = 5 + B$, $A = B$ (where B is a variable), or $A = 5$, respectively.

Event Something that happens in the computer. Typical events include on mousedown, on mouseup, on keydown, and on keyup.

Event-driven object-oriented programming A solution to a problem in which the processing is controlled through events in the computer.

Expression An operation or series of operations performed on variables or constants, as in $5 + B$.

External documentation Instructions to the user in the form of manuals or other written documents.

Field A field is one piece of data in a database table, such as a name or an address. A field is given a name and has the same attributes for all records in a table.

File A collection of related records.

Flowchart A graphic illustration of an algorithm.

Foreign Key A relational field to another table.

Form Allows the user to see all or some of the fields of a record on the monitor.

Function A small set of instructions built into a computer language or applications that enables the user to complete a frequently repeated task with fewer keystrokes than would be required without the function.

Global variable A variable that can be accessed by all modules below and in line (in the interactivity chart) with the module that declared the variable.

Graphical user interface (GUI) An interactive screen in which the user controls what happens in a program.

Hashing A method of using a predefined algorithm to designate the record number for fast retrieval of a given record.

Heuristic solution A solution to a problem that cannot be solved through a single sequence of instructions.

Hierarchical Database Management System (DBMS) Organizes data in a tree-like structure according to record types. The relationship between records is parent–child.

Hierarchy The order in which operations are performed for mathematical, relational, and logical operations.

Identifier A synonym for variable name. It is also synonymous with module name. It identifies the variable or the module.

If/Then/Else **instruction** The instruction to the computer that implements the decision logic structure.

Incrementing The process of counting on the computer by adding a number to a previous number. The instruction for incrementing by one is *Counter = Counter + 1.*

Indicator A value built into a solution by the programmer to redirect the flow of processing.

Information Organized facts.

Inheritance The ability of one object to inherit properties and functionality from another.

Initialization **module** The module containing all of the processing that has to be completed only once and at the beginning of the solution.

Input mask An input mask specifies required characters when entering data into database tables. These characters are automatically entered into a field by the computer.

Instance of a class An object.

Interactive processing Processing that involves user intervention to enter new data as needed, usually at a keyboard.

Interactivity The interaction between classes or between screens.

Interactivity chart A chart, also called a structure chart, showing all of the subtasks, or modules, in a program.

Internal documentation Remarks within a computer solution to explain the processing.

IPO chart Input-processing-output chart; describes the input, the output, and the processing needed to solve a problem on the computer.

Key The field of the records that is used to order a file or search for a record.

Linked list A list that has one field that contains the record number of the next record to be processed.

Local variable A variable accessed by the module that declared the variable. A single variable can be both local and global (see Chapter 4).

Logical data The data set consisting of *True* and *False,* used in making yes-and-no decisions.

Logical file number (LFN) In record processing, a number used to reference a file.

Logical operator An operator within an expression that uses logical data as operands and produces logical data as the resultant. The logical operators include NOT, AND, and OR.

Logic structure A structure for organizing the instructions to the computer that make up a program. There are four logic structures: the sequential structure, the decision structure, the loop structure, and the case structure.

Loop logic structure One of the four logic structures for organizing the instructions to the computer that make up a program. The loop structure enables the computer to process the same set of instructions repeatedly.

Machine language Instructions represented by zeros and ones.

Master file The file in which all of the data needed for processing are kept current.

Mathematical operator An operator that uses numeric data as its operands and produces numeric data as the resultant. The mathematical operators include − (subtraction), + (addition), * (multiplication), / (division), \ (integer division), MOD (modulo division), and ^ (power).

Module A subtask of the larger task the computer performs to complete a whole solution. The modules include the *Control, Initialization, Process,* and *WrapUp* modules.

Multidimensional array A multidimensional block of elements with a single variable name. Each element is designated by element numbers representing row, column, page, and so on.

Multiple control-break A control break on more than one field.

Multiple-thread The concept of more than one process of code operating at the same time, or asynchronously.

Navigational tools Tools including hot spots, hot objects, time, buttons of all types, and others, used to allow a program user to move through and interact with a computer program.

Negative logic A type of decision logic in which the action the computer is to perform follows from the *False* side of the instruction.

Nested *If/Then/Else* A type of decision structure that nests one *If/Then/Else* instruction within another.

Network Database Management System (DBMS) Similar to the Hierarchical Database Management System with the exception that one record type (sometimes called tables) can relate to any number of other record types.

Normalizing Separating data into related database tables.

Null file A file containing no records.

Numeric data The data type that includes all numbers, integers and real numbers, and is the only data type that can be used in calculations.

Object An item, or an instance of a class; an item on the screen when using an event-driven object-oriented programming language.

Object-Oriented Database Management System (DBMS) A DBMS that is newer on the market. It groups data, their attributes, and procedures into complex items called objects.

Object-oriented programming (OOP) A language that supports object-oriented principles; a strategy of program design in which the data parts are the principal items, instead of the process.

One-dimensional array One column of elements with a single variable name. Each element is designated by an element number.

Operator A sign or symbol in an expression or equation telling the computer how to process the data. The three types of operators are mathematical, relational, and logical.

Page break A break in the process of printing to finish one page and begin another.

Parallel arrays Two or more arrays in which the data in the same element numbers are related to each other.

Parameter A variable passed from one module to another module through the calling sequence of the module or function. There are two types of parameters, call-by-value parameters and call-by-reference. Call-by-value parameters cannot be changed in the module. Call-by-reference parameters can be changed and the changed value will be passed back to the calling module.

Pointer technique A programming technique that uses the value in one array to point to an element in another array.

Positive logic A type of decision logic in which the action the computer is to perform follows from the *True* side of the instruction.

Primary key A unique key that is the major key for ordering a file or searching for a record.

Primer *Read* The first record that is read into the internal memory before starting a processing loop, in order to have values to process the first time through the loop.

Print **module** A process module that prints the results of processing.

Problem analysis chart A chart used to begin to break down a problem into parts, including given data, results required, processing required, and solution alternatives.

Process **modules** The modules that process the data. They include *Calculation, Print, Read,* and *Data Validation* modules.

Program A computer solution to a problem; a set of instructions in a given computer language that solves the problem.

Property An attribute of an object or database item. In the case of a database field, it could contain the field type (Integer), allow null, etc.

Pseudocode A set of step-by-step instructions similar to that found in the programming language to be used.

Pushing and popping the stack Adding (pushing) and taking from (popping) a stack.

Query The way to select fields and/or records to be processed.

Query table A query table is the result of a database query. It contains selected records and/or fields from database tables.

Queue A list in which the next value used was the first one to be added. Data are added and used in a first-in, first-out basis.

Read **module** A *Process* module that enters data into the computer.

Record The set of data for one entity in a file or table.

Recursion Recursion occurs when a module or a function calls itself.

Register A high-speed temporary holding area built into the computer to hold instructions and data needed for the current processing.

Relational Database Management System (RDBMS) A system of tables with a common field that relates one table to another. This system is less complex, costs less, and accommodates smaller databases.

Relational operator An operator within an expression or equation that uses numeric or string data as operands and produces logical data as the resultant. The relational operators include: = (equal to), < (less than), > (greater than), <= (less than or equal to), >= (greater than or equal to), and <> (not equal to).

Repeat/Until One of three types of loop instructions; this loop logic structure tests at the end of each loop to see if it should repeat; it repeats the instructions in the loop until the condition is *True*.

Report The printed document of the records in a specific database or query table.

Results The required answers to or output from a problem.

Room Where the objects live when developing electronic games.

Schema The schema of a database is a graphic representation of the tables and their relationships.

Screen The image on the monitor in one instance.

Script A set of instructions given to an object or a sprite.

Secondary key A key, which may or may not be unique, that is used to order a file or to search for one or more records in a file. A secondary key is considered a minor key.

Sequential logic structure One of the four logic structures for organizing the instructions to the computer that make up a solution. The sequential structure processes the instructions one after another in a sequence.

Sequential file updating Adding, deleting, or changing data in records in a file to keep the records current.

Sequential search A method for locating a record in a file in which the computer starts at the first record and continues through the file, record by record, until the needed record is found.

Solution The set of instructions to the computer that will output the results; a computer program before it is coded into a computer language.

Sorting Arranging data in order; the order may be numeric or alphabetical.

Sound The music or other sounds that act as a background or as effects.

Sprite Animated images that are used to represent the objects.

Stack A list in which the value to be added and the value to be used are on the same end of the list. Data are added and used in a last-in, first-out basis.

Static array An array in which the maximum number of elements cannot change during processing.

Storyboard A design tool used to create screens.

Straight-through logic A type of decision logic that processes all decisions sequentially, one after another.

Structure chart A chart, also called an interactivity chart, showing all of the subtasks, or modules, in a program.

Subclass A class of specialized functionality that inherits is general functionality from a super class.

Super Class A super class is a class of generalized functionality and instance variables that can be inherited by a sub class.

Syntax The rules of setting up instructions and commands in an operating system, a programming language, or an application program.

Systems flowchart Shows the overall flow of data throughout the entire computer system, including all peripheral equipment.

Table A group of related records or entities.

Transaction Used by database software to make sure that all of the actions in a batch of database actions are completed. If there is a failure of any of the actions in the batch, then all of the actions are canceled.

Transaction file A file containing all of the updates that need to be made to a master file.

Traversal Methods of accessing data within a tree structure.

Trigger A script used by a database that runs when certain database actions occur: for example, insert Edit or Delete.

Tutorial A program provided with a software package to help the user learn how to use the package.

Two-dimensional array A block of elements with one variable name. Each element is designated by element numbers designating the row and column.

Variable A named memory location in the computer that is given a value that can be changed at any time during the processing.

While/WhileEnd One of the three types of loop instructions; the loop logic structure that tests at the beginning of the loop and repeats as long as a condition is *True*.

Wrapup **module** The module containing all of the processing that has to be completed only once and at the end of the processing.

Index

Primary Key, 250, 307
Primer Read, 136, 383
Problem Analysis Chart, 43
Problem Solving, 3
Problem Solving Steps, 3
Product, 133
Program, 6
Property, 299
Pseudocode, 48

Q

Query, 316
Queues, 241

R

Real Numbers, 17
Record, 250, 299, 306
Recursion, 151
Relational Database Management
 System, 300
Relational Operator, 25
Repeat/Until, 136
Reports, 319
Resultant, 23
Results, 6
Return Values, 75
Rules for Naming Constants and Variables, 15

S

Schema, 314
Secondary Key, 250
Selection Exchange Sort, 234
Sequential Access File Updating
 and Processing, 381
Sequential Logic Structure, 64, 77, 84
Sequential Search, 204
Shell Sort, 239

Solution, 6
Sorting, 234
 Bubble Sort, 236
 Selection Exchange Sort, 234
 Shell Sort, 239
Stacks, 241
 Pop, 241
 Push, 241
Static Arrays, 176
Straight Through Logic, 100, 102
String, 18
Syntax, 42
Systems Flowcharts, 253

T

Table, 299, 306
Table Look-Up Technique, 203
Transaction File, 417
Two-dimensional Array, 185

U

Unified Modeling Language (UML), 451
User-defined Events, 341

V

Variable, 13
 Local Variable, 69
 Global Variable, 69
 Variable Name, 14, 15

W

Warnier Orr Diagrams, 481
While/WhileEnd, 134